# THE FATHERS
# OF THE CHURCH

A NEW TRANSLATION

VOLUME 97

# THE FATHERS OF THE CHURCH

## A NEW TRANSLATION

### EDITORIAL BOARD

Thomas P. Halton
*The Catholic University of America*
*Editorial Director*

Elizabeth Clark
*Duke Univeristy*

†Robert B. Eno, S.S.
*The Catholic University of America*

Frank A. C. Mantello
*The Catholic University of America*

Kathleen McVey
*Princeton Theological Seminary*

Robert D. Sider
*Dickinson College*

Michael Slusser
*Duquesne University*

Cynthia White
*The University of Arizona*

Robin Darling Young
*The Catholic University of America*

David J. McGonagle
*Director*
*The Catholic University of America Press*

### FORMER EDITORIAL DIRECTORS

Ludwig Schopp, Roy J. Deferrari, Bernard M. Peebles,
Hermigild Dressler, O.F.M.

Edward Strickland
*Staff Editor*

# ORIGEN
## HOMILIES ON JEREMIAH
## HOMILY ON 1 KINGS 28

*Translated by*
JOHN CLARK SMITH
*University of St. Michael's College
at the University of Toronto*

THE CATHOLIC UNIVERSITY OF AMERICA PRESS
Washington, D.C.

Copyright © 1998
The Catholic University of America Press
All rights reserved
Printed in the United States of America

The paper used in this publication meets the minimum requirements of the American National Standards for Information Science—Permanence of Paper for Printed Library Materials, ANSI Z39.48-1984.

LIBRARY OF CONGRESS CATALOGING-IN-PUBLICATION DATA

Origen.
    [Homilies on Jeremiah. English]
    Homilies on Jeremiah ; Homily on 1 Kings 28 / Origen : translated by John Clark Smith.
        p. cm.—(The Fathers of the Church ; v. 97)
    Includes bibliographical references and indexes.
    1. Bible. O.T. Jeremiah—Sermons—Early works to 1800.
2. Bible. O.T. Kings, 1st, XXVIII—Sermons—Early works to 1800.
I. Smith, John Clark, 1944– . II. Origen. Homily on 1 Kings 28. English.
III. Title. IV. Title: Homily on 1 Kings 28. V. Series.
  BS1525.07413  1998
  224'.206—dc21
                                    97-46402
  ISBN 0-8132-0097-0 (alk. paper)
  ISBN 978-0-8132-2764-1 (pbk.)

CONTENTS

| | |
|---|---|
| Abbreviations | vii |
| Select Bibliography | ix |
| Introduction | xiii |

## Homilies on Jeremiah

| | |
|---|---|
| Homily 1 : Jeremiah 1.1–10 | 3 |
| Homily 2 : Jeremiah 2.21–22 | 23 |
| Homily 3 : Jeremiah 2.31 | 28 |
| Homily 4 : Jeremiah 3.6–11 | 30 |
| Homily 5 : Jeremiah 3.22–4.8 | 40 |
| Homily 6 : Jeremiah 5.3–5 | 62 |
| Homily 7 : Jeremiah 5.18–19 | 68 |
| Homily 8 : Jeremiah 10.12–14 | 74 |
| Homily 9 : Jeremiah 11.1–10 | 85 |
| Homily 10 : Jeremiah 11.18–12.9 | 94 |
| Homily 11 : Jeremiah 12.11—13.11 | 103 |
| Homily 12 : Jeremiah 13.12–17 | 110 |
| Homily 13 : Jeremiah 15.5–7 | 130 |
| Homily 14 : Jeremiah 15.10–19 | 135 |
| Homily 15 : Jeremiah 15.10 and 17.5 | 157 |
| Homily 16 : Jeremiah 16.16–17.1 | 166 |
| Homily 17 : Jeremiah 17.11–16 | 180 |
| Homily 18 : Jeremiah 18.1–16 | 188 |
| Homily 19 : Jeremiah 20.1–7 | 207 |

| Homily 20 : Jeremiah 20.7–12 | 221 |
| Homily 27 : Jeremiah 27.23–29 | 245 |
| Homily 28 : Jeremiah 28.6–9 | 260 |

# Fragments on Jeremiah

| Fragments from the *Philocalia* | 277 |
| Fragments from the *Catena* | 280 |

# Homily on 1 Kings 28

| Homily on 1 Kings 28 | 319 |

## Indices

| General Index | 337 |
| Index of Holy Scripture | 348 |

# ABBREVIATIONS

## Manuscripts

| | |
|---|---|
| S | Scorialensis manuscript of the Homilies on Jeremiah (xi–xii century) |
| T | Fragment of the Homily on I Kings from Toura |
| M | Monacensis manuscript of the Homily on I Kings |
| Al | Allatius edition of the Homily on I Kings |

## General

| | |
|---|---|
| ANF | A Select Library of the Ante-Nicene Fathers of the Christian Church. New York, 1885–87. Reprint. Grand Rapids, 1969. |
| CWS | Classics of Western Spirituality. New York, 1978–. |
| FOTC | The Fathers of the Church. Washington, D.C., 1947–. |
| GCS | *Die griechischen christlichen Schriftsteller der ersten drei Jahrhunderte.* Berlin, 1901–. |
| LXX | Septuagint |
| NCE | New Catholic Encyclopedia |
| PG | Migne, J.-P., ed. *Patrologiae Cursus Completus: Series Graeca.* Paris, 1857–66. |
| RSV | Revised Standard Version |
| SC | Sources chrétiennes. Paris, 1942–. |
| ThQ | Theological Quarterly |

## Works of Origen

| | |
|---|---|
| *Cels* | *Contra Celsum* |
| *Comm in Mt* | *Commentariorum in Matthaeum* |

## ABBREVIATIONS

*Hom in Is*     *Homiliae in Isaiam*
*Hom in Lc*     *Homiliae in Lucam*
*Hom in Lev*    *Homiliae in Leviticum*
*Jo*            *Commentariorum in Johannem*
*Or*            *De oratione*
*Princ*         *De principiis*
*Sel in Ezech*  *Selecta in Ezechielem*

Abbreviations of Classical and Patristic texts follow H. G. Liddell, R. Scott, and H. S. Jones, eds., *A Greek-English Lexicon* (Oxford, 1940) and G. W. H. Lampe, ed., *A Patristic Greek Lexicon* (Oxford, 1961).

# SELECT BIBLIOGRAPHY

## Texts of and Introductions to the Homilies

Guéraud, O. "Note préliminaire sur les papyrus d'Origène découverts à Toura." *Revue de l'histoire des religions* 131 (1946): 85–108.

Klostermann, E., ed. *Origenes Werke: Jeremiahomilien Klageliederkommentar Erklärung der Samuel- und Königsbücher.* (GCS 6). Leipzig: Hinrichs, 1901. Rev. ed. P. Nautin, 1983.

———., ed. *Origenes, Eustathius von Antiochien und Gregor von Nyssa über die Hexe von Endor.* Bonn: Marcus und Weber, 1912.

Nautin, P., and M.- T., eds. *Origène: Homélies sur Samuel* (SC 328). Paris: Cerf, 1986.

Nautin, P., and P. Husson, eds. *Origène: Homélies sur Jérémie* (SC 232, 238). Paris: Cerf, 1976, 1977.

Schadel, E., ed. *Origenes: Die griechischen erhaltenen Jeremiahomilien.* Stuttgart: Hiersemann, 1980.

## Works of Origen

Geerard, M., ed. *Clavis patrum graecorum.* Volume I. Turnhout, Belgium: Brepols, 1983.

## Biblical References

Allenbach, J., et al. *Biblia Patristica.* Volume 3: Origen. Paris: Éditions de Centre national de la recherche scientifique, 1980.

## Bibliographical References

Crouzel, Henri. *Bibliographie critique d'Origène.* The Hague: Nijhoff, 1971.

———. *Bibliographie critique d'Origène.* Supplément I. The Hague: Nijhoff, 1982.

x   SELECT BIBLIOGRAPHY

―――. "The Literature on Origen 1970–1988." *Theological Studies* 49 (1988): 499–516.

## General

Crouzel, Henri. *Origen*, trans. A. S. Worrall. Edinburgh: T. & T. Clark, 1989.
Nautin, Pierre. *Origène, sa vie et son oeuvre*. Paris: Beauchesne, 1977.
Smith, John Clark. *The Ancient Wisdom of Origen*. Lewisburg, PA: Bucknell University Press, 1992.
Trigg, Joseph. *Origen: The Bible and Philosophy in the Third-Century Church*. Atlanta: Knox, 1983.
Westcott, Brooke Foss. "Origenes." *Dictionary of Christian Biography*, IV (1887), 96–142.

## Origen's Exegesis, Language and Preaching

Borst, J. *Beiträge zur sprachlich-stylistischen und rhetorischen Würdigung des Origenes*. Freising: Datterer, 1913.
Castagno, Adele Monaci. *Origene predicatore e il suo pubblico*. Milan: Franco Angeli, 1987.
Gögler, Rolf. *Zur Theologie des biblischen Wortes bei Origenes*. Düsseldorf: Patmos, 1963.
Gorday, Peter. *Principles of Patristic Exegesis: Romans 9–11 in Origen, John Chrysostom and Augustine*. New York: Edwin Mellen, 1983.
Hanson, Richard P. C. *Allegory and Event: A Study of the Sources of Origen's Interpretation of Scripture*. London: SCM Press, 1959.
Lomiento, G. "'Pragma' und 'Lexis' in den Jeremiahomilien des Origenes." ThQ 165 (1985): 118–31.
Lubac, Henri de. *"Du hast mich betrogen, Herr": Der Origenes-Kommentar über Jeremia 20, 7*. Translated by Hans Urs von Balthasar. Kriterion LXIX. Einsiedeln: Johannes-Verlag, 1984.
―――. *Histoire et Ésprit. L'intelligence de l'écriture d'après Origène*. Paris: Aubier, 1950.
Neuschäfer, Bernhard. *Origenes als Philologe*. Basel: Fr. Reinhardt, 1987.
Poffet, J. M. *La méthode exégétique d'Héracléon et d'Origène commentateurs de Jean 4*. Fribourg, Switzerland: Editions universitaires, 1985.
Peri, V. "Geremia secondo Origene. Esegesi e psicologia della testimonianza profetica." *Aevum* 48 (1974): 1–57.

_____. "L'ordine delle omelie xiv–xi nella tradizione manoscritta delle omelie su Geremia di Origene." *Aevum* 30 (1956): 5–33.

Smelik, K. A. D. "The Witch of Endor: I Samuel 28, in Rabbinic and Christian Exegesis till 800 a.d." *Vigiliae Christianae* 33 (1979): 160–79.

Torjesen, Karen. *Hermeneutical Procedure and Theological Method in Origen's Exegesis.* Berlin: De Gruyter, 1986.

# INTRODUCTION

## *Origen and his Work*

Origen of Alexandria (A.D. ca.185–ca.253) is universally recognized as one of the greatest theologians and religious thinkers of the Christian Church. His work was voluminous and, in the opinion of both his contemporaries and those who followed, unique and profound. Unfortunately, there remain only a few extant works in the original Greek: several sections of the *Commentary on John*,[1] several sections of the *Commentary on Matthew*,[2] the apology *Against Celsus*,[3] *On Prayer, Exhortation to Martyrdom*, the *Dialogue with Heraclides*,[4] twenty homilies on Jeremiah, a homily on 1 Kings (1 Samuel) 28 and a rather large selection of fragments from various works. His philosophical theology *On First Principles*,[5] unfortunately extant for the most part only in a Latin translation, was probably the first such work. *Against Celsus* was, and is, the most thorough and probing defense of Christianity

---

1. A new translation by R. J. Heine has appeared in FOTC 80 (Books 1–10) and FOTC 89 (Books 13–32). A translation is also available complete with fragments in Italian by Eugenio Corsini, ed., *Commento al Vangelo di Giovanni di Origene* (Torino, 1968).

2. Books 2–14 only translated by J. Patrick, ANF 10.

3. English translation by Henry Chadwick, *Contra Celsum* (Cambridge, 1953; rev., 1980).

4. All of the last three works are available in a translation of Henry Chadwick, in a book entitled, *Alexandrian Christianity. Selections from Clement and Origen* (Philadelphia, 1954). The first two have received a more recent translation by R. A. Greer in *Origen* (New York, 1979) in the series Classics of Western Spirituality.

5. English translation by G. W. Butterworth, *On First Principles* (London, 1936).

ever penned. His scholarly word-studies of the Scriptures were astonishing for his time. And his homilies transcend the genre and always surprise and inspire their audience, but they are only available—with the exception of the homilies on Jeremiah and 1 Kings 28—in Latin translations.

(2) Origen was, however, not only a writer. His influence also spread through his teaching and preaching in Egypt and Palestine in the third century A.D. He was the dean of two important Christian academies, and, due to his reputation for wide learning and fairness, he was asked to counsel emperors and royalty, as well as defend the young Christianity before the most able philosophers, pagans, and theologians of his day. More important, perhaps, to his contemporaries and students was his exemplary life. Origen took the demands of the Gospel literally, and probably died from the torture of persecution. Hence both as a man and as a thinker his influence was so extensive that almost every Christian or religious thinker after the third century A.D. owes a debt to him and his work.

(3) Too often that debt has gone unnoticed and been misunderstood. Since many traditional and orthodox interpretations were not established then, Origen felt free to arrive at his own tentative conclusions, and to dare to speculate in areas which either were not discussed or were unclear in the Scriptures, matters such as the motives of God, the origin of souls, the afterlife, the nature of Christ, the universe, the Trinity and the Church. He probed tentatively, but he nevertheless probed, and his answers cost him respect for many generations in orthodox circles. For it is his speculations in these areas which many people tended to stress, remember and misinterpret, and for which he was condemned in councils. They did not thoroughly investigate at that time or even until very recently the countless subtle developments which Origen had anticipated in theology and religious thinking, and which are clear on every page of his writing and preaching. No one would have been more surprised and disheartened than Origen by the labels of those who

INTRODUCTION xv

read him later; some even claimed he was not a Christian, but a heretic who foisted philosophy upon the Scriptures. Yet those who knew him and his scriptural work preserved his memory and translated his work into Latin, as well as incorporated it into their own views.

(4) Though the controversy continues, he is slowly achieving his rightful place among Christians of all sects. Books, articles and even Origen conferences are becoming more and more common. There are now critical texts of many of his writings—though the original Greek texts have mostly disappeared—and many of his works have been translated.[6]

*Homilies on Jeremiah and 1 Kings (1 Samuel) 28*

(5) Of all his works, the most accessible and yet immensely interesting are his homilies. The majority of those that survive are in Latin translations,[7] but there are almost twenty-one complete homilies extant in Greek from the homilies on Jeremiah and 1 Kings, delivered at some stage not too long after A.D. 240, when Origen was in his fifties.[8] We are thankful for anything which survives in Greek, but the homi-

---

6. For further research on Origen's life and thought, see Book VI of Eusebius, *The Ecclesiastical History*, Chapter 13 of *The Philocalia*, translated by George Lewis, *The Philocalia of Origen* (Edinburgh, 1911), the letter of one of Origen's students, preserved in the *Oration* and *Panegyric*, translated in ANF 6.21–39, the *Apology against Rufinus* by Jerome, *Concerning the Adulteration of the Works of Origen* by Rufinus, and, for an entertaining but fictional treatment of the man, see Theodore Vrettos' historical novel *Origen* (New Rochelle, N.Y., 1978). The most thorough recent discussion of these sources is in Pierre Nautin, *Origène, sa vie et son oeuvre* (Paris, 1977), but this should be read critically, since many statements about these times can only be conjectural. See the bibliography for some recent works on Origen.

7. See the homilies on Genesis and Exodus translated by R. J. Heine in FOTC 71, those on Leviticus translated by G. W. Barkley in FOTC 83, and the homilies on Luke translated by J. T. Lienhard in FOTC 94.

8. Cf. Pierre and Marie-Thérèse Nautin, eds., *Origène: Homélies sur Samuel* (Paris, 1986), 60, 235, which reflects Nautin's latest thoughts on both series of homilies. Cf. also Erwin Schadel, ed., *Origenes: Die griechischen erhaltenen Jeremiahomilien* (Stuttgart, 1980), 6.

lies are especially important. They provide a glimpse of Origen which was familiar to his contemporaries but which later centuries sometimes forgot. In them we see the preacher and teacher, the man responding to crises within his community and his own travails, the exegete and especially the religious thinker.

(6) Beyond these important factors, the homilies on Jeremiah comprise a catechism of Origen's view of Christian doctrine and Christian philosophy. In lieu of a long introduction,[9] I have provided a thorough subject index so that the reader can explore Origen directly. Through these homilies one can obtain an overview of Origen's thought and exegesis, and enjoy watching a master grappling with the difficulties and profundities of the text.

(7) As a master of Scripture—though he himself would have disclaimed such a description—Origen is exhilarated by his task. For him, a word of Scripture can have several levels of meaning. He explores nuances and subtleties with an eye awaiting a divine signal in the text. For him, only Scripture held the secrets of God's purpose for man, and he believed that it could be revealed only by the most detailed and patient unraveling of the truths contained therein. We are often amazed at his creativity in dealing with what he would call the "spirit" of the text. But there is no doubt of his sincerity and the depth of his feeling for the dynamics of the Scripture's mysteries. And with his breadth of knowledge and experience, the journey through any of his books is an adventure of ideas.

(8) The journey is particularly interesting in the case of the book of Jeremiah, for it is obvious that Origen in many ways identified with the great prophet and his themes, and thought of Jeremiah as a type for Christ in the Hebrew Scriptures. Beyond these things, there are more than enough dif-

---

9. See the introductions to the translations of Nautin and Schadel, as well as the introduction to R. J. Heine's translation of the homilies on Genesis and Exodus in FOTC 71 and J. C. Smith, *The Ancient Wisdom of Origen* (Lewisburg, PA, 1992).

ficulties to keep him busy. Origen realized that Jeremiah came at a crucial time in the history of Israel, the time of the captivity, and he views this event and the events around it as pregnant lessons for the people of his time. The themes, then, are many: conversion, repentance, the Judgment, spiritual progress, the Fire, the role of Christ, the role of evil, the meaning of Israel, salvation, etc.

(9) The homily on 1 Kings 28 concerns one of the most controversial passages in Scripture, commonly called the Witch of Endor episode, in which a medium conjures up the dead prophet Samuel from Hades. This is a remarkable work of exegesis for many reasons, but primarily because Origen, who is unfortunately infamous for his allegories, stays almost entirely with the historical or literal text from beginning to end. It indicates again that our view of Origen is too often determined by the work which has come down to us, and that perhaps too often we discount the contextual side of his writing. Beyond this, its interest also lies in its being a dialectical work in which Origen debates with those who believe that the episode is questionable.

## Texts and Translation

(10) The critical text for the 20 Greek homilies and the fragments on Jeremiah from the *Catena* is that of Erich Klostermann.[10] The improved Greek text of Pierre Nautin, a reprint of Klostermann with some corrections or different views on the text, has also been referred to constantly.[11] Nautin's suggestions were appended to a reprint of Klostermann's edition in 1983 and then revised again in 1986 when he published his text of the homily on 1 Kings.[12] Beyond these two series, I have used the Nautin edition of the

---

10. Erich Klostermann, ed., *Origenes: Jeremiahomilien*, Volume 3 of Origen's works, GCS 6.
11. Pierre Nautin and Pierre Husson, eds., *Origène: Homélies sur Jérémie*, Vols. 1 and 2 (Paris, 1976, 1977).
12. See pp. 231–37 of this edition.

xviii                    INTRODUCTION

Latin translation of Jerome for two missing Greek homilies, and Robinson's text for the fragments from the *Philocalia*.

(11) I use Klostermann's text because of its more complete critical apparatus, especially for Jerome's suggestions, even though Nautin does occasionally improve on Klostermann. Nautin tries to adhere to the extant Greek rather than accept the modifications of other editors and Jerome. At times Jerome's translations are illuminating in clarifying a phrase, but Jerome is a Latin thinker and his translations sometimes erase the enthusiasm and emotion in Origen's words. As Klostermann shows in his introduction, Jerome can append or excise words or modify the meaning for adjustment to a Latin mentality and vocabulary. I have considered all the modifications of and additions to the extant manuscripts by Klostermann, Nautin, Jerome and other editors.[13] My basic goal was to follow closely what we have in Greek (primarily the Scorialensis manuscript, referred to as S, and the *Catena*) whenever possible, without additions or modifications. However, when this was not possible, I considered the suggestions of others, and when these changes to the manuscript have affected the meaning significantly, I have noted them.

(12) The quality of the fragments on Jeremiah is not certain.[14] Those which survive from existing paragraphs in the *Homilies* show that the scribe of the fragments abridged several lines into a few, though apparently using the same key words that Origen used. But we cannot say with confidence that all of these fragments come from the *Homilies*. Though we know of no other work on Jeremiah outside of the *Homilies*, it remains possible that Origen commented on texts of Jeremiah, perhaps at some length, in other works, and perhaps even with a different exegesis because of a different purpose at hand.[15]

---

13. For the editions of editors other than Klostermann and Nautin mentioned in my notes, see Klostermann's introduction.
14. Cf. Klostermann, xxvi; Nautin, 1.27–32.
15. Unlike the set reproduced in Migne (PG 13.543ff.), the edition of

INTRODUCTION

(13) For the homily on 1 Kings 28, I have used the critical text of Pierre Nautin published in 1986,[16] primarily because of his access to the recently discovered fragments at Toura and because of his nearly always helpful views of the text. However, it has been compared word for word with Klostermann, who had a good sense of how an ancient would write Greek. Once again I have noted all of the major differences in manuscripts and published critical texts.

(14) To my knowledge, this is the first translation of these fragments into a modern language and the first English translation of these homilies. The two homilies which were translated into Latin by Jerome, but which are not extant in the Greek, have also been translated, as well as the fragments in the *Philocalia*. There are also several fragments which appear in the apparatus of Klostermann which have been placed in the notes. These, too, are here translated into English for the first time.

(15) My translation of the homilies benefits from the French translations of Nautin and Husson and the German translation of Erwin Schadel.[17] While Nautin's editions each have a long and worthwhile introduction to the theological and religious place of the works, as well as Origen's style of preaching and language, they remain within the restrictions of the series *Sources chrétiennes*, which was not intended to be a group of commentaries. Notes in that series are as a rule explanatory and theological with occasional mention of Origen's philosophical influences and tendencies.[18] Schadel's edition, with its lengthy notes, is a philosophical commentary on the thought in the homilies, though not ignoring

---

Klostermann includes only those fragments which do not repeat texts in the extant homilies. See Klostermann, xxix–xxxii, for clarification and numbering of the fragments.

16. Pierre and Marie-Thérèse Nautin, *Origène*.
17. Works cited above. Schadel defends his changes to the text on pp. 12ff.
18. Nautin's edition of the homily on 1 Kings is, however, more of a commentary, and essentially guides the reader through Origen's train of thought, as Nautin sees it.

the theological points of interest. He is quite enthusiastic about the ideas contained within these homilies and very diligent to point out the many ways in which Origen will express a matter simply, but at the same time imply a much more complex problem. The total length of Schadel's notes is almost half the length of the translation itself, and, even though this is but a taste of what could have been done, we are fortunate to have it.

(16) The Fathers of the Church is a translation series, and in line with the other translators in the series, I have resisted the attempt to create a commentary, or even to respond to Nautin or Schadel, beyond establishing a text. Of course, every translation is a commentary of a sort. I have restricted myself to clarifying what may be obscure to readers and giving some direction on how I formed my text, since there are many textual problems.

(17) Origen is a difficult author to translate. By any contemporary standard he is a master of his language and the most complex and eclectic writer of any of the early Greek Fathers. My time and attention have been absorbed in understanding and clarifying Origen's language, which, even in homilies, is a mixture of several strands of Greek. This translation is not an attempt to paraphrase or remake Origen's work to suit the ways of a modern-day homily. Nor have I strained to be eloquent or to mold the vocabulary or style to suit how I might want to read or hear it. The translation does, however, try to follow the original very closely and yet be fluid. Every attempt is made to leave difficulties of interpretation to the reader when they are present in the Greek. I have particularly tried to be scrupulous with Origen's vocabulary, and have consciously taken no liberties.

(18) Words quoted from Scripture are noted, thanks to many prior editors of the Greek text. I have almost always followed the Revised Standard Version, except regarding the Old Testament, where Origen's basic text was not the Hebrew, but the Septuagint, an early Greek translation. Thus what I refer to as 1 Kings, for example, will be more familiar

to most readers as 1 Samuel. All references to Old Testament passages are to the Septuagint. Since this text is often different from the Hebrew text from which our modern translations are made today, I have newly translated directly from Origen's text all passages from the Old Testament, using the words of the RSV when possible. I have tried to clarify the scriptural foundation of Origen's interpretations and vocabulary by setting off words with italics when he uses them in an obvious biblical context.

# HOMILIES ON JEREMIAH

# HOMILY 1

## Jeremiah 1.1–10

*When did Jeremiah begin to prophesy and in the time of which kings did he prophesy and what was then said to him by the Lord?*[1]

OD IS READY TO DO GOOD but hesitant to punish those who deserve punishment. In fact, though he can inflict punishment on those whom he has sentenced without saying anything, without prior warning, he never does. For when he sentences, he says so, and the speaking is a way to turn the person to be condemned away from the sentencing. It is possible to take many examples of these sentences from Scripture, but for now it will suffice[2] to mention a few in order to arrive at the vision[3] of the passage just read.

(2) The Ninevites had become sinners and were sentenced by God: *Still in three days and Ninevah will be overthrown.*[4] God did not wish to sentence without saying anything,[5] but *giving them the opportunity for repentance*[6] and conversion, he sent a Hebrew prophet, so that, when he said, *still in three days and Ninevah will be overthrown,* those sentenced might not be sentenced, but would obtain the mercy of God by repenting.

---

1. The title and this description are from Jerome. S has only Ἱερεμίας.
2. "Suffice," from Jerome and Klostermann.
3. See the note on this word (σκοπός) in Schadel, 239, n. 2, who translates it: *Sinnziel.* We have translated it to reflect not only the inner meaning of the passage, but also the object which is to be seen by the work of exegesis.
4. Jon 3.4.
5. "Without saying anything," (σιωπῶν) from Jerome. S has εἰπών.
6. Wis 12.10.

(3) The inhabitants of Sodom and Gomorrah were sentenced, as is evident from the words of God according to Abraham.[7] Nevertheless the angels have done their work, wanting to save those who did not want to be saved, by saying to Lot, *Are there here with you some who are in-laws or sons or daughters?*[8] They realized that the others did not follow Lot but they still did the work *of goodness and loving kindness*[9] of their own, and at the same time[10] of the one who had sent them.

2. You will find the same in what concerns Jeremiah. The time of his prophecy is recorded—when he began, and until when he prophesied. Now, if the reader neither pays heed to the passage nor examines the intent of what was read, he will say that it is a history and it records when Jeremiah began to prophesy and how long before he stopped prophesying. What, then, does this history mean for me? When I read on, I learn that he began to prophesy *in the days of Josiah, the son of Amos, king of Judah, in the thirteenth year of his kingdom.* Then he emerged *in the days of Joachim, son of Josiah, king of Judah* prophesying *to the end of the eleventh year of Zedekiah, son of Josiah, king of Judah.* And[11] I learn that his prophecy continued under three kings *until the captivity of Jerusalem in the fifth month.* What then do we learn from these words, if we attend to the reading?

3. God sentenced Jerusalem for her sins, and those condemned were to be delivered into captivity. Nevertheless, at the appointed time, the benevolent God sends this Prophet under the third king before the Captivity so that those who wish to consider it may repent by means of the words of the Prophet. He had charged the Prophet to prophesy under the second king also after the first king, and under the third king until the times of her captivity. For the patient God was

---

7. Gen 18.  8. Gen 19.12.
9. Titus 3.4.
10. "Of their own, and at the same time," from Jerome.
11. "And," from Jerome.

offering a respite even, so to speak, down to the day before the Captivity, urging hearers to repent so that he may prevent the misfortune of the captivity. Hence it is written, *Jeremiah prophesied until the captivity of Jerusalem, until the fifth month.* The Captivity begins, and still he prophesied, saying something like this: "Become captives, provided in such circumstances you can repent! For when you repent, the misfortunes of the captivity will not transpire, but God's mercy will be realized for you." So from the record about the times of the prophecy we have gained what is useful, that God in his own love for man encourages hearers not to endure the misfortunes of the Captivity.

(2) So it is also for us. If we sin, we also are liable to become captives. For *to deliver such a one to Satan*[12] is no different from delivering those captives from Jerusalem to Nebuchadnezzar. For just as they are delivered to him for sins, so we are delivered for sins to Satan, who is Nebuchadnezzar. And *I have delivered*[13] *them to Satan, so that they may learn not to blaspheme,*[14] the Apostle says concerning other sinners.

4. See then how very bad sinning is, that they may be delivered to Satan, who holds captive the souls of those forsaken by God—though God does not forsake without cause or judgment those whom he has abandoned. For when he sends the rain for the vineyard, and the vineyard bears thorns instead of grapes, what else will God do except order the clouds not to sprinkle rain on the vineyard?[15]

(2) Thus a captivity is also imposed on us for our sins, and, if we do not repent, we are liable to be delivered to Nebuchadnezzar and the Babylonians in order that the spiritual Babylonians may torture us. As these things are imposed, the words of the Prophets, the words of the Law, the words of the Apostles, and the words of our Lord and Savior Jesus Christ, speak to us about repentance, encourage us to-

---

12. 1 Cor 5.5.
13. "I have delivered," from Jerome. S has, "he has delivered."
14. 1 Tim 1.20.    15. Cf. Isa 5.4–6.

ward conversion. If we hear, let us believe in him who said, *I will repent of all the evil which I planned to do to them.*[16] These are comments regarding the preamble.

5. But after the preamble it is written, *The Word of the Lord came to him,* that is, to Jeremiah. And what does the Word of the Lord say to him? It is something special,[17] beyond what is said of the other Prophets. For of none of the Prophets do we find such a thing said. Abraham was called a prophet in the passage, *He is a prophet and he will pray for you.*[18] Yet God did not say to him, *Before I formed you in the womb, I knew you, and before you were born, I consecrated you.* But later on Abraham was exalted, when he went out *from his country and from his kindred and from his father's house.*[19] Isaac was born from a promise, and we do not discover any such word said to him. And what need is there to recount the rest? Jeremiah obtains a special gift, which is: *Before I formed you in the womb, I knew you, and before you came from your mother, I consecrated you.*

6. We are aware that some people refer these words, in that they surpass Jeremiah, to our Lord and Savior. And one can see that while many passages which I will cite accord with him and can refer to the Savior, a few of the words said about Jeremiah are troublesome for this interpretation,[20] since they cannot be fitting, in the view of many, for the Savior. What, then, are those words which are fitting for the Savior? *"To all to whom I send you, you shall go, and whatever I command you, you shall speak. Be not afraid before their face, for I am with you to take you away,"* says the Lord. It does not yet appear that these words refer clearly to the Savior, but the next do: *Then the Lord extended his hand near me, and he touched my mouth, and the Lord said to me: "Behold, I have placed my words in your mouth. Behold, this day I have placed you over nations and kingdoms, to uproot and demolish."* What nations did Jeremiah uproot, and what kingdoms did he demolish? For it is writ-

16. Jer 18.8.
17. "It is something special," from a suggestion of Klostermann.
18. Gen 20.7.      19. Gen 12.1.
20. λόγος.

ten, *Behold, I have placed you over nations and kingdoms, to uproot and demolish.* And what power did Jeremiah have for causing destruction? This was said as if to Jeremiah in the passage *and to destroy.* And what sort of things did Jeremiah build, so that it could be written *and to build?* Jeremiah said, *I did not help, and no one helped me.*[21] How then is it given to him *to build and to plant?* How can *to plant* be fitting for Jeremiah?

(2) Referring these words to the Savior is not troublesome for the interpreter, for Jeremiah in such passages is a prefigure for the Savior. Yet those words which will be cited next are much more troublesome for the interpreter—even one very intelligent—when he wants to show how they also can be fitting for the Savior: *And I said: O you who are, Master and Lord, behold, I do not know how to speak.* How then[22] can *I do not know how to speak* accord with the Savior, the one who is[23] Wisdom, the *power of God,*[24] who brought to us the *fullness of divinity which dwelt corporeally in him?*[25] But also the words *I am a youth* are rejected for the Savior, as he speaks inappropriately; for if the Lord says to him, *do not say* such a thing, it is clear that he rejects it[26] because it is said inappropriately.

(3) These words then are not fitting for the Savior, and those above do not[27] seem to be troublesome for the Savior. Yet it is easy to say[28] that the latter words refer to Jeremiah while the former refer to the Savior. The person of good sense, however, will find it very troublesome in the context, when he realizes that it is senseless to separate in a series of statements[29] words said either to Jeremiah or to the Savior, and state that these do not belong to Christ but to Jeremiah

---

21. Jer 15.10.
22. "Then," an addition of Klostermann from Jerome.
23. "Is," a correction of Klostermann from Jerome. S has ἐν.
24. 1 Cor 1.24.  25. Col 2.9.
26. "It," an addition of Klostermann.
27. "And" and "not," from Jerome.
28. "To say" (εἰπεῖν), a correction from Jerome. S has εἶπον.
29. λόγος.

since they are less than appropriate for Christ,[30] and that these, being greater than Jeremiah, do not belong to Jeremiah but to Christ. Let us refer the whole context[31] then to Jeremiah, and explain what seems to be greater than Jeremiah.

7. Everyone who has received words from God and has the grace of heavenly words has received them in order to *uproot and demolish nations and kingdoms*. But, though everyone who has received words from God is said to *uproot nations and kingdoms*, it is not, it seems to me, said in a bodily[32] sense. For when one has considered human souls which are ruled by sin according to the passage from the Apostle, *Let not sin reign in our mortal body*,[33] and when one sees also the many kinds of sins, he interprets allegorically also the *nations* and the *kingdoms* as the bad movements in the souls of men which are uprooted and demolished by those words of God which are given either to Jeremiah or to whomever. And so one is able to apply to Jeremiah both the first words, which are troublesome for the text with respect to the Savior, and to apply also to Jeremiah the second, when viewed allegorically.

(2) Somebody among our hearers will say to me: "Explain also the other passage[34] and try to clarify the whole passage as applicable to the Savior. With respect to the second, there is no struggle. For it is evident that the Savior uprooted the kingdoms of the Devil and has demolished the pagan nations by destroying the pagan life. Explain how the Savior in any sense is able to say there, in what seems insulting to the

---

30. "Since they are less than appropriate for Christ," an addition of Klostermann from Jerome.

31. "Context," my addition.

32. Origen viewed Scripture as a living entity with usually two dimensions, an outside "body"—the literal and obvious interpretation—and an inner "spirit." Sometimes he includes a third dimension, the soul, which refers basically to the moral side of life. However, he does not follow this approach rigidly in every text. See his chapter (4.2) on Scripture in *On First Principles*.

33. Rom 6.12.   34. λόγος, i.e., "I am very young."

HOMILY 1 9

Savior, the word: *I do not know how to speak, because I am very young* and the rest."

(3) You see that the thought[35] is embarrassing. We know the Savior as Lord. If we seek to bring these words up[36] to the Savior according to the worthiness of the Word and according to the truth, it is necessary to take the Scriptures as *witnesses*.[37] For without witnesses, our interpretations and exegeses are unfaithful.[38] *On the testimony of two or three witnesses shall every word be established*[39] applies more to discussions than[40] to men . . .[41] so that I will establish the words of the interpretation by taking two witnesses from the New and Old Testaments, by taking three witnesses from the Gospel, from the Prophets, from the Apostles. For, in this way, *every word will be established.*

(4) How then can we apply these words to the Savior anagogically? Take the Old Testament as a witness. *For before the child knows either good or evil, it must reject wickedness to choose good.*[42] And this is mentioned explicitly about the Savior in Isaiah: *Behold the virgin will be with child and will bear a son and they will call his name Emmanuel,*[43] and after this comes, *before the child knows.* And if one needs to take an example from the Gospel: Jesus, before he became a man and was still a child, after *he emptied himself,*[44] he progressed—for no one progresses if he has matured,[45] but he progresses if he has need of

---

35. λόγος.
36. ἀναγαγεῖν, literally, to bring, lift or go up, to interpret anagogically, this word and its cognates are often used by Origen to explain his exegetical method.
37. Deut 19.15.
38. After this Klostermann adds, in light of Jerome (*et hoc quod dictum est*), καὶ τό. It seems likely that more text is missing here or was not copied completely.
39. Deut 19.15.
40. "Than" (ἤ) a correction of Cordier from Jerome. S has μή.
41. Probable lacuna here.      42. Isa 7.16.
43. Isa 7.14.      44. Phil 2.7.
45. This word τελειεῖν and its many derivatives in Origen are often routinely translated in English "to perfect" or "to make perfect," but the underlying

progress. He not only *progressed in stature*, he *progressed in wisdom*, he *progressed in grace before God and men*.[46] For if he emptied himself when he came down here, and after emptying himself he was beginning to acquire those aspects from which he emptied himself—since he emptied himself willingly—how amazing is it that he also *progressed in wisdom and in stature and in grace before God and men*. And what[47] I have cited from Isaiah became true concerning him: *Before the child knows either good or wickedness*,[48] *he will choose the good and reject wickedness*.[49]

8. But someone will say: "Even if[50] you are able to refer anagogically to the Savior the words, *He does not know*, and even if you can speak as one who understands the Savior as a child in some sense, is it not a mistake for you to speak this way about the *Only-begotten*,[51] about the *First-born of all creation*,[52] about the one who was proclaimed before conception according to the words, *the Holy Spirit will come upon you and the power of the Most High will overshadow you?*"[53] And does he say, *I do not know how to speak?* See if you can perceive something praiseworthy and great concerning the Savior in a passage which says that when he *does not know* something, it is better not knowing than knowing these things.

(2) I will even use his own voice testifying that he does not know some things. To those who supposedly say to him: "Is it not in your name we ate, and in your name we drank,[54] and

---

meaning for Origen involves more precisely the process of growth from immaturity to maturity. See, for example, his many discussions of Heb 5.14, listed in *Biblia Patristica*, Volume 3, ed. J. Allenbach (Paris: Éditions du Centre national de la recherche scientifique, 1980). Origen often discusses conditions of lapsing for the mature. He did not believe anyone except Jesus could be "perfect," as we understand the term, in this earthly life.

46. Luke 2.52.
47. "And what," an addition of Klostermann from Jerome.
48. Origen quotes a slightly different text here from the LXX.
49. Isa 7.16.
50. "Even if" (εἰ καὶ), an addition of Klostermann from Jerome. S has εἶτα.
51. John 1.14.   52. Col 1.15.
53. Luke 1.35.
54. Cf. Luke 13.26.

## HOMILY 1

in your name we cast out demons and we did many mighty works?" he replies: *Depart from me, for I never knew you.*[55] Does what is said here by the Savior, *I never knew you,* diminish his power? Or does it suggest something greater and more admirable, since he did not know the inferior and lost ones? For he knew what is distinguished and superior, and the Lord *knew his own,*[56] and, *if anyone does not recognize this, he is not recognized.*[57] Hence the sinner is not recognized by God.

(3) Someone listening will say to me: "You have shown that he does not know sinners, you have shown that he does not know *those who have done iniquity,*[58] for they are not worthy of his knowledge. How indeed can you demonstrate that the statement, if made by the Savior, *I do not know how to speak,* is great and glorious?" To speak is a human trait, to speak is to use a language as one speaks the dialect of the Hebrews, for example, or that of the Greeks or some others.[59]

(4) If you approach the Savior and know him as the Word in the beginning with God,[60] you will perceive that he does not know how to speak since to speak is human, but he does not speak,[61] since what he knows is greater than speaking. And if you compare the language of angels to the language of men,[62] you will see also that he is greater than the angels, as the Apostle in the Letter to the Hebrews attested;[63] you will say that he was greater also than the language of angels when he was God the Word with the Father.[64]

(5) So he learns and in some sense takes on a knowledge which is not of great matters but of what is inferior and smaller. And just as I learn, when I exert myself, to babble when I converse with children—for since I, being mature, do not know exactly how to communicate with a child, I

---

55. Matt 7.22–23.
56. 2 Tim 2.19, citing Num 16.5.
57. 1 Cor 14.38.
58. Matt 7.23.
59. "Or" and "others," additions of Klostermann from Jerome.
60. Cf. John 1.2.
61. "He does not speak," an addition of Klostermann from Jerome.
62. Cf. 1 Cor 13.1.
63. Heb 1.4–5.
64. Cf. John 1.1–2.

make an attempt to converse with children—in the same way also the Savior, when he is in the Father,[65] and sharing in the magnificence of the glory of God, does not speak human words—he does not know how to articulate to those below[66] him—but when he comes into a human body, he says, according to the initial words, *I do not know how to speak for I am a youth.* He is a youth because of his bodily birth, an elder according to the words, *first fruit of all creation,*[67] a youth because he came *at the completion of the ages.*[68] And[69] . . . he has appeared later in life.

(6) He says then, *I do not know how to speak.* I know some things greater than speaking, I know some things greater than this human voice. Do you wish that I speak to men? I have not yet adopted human speech; I have your dialect, O God, I am your Word, O God; with you I know how to converse; with men, *I do not know how to speak, for I am a youth.*

9. *Do not say, "I am a youth,"*[70] *for to all those to whom I dispatch you, you shall go.* Then *he extended his hand and touched his mouth, gave to him words,* and he gave him *words* for *kingdoms,* so that he might *uproot.* But he had no need of words of uprooting when he was in the[71] Father;[72] he had no need of words which demolish and those which destroy what is inferior. For there was nothing which merited destroying there,[73] there was nothing which merited uprooting. Thus as the saying, *I do not know you because you are workers of iniquity,*[74]

---

65. Cf. John 14.10–11.
66. Another common spatial metaphor in Origen used theologically: those above and those below.
67. Col 1.15.                      68. Heb 9.26.
69. "And," a correction of Cordier from Jerome. It would seem more likely, in light of the pattern of "youth" and "elder," that "elder" should be given here. Hence there may be a lacuna.
70. "Do . . . youth," an addition of Klostermann from Jerome.
71. "The," an addition of Klostermann.
72. Cf. John 14.10.
73. Another spatial image which is used theologically. See Schadel, 243–44, nn. 11 and 12.
74. Luke 13.27.

HOMILY 1    13

is a great matter, said in this way by the Savior on account of the *immeasurable greatness*[75] of his glory, the words, *I do not know how to speak*, should be equated with: *I do not know how to speak* human words.

10. But, *Before I formed you in the womb, I knew you*, is said either of Jeremiah or of the Savior. You will find, after you read Genesis and observe what is said about the creation of the world, that Scripture, in a way exceedingly dialectic,[76] did not say, "Before I made you in the womb, I knew you." For when he is created *according to the image*,[77] God said: *"Let us make man in our image and likeness"*;[78] he did not say: "let us form." But when he took *clay of the earth*, he did not make man, but he formed man and he *placed the man whom he formed in paradise so that he would work and protect it.*[79] If you can, note[80] the difference between making and forming[81] because the Lord, who speaks either of Jeremiah or of the Savior, did not say: "Before I made you in the womb, I knew you." For what is made does not arise in a womb, but what is formed from the clay of the earth, this is created in the womb.[82]

(2) *Before I formed you in the womb, I knew you*. If the Lord knew all men,[83] he would not say especially to Jeremiah, *I*

75. Eph 1.19.
76. "Dialectic" here means to clarify the use and distinction of certain words and ideas, in this case, the distinction between "to form" and "to make." For more discussion on the dialectic and its philosophical origins, see Schadel, 244, n. 13.
77. Gen 1.27.      78. Gen 1.26.
79. Gen 2.15.
80. "Note" (ὅρα), a correction of Cordier. S has ὁρᾶν.
81. "And forming," an addition of Klostermann from Jerome.
82. For Origen the act of "making" refers to the spiritual creation, the act of "forming" to the bodily creation. He follows here his fellow Alexandrian Philo and others. Schadel, in a long note, 244, n. 14, indicates that this is another example of Origen's use of the inner and outer metaphor so prevalent in his thought.
83. After this phrase in the text, there occur a few words in manuscript S which do not appear in Jerome's translation: πρὸς τὸ οὐκ ἐπίσταμαι λαλεῖν ἐπεὶ πάντας ἠρίστατο ὁ κύριος λεκτέον γάρ. As written they make little sense.

*knew you.* Hence God knows those who are unique, those worthy of his knowledge, and *the Lord knows those who are his*,[84] but God ignores those who are not worthy, as does the Savior when he says, *I never knew you.*[85] Since we are men, to the extent we progress, we judge that certain things are worthy of our knowing them. And we do not want to hear some things, so we neither know nor see these things, but we want to know others. What follows? The God of the universe wants to know Pharaoh, he wants to know the Egyptians, but they are not worthy of the knowledge of God. But Moses is worthy, and each of the Prophets are likewise honored. You need to set many things right in order that God may begin to know you. For he knew Jeremiah before being formed in the womb, but another he may begin to know after he has lived thirty years, another[86] after he has lived forty years.

(3) These are esoteric words,[87] not to be investigated concerning the Savior, but requiring to be understood concerning Jeremiah *by those who have ears.*[88]

11. How can he say: *Before I formed you in the womb, I knew you, and before you appeared from your mother, I sanctified you?* God sanctifies some people for himself. He did not await this person so that he could sanctify him after he was born, but he had already sanctified him before he appeared from his mother. If you apply this to the Savior, there is no difficulty saying that he was sanctified before he was born: he was sanctified not only before he appeared, but he was also sanctified even prior to this. But Jeremiah himself was sanctified before he appeared from his mother.

12. *I have appointed you as a prophet to the nations.* If you in-

---

Schadel omits them. Nautin amends them, ignoring several words and adding a couple of others.

84. 2 Tim 2.19.                         85. Matt 7.23.
86. "Another," an addition of the editor from Jerome.
87. They are "esoteric" probably because existing before being in the womb implies for Origen pre-existence of souls, a subject not discussed in the doctrine of the Church.
88. Matt 11.15.

## HOMILY 1

vestigate the words, *I have appointed you as prophet to the nations*, with respect to Jeremiah, observe that in what follows he is called to prophesy *to all the nations*, and there is the subtitle: *what Jeremiah prophesied to all the nations*,[89] *to Elam, to Damascus*,[90] *to Moab*.[91] And because he has prophesied to *all of the nations*, we hold that in a literal sense *I have appointed you as prophet to the nations* is in reference to him.

(2) Whether in an anagogical sense it applies to Jeremiah, we have dealt with already,[92] and whether it applies to the Savior, what do we need to say? He really did prophesy to *all of the nations*. As he has many thousands of other roles, so also is he a prophet. As he is a *high priest*,[93] as he is a savior, as he is a healer, so also is he a prophet. Moses, in fact, when he prophesies concerning him, is not only a prophet, but spoke especially as one when he said, *The Lord God will cause to rise up for you from your*[94] *brothers a prophet such as I; listen to him. And if there is one who does not listen to that prophet, he will be rooted out of his people*.[95] He then is also a prophet appointed to *all of the nations*, and he received grace *from God which was poured forth on his lips*,[96] so that not only when he was present in the body, but also now, when he is present in power and in the Spirit,[97] he prophesies to *all of the nations*, so that from all nations he accomplishes his prophecy and draws men to salvation.

13. *And I said: "O you who are, Master and Lord, behold: I do not know how to speak, for I am a youth." And the Lord said to me: "Do not say, 'I am a youth,' for to all to whom I will send you, you will go."* Often we have said that with respect to the inner man[98] one can be a child even if he is old in body. Yet some-

---
89. Jer 25.14 (49.34).  90. Jer 30.29 (49.23).
91. Jer 31.1 (48.1).  92. See 6.(2) above.
93. Heb 2.17.
94. "Your," an addition of Klostermann from Jerome.
95. Acts 3.22–23; Deut 18.15, 19.  96. Ps 44.3 (45.2).
97. Or: Spirit.
98. Inner/outer man: A favorite theological metaphor of Origen, used in many ways, but especially in terms of the spirit/body.

times one might be a child with respect to the outer man, but an adult with respect to the inner. Such a one was Jeremiah, who already had grace from God while still a child in body. For that reason the Lord said to him, *Do not say, "I am a youth."* It is a sign he is not a youth, but a mature man,[99] so that *to all to whom I will send you, you will go, and whatever I command you, you will speak. Be not afraid before their face.* The Word of God knew that those who are ambassadors of the Word take risks with those who hear them. For, being reproved, they hate them; being reproached, they persecute them. The Prophets underwent every kind of suffering: *A prophet is not without honor except in his own country and in his own house*[100] which[101] we also discussed just recently.[102]

(2) Thus when he sent the Prophet, God knew all the dangers he would incur, and he says to him, *"Be not afraid before their face, for I am with you to take you away," says the Lord.* What Jeremiah did suffer has been described: he was cast into a cistern of mud,[103] he remained there, drinking only water, while eating *one loaf of bread*[104] *for a day*,[105] yet his prophecy has shown what myriad other things he also has suffered. *Which of the prophets did your fathers not persecute?*[106] has been said to the Jews. And of necessity *those who wish to live piously in Christ Jesus in every sense will be persecuted*[107] by opposing powers through every kind of means they can find. On account of this, not being dismayed, let those persecuted

---

99. Cf. Eph 4.13. Τέλειος ("mature") is an important word in Origen's thought and is often contrasted with the immature, the youthful or the childish, and refers to the spiritual as well as the physical state. The common translation "perfect" fails to reflect the ongoing spiritual growth.
100. Matt 13.57.
101. "Which," an addition of Huet from Jerome.
102. It is uncertain to what work he is referring here. Klostermann suggests perhaps *Jo* 13.55, *Hom in Lc* 33.2 or *Comm in Mt* 10.18, though this last was composed after the homilies.
103. Cf. Jer 38.6 (45.6).
104. "One loaf of bread," from LXX. S has τ`` ἀρτίων. Jerome has *panem*.
105. Jer 44.20 (37.20).          106. Acts 7.52.
107. 2 Tim 3.12.

## HOMILY 1

continue to do all things, only let them pray that they are persecuted unjustly and not justly, not on account of injustice, not on account of sin, not on account of greed. And if anyone is persecuted for righteousness, let him hear this: *Blessed are you when men revile you and persecute you and say all kinds of evil against you for my sake. Rejoice and be glad, for your reward is great in the heavens, for so they persecuted the prophets before you.*[108]

14. *"Because I am with you to take you away,"* says the Lord. *Then the Lord stretched forth his hand to me and touched my mouth, and the Lord said to me.* Observe the differences between Jeremiah and Isaiah. Isaiah said: *I am one who has unclean lips, and I dwell in the midst of a people who have unclean lips and I have seen the King, the Lord of Sabaoth, with my eyes.*[109] And since he did not confess to having unclean works but only words—for until this point he was a sinner—the Lord did not *stretch forth his hand,* but *one of the Seraphim touched his lips with his hand and said, "Behold, I have taken away your iniquities."*[110] But since Jeremiah was sanctified *from the womb of his mother,* tongs are not sent for him, nor a *coal from the altar*[111]—he had nothing worthy of the fire—but the hand itself of the Lord touched him.

(2) Therefore he says, *The Lord stretched forth his hand to me and touched my mouth, and the Lord said to me: "Behold, I have placed my words in your mouth. Behold, this day I have placed you over nations and kingdoms, to uproot."*

(3) Who is so blessed to uproot with the words given by God the numerous kingdoms which *the Devil displayed,*[112] kingdoms of opposing powers, kingdoms of sins? Yet it was written, *Behold, I have placed my words in your mouth. Behold, this day I have placed you over nations and kingdoms to uproot.*[113] And just as there are kingdoms so there are also nations.[114]

---

108. Matt 5.11–12.
109. Isa 6.5.
110. Isa 6.7.
111. Isa 6.6.
112. Matt 4.8.
113. "To uproot," from Jerome.
114. The sentence in Jerome continues: "It is not able to be called a kingdom unless it has nations under it."

As there is a kingdom of fornication, so each act of fornication is a nation of fornication.[115] The same types of sin—covetousness, robbery—form a single kingdom, and there are many kingdoms in those who have many kinds of sins. So then, with respect to each of the sins, conjure up for me the nations that are subject to the kingdoms. For example, a certain one has many nations subject to the kingdom of fornication, another has many nations subject to the kingdom of robbery, another to slander, and another to anger.

(4) There is need of the words of God which are sent out to the nations and kingdoms to uproot and demolish. To uproot what? The Savior taught us when he said, *Every plant which my Father in heaven has not planted will be uprooted.*[116] There are some things in[117] souls which *my Father in heaven has not planted.* For all of the *evil thoughts, murders, adulteries, fornications,*[118] *thefts, false witnesses, slanders*[119] are plants not planted by the heavenly Father. If you want to see whose plants such thoughts are, hear that *an enemy has done this,*[120] the one who has sown *weeds among the wheat.*[121] Thus God, who has the seeds, awaits us, as well as the Devil. If we give *a place to the Devil,*[122] the enemy sows a *plant which the Father in heaven did not plant,* and it will be utterly uprooted. If we do not give *a place to the Devil* but give a place to God, God rejoicing sows his seeds in our hearts.[123]

---

115. Jerome has for this sentence: "Just as fornication rules in the sinful man, it is necessary that the kingdom of fornication has its own nations." Klostermann believes there is a lacuna here.

116. Matt 15.13.

117. "In," an addition of Klostermann.

118. "Fornications," from the Catena and Jerome.

119. Matt 15.19.     120. Matt 13.28.

121. Matt 13.25.     122. Eph 4.27.

123. For Origen, the ἡγεμονικόν, the Stoic philosophical term for heart, which meant a governing power or principle within man, refers to the seat of spiritual force in man. It is the superior ruling or higher part of the soul and the center of the καρδία, the biblical term for heart. Jacques Dupuis, *"L'ésprit de l'homme." Étude sur l'anthropologie religieuse d'Origène* (Paris, 1967), 70. Rufinus, the translator into Latin of many of Origen's works, often translates it: *principale cordis.*

## HOMILY 1

(5) And do not suppose that Jeremiah has received some sort of unfortunate gift from God because[124] he has been *placed over nations and kingdoms, to uproot*. God is good when he uproots what is bad through words, the iniquitous kingdoms by the kingdom of Heaven, the hostile nations by the nation of God. *To uproot and demolish.*

15. There is a building of the Devil, there is a *building of God*.[125] The building *on sand*[126] is of the[127] Devil. For it stands on nothing firm, secure, and unified. But the *building of God* is *on rock*.[128] See what is said to those who belong to God: *You are a field of God, a building of God*.[129] In addition, the words of God are *over nations and kingdoms to uproot, demolish, and destroy*. If a person uproots, the thing uprooted is not destroyed, but is uprooted. If one demolishes, the rocks of what is demolished are not destroyed; they are what is demolished. Hence there is need of the goodness of God after the uprooting, to destroy what has been uprooted, after the demolition to destroy what has been demolished. With respect to what is destroyed and what is uprooted, read carefully how such things are destroyed: *And the chaff you will burn with unquenchable fire*, and *bind the bundles, bundles of weed and deliver them to the fire*.[130] In this way, it is destroyed after the uprooting.

(2) If you also wish to see, after the demolition, what is destroyed in the building made of poor material, that house, demolished on account of a leper,[131] becomes dust[132] and as dust which is *outside the city*, it is *cast out*, so that not a *rock*[133] will remain. It is similar to the passage: *As the mud of the streets I will grind them*.[134] For it is necessary that the inferior does not ever survive, and once destroyed the rocks do not[135]

---

124. "Because" (ὅτι), a correction of Huet from Jerome. S has ἔτι.
125. 1 Cor 3.9.
126. Matt 7.26.
127. "The," an addition of Klostermann.
128. Matt 7.25.
129. 1 Cor 3.9.
130. Matt 3.12; 13.30.
131. Cf. Lev 14.33ff.
132. Cf. Ps 17(18).42.
133. Lev 14.40.
134. Ps 17(18).42.
135. "Not," from Jerome.

prove useful for another building upon which the evil one could build. It was uprooted so that he may not again discover seeds in what was uprooted in order to sow weeds[136] again. For in every case when he had the seeds of weeds, he sowed them. Thus *bind the weeds and burn them completely in the fire*,[137] so that the uprooted is destroyed, and once demolished, the building of the Devil is destroyed.

16. But the words of God do not end with these: to *uproot, demolish and destroy*. For let what is bad be uprooted from me, the inferior demolished! If the superior was not planted before the others were uprooted, what does it matter to me? What does it matter to me if what is distinguished cannot be built up before these others? On account of this, first the words of God fulfill the need to *uproot, demolish and destroy*, then to build[138] and to plant. In Scripture we always note that those acts which are "unpleasant-seeming,"[139] as I will name them, are listed first, then those acts which seem gladdening are mentioned second. *I will kill and I will make alive.*[140] He did not say, *I will make alive* and then *I will kill.*[141] For it is impossible that what God has made to live would be taken away by himself or by someone else. But, *I will kill and I will make alive.* Whom will I kill? Paul the traitor, Paul the persecutor. *And I will make alive* so that he becomes *Paul the Apostle of Jesus Christ.*[142]

(2) If the miserable heretics[143] had understood this, they would not continually produce for us these words, saying, "Are you not aware how the[144] God of the Law is crude and inhuman when he says: *I will kill and I will make alive?*" Do

---

136. Cf. Matt 13.25.         137. Matt 13.30.
138. "To build," an addition from Jerome.
139. Origen appears to have invented a word here: σκυθρωποφανῆς.
140. Deut 32.39.
141. This sentence is an addition from Jerome.
142. 2 Cor 1.1.
143. In light of the following statements, we would assume Origen is referring to the Gnostics, especially Marcion, Valentinus and Basilides, who diminished the power and quality of the God of the Old Testament.
144. "The," an addition of Klostermann.

## HOMILY 1

you not see in the Scriptures, the promise[145] of the resurrection of the dead? Or are you not aware that the resurrection of the dead is already foreshadowed for each person? *We were buried* with Christ *through baptism,* and we have risen with him.[146]

(3) He begins then in more gloomy but necessary tones with *I will kill,* then, after he has killed, *and I will make alive. I will wound, and I will heal.*[147] *For the Lord disciplines the one he loves, and every son he receives he chastises.*[148] First he wounds, and then he heals. *For he brings pain, and he restores again.*[149] And similarly here: *I have set you today over nations and kings to uproot and to demolish and to destroy, and to build and plant.* Regardless, that which is bad needs to be removed[150] from us first. God cannot build where there is a worthless building. *For what partnership have righteousness and iniquity? Or what fellowship has light with darkness?*[151] It is necessary to uproot evil at its roots; it is necessary to demolish the building of evil from our souls so that then the words may build and plant.[152] For I can understand in no other way what was written, *Behold, I have given my words into your mouth.* What do the words do? They *uproot and demolish and destroy.* Words uproot nations, words demolish kingdoms—but not the corporeal and worldly kingdoms.[153] Since words worthily uproot, since words worthily demolish, understand what is uprooted by words and what is demolished by words. Is there not a power in what was said just now—if God provides according to the passage, *The Lord will provide a word for those who preach the Gospel with great power*[154]— a power which uproots if there is a lack of faith, if there is hypocrisy, if there is wickedness, if

---

145. "Promise" (ἐπαγγελία), a correction from Jerome. S has ἀπαγγελία.
146. Rom 6.4; cf. Eph 2.6.   147. Deut 32.39.
148. Heb 12.6.   149. Job 5.18.
150. "To be removed" (ἀφαιρεθῆναι), a correction of Klostermann from Jerome. S has ῥηθῆναι.
151. 2 Cor 6.14.
152. "And plant," an addition of Klostermann from Jerome.
153. "Though . . . kingdoms," an addition of Klostermann from Jerome.
154. Ps 67.12.

there is licentiousness? Is there not a power which demolishes if anywhere an idol temple has been built in the heart, so that, when that temple is destroyed, the *temple of God*[155] is built, and the glory of God is found in the temple which was built up? And there appears not a *grove*[156] but a *plantation*[157]—a paradise *of God*—where the temple of God is in Christ Jesus, *to whom is the glory and the power for the ages of ages. Amen.*[158]

155. 1 Cor 3.16.
156. In Scripture, a pagan place incompatible with the altar of God. Cf. Deut 16.21; 7.5, 12.3; Jer 3.6; 33.18, etc.
157. Matt 15.13.   158. 1 Pet 4.11.

## HOMILY 2

*Jeremiah 2.21–22*

*On "How did you turn to bitterness, you strange vine?" up to, "'If you wash in lye and wash yourself with soap, you remain stained in your iniquities before me,' says the Lord."*

OD DID NOT MAKE *death and he does not delight in the destruction of living things; for he created all things that they might exist and the creatures of the world are wholesome and there is no destructive poison in them and the dominion of Hades is not on earth.*[1] Passing over, then, a little passage, I will ask: From where, then, did death come? *By the envy of the Devil death came into the world.*[2] If, then, there is something excellent[3] in our regard, God has made it, but we have created evil and sins for ourselves. For the same reason, the beginning of the passage just read from the Prophet speaks in a rhetorical sense to those who have bitterness in the soul contrary to the sweetness which God fashioned for it: *How have you turned to bitterness, you strange vine?* as if he was saying: God did not make lameness, but he has made all things swift of foot, yet what cause arose which has made the lame lame? And God has made all limbs absolutely sound, but what cause arose which makes things suffer? In the same way, the soul, not only of the first man but of all men, arose *according to the image*—for the statement, *Let us make man according to our image and according to our likeness,*[4] applies to all men.

---

1. Wis 1.13–14.     2. Wis 2.24.
3. "Excellent" (ἄριστον), a correction of Delarue. S has ἀρεστὸν.
4. Gen 1.26.

And, just as in Adam, what most people think of as *according to the image* is prior to what was superimposed upon it when he bore *the image of the earthly*[5] due to sin, so in all people what is according to the image of God is prior to the inferior image. *We have borne*, being sinners, *the image of the earthly, let us bear*, after we repent, *the image of the heavenly*.[6] Indeed, creation was made according to the *image of the heavenly*.[7]

(2) Hence there is a concern here when the Word says reprovingly to sinners: *How did you turn to bitterness, you strange vine?* For *I planted you as a fruitful vine, wholly true*. In those things said before and when I resume after a little, I will convince you that God planted the human soul as a good vine, but each soul turned contrary to the plan of the Creator. *I planted you as a fruitful vine, wholly*, not partly, *true*, not true in one sense, false in another, rather, *I planted you as a fruitful vine, wholly true. How did you turn*, you whom I created as a wholly true vine, *how did you turn to bitterness and become a strange vine?*[8]

2. After this let us look at the words: *"Even if you wash in lye and cover yourself with soap, you are yet stained in your iniquities before me,"* says the Lord. Does a sinful soul, which has taken up lye and which washes itself in bodily lye, suppose that it will put an end to its filth and put an end to its sin? Does anyone assume that when he has taken up soap that arose from the earth and washed himself and cleaned himself the soul is purified, because the Word then says to the one who has

---

5. 1 Cor 15.49.   6. 1 Cor 15.49.

7. Origen's ideas on the "image," discussed in all of his works, are a significant contribution to theology. See Henri Crouzel's study, *Théologie de l'image de Dieu chez Origène* (Paris: Aubier, 1956).

8. This section is filled with unanswered questions, because for Origen there are no answers to this, perhaps the most profound, quandary of man: If man was created good, how could he not be good? The precise inner cause of perversion and evil is never developed, though in *On First Principles* and in other works, Origen indicates that man's good is not his; only God is truly good. In that sense man can ignore it in the same way he can refuse to see the light by closing his eyes. Eventually he will go blind. But a question still remains: Why would one ignore the good?

## HOMILY 2

turned to bitterness and become like a strange vine: *"Even if you wash yourself in lye and cover yourself with soap, you are yet stained in your iniquities before me,"* says the Lord?

(2) Hardly, but one needs to see that the Word[9] has every power, and just as he has the power of every Scripture, so the Word has the power of every ointment and he is the most cleansing power of any purifying agent. *For the Word of God is living and active and sharper than any two-edged sword*[10] and whatever you mention, if there is a need, it is in the power of the Word.

(3) Thus there is a *lye* Word and a *soap* Word which, when it has been spoken, purifies that sort of filth. But since the Word which is lye and the Word which is soap does not cure every kind of sin, and there are sins which need neither lye nor soap, it is said to him who thinks that he has sins which can be washed away in lye and soap: *"Even if you wash in lye and cover yourself with soap, you are yet stained in your iniquities before me,"* says the Lord. And just as certain wounds are cured by emollients and others by oil and others need a bandage and hence are healed, yet others are wounds about which it is written: *It is not closed with ointments or oil or bandages; but your country is a desert, your cities are burnt up,*[11] so there are certain sins which foul the soul, and man needs for such sins the lye of the Word, the soap of the Word, yet there are some sins which are not cured in this way, for they are not comparable to filth.

(4) Accordingly, when one has understood the differ-

---

9. The use of the Greek word λόγος in this and the following sentences is difficult to translate, but we should note that Origen, like others of his time, uses the word λόγος in many ways, and many of them are found in these homilies. I have tried to note when he uses the term in a way which cannot be translated as "word." But even as "word," there are many implications. Generally, Origen viewed λόγος as a power within man which shares with a greater universal Λόγος, whom Origen believed, of course, to be the Λόγος of the Gospel of John who became flesh and dwelt among men. A good place to begin a study of this concept is Rolf Gögler, *Zur Theologie des biblischen Wortes bei Origenes* (Düsseldorf: Patmos, 1963).

10. Heb 4.12.   11. Isa 1.6–7 (LXX).

ences in sins, see how the Lord says in Isaiah, *The Lord will wash away the filth of the sons and daughters of Zion, and will cleanse the blood from their midst by a spirit of judgment and a spirit of burning.*[12] Filth and blood; filth by a spirit[13] of judgment, blood by a spirit of burning. Even if you have not[14] committed a sin which leads to death,[15] you nevertheless have sinned, you have become filthy. Thus, *the Lord will wash away the filth of the sons and daughters of Zion, and he will cleanse the blood from their midst,* then a *spirit of judgment* as a recompense for the filth, a *spirit of burning* for the blood.[16] And most of us, whenever we sin more grievously, need not lye or the washing with soap, but the *spirit of burning.*

3. On this account, Jesus—now perhaps I discover the reason[17]—baptizes *in the Holy Spirit and in fire,*[18] not the same man *in the Holy Spirit and in fire,* but the holy man *in the Holy Spirit,* while another man, after he has believed, after he has been deemed worthy of the Holy Spirit, after he has sinned again, Jesus washes in fire, so that it is not the same man who is baptized by Jesus in the Holy Spirit and in fire.

(2) Blessed, then, is the one who is baptized in the Holy Spirit and does not need the baptism by fire, but three times unhappy is that man who has need to be baptized in fire, though Jesus takes care of both of them. For *a shoot from the stump of Jesse will come forth, and a branch will grow out of the root,*[19] a shoot for those who are punished, a branch for the righteous.[20] So God is a consuming fire[21] and God is light,[22] a consuming fire to sinners, a light to the just and holy ones.

12. Isa 4.4.
13. "By a spirit," an addition of Klostermann from Jerome.
14. "Not," an addition of Klostermann.
15. Cf. 1 John 5.16–17.
16. "Spirit of burning for the blood," an addition of Blass.
17. λόγος.   18. Luke 3.16.
19. Isa 11.1.
20. "A branch ... righteous," an addition of Klostermann from Jerome. Klostermann notes that Origen offers the same distinction in *Jo* 1.36; *Sel in Ezech* 7.10 and *Hom in Is* 3.1.
21. Cf. Heb 12.29.   22. Cf. 1 John 1.15.

## HOMILY 2

(3) And blessed[23] is he *who shares in the first resurrection,*[24] he who has kept the baptism of the Holy Spirit. Who is he who is saved in another resurrection? He who needs the baptism from fire, when he comes before that fire and the fire tests him, and when that fire finds wood, hay and stubble to burn.[25]

(4) Now because of this, since these things are said, since we have brought together as far as we can the words of Scripture, let us put away these things into the heart and let us try to live in light of them, to see if we can become pure before our final departure and, after we prepare our works for the final departure, after we depart, be accepted among those who are good[26] and be saved in Christ Jesus, *to whom is the glory and the power for the ages of ages. Amen.*[27]

---

23. "Blessed" (μακάριος), a correction of Cordier from Jerome. S has μακαρίοις.
24. Apoc 20.6.
25. Cf. 1 Cor 3.12–13. The discussion of the two resurrections indicates that Origen believes that people are treated according to the gravity of their sins, and according to whether they keep the original baptism, the baptism of the Holy Spirit, without mortal sins. Those that sin gravely after this baptism will first receive the baptism of fire and then "another" resurrection. The wood, hay, and stubble are the impurities of soul which need to be annihilated in the baptism of fire before blessedness can be received. There are many other texts which discuss the same ideas. See, for example, *Cels* 4.13, 5.15; *Jo* 13.23; *Hom in Lev* 15.3; and *Princ* 2.10.4, as well as *Hom in Jer* 16.6 and 20.3.
26. Cf. Matt 22.10.
27. 1 Pet 4.11.

## HOMILY 3

*Jeremiah 2.31*

On *"Did I become a wilderness to the house of Israel,"*
up to, *"or a dry land?"*

THE LORD SAYS in the beginning of the reading that he had neither become a desert nor a land made dry to Israel. Who then, faced with this reading, would not scrutinize it to seek the purpose of what was written? Suppose that God had not become a desert to Israel, had not become to Israel a land made dry. Does this mean then that the Lord has become a desert to Israel today or is now a land made dry to it? What then? When he was not a desert or a land made dry to Israel, was he a desert and land made dry to the pagan nations? For if he was not always and for all a desert and always and for all a land made dry, what need is there of the statement he makes especially for Israel: *Did I become a desert or a land made dry to the house of Israel?* But it is necessary to come to the universal benefits[1] of God, and then, after his universal benefits, to what is particular.

2. The God who *brings forth the sun on the evil and the good* is a desert to no one. To no one is he who *rains on the just and unjust* ever a land made dry.[2] How is he a desert, when he brings forth the day and causes the night to rest? How is he a desert, when he causes the land to bear fruit? How is he a desert, when he provides for each person in his soul so that it is endowed with reason, so that it can grasp knowledge and exercise its intelligence, and in the body so that it has

---

1. εὐεργεσίας.   2. Matt 5.45.

healthy sense faculties?[3] Hence with respect to the way[4] of what is universal, God is not a desert.

(2) But with respect to what is particular, I come to the deeds of Israel and I say: He was neither a desert nor a land made dry when he was accomplishing signs and wonders for the people in Egypt. But if any time arose when they would be abandoned, he would become to them like a desert without being a desert himself.

(3) So when he was not a desert or a land made dry to Israel, he was, with respect to what is particular, a desert and land made dry to the pagan nations. But when he turned away from Israel and became to that Israel like a desert and a land made dry, then grace was poured forth on the pagan nations, and Jesus Christ became now to us not a desert but an abundance, and not a land made dry, but one which bears fruit. For *the children of the desolate*[5] *are many more than of one who has a husband.*[6] And he threatens them for whom he has neither become a desert nor a land made dry when he says, "I have not become to you a *desert* or a *land made dry*, but you have said: *We will not be ruled over and we will not go to you anymore.*"[7] Have not the sons of Israel spoken from desperation in the text: *We will not be ruled over....*[8]

---

3. Cf. Heb 5.14.   4. λόγος.
5. This same Greek word (ἔρημος) is also translated "desert."
6. Isa 54.1; Gal 4.27.   7. Jer 2.31.
8. The remainder of this homily is missing.

# HOMILY 4

## Jeremiah 3.6–11

*On "The Lord said to me in the days of Josiah," up to,
"Israel justified her soul in comparison to the perfidious Judah."*

THE LETTER[1] ITSELF OF THE TEXT just read has something unclear that we need to understand first. Then, after this, if God wills, we shall know his mystical[2] plan.

(2) He wants us then to know in these words, just as it is written in Kings,[3] that the people were divided in those times into the kingdom of ten tribes under Jeroboam and the kingdom of two tribes under Roboam. And those under Jeroboam were called Israel, and those under Roboam Judah. And the division of the people persisted, according to the history, until today. For we know of nothing in the history which united Israel and Judah *into the same nation*.[4] Then Israel first,[5] under Jeroboam and under his successors, sinned excessively, and Israel sinned so much beyond Judah that they were sentenced by Providence to become captives *to the Assyrians until the sign*, as the Scripture says.[6] After this, the sons of Judah also sinned, and as captives they were sentenced to Babylon, not until a sign as Israel, but for *seventy years*, which Jeremiah prophesied,[7] and Daniel also mentioned.[8]

---

1. ῥητὸν, i.e., the literal interpretation.
2. Here Origen refers to the deeper, spiritual interpretation.
3. 3 Kings (1 Kings) 12ff.   4. Jer 3.18.
5. "First" (πρῶτον), a correction of Delarue from Jerome. S has πρὸς τὸν.
6. 4 Kings (2 Kings) 17.23.
7. Jer 25.11.   8. Dan 9.2.

(3) If we understand these matters with respect to that people then, consider whether the passages of the Prophet do not signify something such as this: For as a basis[9] he decries the faults of Israel,[10] and he says that after all the sins had been committed by Israel, the community of Judah, who had heard of the faults of those people and the manner in which I have indicated they came to captivity, did not learn[11] but added to the sins, to the point that, when their sins were compared to the sins of Israel, he found, on account of the adding, more righteousness in Israel than in Judah. Then the Prophet is ordered to prophesy to them that Judah is worse than Israel, so that Judah might turn back from her sins.[12] Thus after the prophecy to exhort Israel to turn back, the Prophet prophesies that Israel and Judah will be together and there will arise at the same time one kingdom from both.[13]

(4) Let him who finds interest in the reading take the words of everything read today and then he will see that the thoughts have been clarified: *And the Lord said to me in the days of Josiah the king: "Have you seen what the assembly of Israel*—not Judah, but first *Israel*—*has done to me? She has gone up on every high mountain and under every green tree and there*[14] *she prostituted herself. And then after all her prostituting, I said all these things: 'Return to me.' And she did not return.*[15] *And the Judah the Covenant-breaker saw her breach of covenant*—that of the assembly of Israel—*and they*—the people from Judah—*saw all those things in which she committed adultery for which the assembly of Israel was abandoned, and I sent her away and I gave her a bill of divorce."*[16] It was necessary that Judah be taught, for *I sent away* Israel, the synagogue of Israel, and *I gave them* to the Assyrians. *And I gave to her a bill of divorce into her hands. And the perfidious Judah was unafraid.*[17] But after these things

9. ὡς λόγος.   10. Jer 3.6.
11. Jerome here has: "had no repentance nor converted to me."
12. Cf. Jer 3.7ff.   13. Cf. Jer 3.18.
14. "There," an addition of Klostermann from Jerome.
15. "And she did not return," an addition of Cordier from LXX.
16. Jer 3.6–8.   17. Jer 3.8.

which he did to Israel, after sending her away, after giving a *bill of divorce*, it was necessary that Judah's synagogue should have learned from what the latter suffered; but not only did Judah not learn, but they added to the sins to the extent that it appears the sins of the synagogue of Israel were righteous compared to the sins of the synagogue of Judah. *And he has given a bill of divorce into her hands. And the perfidious Judah,* her sister, *was unafraid. And she, too, went and prostituted herself, and the prostitution was nothing to her, and she was adulterous with the tree and the rock. And in all of these events, perfidious Judah did not turn to me with her whole heart, but on pretense*[18] she turned to me. She was not afraid of me because of what I had done to Israel in order that she might turn back maturely.[19] But though it was necessary that she turn back in truth, she turned back *on pretense. And in the midst of all these things the perfidious Judah did not turn with her whole heart to me, but on pretense. And the Lord said to me, "Compared to the perfidious Judah, Israel has justified her soul."*[20] The sins of Israel compared to the errors of Judah effected a justification of the soul of the synagogue of Israel.

2. *Go, then, and proclaim these words to the North.*[21] If the letter is understood, let us see what he plans to clarify in these words. The calling[22] of the pagan nations has its beginning in the transgression of Israel. And the Apostles, when they preached, said in the synagogues of the Jews, "The word of salvation was sent to you, but since you deemed yourselves unworthy, behold, we have turned to the pagan nations."[23] And the Apostle who realized these things spoke what he knew: *By their trespass, salvation has come to the pagan nations so as to make them jealous.*[24] Therefore the many sins of that peo-

---

18. Jer 3.8–10.
19. "Maturely." This word (τελείως) and its cognates are often translated with the absolute idea of "perfect." But Origen expects no one on earth to be "perfect" as we understand the term. The term is often contrasted with what is childlike or infantile.
20. Jer 3.10–11.   21. Jer 3.12.
22. "The calling," an addition of Klostermann from Jerome.
23. Cf. Acts 13.26, 46.   24. Rom 11.11.

ple have forced it to be forsaken, and for us to come to the *hope of salvation*,[25] *strangers of the covenants, aliens of the promises*.[26] Yet how does it happen that I who arose outside as a *stranger* to that so-called holy land[27] now discourse concerning the *promises* of God, and believe in the God of the patriarchs Abraham, and Isaac, and Jacob, and receive by the grace of God Jesus Christ who was foretold by the Prophets? If you comprehend these two peoples,[28] one from Israel, the other from the pagan nations, look with me at the exile of Israel also with respect to the people of Israel. Note with me that it is written concerning that people: *I sent her away and I gave to her a bill of divorce*. For God *sent away* that people and gave to it a *bill of divorce*, which is given to those who are married. The Law of Moses says that if the wife is displeasing to the husband, the woman gets a *bill of divorce* from the husband and is sent away, and the man who sent away the former wife because she seemed to act improperly is allowed to marry another woman. So, note in the word those who receive the *bill of divorce*, and since they received the *bill of divorce*, they were forsaken in everything due to this. For where are the Prophets now among them? Where now are the signs among them?[29] Where is the manifestation of God? Where is the ritual, the Temple, the sacrifices?[30] They were driven away from their own place. Hence he gave to Israel a *bill of divorce*. Then we, Judah, turned to the Lord—Judah because the Savior arose from the tree of Judah, for it was declared beforehand that *our Lord arose from Judah*.[31] And our last days—if only they were not already here—seem to become similar to the last days of those people, perhaps even worse.

3. That such events will happen also for us at the *perfection of this age*[32] is clear from what the Savior says in the Gospel:

25. Cf. 1 Thess 5.8.  26. Cf. Eph 2.12.
27. It is "so-called" because the true holy land for Origen is in heaven and the home of God, the angels, etc. See *Princ* 2.3.6.
28. This theme of the "two peoples" is a recurring theme in Origen's exegesis.
29. Cf. Ps 73.9.  30. Cf. Hos 3.4.
31. Heb 7.14.  32. Matt 13.49.

*Because wickedness has multiplied, the love of many will grow cold, but he who endures to the end will be saved.*[33] And *he who will come will do signs and wonders so as to lead astray, if possible, even the elect.*[34] Also applicable to us is[35] the statement by the Savior concerning his return, that soon a faithful man will not be found out of so many churches: *Except the Son of Man come, will he find faith on the earth?*[36]

(2) And if we truly judge the matters in truth and not by numbers, if we judge the matters by intention and not from the spectacle of many gathered, we will see that we are not now faithful.[37] But when noble martyrdom arose, when we came to the gathering after conducting the martyrs to their graves and the entire church, unafflicted, was present, and the catechumens were taught by the martyrdoms and by the deaths of those who confessed the truth *unto death*,[38] neither *frightened*[39] nor troubled by the *living God*,[40] then there were faithful. Then also we knew those who had seen strange and marvelous signs, then the faithful were few but truly faithful, who traveled *a way narrow and hard which leads to life*.[41] But now, when we have become many, since there cannot be many elect—for Jesus did not speak falsely when he said, *Many are called but few are chosen*[42]—out of the mass of those who profess religion, there are very few who attain the selection of God and blessedness.

---

33. Matt 24.12–13.
34. Cf. Matt 24.24.
35. "Is," from S. Jerome has "will be."
36. Luke 18.8.
37. The repetition, "truly" and "truth," is a door to the mind of Origen and his wish to stress a critical yardstick of how to see the spiritual basis of Christian life and thought. We translate "truly" and "truth" to be consistent with our translation of ἀληθῶς and ἀλήθεια in the homilies, but the meaning is broader. Origen, while not at all unaware of the value and place of the external, sought what was most profound in the situation, action, or thought as his standard. This paragraph shows how he applied that rigorous standard to the "Church" and to those who are "faithful." Two of the principles of this yardstick are: 1) "many" does not imply quality of faith, and 2) hardship and visions are more important than professions.
38. Apoc 2.10.
39. Phil 1.28.
40. Cf. Acts 14.15.
41. Cf. Matt 7.14.
42. Matt 20.16.

## HOMILY 4

4. So when he speaks first[43] that I sent away Israel due to her sins and I sent her into exile, but Judah did not turn back when she heard about what happened to Israel,[44] he speaks about our sins. When[45] the events which refer to Israel and the mistakes of that people are known, we should be fearful and say: "If he did not spare the natural branches, how much more will he not spare us."[46] If the kind and at the same time benevolent God, who does not *spare* those rooted firmly in the *root* of the Patriarchs Abraham, Isaac, and Jacob, cuts off those who boast to be *cultivated*, "how much more will he not spare us!"[47]

(2) For *note the kindness and severity of God.*[48] For he is not *kind* without being *severe* nor *severe* without being *kind*. For if he was only *kind* and he was not *severe*, we would not think much *of his kindness.*[49] If he was *severe* and he was not *kind*, perhaps we would also despair in our sins. But now as God[50] is both a *kind* and[51] a *severe* God—for we men who repent need his kindness, but those of us who persist in sins need his severity—he also speaks to us through the Prophets and says: *You saw what the assembly of Israel*—Israel means to me that people[52]—*has done to me. She has gone on every high hill and under every overshadowing tree.*[53] If you see the Pharisee going up[54] to the temple in an arrogant way and neither beating his breast nor showing concern for his own faults, but saying, *I am thankful that I am not like the other people, extortioners, unjust, adulterers, or even like this tax collector. I fast twice a week, I give tithes of all that I get,*[55] you will know that he has

---

43. "First" (πρῶτον), a correction of Delarue from Jerome. S has πρὸς τὸ.
44. Cf. Jer 3.8ff.
45. "When" (ὅτε), a correction of Cordier. S has ὅτι.
46. Cf. Rom 11.21–24.
47. Cf. Rom 11.18, 21, 24.
48. Rom 11.22.
49. Rom 2.4.
50. θεός, a correction of Cordier. S has θεοῦ.
51. "And" (καί), is a correction of Huet from Jerome. S has εἰ.
52. The Jews.
53. The LXX text is different here.
54. "Going up" (ἀναβαίνοντα), from Jerome. S has ἐστι.
55. Luke 18.11–12.

blameworthily gone up *on every high hill*[56] as one who has loved being haughty and *for boasting and arrogance.*[57] But he has gone up also *on every high hill,*[58] and appeared *under every tree* which is not fruit-bearing but *sacred wood.*[59] For one tree is a *sacred wood* kind, another is a fruit-bearing type. Whenever they plant trees for *sacred wood,* they do not plant fruit, fig or grape trees, but they plant fruitless trees only for delight. You find that such are the words of the heretics and the beauties of their most persuasive thoughts which do not reform[60] hearers. Thus, whenever someone gives himself up to such words, he has gone *under every tree of sacred wood.* He has not said "every tree" and then said no more, nor again added every fruit-bearing tree, but he has said *under every tree of sacred wood.* On account of this, you can understand why the Lawgiver once said: *You will not plant every tree before the altar of the Lord your God, and you will not make a sacred wood.*[61] For you have rejected even the name of *sacred wood.*

5. *And there she prostituted herself. And I then said, after she prostituted herself in all of these things: "Return to me." And she did not return to me, and perfidious Judah saw her perfidy.*[62] We also have blasphemed; I mean those who sin and do not keep their agreements with God nor see that those people have broken the Covenant,[63] even though being of noble race, being from Abraham, though receiving a promise. Thus we need to consider that if[64] they have fallen from the blessings and the promises and it has profited them nothing to be from the Fathers, how much more will we, if we sin, be forsaken? *If you were children of Abraham, you would do the works of Abraham,*[65] the Savior says to them, and again John: *Do not begin to say to yourselves that we have Abraham as our father, for I*

---

56. Jer 3.6.
58. Jer 2.20.
60. ἐπιστρεφόντων.
62. Jer 3.7.

57. Cf. Jer 31.29 (Lucian).
59. Jer 3.5.
61. Deut 16.21.

63. Origen distinguishes the baptismal "agreements" of the Christians from the "Covenant" of the Jews.

64. "If," an addition of Wendland.   65. John 8.39.

## HOMILY 4

*tell you, God is able from these stones to raise up children of Abraham.*[66] He understands us as *stones* because we have a *stony heart*[67] and because we are *hardened*[68] against the truth, and truly[69] the powerful God *raises up children* of Abraham from the *stones* if we *continue* in *childbearing*[70] and we keep the *spirit of sonship*.[71]

(2) Then *the perfidious Judah*, who had not kept the agreements with God, *saw the perfidy* of the assembly of Israel, *and she saw all of those things for which that people was forsaken*. For like Judah we also see all of these things, if[72] we read the Scripture: *Concerning all these things for which the assembly of Israel was forsaken, in which she committed adultery, God sent her away and gave to her a bill of divorce*.[73] And we need to be taught from the way he treated them, when he separated them according to their sins, when he forsook them and delivered them to captivity, and delivered them to murder and delivered them to enemies. We need to turn away from these things and each of us consider that "if God did not spare the natural branches, how much more will he not spare us?"[74] If he thus rejected those from the fathers who became sinners, what will we suffer, we who were called from the pagan nations? We have considered nothing of this, we who were called so that that people might become jealous[75] when they see the servant honored, when they see one low-born advanced. If these people have already suffered such, how much more, if we sin, will we be forsaken?

(3) *In these things the house of Israel committed adultery. I sent her away and gave her a bill of divorce into her hands. And the per-*

---

66. Luke 3.8.  
67. Ezek 11.19, 36.26.  
68. Cf. Exod 10.27.  
69. Note again the use here of "truth" and "truly." See the footnote above on 3.2.  
70. Cf. 1 Tim 2.15. Origen often sees an inner union of soul and spirit where the "sons" are good thoughts. See *Hom in Gen* 1.15 and *Hom in Jer* 5.7.  
71. Cf. Rom 8.15.  
72. "If," an addition of Klostermann from Jerome.  
73. Jer 3.7–8.  
74. Cf. Rom 11.21–24.  
75. Cf. Rom 11.11.

*fidious Judah was unafraid* of what I had done to the assembly of Israel, that *I sent her away and gave her a bill of divorce, she was unafraid of* what happened to those people. Someone entered into the service of a master of a house. He is recently bought. He inquires which of the preceding servants he respects and why, and which of the servants he disrespects and why. After he has learned this, if he wishes to be in the service of the master, he prevents himself from falling into what the preceding servants did, they who were cast out and given punishment when they erred. Then after learning what the former servants had done and those who were considered of good repute, and how they found their freedom, he will emulate[76] them.[77] But we were not servants of God but of idols and demons, pagans just recently come to God. Let us read the Scripture, let us see who was justified, who was not, let us imitate those who were justified, let us prevent ourselves from falling into those things by which those who were made captives have fallen, those sent away from God.

6. *And the perfidious Judah was unafraid, and she went and prostituted herself, she also.* First Israel went and prostituted herself and later Judah prostituted herself, *and her prostitution was nothing, and she committed adultery with the tree and the rock.*[78] Whenever we sin, with hearts of stone we do nothing other than commit adultery with the *stone.* Whenever we sin and prostitute ourselves *under every woody tree,*[79] we commit adultery with the *wood.*

(2) *And the perfidious Judah did not turn to me with her whole heart, but on pretense.*[80] If we have turned to God but not fully, we are accused as one who has not turned *with a whole heart.* Thus *the perfidious Judah did not turn to me with her whole heart.*[81] He did not[82] say: "The perfidious Judah did not turn,

76. Cf. Rom 11.11.
77. This is developed more in *Hom in Ezech* 7.1.
78. Jer 3.8–9.                                               79. Jer 3.6.
80. Jer 3.10.
81. "The . . . heart," an addition of Klostermann from Jerome.
82. "Not," an addition of Klostermann from Jerome.

and remained there," but: *The perfidious Judah did not turn to me with her whole heart, but on pretense* she turned.

(3) So the true conversion is to read the books of the Old Testament[83] to see those who have become righteous, to imitate them; it is to read those, to see who have been reproached, to prevent oneself from falling into such reproaches; it is to read the books of the New Testament, the words of the Apostles; after the reading, it is to write all of this into the heart, to live according to it so that a *bill of divorce* may not be given to us, but we can belong to the holy inheritance, and,[84] with the full number saved of the pagan nations, Israel may be able then to enter. *For if the full number of Gentiles have entered, then even Israel will be saved,*[85] *and there will be one flock, one shepherd,*[86] who teaches us to glorify Almighty God in the same Christ Jesus, *to whom is the glory and the power for the ages of ages. Amen.*[87]

83. "Books of the Old Testament," literally, "the old or ancient [books]" (τὰ παλαιά), implying also what is venerable. Cf. *Hom in Jer* 5.8.
84. "And," an addition of Klostermann from Jerome.
85. Rom 11.25–26. 86. John 10.16.
87. 1 Pet 4.11.

# HOMILY 5

## Jeremiah 3.22–4.8

On *"Return, you sons, and when you return I will heal your afflictions,"* up to, *"for these things gird yourselves with sackclothes."*

**I**T IS WRITTEN CLEARLY in the Acts of the Apostles that the Apostles first came into the synagogues of the Jews,[1] announcing to them, as descendents of Abraham and Isaac and Jacob,[2] what had been written concerning the coming of Jesus Christ.[3] But when these did not receive what was said, it was necessary that there be other hearers of what was said. Then after explaining to them, they left them. For it was written that *there ought to be announced to you the word of God. But since you did not think yourselves worthy, behold we turn to the pagan nations.*[4] Though this is clearly mentioned in the Acts of the Apostles, it has been said implicitly very often by the Prophets. For the Holy Spirit primarily speaks through the Prophets to those people, but if at some point, after having said many things, he is not heard, he prophesies to the pagan nations the word which was preached.

(2) And this is also reflected at the beginning of what was read today, since it is said just before to those from Israel: *"And you will call me father and not turn away from me, for as a wife shows disdain toward him who lives with her, so also the house of Israel has shown disdain toward me," says the Lord.*[5] And when these statements concerning Israel were originally said and

---

1. Cf. Acts 13.14.
2. Cf. Acts 13.26.
3. Cf. Acts 13.33–35.
4. Cf. Acts 13.46.
5. Jer 3.19–20.

the sons of Israel heard *that*[6] *they were unrighteous in their ways and forgot their holy God*,[7] then the Holy Spirit next places the word among us who are from the pagan nations and says, *Return,*[8] *you sons, and when you return I will heal your afflictions.*[9] For we are those who are filled with *afflictions*. For each, once cleansed and recovered from the *afflictions*, would say: *We were once unbelieving, foolish, deceitful, slaves to many desires and pleasures, passing our days in malice and envy, a loathed people who hated others. But when the goodness and loving kindness of God our Savior appeared, by a washing of regeneration, he poured out his mercy upon us.*[10] And indeed, though that text of the Apostle was mentioned once before, I am persuaded to present it more clearly. For he did not say: "for we then were foolish and deceitful." But Paul, the Apostle from Israel, one *blameless according to the justice in the Law*[11] does say: *For we also,* those from Israel, *were then deceitful, foolish*.[12] So not only those from the pagan nations[13] were *foolish*, nor only those from the pagan nations were *deceitful*, nor only sinners, but we *also*, who have been taught the Law, were such before the coming of Christ. Thus, after the words are spoken to Israel, it is said to us from the pagan nations: *Return, you sons, and when you return, I will heal your afflictions.*[14]

---

6. "That" (ὅτι), a correction of Cordier from LXX. S has ἔν.
7. Jer 3.21.
8. "Return." The words ἐπιστρέφειν and ἐπιστροφή have many levels of meaning and tone in such a work as this. The common English translation is "to convert." While there are places where this seems right, I avoid it because it has certain unfortunate connotations. It has, for example, a very forceful religious tone and does not reflect the movement. Usually I translate with the more literal and root meaning: to turn back or to return (to where you once were). This translation also conforms to the idea in Origen's thought of how souls were, before the fall, with God, and will "return" to God.
9. Jer 3.22.
10. An abridged version of Titus 3.3–6.
11. Phil 3.6.   12. Titus 3.3.
13. "From the pagan nations": I have translated this phrase literally, since it is unlikely that Origen means to include all of those from the pagan nations, nor all of the Israelites, but only those "from" these peoples who do or will accept God's invitation and teaching.
14. Jer 3.22.

2. But someone will say: "These statements are said to Israel, but you apply them to those from the pagan nations." We wish to suggest that when he wants to speak to Israel about what concerns conversion, he applies the name of Israel not after[15] many words, but immediately.

(2) So next he says: *"If Israel returns to me," the Lord says, "he will return himself, and if he takes away his abominations from his mouth, and he is awed by my presence, and he will swear: 'The Lord lives, with truth and in justice and in righteousness,' then the pagan nations will bless themselves in him."*[16] The former was said to those from the pagan nations, then the following to Israel,[17] since, according to the statements made by the Apostle in the Epistle to the Romans, *if the full number of the pagan nations come in, then all of Israel will be saved.*[18]

(3) Note how God encourages us who *return* to return completely, promising that if we who return will return to him, he will heal our *afflictions* through Jesus Christ. But we are neither hesitant nor slow to act with respect to salvation, as that Israel was, and in reply, say: *Behold, we will be yours.*[19] God said, *Return, you sons, and when you return, I will heal your afflictions,* but those from the pagan nations, those who formerly were not yours but belonged to pagan gods, but belonged to opposing powers, said: *We will be servants to you.* For *when the Most High apportioned the nations,* we did not arise as your *portion* nor among the people of Jacob, your *allotted heritage;*[20] but we became the portions of others.[21] Nevertheless, we, who were then the portions of others when you said to us, *Return you sons and when you return, I will heal your afflictions,* answer, *Behold*[22] *us.*[23] For we were only awaiting one

---

15. "Not after" (οὐ μετά), a correction of Huet. S has μετ' οὐ.
16. Jer 4.1–2.
17. "The following to Israel," I have added on a suggestion of Nautin.
18. Cf. Rom 11.25–26.   19. Cf. Jer 3.22.
20. Cf. Deut 32.8–9.
21. Origen, in his interpretation of Deut 32.8–9, refers here to angels appointed to look after each nation. For more discussion, see C. Blanc, "L'angelologie d'Origène," *Studia Patristica* 14 (1976): 79–110.
22. "Behold," an addition of Klostermann.
23. Cf. Jer 3.22.

## HOMILY 5

thing: the call. Unlike those who were called and excused themselves, when called, we did not excuse ourselves. For we see in the Gospel parables that, among those who were originally called, one said, "I have married a woman, please excuse me," and another said, "I have bought five yoke of oxen, I go to examine them, please excuse me."[24] We from the pagan nations were not called in this manner and did not excuse ourselves. Why? To work what *field?* Because of what wise *woman?*[25] But for what other reason are we involved?

(4) God has then said to us: *Return you sons, and when you return I will heal your afflictions.* And when we see our *afflictions* and the promise of *healing,* we answer and say immediately: *Behold we will be yours because you are the Lord our God.*[26] So when we obey and say, *We will be yours,* let us remember that we submitted ourselves to God in saying, *We will be yours.* And by saying, *We will be yours,* we belong to no other, not to the spirit of anger, nor the spirit of grief, nor the spirit of desire, let us not belong to the Devil nor his angels.[27] But after we were called and said, *Behold we will be yours,* let us show by works that when we have promised to become his, we have devoted ourselves to none other than him.

(5) And we say: *Because you are the Lord our God.* For we confess no other god, as the gluttonous do the belly: *The belly is god;*[28] nor silver as do the lovers of money, nor greed which is idolatry, nor do we make anything else God and divinize it, as the multitude do. For us God is above all, the God *above all, through all and in all.*[29] And since[30] we attached ourselves with love to God—for love joins us to God—we say: *Behold, see us, we will be yours, because you are the Lord our God.*

3. Then denouncing our former evils—when we considered these idols mighty and lofty, we worshipped and consid-

---

24. Cf. Luke 14.18–20.
25. Cf. Luke 14.20. Origen perhaps considers the "woman" of the parable the wisdom of philosophers. Cf. *Fr in Lc* 69.
26. Jer 3.22.      27. Cf. Matt 25.41.
28. Phil 3.19.      29. Eph 4.6.
30. "Since," an addition of Klostermann.

ered those we were serving as wondrous, but now we realize that all of them were false and actually nothing—we speak as those *who return*.[31] *Truly the hills were directed toward what is false*,[32] when we denounce what was previously lofty and what was previously wondrous. And perhaps if we are skillful, we will discover the difference among the pagan nations between the hills and the mountains, which those who said, *Behold we will be yours because you are the Lord our God*,[33] left behind. They spoke against them both, the hills and the mountains, as false.

(2) So what is the difference among the pagan nations between the mountains and the hills about which, when we realized them, we say: *Truly the hills and the power of the mountains were directed toward what is false?*[34] We say this when we condemn the former mistakes. Among the pagan nations, some of those things that are worshipped are worshipped as god but others as heroes. They also claim about some of them that they were men[35] at one time and then were deified. They worship Heracles not as one born a god, but as one who was changed from a man into a god. They worship Asclepios as one who has been transformed from a man into a god through virtue. But when they worship the fathers of these heroes, fathers who are called by them gods, they worship not as ones transformed from men to gods, but, as they suppose, those who were gods from the beginning. Thus those who are supposed by the pagan nations to be gods from the beginning are the mountains and the *power of the mountains*, while those who are supposed among them to be gods now, but were once men, they are *the hills*.

(3) Thus knowing both kinds of beings which they worship, they say: *Truly the hills and the power of the mountains were directed toward what is false*.[36] For those who serve these beings do not understand that they are *false*. So they suppose that

---

31. Jer 3.22.
32. Jer 3.23.
33. Jer 3.22.
34. Jer 3.23.
35. "That they were men," an addition of Klostermann.
36. Jer 3.23.

## HOMILY 5

these oracles are true[37] oracles and the cures are true cures, not seeing a difference between "every false power, both of signs and of wonders, which occur in every deceit of injustice on those who are lost"[38] and every power of signs and wonders of truth. What Christ Jesus did, these were signs of truth, and before him, what Moses was doing, was a power of truth; but the Egyptians did *false* signs and wonders,[39] and truly after Jesus what Simon Magus was doing so that the people of Samaria were deceived into supposing he was the "power of God,"[40] these also were *false* signs and wonders. And so, when we denounce these things we say as those who have denounced: *Truly the hills and the power of the mountains were directed toward what is false.*[41]

4. Since then we from the pagan nations know that *in the stumbling of Israel we have acquired the way of salvation,*[42] and they who have been rejected[43] are outside until the full number of us enter, and we know that *if the full number of pagan nations enter, every one of Israel will, after this, be saved,*[44] we state, first, that *truly the hills and the power of the mountains were directed toward what is false,*[45] but, second, with respect to the Israel who will be saved after the full number of pagan nations, *the salvation of Israel is only through the Lord God.*[46] And since we remembered once the statement of the Apostle which says, *By their transgression for which Israel has stumbled, salvation has come to the pagan nations,* and when *the full number of pagan nations has entered,* although Israel remains outside, after the full number of pagan nations have entered *then all of Israel will be saved,* well, let us bring to light the matters referred to in these passages.

(2) There was a certain[47] Israel which was saved. Most of

---

37. "Oracles are true," an addition by Lietzmann.
38. Cf. 1 Thess 2.9–10.
39. Cf. Exod 7.8 ff.
40. Cf. Acts 8.9–10.
41. Jer 3.23.
42. Cf. Rom 11.11.
43. Cf. Luke 13.28.
44. Cf. Luke 13.28; Rom 11.25–26.
45. Jer 3.23.
46. Jer 3.23.
47. "A certain," an addition of Nautin.

Israel has fallen, but *there is a remnant chosen by grace*,[48] the *remnant* concerning which it is said *in mystery in Elijah*:[49] *I have kept for myself ten thousand men who have not bowed the knee to Baal*.[50] And remembering this *remnant*, the Apostle said, *So too at the present time there is a remnant chosen by grace*.[51] So even though a remnant of Israel was saved, Israel was abandoned. Apply also these two categories, if you can, to the pagan nations. For he did not say, "When all the pagan nations are saved, then all of Israel will be saved," but, *When the full number of pagan nations enter, then all of Israel will be saved*.[52] For a certain Israel will be saved, not after all of the pagan nations, but after the *full number* of pagan nations.

(3) If anyone is able, insofar as he has found that Israel is saved *after the full number of pagan nations*, let him consider, having passed over by reason the remaining period, when it is that *all serve God under a single yoke*, according to what is said in Zephaniah, *And from the ends of Ethiopia they offer sacrifices to him*, when, as it is said in the sixty-seventh Psalm, *Ethiopia stretches forth her hand to God*, and *to the kings of the earth* the Word commands, saying, *Sing to the Lord, raise a psalm to the God of Jacob*.[53]

5. Therefore we from the pagan nations, who repent about those false things which we supposed to be true, say this concerning ourselves: *Truly the hills and the power of the mountains were directed to what is false*, but concerning Israel who will be saved through us, *the salvation of the house of Israel is above all through the Lord God*. Then, after we confessed concerning the sins in which both our fathers and we shared, when we ourselves were serving idols, we say: *But the shame has devoured all of the labors of our fathers by their youth, their*

---

48. Rom 11.5.
49. Rom 11.2.
50. Rom 11.4; 3 Kings 19.18.
51. Rom 11.5.
52. Rom 11.25–26.

53. Zeph 3.9–10; Ps 67.32–33. Since Ethiopia is often a symbol for Origen for the home of the Devil, the text here implies that even the home of the Devil, indeed all nations, will be unified and "serve God." Is Origen also implying that the Devil himself will be saved? Cf. *Hom in Jer* 11.6, *Cels* 8.72, and *Or* 22.11.

*flocks and their herds, their sons and their daughters.*[54] *The shame has devoured the labors of our fathers* and the other things which are said. Hence if the laborious labor and the false work of our fathers is to be *devoured, shame* must arise; for until *shame,* the *labor of our fathers* and the other matters which follow are not *devoured.* For this reason let us note the differences of those who sin. There are even sinners who are neither ashamed nor have any fear, who do not blush for their sins. Of this sort are *those without feeling and those who give themselves over to every licentiousness and every uncleanness.*[55] For you see how those from the pagan nations in some sense recount as deeds of honor their fornication and adulteries, without being embarassed to admit that they have done such things, and they do not call them sins. Insofar as they have no *shame,* their *labors are not used up, their sins are not used up.* The beginning of good is to be ashamed about something one was not ashamed of. Because of this I do not think in those prophecies that a curse is said in the text: *All those who hate Zion, may they be put to shame and turned backwards.*[56] For it is prayed that those who are unaware of the works of shame come to the awareness that those ashamed can lose the labors of their sins.

6. The movements without reason in the fathers were called *sheep* and *calves.*[57] For not everything without reason was praiseworthy, but certain ones without reason are blamed, as are the *sheep* of the fathers who have sinned, but there are certain praiseworthy sheep without reason, as in, *My sheep hear my voice.*[58] These are also *sheep* for which we have a corresponding faculty of reason, since we have the *good shepherd* in our souls. For when the Savior says, *I am the good shepherd,*[59] I do not hear this only in a general sense, as all hear it, that he is the *shepherd* of believers—though this also is both sound and true—but also in my soul I ought to have

54. Jer 3.24.
56. Ps 128(129).5.
58. John 10.27.

55. Cf. Eph 4.19.
57. Jer 3.24.
59. John 10.11, 14.

48                    ORIGEN

Christ within me, the *good shepherd* within me, tending in me the movements without reason, so that no longer do they come by chance to the pasture, but when these which were once alien to him are led by the *shepherd,* they become his own. Now because of this, if the shepherd is in me, he rules my senses.⁶⁰ They are no longer under an alien purpose or under Pharaoh, or under Nebuchadnezzar,⁶¹ but under the *good shepherd.*

7. *The shame, then, has devoured the labors of our fathers from their youth, their sheep and their calves.*⁶² There is something⁶³ in us to cultivate us, and either it cultivates in an evil way—if one can indeed say that evil corresponds to one who cultivates⁶⁴—or⁶⁵ it cultivates in a good way. If then it cultivates in an evil way, the *labor of the fathers is devoured by their shame.* But if it cultivates in a good way, there is no *labor of the fathers.* For the *labor* is by those who are offered as the first-born on the altar of God.⁶⁶

(2) They say *their sons and daughters.* Of whom is *their* except of the *fathers* of the⁶⁷ *sons and the daughters devoured* by their *shame?* Often we have spoken of the children of the soul, that the thoughts are the sons and the works and deeds are the daughters through the body. Since there are then certain wicked thoughts, like those from the pagan nations have thought, and there are also wicked works, the *sons and daughters* are *devoured* by their makers, if *shame* arises in them for their sins. But let us not⁶⁸ make *sons and daughters* which require the waste of what is from *shame.*

8. Next those who have confessed say, *Let us lie down in our*

---

60. Klostermann and Schadel note here the probable influence of the exegesis of Philo. See *De sacrificiis Abelis et Caini* 45, and *Legum allegoriarum libri* 3.188.
61. Both of these kings are for Origen people who are evil.
62. Jer 3.24.                                63. "Something," from the Catena.
64. Perhaps Origen is influenced here by Philo, *De agricultura* 20–21, where the word "cultivates" (γεωργοῦν) refers to good work.
65. "Or" (ἤ), a correction of Ghisleri. S has ἡ.
66. Cf. Num 18.17.
67. "The," an addition of Klostermann.
68. "Not," from the Catena.

## HOMILY 5

*shame,* and then they say, *and our dishonor has veiled us.*[69] We have spoken often about the *veil* placed over the face of those who do not turn to the Lord.[70] On account of this *veil, if Moses is read,*[71] the sinner will not understand him. For a *veil rests*[72] *over his heart.*[73] On account of the *veil,* if the Old Testament is read, he who hears will not understand. Also on account of the *veil,* the *Gospel is hidden to those who are lost.*[74] Hence we say about the *veil* that *shame* is the *veil.* For insofar as we have the works of *shame,* it is clear that we possess the *veil,* according to the forty-third Psalm: *And the shame of my face veiled me.*[75] I have set forth that he who does not have the works of *shame* does not have a *veil,* which was just what Paul says: *But we all with an unveiled face behold the glory of the Lord.*[76] Thus Paul has an unveiled face. For he does not have the works of *shame.* He who is not like Paul has a veiled face.

(2) As it is then said there, *The shame of my face veiled me,*[77] so in the same way it is said here, *Our dishonor veiled us.*[78] To the degree that we do the works of dishonor, we have a *veil* resting upon our *heart.* If we want the veil of dishonor to be lost, let us come to the works of honor and consider that statement of the Savior, *that all may honor the Son even as they honor the Father,*[79] and the statement made by the Apostle, *by breaking the Law, you dishonor God.*[80] The righteous man, *as he honors the Father honors the Son;*[81] the dishonor, when I dishonor the Son (the dishonor itself through which I dishonor the Father or the Son) becomes a covering over my appearance and I say: *And dishonor concealed us.*[82]

(3) Hence when we have considered the *veil* which hangs

---

69. Jer 3.25.
70. Cf. 2 Cor 3.16. On the "veil," see, for example, *Princ* 1.1.2, *Comm in Mt* 10.14, and *Cels* 4.50.
71. 2 Cor 3.15.
72. "Rests," an editorial correction. S has κει(?).
73. 2 Cor 3.15.
74. 2 Cor 4.3.
75. Ps 43.16.
76. 2 Cor 3.18.
77. Ps 43.16.
78. Jer 3.25.
79. John 5.23.
80. Rom 2.23.
81. Cf. John 5.23.
82. Jer 3.25.

over from the works of *shame* and by the deeds of dishonor, let us remove the *veil*. It is in our power to remove the veil; it is for no one else. When Moses turned to the Lord, he removed the *veil*.[83] Do you see then how Moses is also received before the people? Whenever he did not turn toward the Lord—as a symbol of those people who did not turn to the Lord—he placed over his face a *veil*. But when he turned to the Lord—as a symbol of those turning to the Lord—then *he removed the veil*.[84] And as God did not order him, "Put on the veil"—for the Lord did not say to Moses, "Put on the veil"—but Moses, knowing that the people could not see his glory, then rested *the veil over his face*.[85] And he did not wait for God to say, "Remove the veil," whenever he might "turn to the Lord."[86]

9. So this has been written so that you also, who have placed upon your face the *veil* due to the works of *dishonor* and *shame*, might yourselves work to take away the *veil* and will say no longer, *Our dishonor veiled us*. If you turn toward the Lord, then you remove the *veil*, and you no longer say, *Our dishonor veiled us*. When anger against someone hangs over our soul it hangs as a *veil* over our face. So, if we wish to say when we pray, *The light of your face has been manifested upon us, Lord*,[87] let us remove the *veil* and fulfill that apostolic exhortation: *I desire then that in every place the men should pray, lifting holy hands without anger or quarreling.*[88] If we remove the *anger*, we remove the *veil*, if all passions.[89] Insofar as these things are in our mind, in our understanding, the *veil* and the *dishonor* are hanging over the inner face, over our heart, we do not see the shining glory of God. It is not God who hides his glory from us, but it is we who put the *veil* over our heart from evil.[90]

83. Cf. Exod 34.34.
84. 2 Cor 3.16.
85. Exod 34.35.
86. Cf. Exod 34.34.
87. Ps 4.6(7).
88. 1 Tim 2.8.
89. This sentence seems incomplete.
90. Origen in this paragraph lists the majority of the most important terms of his anthropology. They include ψυχή (soul), πάθος (passion), νοῦς (mind or

## HOMILY 5

10. *Therefore, we and our fathers sinned against God.*[91] Oh, let us also say as those in the dramatization of the Prophet, *We sinned*. *We sinned* is not the same as: "We are sinning." For the one who is still in sin does not say, *We sinned*, but he who was in sin but has really repented says, *We sinned*, just as the confession is also written in Daniel of those who no longer sin, who say: *We have sinned, we have transgressed the Law*,[92] and in the Psalms the Prophet said, *Do not remember our ancient iniquities*.[93] So let us also confess sins; oh not just yesterday or the day before yesterday, but when we confess let us confess about sins fifteen years ago so that we have no sin after those for fifteen years. But if we sinned yesterday, we are by no means trustworthy when we confess our sins, nor is it possible that these sins of ours are erased.

(2) *Therefore we and our fathers sinned from our youth until this day.*[94] That other phrase[95] is stated for a teaching on the best way of confession, but this is a denouncement of prolonged sinning. *From youth*, he says, *until this day, and we did not listen to the voice of the Lord our God*.[96] *We sinned and we did not listen* until now; then when they turn and begin conversion, they say, "We were sinning and we did not listen." For it does not happen that to want to listen means we simultaneously do immediately listen. For just as time is still[97] required with a cure for wounds, so is it also with turning maturely[98] and purely to God for conversion.

11. Next God says concerning Israel: *"If Israel returns to*

---

intellect), λογισμός (understanding) and ἡγεμονικόν (heart). Others mentioned elsewhere in the homilies are πνεῦμα (spirit), σάρξ (flesh), σῶμα (body) and καρδία (heart). With these terms Origen describes the battle which goes on in man's soul when it encounters various influences.

91. Jer 3.25.  
92. Dan 9.5.  
93. Ps 78.8.  
94. Jer 3.25.  
95. "We and our fathers sinned."  
96. Jer 3.25.  
97. "Time" (χρόνος) and "still" (ἔτι), the result of a correction of Klostermann. S has ἐπιχρόνος.  
98. τέλειος. As noted previously, this word is used as a term of process or growth rather than perfection when it refers to conversion. Hence Origen contrasts it with being like an infant or child.

me," the Lord says, "then he will also return,"⁹⁹ that is, if¹⁰⁰ he turns maturely, he also will be turned to a conversion, as if he has only begun to turn. Then he says: *And if he removes his abominations from his mouth, and he is awed by my presence, and he will swear: "May the Lord live in truth and in judgment and righteousness," and the nations shall bless in him.*¹⁰¹ If they do these things, the *nations bless in him.* What things do they do so that *the nations bless in him?* *If he removes his abominations from his mouth.*¹⁰² But how to remove *the abominations from his mouth?* Whatever we say in an evil way, they are *abominations* in our *mouth.* So let us remove the *abominations* from our *mouth* by getting rid of the slanders, the profane words, idle words which are destined to accuse us *on the day of judgment. For by your words you will be justified and by your words you will be condemned.*¹⁰³ Thus if we wish to arrive for ourselves where *the nations bless in him, and in him they praise God in Jerusalem,*¹⁰⁴ let us do the things stated at the beginning. But what do we do first? We remove *the abominations from our mouth.*

(2) Next there is the passage: *He is awed by my presence.*¹⁰⁵ Let us do this second thing not simply that we may *be awed.* For perhaps it is awe which appears, but not by the *presence of God.* Indeed they who *are awed* without knowledge but by intending to be awed are not *awed by the presence of God.* But when they *are awed* with knowledge by always seeing and recognizing for themselves *the presence of the God who appears to those who do evil in order to cut off their memory from the earth,*¹⁰⁶ these are those who *are awed by the presence of God.*

---

99. Jer 4.1. The words for "turn" and "converted" or "conversion" in this section arise from the same Greek word (ἐπιστρέφειν) which literally means to turn back or return to a place or state in which one was at one time. I generally avoid the translation "conversion" or "converted" in favor of the more primitive "turn" or "return" because "convert" or "conversion" seem static and weaken the motion process involved in the word, namely, the turning and progression or regression this implies. This is similar to the usage described for the word τέλειος.

100 "If," an addition of Cordier.     101. Jer 4.1–2.
102. Jer 4.1.     103. Matt 12.36–37.
104. Jer 4.2.     105. Jer 4.1.
106. Cf. Ps 33.17 (34.16).

## HOMILY 5

12. *If he removes his abominations from his mouth, and he is awed by my presence, and he swears, "May the Lord live in truth and in judgment and in righteousness."*[107] Let us, those who *swear,* see for ourselves in what way we do not *swear in judgment* but without judgment, so that our oaths arise by habit more than by judgment. In fact we are carried away[108] and when he reproves this the Word says: *And if he swears: "May the Lord live in truth and in judgment and in righteousness."* We know what is said to the disciples in the Gospel by the Lord: *But I say to you: do not swear at all,*[109] but let us also consider that word, and if God will permit, both views will be examined. For perhaps first it is necessary to swear *in truth and in judgment and in righteousness* so that after this, after having progressed, a worthy person may come not to *swear at all,* but to have a *yes* which needs no witnesses[110] to be this,[111] to have a "no" which needs no witnesses for it to be truly *no.*[112]

(2) *And he swears,* then, *"May the Lord live in truth."*[113] First, in the swearing, let not the false but the true live, so he may swear with truth—for we wretches also give false oaths. But suppose it is *with truth,* the oath is still[114] not proper, but *in judgment.* For it may happen that I swear from habit, I do not swear[115] *in judgment.* If one would need to take for some oath the witness of the God of the universe and[116] his Christ with respect to some matter, how great must be the matter to get down on one's knees and swear? To cure the[117] unbelief which arises in some concerning my discourse[118] I might at

---

107. Jer 4.1–2.
108. We are "carried away" in confusion, because we cannot distinguish when we provide true oaths and when we swear by habit without thinking.
109. Matt 5.34.
110. "Witnesses," an addition of Cordier.
111. "This," a correction of Klostermann. S has τὸ οὔ.
112. Cf. Matt 5.37.
113. Jer 4.1.
114. "Still," is my addition.
115. "I do not swear," an addition of Klostermann.
116. "And," an addition of Cordier.
117. "The" (τήν), a correction of Ghisleri. S has ἤν.
118. λόγος.

some point do this, but if it is a risk if I swear thus, I would sin.

(3) *If*, then, *he swears, "May the Lord live with truth and in judgment,"* not without judgment, *and in righteousness*, not with unrighteousness, *and the nations will bless in him.*[119] He unified diverse peoples, those from the pagan nations and Israel; he spoke concerning the pagan nations and he spoke[120] also concerning Israel.

13. He adds: *And the nations will bless in him, and in him they will praise God in Jerusalem. For this is what the Lord says to the men of Judah and to the inhabitants of Jerusalem.*[121] He has spoken to those from the pagan nations, he has spoken also to those from Israel, he speaks to those from Judah. I recall the allegories said recently[122] concerning Judah and the inhabitants in Jerusalem. For we live, God willing, in Jerusalem. Since, *where the treasure is, there also is the heart*,[123] if we have our treasure in heaven,[124] also we have the *heart* in *Jerusalem above*, concerning which the Apostle said, *The Jerusalem above is free, and she is our mother, for it is written,* and so forth.[125]

(2) This then *is what the Lord says to the men of Judah and to the inhabitants of Jerusalem: "Break up fallow ground and sow not among thorns."*[126] This word is especially directed to those who teach, lest they entrust what is said to the pupils too soon before they have prepared the *fallow ground* in their souls. For whenever they put the *hand to the plow*,[127] they make the *ground fallow* in their souls, according to the *beautiful*[128] and the *good earth*[129] of those who hear. Then when they sow, the sowers do not sow *among thorns*. But if prior to the *plow* and prior to the making of *fallow ground* in the heart[130]

---

119. Jer 4.2.
120. "Spoke" (εἶπεν), from another manuscript. S has εἴπερ.
121. Jer 4.2–3. 122. See *Hom in Jer* 4.2.
123. Cf. Luke 12.34. 124. Cf. Matt 6.20.
125. Gal 4.26. 126. Jer 4.3.
127. Cf. Luke 9.62. 128. Matt 13.8.
129. Luke 8.8.
130. Origen does not follow the Scriptural text given above (Luke 12.43): he does not use καρδία but ἡγεμονικόν.

## HOMILY 5

of those who hear, someone takes the holy seeds, the word concerning the Father, concerning the Son and Holy Spirit, the word concerning the Resurrection, the word concerning the punishment, the word concerning the final rest, concerning the Law, the Prophets and in general each of the Scriptures, and sows them, he disobeys the first commandment which states first: *Break up their fallow ground;* second: *and do not sow among thorns.*

(3) But someone among the hearers will say: "I do not teach, I am not covered under this commandment." And you,[131] be a farmer of yourself, and do not *sow* among *thorns*, but make for yourself the field as *fallow ground*, which the God of the universe has trusted with you. Consider the field, behold where there are thorns, where there are *cares of life and guile of riches and love of pleasure*.[132] And after considering the *thorns* in your soul, seek out the spiritual[133] plow, concerning which Jesus said, *No one who puts his hand to the plow and looks back is worthy of the kingdom of God*.[134] After having sought and found it, gather from the Scriptures the *bulls*, the pure workers; plow and break up the earth. And in order that it may no longer be old, make it new by *putting off the old man with his practices and putting on the new man which is renewed for knowledge*.[135] Make for yourself *fallow ground*, and if you make the *fallow ground*, take the seeds from those who teach, take seeds from the Law, take from the Prophets, from the Gospel writings, from the[136] words of the Apostles, and when you have taken these seeds, sow the soul through

---

131. "You" (σύ), a correction of Ghisleri. S has σοῦ.
132. Cf. Mark 4.19; Luke 8.14.
133. λογικός. This word comes from λόγος, which has no single English equivalent, but it concerns the rational and contemplative thinking which lies behind and issues in expression and discourse. Origen's purpose is probably quite straightforward. He is concerned that his hearers may think he is referring literally to a plow. So he specifies that he means that plow of this faculty.
134. Luke 9.62.
135. Col 3.9–10.
136. "From the," an addition of Klostermann.

memory and exercise.[137] It may appear that these seeds sprout on their own,[138] and it is not true[139] that they[140] sprout after the memory of them, but God will cause them to grow. *I planted, Apollos watered, but God caused them to grow.*[141] And if one has been able to comprehend Scripture, he has made *fallow ground,* and after making *fallow ground,* he did not sow among *thorns.* These seeds are not built up by God to become plants suddenly, but,[142] as in the Gospel according to Mark, *first the blade then the ear,*[143] then it is *ready for harvest.*[144] When it is *ready for harvest,* those sent out for harvest will come.[145] When it is *ready for harvest,* they will come to those to whom the Word said: *Raise up your eyes and see the fields, that they are already white for harvest.*[146] Thus he says to us, *Make of yourselves fallow ground and do not sow among thorns,*[147] but if before you purge your soul, still having *thorns,* you go to one who is able or claims or professes to teach and ask for lessons and spiritual seeds,[148] you transgress the commandment which said, *Do not sow among thorns.*

14. And next after this it is said: *Circumcise yourselves for your God and circumcise the foreskin of your heart.*[149] *Circumcise yourself for your God. Circumcise yourselves. For your God* is necessarily added, and you will understand it from the example of the corporeal.[150] They are *circumcised,* I say, according to the corporeal, not only those with a circumcision according to the Law of Moses, but also many others. The priests of the

---

137. Nautin offers *Fr in Luc* 68 as a parallel text. Schadel, 265, n.57, sees here a reflection of philonic-neoplatonic terminology. Cf. Philo, *De plantatione* 31, and Plotinus, *Enneades* 4.6.3
138. Cf. Mark 4.28.
139. "And" and "true" (δ' ἀληθές), additions of Klostermann. S has ἀληθῶς.
140. "They" (αὐτά), a correction from another manuscript. S has ἅττα(?).
141. 1 Cor 3.6.
142. "But," an addition of Cordier.   143. Cf. Mark 4.28.
144. John 4.35.   145. Cf. Matt 9.38.
146. John 4.35.   147. Jer 4.3.
148. Origen uses the general phrase "spiritual seeds" in contrast to the more specific "holy seeds" used above. The "holy" teachings have already been mentioned by him. But there are other teachings of a "spiritual" nature, too.
149. Jer 4.4.   150. αἰσθητός.

## HOMILY 5

Egyptians are *circumcised* for idols, but that circumcision is a circumcision for idols, not a circumcision done *for God*. And perhaps the circumcision of the Jews is done *for God;* it was at that time anyway. If then the Word says, *Circumcise yourselves for your God*, having understood the literal meaning, pass over now to the allegorical, so that you can discover how, among those circumcised allegorically—so that some of them may perhaps say, *We are the circumcised*[151]—there are those *circumcised for God*, but also those *circumcised* yet not *for God*. There are also other words[152] outside the word of truth, outside the word of the Church. Those who practice philosophy *circumcise* their habits and the heart so that they have, you could say, self-control. Those from the heresies have self-control and there is a circumcision for them, but it is a circumcision not *for God*. For circumcision happens among them for a false reason. And whenever you share in communion in accord with the rule of the Church, in accord with the purpose of sound teaching, it is not only to circumcise, but to circumcise *for God*.

(2) *Circumcise yourselves* then *for your God and circumcise the foreskin of your heart.*[153] Who does not pass over these words as clear? There is then[154] a *foreskin* of the heart, and it is necessary to circumcise it. If he seeks for such things in the text, he who understands thoroughly[155] the meaning will discover: The *foreskin* is inborn, the circumcision comes later, and whatever has appeared from birth, the circumcision strips this away. So if the Word exhorts to strip away *the foreskin of the heart*, there ought to be something inborn in the heart, which he calls the *foreskin* which is necessary to strip away so that one may *circumcise the foreskin of the heart*. If one will consider that *we were children of wrath by nature, like the rest of mankind*,[156] if one will consider *the body of humility*[157] in which

---

151. Phil 3.3.  152. λόγοι.
153. Jer 4.4.
154. "Then" (οὐκοῦν) is a correction of Cordier. S has οὐκ ἄν.
155. "Understands thoroughly": ἀκριβώσας.
156. Eph 2.3.  157. Phil 3.21.

we were born, if one will consider that *nothing clean is from dirt, even if*[158] *his life is only one day; yet his months are numerous,*[159] he will see in some sense that we have been born with uncleanness and a *foreskin over our heart.*[160]

15. But in order to speak with a simpler example so that you all can be brought to see *the foreskin of the heart,*[161] I will state that in the first stage of growth false teachings certainly arise in the soul, for it is impossible from the beginning that man receive pure and[162] true doctrines. But the divine Word has provided history and Scripture with what is according to letter in order that he could nourish first the one born to Abraham *according to the flesh* on those doctrines *according to the flesh.* And *the one from the slave* would arise first, so that the one *of the free woman* and the one *through the promise* could be born after him.[163] If one has considered this in light of what has been heard, the *foreskin of the heart* coming before the circumcision can be understood.[164]

(2) Hence there is need for us to receive the Word who purifies doctrines and who strips away all those things arising in us in accord with false opinion. This means then to put away the *foreskin* of our *heart.* For if it is our *heart* which contains the governing power,[165] wherever there are thoughts,

158. "If" (εἰ), a correction from manuscript. S has ἡ.
159. Job 14.4–5.
160. Origen clearly states that before we were born we had in some way acquired "dirt." How? He does not explain here, but there are at least two possibilities. First, he may be implying his idea of a pre-existent fall of souls with the "foreskin" as its taint, or this may also be a reflection of the Pauline concept of man's taint from the fall of Adam.
161. Jer 4.4.
162. "And," an addition of Ghisleri.   163. Gal 4.23.
164. This paragraph applies Origen's polarity of flesh and spirit to education. The Scripture's outer "foreskin" are teachings which together are a kind a covering which needs to be "circumcised" in order for one to see the spiritual seeds beneath, just as the "slave" is born before the one "of freedom." However, it should be noted that Origen says that these early "teachings" are, in fact, "false" in comparison to what will come. Which teachings? Which scriptural writings? Origen does not specify here.
165. Here is a rare instance when Origen uses καρδία and ἡγεμονικόν in contrast and in the same sentence. As noted above, καρδία for Origen is often

## HOMILY 5

there *wicked reasonings come forth.*[166] He who strips away the *wicked reasonings* strips away *the foreskin of the heart*, he who takes away false opinion *circumcises* the *foreskin* of his *heart*, and by circumcising purely becomes a *man of Judah* and an *inhabitant of Jerusalem.*[167] But if someone does not put away the *foreskin* of his *heart*, let us see how the Word threatens him: *lest my wrath go forth like fire*, he says, *and burn with no one to quench it.*[168] Like *fire* the *wrath* of the Lord *goes forth* upon those who were not circumcised *for God*, on those who have not removed *the foreskin* of their *heart, and there is no one to quench it in the face of the wickedness of their habits.*[169] That *fire* has as fuel *the wickedness* of your *habits*. Where there is no *wickedness of habits*, the *fire* has no place to dwell. But because the fuel of that *fire* is the *wickedness* of your *habits*, hear the Prophet when he says: *And there will be no one to quench it in the face of the wickedness of your*[170] *habits*.

(3) *Proclaim in Judah, and let it be heard in Jerusalem. Speak, proclaim,*[171] *signify it with the trumpet through the land, and cry out loud.*[172] Speak these proclamations, he says, *in Judah*, to those from the tribe of Judah, of Christ, *for it is evident that our Savior was descended from Judah.*[173]

16. *Signify it with the trumpet over the land.* The exalted Word, he who arouses the hearer, he who prepares him for the *war* against the passions, for the *war* against the opposing forces, he who makes him ready for the heavenly *feasts*[174]—for to both conditions these things are said—is understood as a *trumpet*. In the book of Numbers there is such a Word, a *trumpet*. When the Word commands me and some

---
the scriptural equivalent of the philosophical term ἡγεμονικόν, and I have translated both as "heart" throughout, but here I specify the philosophical meaning of ἡγεμονικόν. However, the connection between these two terms is clearly explained here.

166. Matt 15.19. 167. Jer 4.4.
168. Jer 4.4. 169. Jer 4.4.
170. "Your," a correction of Cordier. S has "our."
171. "Proclaim," is an addition from LXX.
172. Jer 4.5. 173. Heb 7.14.
174. Cf. Num 10.9, 10.

others—for he has given it to him who wishes for and seeks the sense of Scripture—he commands to make *beaten silver trumpets.*[175] So also the Word says, *Signify it with the trumpet over the land, and cry out loud. Say: "Assemble and let us go into the fortified cities."*[176] The Word of God does not wish us to enter into an unfortified city, but into one *fortified. The Church of the living God* is *fortified* by *the truth* of the Word.[177] For he is the *wall*, as[178] it is said in the seventeeth Psalm that God also is a *wall.*[179]

(2) *Get up, flee to Zion.* Whoever of you are outside Zion, *get up, flee to Zion.* You who are in progress, *press on and do not remain.* Hasten to the watchtower, *because I bring evil from Borra and great destruction.*[180] While he *brings evil from Borra*—Borra being, as it is often said,[181] the adversary—if he who has neither hastened nor come into the *fortified cities* should be found, not being *in the churches of God*[182] but standing outside, once caught by the enemies he will be destroyed. But who is the enemy? Let us see from the next words how it is said: *A lion went up from his thicket; he who destroys nations has set out.*[183] He is the enemy whom we need to flee. *A lion* pursues us. Who is this? Peter teaches us by saying, *Your adversary the Devil prowls around like a roaring lion seeking someone to devour. Resist him, be firm in the Faith.*[184] And according to the ninth Psalm, *he lurks in secret, he lurks like a lion in his covert,*[185] and he the *lion* does not *lurk* during the day, but he even arises at night. For according to the hundred and third Psalm, *You make darkness and it becomes night; in it all the beasts of the forest creep forth, lions roar for prey and seek food for themselves from God.*[186]

17. Thus, *the lion went up from his thicket.* Where? When? Af-

175. Num 10.2.
176. Jer 4.5.
177. Cf. 1 Tim 3.15.
178. "As," a conjecture of Klostermann.
179. Ps 17(18).30.
180. Jer 4.6.
181. That is, by Origen himself.
182. 2 Thess 1.4.
183. Jer 4.7.
184. 1 Pet 5.8–9.
185. Ps 9.30 (10.9).
186. Ps 103(104).20–21.
187. Jer 4.7.

ter falling down, he has gone down into the depths of the earth. *The lion went up from his thicket.* You are a man, you are higher than the Devil. For you are greater than he, whatever you may be. That one is lower due to evil.

(2) *The lion,* then, *went up from his thicket; he who destroys nations has set out.* After he has *gone up from his thicket,* from his own place, for his punishment, *he who destroys nations has set out. He has set out from his place to reduce your land to a desert.*[187] He wants to enter into the *land* of you, about which we were speaking briefly before.[188] Each of us he wants to dwell in. Thus he comes *to reduce your land to a desert,* so that he may trample on the seeds, so that he may make a *desert land of you. And your cities will be ruined without any inhabitants. For this gird yourself with sackcloth.*[189] Since then the *lion* has come up and the *lion* threatens you and wants to obliterate your *land, gird yourself* with *sackcloth,* cry out and mourn, implore God through prayers to remove this *lion* from you, and you may not fall in with him into the pit. *In the way the shepherd reserves from the mouth of the lion two legs or a piece of an ear,*[190] this *lion* seeks to take your *ears* in order that through your gluttony, when he deceives you with false words, he may pluck you out from the truth. He wants you away from the truth to seize the feet and eat you up. But *gird yourself with sackcloth* and beat your chests and cry out and shout when you see the opposing enemy, so that the *wrath of anger of the Lord may turn away from you,*[191] and after having *turned aside* the *wrath,* you can be without anxiety, for no longer does the *lion* attack you unawares; you have entered into the *fortified city* and glorify the God who rescues[192] you in Christ Jesus, *to whom is the glory and the power for the ages of ages. Amen.*[193]

---

188. Cf. Hom in Jer 5.13.
189. Jer 4.7–8.
190. Amos 3.12.
191. Jer 4.8.
192. ῥύομαι. Or, in light of the fortified city, "protects."
193. 1 Pet 4.11.

## HOMILY 6

*Jeremiah 5.3–5*

On "Lord your eyes are toward faith," up to,
"I will go to the strong and I will speak to them."

ORD, HE SAYS, *your eyes are toward faith.*[1] As *the eyes of the Lord are on the righteous,*[2] for from unrighteous things he turns them, so the *eyes* of the Lord *are toward faith,* for he turns them away from unbelief. Thus it has been well stated, by one who understands, what he says in the prayer: *Lord, your eyes are toward faith.*

(2) Here then it is written: *Lord, your eyes are toward faith.* But since, *if someone of understanding hears a wise saying, he will praise it and add to it,*[3] let us see how much there is to make from the statement: *Lord, your eyes are toward faith.* Paul says, *But now these three remain, faith, hope and love. But the greatest of these is love.*[4] As *eyes* of the Lord *are toward faith, eyes* of the Lord are *toward hope, eyes* of the Lord are *toward love.* But since he is the spirit *of power and of love and of self-control,*[5] just as *eyes* of the Lord are *toward love,* so *eyes* of the Lord are *toward power,* so it is that *eyes* of the Lord are *toward self-control*[6] ... *eyes* of the Lord are *on righteousness,*[7] so it is that *eyes* of the

---

1. Jer 5.3.    2. Ps 33(34).16.
3. Sir 21.15.   4. 1 Cor 13.13.
5. 2 Tim 1.7.

6. After "self-control," Klostermann believes there is missing text, something, he believes, such as this: "... but since there is also a 'righteousness from faith,' (Rom 10.6), as the 'eyes' of the Lord are 'toward faith' [or on the righteous] ... so it is that...." While Nautin is silent, see Schadel's discussion, 267, n. 63.

7. Ps 33.16.

Lord are *on* all virtues. If therefore you want to anticipate the rays of the spiritual *eyes* of God on you, take up virtues, and just as there will be the text, *Lord, your eyes are toward faith,* so also, *Lord, your eyes are toward* each of the goods which you may acquire. And if you are of such greatness that the *eyes* of the Lord shine on you, you will say, *The light of your countenance was impressed upon us, O Lord.*[8]

2. Then let us note what is said concerning sinners: *You have whipped them, but they did not suffer.*[9] Those perceivable whips, when applied to the living body, whether those whipped want them or not, cause pain in them. But the whips of God are of a kind that some of those whipped suffer pain, but others who are whipped do not.

(2) Let us see if we can determine what it means to suffer pain and not to suffer pain from the whips of God, and why those with evil natures are those who do not suffer pain from the whips of God, but blessed are those who do suffer pain from the whips of God. For Wisdom says, *Who will place whips on my thoughts and seals of prudence on my lips so that they may not spare me in my errors, and my sins will not pass me by?*[10] Note especially the passage, *Who will place whips on my thoughts?* Thus there are *whips* to *whip* the thought. The *whips* of God *whip* the thought. For the[11] Word, by guiding the soul to a perception[12] of how it has sinned, *whips* it. But he *whips* the blessed man who suffers pain from the *whips,* for the words reach him and he does not complain about the one who reproves him. But when someone is found, let us say, without sensitivity it will be said about him: *You have whipped them, but they did not suffer.* Though the same word is said reprovingly to touch, so to speak, the thoughts of one who has "defiled the conscience"[13] by some sin, if one person who hears does suffer pain from that word so that it is said about him, *you have seen that* such a man *was moved deeply,*[14] and another

---

8. Ps 4.7(6).  9. Jer 5.3.
10. Sir 23.2, 22.27.  11. "The," I have added.
12. "Perception" (συναίσθησις), a correction from the Catena. S has σύνεσιν.
13. Cf. 1 Cor 8.7.
14. Cf. 3 Kings 20.29.

hearer does not suffer but is without a sensitivity of the reproof, it is clear that it will be said about him who is without sensitivity: *You have whipped them, and they did not suffer.*

(3) This then is one viewpoint concerning whether *they did not suffer* or they did suffer. But let us see if we have another. In the bodies of certain members,[15] a kind of deadness and dryness arises, and often the condition of the dead member, compared to the living, is such that when the capacity to make one suffer is applied to a living member, that person on whom the making of the pain is inflicted suffers. But if the making of pain is applied to a member with no sensitivity, that limb feels nothing, when there is a deadness in it. If you have seen this for the body, change over to the soul and see that there is also a kind of soul, its members dead, with the result that it does not feel from the *whips*, even if certain painful ones are applied. Such *whips* are applied,[16] but such a soul will not feel them, but another will feel them. And perhaps just as the one who does not feel the sufferings applied to him is affected more for not being sensitive than for being sensitive, he should pray more to suffer whenever painful *whips* are produced, since this is a sign of living itself, but be disgusted for not feeling the pains. As indeed this happens for bodies, so I suppose in the passage, *They wanted to be the fuel for the fire*[17] something such as this is made clear: Insofar as the fire is applied to someone and the burning is not felt, these persons, if they discover the difference of not feeling and feeling the pains, may *want* to feel the fire more than not feel it. And someone, though that judgment fire is applied to the sinners, may pray more to feel than not to feel it.[18]

(4) These things we have said on the passage, *You have whipped them and they did not suffer.*[19]

15. "Members" (μέλων), a correction of Klostermann (348). S has μερῶν.
16. "Such whips are applied" (δεινὰ προσφέρεται), a correction of Ghisleri. S has διαπροσφέρεται.
17. Isa 9.4.   18. Cf. *Hom in Jer* 19.9.
19. Jer 5.3.

## HOMILY 6

(5) *You have brought them to completion, and they did not want to receive instruction.*[20] Whenever the God whose Providence is for the universe does what is purifying for the salvation of a soul, he has *brought to completion* what depends on him.[21] But understand the passage, *You have brought them to completion and they did not wish to receive instruction*, from the example of one who offers knowledge and one who does not wish to receive the knowledge from the one who offers it. For suppose the teacher does everything which is possible for him and *brings to completion* everything for the transference of knowledge, but that person does not *receive* the things said. I would say to the teacher concerning such a one: "You have brought him to completion and he does not want to receive instruction." Whenever then everything arises for us from Providence so that we may be *brought to completion* and made mature, yet we do not *receive* what belongs to the Providence which draws us to maturity, then it would be said to God by one who understands: *Lord, you have brought them to completion and they did not want to receive instruction.*[22]

3. *They have hardened their faces into rock.*[23] You can understand this from the more bodily sense.[24] Among sinners those who hear reproving words for sin blush and hide themselves and cringe when the reproving word touches them. But others are such that they are unashamed, unafraid about why they are reproved, about how they have sinned. You might say then concerning these, the unashamed, *They have hardened their faces into rock.* If you have understood the bodily sense, change over with me in meaning[25] to the soul to understand the *face* about which it is spo-

20. Jer 5.3.
21. "Him" (αὐτῷ), a correction of Ghisleri. S has αὐτό.
22. The two words for "brought to completion" and "maturity" are related in Greek and are from a similar root (τέλειος, τέλος), but it is difficult to reveal this in English.
23. Jer 5.3.
24. The literal sense. Origen saw the Scripture as a kind of living being with a body, soul, and spirit.
25. λόγος.

66        ORIGEN

ken, *and then you will see*[26] *face to face.*[27] And see the hard soul as the *hardened* heart of Pharaoh[28] so that it remained hard in the face of reports, and as it rejected what was said, it was not formed according to the reports. For here you find that it accords with the text, *They have hardened their faces into rock.*

(2) *And they did not want to return. And I said: "These are perhaps poor because they do not want to know the way of the Lord and the judgment of God. I will go to the strong and I will speak to them."*[29] Since he has understood these things concerning those not wanting to be instructed and not understanding the *whips* of God, he understandably states the reason for this: Their soul is *poor.*

(3) *And I said: "These are perhaps the poor, hence they were not capable because they did not know the way of the Lord and the judgment of God. I will go to the strong and I will speak to them."*[30] The *strong* in souls are spoken of with approval. For also among the Greeks the *strong* and the greatness of the rational soul is continually named. For whenever anyone throws himself into great deeds, has worthwhile objectives,[31] always considers what is right, and how he can live in accordance with right reason, wishing not to know[32] anything abject and small, such a person has in the soul the *strong* and the great. The others then, the ones the Word disparaged since they were *poor,* did not hear, the Prophet said; they did not hear for this reason: since they were *poor. I will go to the strong and speak to them,* and if it is so that the blessed man is meant in the saying *the ears of those who hear,*[33] one is blessed if he should ever meet[34] a *strong* and great listener.

(4) Due to these things being said in this way, when we

26. "You will see," I have added.
27. 1 Cor 13.12.
28. Cf. Exod 4.21.
29. Jer 5.3–5.
30. Jer 5.3–5.
31. "Objectives" (προθέσεις), a correction of Cordier. S has προσθέσεις.
32. "To know" (ὁρᾶν), a correction of Klostermann. S has ὁρῶν.
33. Sir 25.9.
34. "If he should ever meet" (ἐάνπερ τύχῃ), a correction of Klostermann. S has ἐὰν πορεύσῃ.

## HOMILY 6

see that the fault is not with those who speak as with those who hear for not receiving the reports, and when we see that[35] he accuses the "poorness" of their[36] mind and thought, let us ask from God to receive strength and greatness as the Word grows in us so that we can hear the sacred and holy words in Christ Jesus, *to whom is the glory and the power for the ages of ages. Amen.*[37]

35. "When we see that," I have added.
36. "Their" (αὐτῶν), a correction of Klostermann. S has αὐτοῦ.
37. 1 Pet 4.11.

# HOMILY 7

## Jeremiah 5.18–19

On "'And it will happen in those days,' says the Lord your God, 'that I will never smite you until a consummation,'" up to, "'so you will serve as aliens in a land not your own.'"

**G**OD, WHO JUDGES *little by little* those punished, *gives a chance of repentance*,[1] and, by not punishing all at once for the sinning, holds off for the sinner the *consummation*[2] of the punishment. Because of this, by *judging*[3] *little by little* he punishes, and the example of this[4] is in Leviticus. For in the curses on those who transgress the Law there is written after the prior punishments: *"And it will happen, if after these things you do not return," says the Lord, "I will also bring upon you seven plagues."*[5] And again he speaks of another punishment: *And it will happen, if after these things you do not return but walk contrary to me, I also will walk with you with a con-*

---

1. Wis 12.10.
2. The word "consummation" (συντέλεια) discussed here is one of the most complex in all of Origen's complex theology. It is another word in that series of words based on τέλος. Much of Origen's thought is "goal-directed." Each interpretation or reflection is part of a process toward some end. The idea of the consummation is especially intriguing to him because so many biblical texts seem to him to refer to some future afterlife experience. The chief questions are then: When is the consummation? What will happen at the consummation? What does it concern? Whom does it concern? Why is there a consummation? Is it literally an end to something or some event or people, or is it an allegory for some other experience?
3. "Judging," a correction of Klostermann. S has "punishing."
4. "Of this" (τούτου), a correction of Huet. S has τοῦτο.
5. Cf. Lev 26.21.

*trary heart.*[6] So you will find God measuring out punishments with caution, since[7] he wants to lead the one who has sinned to a return and not render what is due[8] for everything all at once.

(2) These things then happened concerning the people according to the letter.[9] And the Word, by threatening them with what they will suffer, says after this, *"And it will happen in those days,"* says the Lord your God, *"I will never smite you until a consummation."*[10] And if these things directly anticipate also the future punishments . . . ,[11] if not, let him who can pass from what has happened in this life concerning the people to those punishments.[12] For I may say with confidence[13] that just as *they serve as a copy and shadow of the heavenly,*[14] so that people were punished in this way for their sins by a *copy and shadow* of the true punishments, so that every punishment which is mentioned according to the[15] Law and Prophets concerning the people includes a *shadow* of the true punishments.

(3) Thus just as a *consummation* for sins for them has not occurred, but will occur then at an end, so perhaps the punishment also for sinners will be after the final departure. But it was a *consummation* for Jerusalem when the Captivity oc-

---

6. Cf. Lev 26.23–24.

7. "Since" (ἐπεί), a correction of Lietzmann and Klostermann. S has ἢ εἰ.

8. "Render what is due" (ἀποδιδόντα), a correction of Ghisleri. S has ἀποδιδόντι.

9. The first dimension of scriptural interpretation by which Origen often means what concerns the historical, namely, the Jews.

10. Jer 5.18.

11. According to Klostermann, some text is evidently missing after "punishments."

12. We can gather from what remains of this thought that either it is a direct reference to the end times or, if not, it is, through the Hebrew people, a figure for the future punishments.

13. "With confidence" (πειθόμενος), a correction of Blass. S has πειθομεθόμενος.

14. Heb 8.5.

15. "The," an addition of Klostermann.

curred under Nebuccadnezzar. And yet[16] someone will say that it was not a *consummation* then, nor even in the time of the Maccabees, but a *consummation* for the people was at the time of the appearance of the Lord Jesus Christ. For insofar as the Savior was not saying to them, *Behold your house is forsaken,*[17] it was not forsaken. But when he cried out to Jerusalem saying, *Jerusalem, Jerusalem, who killed the Prophets and stoned those sent to you! How often I wished to gather your children together, as a hen*[18] *gathers her brood under her wings, and you would not! Behold your house is forsaken, a desert.*[19] The *house is forsaken, Jerusalem* is surrounded *by armies,*[20] since the *house* has been *forsaken* and *its desolation has come near.*[21] Subsequently, after the transgressions of those people, *salvation* came to us, to the *pagan nations.*[22] Thus those were punished, and a *consummation* was not realized by them until the coming of my Lord Jesus.

2. But I also inquire whether such things are not about us, and that there occur some punishments whose effect is such that some do not have to endure second punishments but are satisfied with the first, but such that others also come to the second, even indeed also to the third, while still others go on to the fourth. For the text, *I will bring upon seven plagues,*[23] makes evident some kind of mystery[24] of one *plague* happening, then two and three, until it speaks of seven for some. And not all seven *plagues* are struck, for I think that

---

16. "And yet" (καίτοιγε), a correction of Klostermann. S has καὶ τότε.
17. Matt 23.38.      18. "Hen," an addition of Cordier.
19. Matt 23.37–38.      20. Luke 21.20.
21. Luke 21.20.      22. Rom 11.11.
23. Lev 26.21.

24. Origen uses the word "mystery"(μυστήριον) often when he is implying a matter beyond what is specified in the rule of faith of his time and a matter open for speculation. He indicates in the previous section that the text could be referring to punishments after the "final departure" (death). But how and when does this happen? Origen does not know; hence it is mystery. He believes that the plagues may be a succession of punishments after death to purify fully the soul, depending on its degree of sin. But when these occur and how they are determined is not specified either in the Bible or in Origen.

## HOMILY 7

some are struck by six *plagues,* others by five, others four, others three or[25] two, but all of those who are subjected to punishments I suppose are struck by one *plague.*

(2) Thus God knows also what concerns the *plagues.* For that reason it is written here at the beginning of the text: *And it will happen in those days,* in the days[26] during which it is said, *I will never act upon you until a consummation.*[27] But a *consummation* will not occur *in those days.* For there are certain *days* when he does what he does *until*[28] a consummation.

3. *And when you say: "Why did the Lord God do all of these bad things to us?" And you will say to them: "As you have forsaken me and served other gods in your land, so you shall serve in a land not your own."*[29] Let one consider the literal sense, and it will suffice at the present to refresh the memory from the literal sense for those who can understand. Surely then, the sons of Israel possessed the holy land, the Temple, the house of prayer. They ought to have served God but when they transgressed the divine commandments they served idols, both the idols acquired from Damascus, as it is written in Kings,[30] and the other idols brought from other pagan nations into the holy land. Due to the fact that they received these pagan idols, they made themselves worthy to be rejected to the land of the idols, to dwell there where they worship the idols.

(2) Thus the Word literally said to them: *As you have forsaken me and served other gods in your land, you shall serve in a land not your own.*[31] But every person who makes something a god[32] serves alien[33] gods. Do you deify food and drink? Your

---

25. "Or," an addition of Cordier.  26. "Days," I have added.
27. Jer 5.18.
28. "Until" (εἰς), an addition of Blass and Klostermann.
29. Jer 5.19.  30. Cf. 4 Kings 16.10.
31. Jer 5.19.
32. "Makes a god" (θεοποιῶν), a correction of Cordier. S has ποιῶν.
33. "Alien" (ἀλλότριος). The term is used throughout this homily, but Origen does not offer a scriptural source until the end of the homily. It is Ps 136.4: "How should we sing the Lord's song in an alien land?"

*god* is *the belly*.³⁴ Do you honor silver and the wealth here below as a great good? Your god and lord is Mammon. For Jesus spoke of the lord himself of the love of money when he said: *You cannot serve God and Mammon. No one can serve two masters.*³⁵ Thus he who honors money and esteems wealth and supposes that it is good and accepts the rich as gods and despises the poor as not possessing god in their character, deifies silver. If anyone in the land of God, in the Church, should worship alien gods by making things worthy to be god which are not to be made god, he will be rejected to an alien land and worship gods which he worshipped when he was inside. Outside let him be rejected by the Church as a lover of money; let the one who is a glutton be outside the Church.

(3) This accords with one allegorical interpretation, lest I now inquire more deeply into what is beyond me³⁶ and what concerns that *land* about which the Savior said: *Who will give to you that which is ours?*³⁷ When someone becomes a worshipper in the *land*, God has arranged³⁸ that some are rejected from their own and come to the *land* about which it is written: *Hear, Israel: "Why is it that you are in the land of enemies, that you are counted among those in Hades? You have forsaken the fountain of life, the Lord. If you had walked in the way of God, you would have dwelt in peace forever."*³⁹

(4) Therefore we are now in an alien land and pray to do the opposite of what the sons of Israel did in the holy land. For they in the holy land gave worship to alien gods, but we in an alien land worship the God who is an alien to the *land*,

---

34. Phil 9.19.   35. Luke 16.12.

36. What is "beyond" Origen's present concerns are those deeper mysteries of what the "land not your own" truly is, namely, that aboriginal "land" prior to the Fall. A deeper inquiry would examine what the original land of man was and why man is no longer in it. But the matter is "beyond" Origen in this context because it is speculative.

37. Luke 16.12.

38. οἰκονομέω. The word implies that the rejection of some is foreknown by God.

39. Bar 3.9–13.

## HOMILY 7

an alien to earthly concerns. For the *ruler of this age*[40] rules here, and God is an alien to his sons. But if I say *alien* I do not mean this as one who has not created the world, but as one who is an alien to the lord of evil, an alien to present sins. And yet when we wish to worship the god alien to the things of evil in this land of affliction, let us see what we do. We do not say, *How shall we sing the Lord's song in an alien land?*[41] but, *How do we sing the Lord's song* not being *in an alien land?* We seek the *place* to *sing the Lord's song,* that *place* to worship the Lord our God in an alien land. What then is this *place?* I have *found* him.[42] He came to this land[43] bearing the body which saved, adopting *the body of sin*[44] *in the likeness of the flesh of sin,*[45] so that in this *place,* through Christ Jesus who sojourned and *nullified*[46] the *ruler of this age*[47] and *nullified* the sin, I can worship God here, and after this I will worship in the holy *land.* For anyone who has worshipped idols in the holy *land* went to an *alien land,* anyone who has worshipped God in an *alien land* will go to the holy *land* in Christ Jesus, *to whom is the glory and the power for the ages. Amen.*[48]

40. John 12.31.
41. Ps 136(137).4.
42. Cf. Bar 3.15.
43. "Land," I have added.
44. Rom 8.3.
45. Rom 8.3.
46. Cf. 1 Cor 15.24.
47. Cf. John 12.31.
48. 1 Pet 4.11.

# HOMILY 8

## Jeremiah 10.12–14

*On "The Lord who made the earth in his strength," up to, "every man who was made foolish by his knowledge."*

THE PROPHET, when he reports three so-called virtues of God—his strength and his wisdom and his prudence—assigns[1] to each of them a certain work of their own: to his strength earth, and to his wisdom the inhabited world, and to his prudence heaven.[2] For hear the text which says: *The Lord who made the earth in his strength, who set right the inhabited world in his wisdom, and in his prudence he stretched forth the heaven.*[3] And we need the *strength* of the Lord with respect to our *earth* (for it is written regarding Adam, *You are earth*),[4] for without the power of God we are unable to accomplish what does not concern the *mind of flesh.*[5] *Putting to death* the *members* which are *on the earth*[6] will be what concerns the will of the spirit, since,[7] according to the Apostle, the *practices* of the *flesh* are *killed* by the *spirit.*[8] Thus we read, *the Lord who made the earth in his strength.*[9] But if you also come over this earth, if you can see what was written in Job—as we find it in the most accurate copies—that he stood it *upon nothing,*[10] you will see that it rested by the strength of God perfectly in the middle.

---

1. "Assigns," an addition of Klostermann from Jerome.
2. "Heaven" (οὐρανόν), a correction of Cordier from Jerome. S has ἄνου.
3. Jer 10.12.
4. Gen 3.19.
5. Rom 8.6.
6. Cf. Col 3.5.
7. "Since" (ἐπεί), a correction of Cordier. S has ἐπί.
8. Rom 8.13.
9. Jer 10.12.
10. Job 26.7.

## HOMILY 8

(2) I come also to the *inhabited world*. I know the *inhabited* soul, I know the "deserted" soul. For if a soul does not have God, if[11] it does not have the Christ who said, *I and my Father, we will come to him and we will make our dwelling with him*,[12] if it does not have the Holy Spirit, it is a desert. But it is *inhabited* when it is filled with God, when it has Christ, when the Holy Spirit is in it. Yet that the Father and the Son and the Holy Spirit are in the soul of man is said variously and diversely in the Scriptures. So David, in the psalm of the confession concerning these spirits, asks the Father, when he says, *with a governing spirit uphold me*,[13] *a right spirit renew in me*,[14] *and take not your holy spirit from me*.[15] What three spirits are these? The Father is the *governing spirit*, Christ is the *right spirit*, and the Holy Spirit is the *holy spirit*.[16]

(3) These to prove that the *inhabited world* arises in no other way than[17] in the *wisdom* of God. For, *wisdom gives strength to the wise man beyond ten rulers who live in the city*.[18] *And the one who despises wisdom and instruction is miserable, and his hope empty, and his labors unprofitable, and his works useless*, says the book of Wisdom ascribed to Solomon.[19] Hence insofar as possible, since the *inhabited world* is *set aright* in the *wisdom* of God,[20] let us ourselves desire that our *inhabited world*, which perhaps has fallen, be *set aright*. For this *inhabited world* has fallen whenever we went to the place of affliction. This *inhabited world* has fallen whenever *we sinned, did wrong, acted wickedly*,[21] and it has need of being set aright.

(4) Thus God is *he who sets aright the inhabited world*.[22] But if you do not take the passage *he who has set aright the inhabited world* in that sense, but you understand the *inhabited world* in a more ordinary sense, seek how it could be that he *sets*

---

11. "If," an addition of Klostermann from Jerome.
12. John 14.23.    13. Ps 50.13 (51.12).
14. Ps 50.12 (51.10).    15. Ps 50.13 (51.11).
16. "Is the holy spirit," an addition of Klostermann from Jerome.
17. "Than" (ἤ), a correction of Cordier. S has ἡ.
18. Eccles 7.20.    19. Wis 3.11.
20. Cf. Jer 10.12.    21. Cf. Dan 9.5.
22. Jer 10.12.

*aright the inhabited world*, seek the fall of the *inhabited world* so that when you have discovered its fall, you may see its setting aright. Therefore if anyone is in this *inhabited world*—if you understand *inhabited world* in this way[23]—it is clear that it has need of being *set aright*.[24] For no one who has not fallen has need of being *set aright*.[25] It is clear that each of those in the *inhabited world* has fallen through sin, and the Lord is *he who sets aright* those who have collapsed and raises up all of those who have fallen down.[26] *In Adam all die*,[27] and so the *inhabited world* has fallen and has need of being *set aright*, in order that *in the Christ all* may be *made alive*.[28]

(5) So in two ways I have explained what concerns the *inhabited world*: I have shown, on the one hand, how for each person each soul is either inhabited or deserted; and I have set down, on the other hand, the meaning of the *inhabited world* itself.[29]

2. *And in his prudence he stretched forth heaven*.[30] Not by chance did he include *prudence* for *heaven*. For you will find it said in Proverbs, *God by wisdom founded the earth, and by prudence he prepared the heaven*.[31] Thus there is a certain *prudence* of God which one does not seek except[32] in Christ Jesus. For all such virtues,[33] insofar as they are of God, are Christ: he is

---

23. The way Origen has first explained it.

24. Jerome's translation is slightly different: ". . . if you understand 'inhabited world' in this way, he has fallen prior to being set aright. But if he has fallen, it is clear. . . ."

25. After this sentence, Jerome has: "But if it has been set aright, let us see what sort of fall preceded it."

26. Cf. Ps 144(145).14.   27. 1 Cor 15.22.

28. 1 Cor 15.22.

29. It is possible to apply these last paragraphs to the speculations on pre-existence found in *On First Principles* and see these comments as referring to the fall of souls. But since Origen's code words—"mystery," what is "daring," "what surpasses" the ordinary, what is troublesome, the presentation of several alternatives—are not employed, it is probable that here he is merely reflecting the Pauline doctrine of 1 Cor 15.22.

30. Jer 10.12.   31. Prov 3.19.

32. "Except," an addition of Klostermann from Jerome.

33. "Virtues" added in light of the beginning of the homily.

## HOMILY 8

the *wisdom* of God, he is the *power* of God, he is the *righteousness* of God, he is *sanctification*, he is *redemption*.[34] In this way he is the *prudence* of God. But though there is one substance, for differences in the aspects[35] the names are many.[36] You do not understand the same thing about Christ when you understand him as *wisdom* and when you understand him as *rightousness*. For when he is *wisdom*, you mean the knowledge of things divine and human, but when he is *righteousness*, he is that power which allots to every person according to worth. And when he is *sanctification*, he is what enables those faithful and dedicated to God to become holy.[37] In this way also then you will understand him as *prudence*, when he is the knowledge of what is good and evil, and what is neither.[38]

(2) Since then he caused a separation for those who dwell in heaven[39] or for those who *bear* the heavenly man[40]. . .[41] having separated what is evil from the good so that neither that heaven, due to the heaven *stretched forth* by the *prudence of God* might be stained, nor the righteous one who is heaven. For the righteous man is also heaven, as I will show; it has been said: *And he stretched forth in his prudence the heaven.*

(3) How then is the *heaven stretched forth?* Wisdom *stretches it forth.* For it is clear that *wisdom stretches* it *forth* in the text: *Since I stretched forth words and you did not pay attention.*[42] He speaks of words being stretched forth; in this way the heaven is *stretched forth*. And one reads in the one hundred-third Psalm: *He stretches forth the heaven like a tent.*[43] But also our

---

34. Cf. 1 Cor 1.24, 30.   35. ἐπίνοια.
36. See Schadel, 277, n. 79, on this definition. He notes the similarity to Philo, *quis rer. her.* 22.
37. "Holy" (ἁγίους), a correction of Klostermann from Jerome. S has ἁγίου.
38. The definition of wisdom and prudence in this paragraph are from the Stoics, and the other definitions are traditional. See Nautin's notes here, 1:358–59, nn. 2–3, and Schadel, 278.
39. Cf. Phil 3.20.   40. Cf. 1 Cor 15.49.
41. Klostermann suspects a lacuna here. Also the entire text up to the end of the paragraph is curiously missing in Jerome's translation.
42. Prov 1.24.
43. Ps 103(104).2.

78   ORIGEN

soul, formerly retracted, is stretched forth so that it can receive the wisdom of God.

(4) Yet let us go back to a prior statement. We were speaking about the *heaven* which emerges by *prudence,* and we said that those who carry the heavenly[44] man are also themselves *heaven.* For if it is said with respect to sinners, *You are earth and to earth you will return,*[45] might it not be said with respect to the righteous, to whom belongs *the kingdom of heaven,*[46] "You are *heaven* and to *heaven* you will *return"?* Or[47] due to the *dust,* it will be said to him who bears the *image of dust,*[48] *You are earth and to earth you will return,* yet due to the heavenly, whenever you bear the *image of the heavenly,*[49] will it not be fitting to say, "You are heaven and to heaven you will return"? Each of us thus has earthly and heavenly works. The earthly are works which lead down to the earth (it has the same nature as they), to the one who stores up things on *earth* and does not store up things in heaven.[50] Likewise the practices done according to virtue lead up to places of the same nature as the works, to what is in *heaven,* to one who *stores up treasure in heaven,* one who *bears the image of the heavenly.*

3. *And he has raised up the clouds from the last of the earth.*[51] This text also not long ago came to mind in the Psalms,[52] and we were saying how God *has raised up clouds from the last of the earth.* Yet there is some need to review again both for those who have known what I said with some clearness and recall, and for those who have forgotten or were not present for the clarification of this passage, either by it being uncovered and becoming evident or understood in some sense. We were saying[53] that the holy ones were clouds. For *Your*

---

44. "Heavenly" (οὐράνιον), is a correction of Cordier. S has ὀυνὸν.
45. Gen 3.19.  46. Matt 5.3.
47. "Or" (ἤ), a correction of Cordier. S has ἡ.
48. Cf. 1 Cor 15.49.
49. 1 Cor 15.49.  50. Cf. Matt 6.19–20.
51. Jer 10.13.  52. Ps 134.7.
53. "We were saying" (ἐλέγομεν), a correction of Klostermann from Jerome. S has λέγομεν.

## HOMILY 8

*truth goes*[54] *up to the clouds*[55] cannot refer to the *clouds* without souls, but the *truth* of God is *up to the clouds* when they hear the commandment of God and know where they may send rain and from where they would hold it back. Since they are clouds which God commands either to rain or not, it is written: *I command the clouds not to pour rain on it.*[56] With respect to these clouds, if there is no rain, it is not that God orders the clouds not to rain on the vine or the field, but that clouds do not appear at all, as it is written in the third book of Kings, where[57] around the time of drought no clouds appeared and where, according to the word of the prophet Elijah, the rain began to arise, a trace of a cloud appeared *like a trace of a man* and clouds started to make rain.[58] But that clouds exist which are ordered not to rain when the soul is unworthy[59] of rain, it is said in the text, *I will command the clouds not to pour rain on it.*[60]

(2) Thus each of the holy ones is a cloud. Moses was a cloud and as a cloud he was saying, *Attend, O Heaven, and I will speak. And let the earth hear the words of my mouth, let my message be awaited as rain.* If he were not a cloud, he would never have said, *Let my message be awaited as rain,*[61] *and let my words fall as drops of rain.*[62] As a cloud he says, *As the storm on the grass and as the showers on the herb, for I have proclaimed the name of the Lord.* Likewise as a cloud Isaiah also says, *Hear O Heaven, and listen, O Earth, for the Lord has spoken.*[63] And since he himself also was a cloud, and he was speaking about clouds which prophesy together with him, he said, when he prophesied, *To the clouds I command not to pour rain on it.*[64]

4. But if it is understood by us that some are *clouds*, let us

---

54. "Goes," I have added.      55. Ps 35.6 (36.5).
56. Isa 5.6.
57. "Where" (ὅπου), a correction of Klostermann. S has ὁ τὸν.
58. 3 Kings 18.44.
59. "Unworthy," a correction of Cordier. S has "worthy."
60. Isa 5.6.
61. "If . . . rain," an addition of Klostermann from Jerome.
62. Deut 32.1–2.      63. Isa 1.2.
64. Isa 5.6.

see how God is one who *raises up clouds from the last of the earth*.⁶⁵ How *from the last of the earth?* The Savior says, *He who wants to be first among you will be last of all*.⁶⁶ Paul observed this commandment and was *last* in this world. So he said, *For I think God has exhibited us Apostles as last of all, like those sentenced to death, because we have become a spectacle to the world, to angels and to men*.⁶⁷ Hence if there is anyone who observes the commandment of the Savior and becomes *last* with respect to this life, he becomes a *cloud* and God raises up *clouds* not from the first ones of the earth, he raises up *clouds* not from those of consular rank, he raises up *clouds* not from governors, nor from rich folk. For *blessed are the poor, for yours is the kingdom of God*.⁶⁸ Do you see how from the *last* ones God *raises up* and represents the clouds physically? Thus if we wish to become *clouds* to whom the truth of God comes,⁶⁹ let us become *last* of all and say by works and by disposition, *For I think God has exhibited us Apostles as last*.⁷⁰ Even if I cannot be an *Apostle*, it is possible for me to become *last*, so that God who *raises up clouds from the last of the earth* may raise me up.

(2) *And he made lightning for the rain*.⁷¹ Certain people say concerning these things that the production of lightning from the clouds arises from clouds which are rubbed against one another. For what happens with flintstones on earth, that when two stones strike against each other fire arises, they say this happens also for clouds. When the clouds are struck against one another in storms, lightning occurs. Furthermore, lightning generally occurs at the same time as thunder: the thunder, on the one hand, the result of the sound of the collision of the clouds, the lightning, on the other hand, being the light.

5. If you have grasped the example, consider with me also the spiritual *cloud*. Moses was a *cloud*, Joshua was a *cloud*. And these converse together, and from their words arise *lightning*.

65. Jer 10.13.
67. 1 Cor 4.9.
69. Cf. Ps 35.6.
71. Jer 10.13.

66. Mark 9.35.
68. Luke 6.20.
70. 1 Cor 4.9.

## HOMILY 8

Jeremiah was a *cloud*, Baruch was a *cloud*. They dialogue with one another. The *lightning* came from the words of Jeremiah and the words of Baruch. So, if you are able, bring together from the Scriptures whatever produces *lightning*. And in the New Testament Paul and Silvanus were two *clouds*. They came together and the *lightning* of the letter arose.[72]

(2) So God *made lightning for the rain and he brought forth the winds from the storehouse*.[73] These *winds* are then in the *storehouses*? Or[74] is it that it is not clear in what consists the nature of these things which blow on earth? But there are certain *storehouses* of *winds* as storehouses of spirits: *a spirit of wisdom and understanding, a spirit of counsel and might, a spirit of knowledge and piety, a spirit of the fear of God*,[75] *a spirit of power and love and of temperance*.[76] And you yourself can bring together from the Scriptures these *winds*.

(3) These spirits are in the *storehouses*. What are the *storehouses*? *In whom are the storehouses of wisdom and knowledge hid?*[77] These *storehouses* are in Christ. So from there these *winds* come, these *spirits*, so that one may be wise, and another may be faithful, and another may possess *knowledge*, and another is one who receives some kind of gift of God. *For to one is given through the spirit the word of wisdom, and to another the word of knowledge according to the same spirit, to another faith by the same spirit*.[78]

6. Thus, *he raised up clouds from the last of the earth, and he made lightning for the rain, and he brought forth the winds from the storehouses*.[79] And we through God hope to arrive at these *storehouses*, and since[80] there are many *storehouses*, perhaps according to the order of those who are raised there will be positions of rest in the *storehouses* of God. But what I mean is this: The resurrection of the dead occurs by orders—for the

---

72. Cf. 1 Thess 1.1; 2 Thess 1.1.　　73. Jer 10.13.
74. "Or" (ἤ), a correction of Cordier. S has ἡ.
75. Isa 11.2–3.　　76. 2 Tim 1.7.
77. Col 2.3.　　78. 1 Cor 12.8–9.
79. Jer 10.13.
80. "Since," an addition of Klostermann from Jerome.

Apostle said, *but each in his own order*[81]—and since the *orders* are not brought together by chance, one *order* will be in a certain *storehouse* of God and another *order* will be in another *storehouse* of God, and a third different *order* will be in another *storehouse*. Yet all of these *storehouses* have one *storehouse* in whom they dwell. Thus it was said by Paul: *In Christ are hid the storehouses of wisdom and knowledge*.[82] And just as I may acquire *one pearl of great value* out of many pearls,[83] so I come to the *storehouse* of the *storehouses*, the Lord of lords, the King of kings[84] whenever I become worthy of the *spirits* from the *storehouses* of God. For, *he brought forth the winds from his storehouses*.

7. *Every man has become foolish from knowledge*.[85] If *every man has become foolish from knowledge*, and Paul is a man, Paul *has become foolish from knowledge* because he knows in part, prophesies in part,[86] *has become foolish from knowledge* because he sees *through a mirror*, sees *dimly*,[87] sees and comprehends matters in small part and—if one can say—an infinitely tiny part. And seen from the opposite, you will understand that *every man has become foolish from knowledge*. There are sins of Jerusalem, sins also of Sodom, but in comparison to the worse sins of Jerusalem, the sins of Sodom are righteousness. *For Sodom*, he said,[88] *was justified due to you*.[89] Thus as the sins of Sodom are not righteousness but injustice, and[90] as there arises righteousness when compared to a greater injustice, so this is understood as[91] knowledge seen from the opposite. The *knowledge* which is in Paul, with respect to that knowledge which is in the heavens, is as foolishness compared to the mature knowledge. Hence, *every man was made foolish by*

---

81. 1 Cor 15.23.
83. Matt 13.46.
85. Jer 10.14.
87. Cf. 1 Cor 13.12.
82. Col 2.3.
84. Cf. Apoc 17.14.
86. Cf. 1 Cor 13.9–12.
88. To Jerusalem.
89. Cf. Ezek 16.51–53. The word translated "was justified" (ἐδικαιώθη) is from the same root as "righteousness" (δικαιοσύνη) and "injustice" (ἀδικία).
90. "And," an addition of Cordier from Jerome.
91. "This is understood as," I have added.

*knowledge*. In considering I think something such as this, the Preacher said, *I have said: "I will become wise." And it was made far from me, beyond what was, and deep, so deep; who will discover it?*[92]

8. The Word intends to be somewhat daring in saying that he *emptied* himself to sojourn in this life in order that in his *emptying* the world might be filled.[93] But if that one who sojourned *emptied* himself in this life, that empty vessel was wisdom itself, *for the foolishness of God is wiser than men*.[94] If I spoke of the *foolishness of God*, how the faultfinders would misquote me! How they would blame me! How can things supposed good by them be said a thousand times, but when what they suppose is not good is said, I would be denounced, since I said, *the foolishness of God!* But Paul as one wise and one who has apostolic stature has now dared to say that every wisdom on earth, the wisdom in him and in Peter and in the Apostles, every kind of wisdom which dwells in the world is the *foolishness of God*. For as with that wisdom which no[95] place on earth contains, as with that wisdom which is supra-heavenly, supra-worldly, this wisdom which dwells among us[96] is the *foolishness of God*. But this *foolishness of God is wiser than men*. Wiser than what sort of men? I do not speak of fools, but rather it is wiser than wise men. Even if you speak of the wise ones *of this age*, either the *rulers* or the prophets of the *rulers of this age*,[97] the *foolishness of God* which I have described *is wiser than men*.[98]

9. The Word intends to say something paradoxical, that *the wisdom of the world is folly with God*,[99] and *God has made foolish the wisdom of the world*.[100] So then has he in wisdom *made foolish the wisdom of the world?* And is *the wisdom of the world* able to contain Wisdom in order that it[101] is refuted as *foolish?* For

92. Eccles 7.23–24.
93. Cf. Phil 2.7.
94. 1 Cor 1.25.
95. "No" (οὐ), a correction of Klostermann from Jerome. S has οὖν.
96. "Among us," I have added.
97. 1 Cor 2.8.
98. 1 Cor 1.25.
99. 1 Cor 3.19.
100. 1 Cor 1.20.
101. The wisdom of the world.

does the wisdom of God challenge *the wisdom of the world* so that it may refute it? But there is need of some little thing, an insignificant *foolishness of God,* in order that, by this shallow *foolishness of God the wisdom of the world* may be *made foolish* and refuted. For the wisdom of this world has not carried the wisdom of God.

(2) For example, in order that you may understand that the *foolishness of God has made foolish the wisdom of the world,* allow me—assuming that I know many and great things—to challenge one who is unintelligent and untaught and acquainted with nothing and has not been challenged about any sort of sophisticated subject. If his thoughts thus are foolish, do I need an argument or deep principles? Is there not need only of one phrase a little smarter than his speech for me to refute the foolishness of that one? Similarly in order that the wisdom of this world is *made foolish,* there is no need for the wisdom of God when it challenges it—for the wisdom of this world is below it—but the *foolishness of God* suffices, because *the foolishness of God is wiser than men, and the weakness of God is stronger than men.*[102]

(3) And my Savior and Lord has assumed all of the opposites so that by the opposites he might dissolve[103] the opposites, and we might be made strong from the *weakness* of Jesus, and we might know wisdom from *the foolishness of God,* and after we have been introduced in these things, we might be able to mount up to *wisdom,* to the *strength* of God, Christ Jesus, *to whom is the glory and the power for the ages. Amen.*[104]

102. 1 Cor 1.25.
103. λύειν.
104. 1 Pet 4.11.

## HOMILY 9

### Jeremiah 11.1–10

*On "The word that came to Jeremiah from the Lord, saying,
'Hear the words of this covenant'" up to, "'They have turned
back to the wrongdoings of their forefathers.'"*

ACCORDING TO THE APPEARANCE of our Lord Jesus Christ as historically told, his dwelling was in a body and a kind of universal event which illuminated the whole world, when *the Word was made flesh and dwelt among us.*[1] For *he was the true light which enlightens every man who comes into the world. He was in the world and the world arose through him, and the world did not know him. To his own he came, and his own did not receive him.*[2] However, it is necessary to know that he was also dwelling prior to this, yet not in a body, in each of the holy ones. And after this visible dwelling, he dwells in us again. And if one wishes to have proof of this, take note of the passage, *The word which came to Jeremiah from the Lord saying: Hear...*, and so on.[3] For who is *the word which came from the Lord* to Jeremiah or to Isaiah or to Ezekiel or anyone except[4] the one *in the beginning with God?*[5] I do not know any *word* of the Lord other than the one concerning whom the Evangelist said, *The Word was in the beginning, and the Word was with God and the Word was God.*[6]

(2) But we need also to see that the dwelling of the Word

---

1. John 1.14.  
2. John 1.9–11.  
3. Jer 11.1.  
4. "Except," an addition of Lietzmann.  
5. John 1.1.  
6. John 1.1.

86   ORIGEN

is with each of those who can especially benefit.[7] For what profit is it for me if the Word has dwelt in the world and I do not have[8] him? And, conversely, if he has not yet also dwelt in the whole world, but grants that I have become as the Prophets, I have the Word. And I could say that Christ was with Moses, with Jeremiah, with Isaiah, with each of the righteous, and what he said with the disciples, *Behold I am with you all the days until the end of the age*[9] is observed in fact and realized before his sojourn. For he was with Moses and he was with Isaiah and with each of the holy. How can they have spoken the word of God if the Word of God did not dwell in them? But these things must be understood especially with respect to us of the Church, who want God of the Law and the Gospel to be the same, Christ to be the same both then and now and[10] for all of the ages. For there will be[11] those who will cut in two, in their opinion, the divinity previous to the dwelling of the Savior and the divinity proclaimed[12] by Jesus Christ, but we know one God both then and now, one Christ both then and now.[13]

(3) These thoughts are due to *the word which came to Jeremiah from the Lord saying.* ...[14]

(4) What then also may we hear? *Hear the words of this covenant, and speak to the men of Judah and to those who dwell in Jerusalem.*[15] We are *the men of Judah* due to Christ. *For it is evident that our Lord was descended from Judah,*[16] and the name *Ju-*

---

7. As Origen states in many places, each man has the Word (λόγος) because he has reason (λόγος). But some "benefit" more because they are more prepared or willing.
8. "Have" (ἔχω), a correction of Huet from Jerome. S has ἔγνων.
9. Matt 28.20.
10. "And," an addition of Klostermann from Jerome.
11. "There will be" (ἔσονται), a correction of Cordier. S has ἴσονται.
12. "Proclaimed" (ἀπαγγελλομένης), a correction of Klostermann from Jerome. S has ἐπαγγελλομένης.
13. Jerome continues: "and one Holy Spirit with the Father and the Son forever."
14. Jer 11.1.                    15. Jer 11.2.
16. Heb 7.14.

*dah*, if I present it according to[17] the Scripture, refers to Christ. *The men of Judah* will not be the Jews who do not believe in Christ, but all of us who believe in Christ. *Judah, may your brothers praise you.*[18] *Your hands are on the neck of your enemies.*[19] *May they praise you.* His brothers *praised* not that Judah who is the son of Jacob, but the brothers praise this Judah, since this Judah says, *I will tell your name to my brothers, in the midst of the Church, I will praise you.* It is not said to that Judah, *Your hands are on the neck of your enemies.* Where is that Judah who has *placed his hands on the neck of the enemies* discovered? History has recorded nothing such as this about him. But if you consider the dwelling of the Lord Jesus who *renders harmless*[20] the Devil, when he disarmed *the principalities and powers* and he made an example and triumphed on the wood,[21] you see how the prophecy which speaks with respect to this Judah, *Your hands are on the neck of your enemies* has been fulfilled. If this[22] is so, and the word now speaks *to the men of Judah*, to whom else could he speak than[23] to us who believe in the Christ, who is called Judah in any case also due to the tribe Judah?

2. The word is spoken *to the men*[24] *of Judah and to the inhabitants of Jerusalem.*[25] This is the Church. For the city of God,[26] the Vision of Peace,[27] is the Church, the peace which he brought to us is in her, and is completed and beheld if we are children of peace.

(2) *Hear then the words of this covenant and speak to the men of Judah and the inhabitants of Jerusalem. And you will say to them: "Thus says the Lord God: 'Cursed is the man who does not hear the words of the covenant which I commanded to your fathers.'"*[28] Who

---

17. "According to" (κατά), a correction of Klostermann from Jerome. S has καί.
18. Cf. *Hom in Jer* 4.2, 5.15. 19. John 49.8.
20. Cf. 1 Cor 15.24. 21. Cf. Col 2.15.
22. "If this" (εἰ τοῦθ'), a correction of Cordier. S has εἶτ' οὖθ'.
23. "Than" (ἤ), a correction of Cordier. S has ἡ.
24. "Men" (ἄνδρας), a correction of Cordier. S has ἄνδρα.
25. Jer 11.2. 26. Cf. Apoc 3.12.
27. The meaning of the word "Jerusalem."
28. Jer 11.2–4.

especially hears *the words of the covenant which God commanded to the fathers?* Is it then those who believe in him or is it those who have proven that they do not believe Moses[29] from their having not believed in the Lord? For the Savior said to them: *If you believe in Moses you would believe in me. For about me he wrote. But if you do not believe in the writings of him, how can you believe in my words?*[30] Hence they have not believed in Moses, but we who believe in Christ believe in the Covenant through Moses, and it is said to us, lest we become accursed, *Cursed is the man who does not hear the words of the covenant, which I commanded to the fathers.*

(3) They then possess what is *cursed*. For they have not heard the *covenant* which God *commanded to the fathers in the day*, he said, *I brought them from the land of Egypt, from the furnace of iron*.[31] And God brought us *from the land of Egypt, from the furnace of iron*, especially what is understood according to the passage in the Apocalypse of John, that the place *where their Lord was crucified is called spiritually Sodom and Egypt*.[32] For if it is *called Egypt spiritually*, and this Egypt is not the one *called Egypt spiritually*, for it is perceptible, it is evident that if you understand the Egypt which is *called spiritually* and you depart from it, you are he who departs *from the land of Egypt and from the furnace of iron* and it is said to you, *Hear my voice and do all* these things.[33]

(4) Next[34] the promise of God is said for those who hear, if they do what is *commanded: And you will be my people and I will be your God*.[35] Not everyone who says they are a people of God are a *people* of God. Hence, that people who were proclaimed to be a people of God heard, *You are not my people*, in

---

29. "Not" (μηδὲ Μωσεῖ), a correction of Klostermann from Jerome. S has μηδαμῶς.

30. John 5.46–47.   31. Jer 11.4.

32. Apoc 11.8.

33. Jer 11.4. "Egypt" in Alexandrian thought often represented the evil world or a place of darkness. See *Hom in Ex* 2.1, 3.3.

34. "Next" (εἶτ'), a correction of Klostermann from Jerome. S has ἤ τ'.

35. Jer 11.4.

## HOMILY 9

the passage, *Therefore you are not my people*. And it has been said to that people you are *not my people*,[36] and elsewhere this people was called a *people*.[37] For, *they have provoked me to jealousy with what is not God*—he speaks concerning the former—*they have provoked me with their idols. So I will provoke them to jealousy with those who are not a people, with a senseless nation I will provoke them*.[38]

3. Thus we were made into a people for God, and the *righteousness* of God was *proclaimed to the people who will be born*,[39] to a *people* from the pagan nations. For this people is *born* suddenly, yet in the Prophet it also is said: *Has a nation been born all at once?*[40] But *a nation was born all at once* when the Savior dwelt among them, and *five thousand* believed in one day,[41] and three thousand were added in another day,[42] and we see that a whole *people* is *born* to the Word of God, and it is said to the barren woman who suddenly bears, who formerly could not give birth before: *Be glad, O barren woman who did not bear, break forth and cry in joy you who have not had birth pains, for the children of the deserted woman are much more than she who has a husband*.[43] She was *deserted* from the Law, *deserted* from God, but that Synagogue is spoken of as one who has the Law as a *husband*.

(2) What then does God promise me? *You will be my people and I will be your God*.[44] He is the God of none except those whom he himself favors, as he himself favors the Patriarch to whom he said, *I am your God*,[45] and again to another, *I will be your God*,[46] and for others, *I will be their God*.[47] At what point then do we reach a condition, I mean for each person, that God is our God? But if we wish to learn of whom he is God, and whom he favors with his own name, he said, *I am the God of Abraham, the God of Isaac, the God of Jacob*, and commenting

---

36. Cf. Hos 1.9.
37. Hos 2.25.
38. Deut 32.21.
39. Cf. Ps 21.31 (22.31).
40. Isa 66.8.
41. Cf. Acts 4.4.
42. Acts 2.41.
43. Isa 54.1; Gal 4.27.
44. Jer 11.4.
45. Gen 17.1.
46. Gen 35.11.
47. Exod 29.45.

on this, the Savior said, *God is not of the dead, but of the living.*⁴⁸ Who is the *dead*? The sinner, who does not have the one who said, *I am the life*,⁴⁹ the one who has *dead works*, who has never repented from *dead works*, concerning which the Apostle said, *Not laying again a foundation of repentance from dead works.*⁵⁰

(3) If then *God is not of the dead but of the living*, and we know who is the one who is *the living*, because he is governed according to Christ and remains with him, if we wish that he be our God, let us say good-bye to the *works* of death, so that he fulfill his promise which said, *And I will be your God, that I may maintain my oath which I swore to your fathers, to give them a land flowing with milk and honey.*⁵¹ For note when he says, *I will maintain my oath which I swore to your fathers, to give them a land flowing with milk and honey*, that he has never given them the *land flowing with milk and honey*. For this is not the *land flowing with milk and honey* which God promised, but it is that⁵² earth about which the Savior taught saying: *Blessed are the meek, for they shall inherit the earth.*⁵³

4. Next the Prophet responds to what was mentioned previously by the Lord. To the words, *Cursed is the man who does not hear the words of this Covenant,*⁵⁴ he says, *And I answered and said: "So be it, Lord."*⁵⁵ What does *So be it, Lord* mean? That he is indeed *cursed* who does not abide in the *words of the Covenant*.

(2) *And the Lord said to me: "Read these words in the cities of Judah and outside Jerusalem."*⁵⁶ And to those *outside* we *read* the *words* of God when we summon them to salvation *saying, "Hear*⁵⁷ *the words of the Covenant and do them." And they did not do them. And the Lord said to me: "A bond was found in the men of*

---

48. Matt 22.32.  49. John 11.25.
50. Heb 6.1.  51. Jer 11.4–5.
52. "But it is that" (ἀλλ' ἔστιν ἐκείνη), a correction of Klostermann from Jerome. S has ἀλλὰ περὶ ἐκείνης.
53. Matt 5.5.  54. Jer 11.3.
55. Jer 11.5.  56. Jer 11.6.
57. "Saying, hear," an addition of Klostermann and Nautin.

## HOMILY 9

*Judah and in the inhabitants of Jerusalem.*"[58] Do we intend to repent for the sin mentioned concerning the *men of Judah*, since we know that we are *the men of Judah* because of Christ, who was prophesied and called[59] Judah?[60] For perhaps since there are some sinners among us who act contrary to right[61] reason, because of this the Prophet says, *A bond was found among the men of Judah and among the inhabitants of Jerusalem.*[62] For whenever a *bond* of unrighteousness[63] and a *bond* of sins were *found* in any who in name come from the Church, with the result that one can apply to the sinner the statement that *each is caught in the snares of his sins,*[64] God could say, *A bond was found in the men of Judah.* But may no *bond* be found in us. Yet how could a *bond* not be *found* among us if[65] a *bond* is even in some up till now? *Loose every bond of wickedness, free the yokes of forced agreements, break every wicked contract. Distribute to the poor his bread.*[66]

(3) Thus, *a bond was found in the men of Judah and in the inhabitants of Jerusalem. They have turned back to the wrongdoings of their forefathers.*[67] *To the wrongdoings* of whom did they *turn back?* He does not[68] say merely: of the fathers. Who is added? *They turned back to the wrongdoings of the forefathers.* We were saying that these things are said to us and to those who sin among us. Then how did those who sin among us *turn back to the wrongdoings* not of the fathers, but of the *forefathers?*

---

58. Jer 11.6–9.
59. "Called" (λεχθέντα), a correction of Cordier. S has ἐλεγχθέντα.
60. S has at the beginning of this sentence "if" (εἰ), as does Jerome. Klostermann corrects εἰ to "which" (ἥ) and Nautin corrects to "or" (ἤ). Jerome's translation is, "if we sin, we who are called men of Judah because of Christ, and sinners have been found in our numbers, it is said concerning us." It is quite different from the Greek. None of this seems to help, so I, along with Schadel, have translated without it.
61. "Right" (τὸν ὀρθόν), a correction of Cordier. S has τῶν ὀρθῶν.
62. Jer 6.9.  63. Cf. Isa 58.6.
64. Prov 5.22.
65. "If" (εἰ), a correction of Klostermann from Jerome. S has ἥ.
66. Isa 58.6–7.  67. Jer 11.9–10.
68. "Not," an addition of Klostermann from Jerome.

Perhaps then our fathers are of two kinds, and the inferior kind of fathers is in us; for prior to believing we are sons in some sense of the Devil, as[69] the word of the Gospel points out when it says, *You are of your father the Devil*,[70] but when we believe, we become *sons of God*.[71] Hence, whenever we sin, we *turn back* to the *wrongdoings* not only of the fathers, but of the *forefathers*. But in order to prove that our fathers are of two kinds, I will use words from the forty-fourth Psalm which grasps the matter in this way, *Hear, O daughter, and consider and incline your ear, forget your people and the house of your father*.[72] One father says, *Forget the house of your father*, whereas another father says, *Hear, O daughter*. So our fathers are of two kinds, but *Forget the house of your father* refers to the first. If you *turn back* again to your sins after you have *forgotten* the house of your first, you[73] have done the sins discussed here.

(4) *They have turned back to the wrongdoings of their forefathers*.[74] I was saying that the Devil also was our first father before God became our Father—if indeed the Devil is not also our father now. We will support this from the Catholic Epistle of John in which it is written, *Everyone who does sin is begotten of the Devil*.[75] If everyone who does sin is begotten of the Devil, just as many times as we sin we *are begotten of the Devil*. Thus he is miserable who is always born from the Devil, just as again he who is begotten[76] by God is always blessed. For I will not say that the righteous man is begotten just once by God, but that he is always begotten in each good act in which God begets the righteous man. If then I set before you, with respect to the Savior, that the Father has not begotten the Son and then severed him from his generation, but always begets him, I will also present something similar for the righteous man.

---

69. "As" (ὡς), a correction of Klostermann from Jerome. S has οὓς.
70. John 8.44.   71. Rom 8.14.
72. Ps 44.11 (45.10).
73. "You" (σύ), a correction of Klostermann. S has οὐ.
74. Jer 11.10.   75. 1 John 3.8.
76. See Schadel's note on how Origen understood this concept, 281, n. 96.

(5) But let us consider who is our Savior: a *reflection of glory*.[77] The *reflection of glory* has not been begotten just once and no longer begotten. But just as the *light*[78] is an agent of *reflection,* in such a way *the reflection of the glory* of God is begotten. Our Savior is the *wisdom of God*.[79] But the *wisdom* is the *reflection of everlasting light*.[80] If then the Savior is always begotten—because of this he also says, *Before all the hills he begets me,* (and not, "*Before all the hills* he has begotten me," but, *Before all of the hills he begets me*)[81]—and the Savior is always begotten by the Father, and likewise also if you have the *spirit of adoption,*[82] God always begets you in him according to each work, according to each thought. And may one so begotten always be a begotten son of God in Christ Jesus, *to whom is the glory and the power for the ages of ages. Amen*.[83]

77. Heb 1.3.
79. Cf. 1 Cor 1.24.
81. Prov 8.25.
83. 1 Pet 4.11.

78. Cf. Wis 7.26; 1 John 1.5.
80. Wis 7.26.
82. Cf. Rom 8.25.

## HOMILY 10

### Jeremiah 11.18–12.9

*On "Make it known to me, Lord, and I will know," up to, "Gather together all the beasts of the field, and let them come to devour her."*

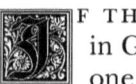F THE ORACLES OF GOD are in Law and Prophets, in Gospels and Apostles, it will be necessary that the one who is instructed in the oracles of God assign God as teacher. For, *the one who teaches men knowledge* is God, as is written also in the Psalms,[1] and the Savior testifies also that you do not need to be assigned a certain teacher on earth when he says: *And do not call anyone a teacher on the earth. For there is one who is your teacher, the Father who is in heaven.*[2] And the "Father who is in heaven"[3] teaches either by himself or through Christ or in the Holy Spirit or through Paul, or for that matter, through Peter or through one of the other saints, provided only that the Spirit of God and the Word of God dwell and teach.

(2) For what purpose are these matters discussed by me? Because the Prophet said: *Make it known to me, Lord, and I will know.*[4] For I will not *know* unless you *make it known to me*, but if, when you *make it known to me, I know*, then I will see *their*

---

1. Ps 93(94).10.
2. Matt 23.8–9. Origen has substantially manipulated our currently accepted text. It reads: "But you are not to be called rabbi, for you have one teacher, and you are all brethren. And call no man your father on earth, for you have one Father who is in heaven." There are other, less attested, readings which Origen may have followed here.
3. "The . . . heaven," an addition of Klostermann from Jerome.
4. Jer 11.18.

# HOMILY 10

habits[5] and I will understand what each does and the nature of his motives.

(3) The Prophet said these things. Next[6] let us consider what the Savior says in the Prophet: *Like a lamb without evil who is led to be sacrificed, I did not know. They have plotted a scheme against me, saying: "Come and let us put wood into his bread, and let us erase him from the land of the living, that his name be no longer remembered."*[7] As also the Prophet Isaiah said: Christ *was led as a sheep to slaughter, and as a lamb before the shearer was silent, so he does not open his mouth.*[8] Isaiah is there speaking concerning him, but here Christ speaks about himself:[9] *Like a lamb without evil who is led to slaughter to be sacrificed I did not know.*[10] He did not say what he *did not know.*[11] For he has not said: *I did not know* evil things. He has not said: *I did not know* good things. Nor has he said: *I did not know* sin,[12] but simply, *I did not know.* To you then he leaves to examine what he *did not know* and learn what he *did not know* from the text: *On our behalf he made him to be sin who did not know sin.*[13] For to *know sin* is to sin, just as to *know* righteousness is to act righteously. Thus he who proclaims what concerns righteousness and does not act righteously *did not know* righteousness.

2. *Against me they plotted a scheme, saying: "Come and let us put wood into his bread."*[14] That the Jews crucified him, this fact is clear and we preach this openly. But how this applies to the statement, *They plotted a scheme against me, saying: "Come and let us put wood into his bread,"* is a matter to consid-

---

5. Jer 11.18.
6. "Next" (εἶτα), a correction of Klostermann from Jerome. S has εἰ δέ.
7. Jer 11.19.   8. Isa 53.7.
9. "Himself" (αὐτοῦ), a correction of Klostermann from Jerome. S has αὐτοῦ.
10. Jer 11.19.
11. "He did know" (ἔγνω), a correction of Cordier from Jerome. S has ἔγνων.
12. Cf. 2 Cor 5.21.   13. 2 Cor 5.21.
14. Jer 11.19.

er. The *bread* of Jesus is the word in which we are nourished. However, since they wanted to impute scandal in[15] his teaching, when he was teaching among them, by crucifying him, they said: *Let us put wood into his bread.* For whenever on account of the word of the teaching of Jesus one fixes on crucifying the teacher, the *wood* has been *put into his bread.* Thus, let those who have planned secret plots say, *Come and let us put wood into his bread.*

(2) But I will say even more paradoxically: The *wood* which has been *put into his bread* has made the *bread* greater. Let me take an example from the Law of Moses: The *wood* which was put into the bitter *water* made it sweet.[16] So the *wood* of the Passion of Jesus Christ when it entered into the word has made its *bread* sweeter. In fact, before the *wood* entered into his *bread,* when it was *bread* alone and there was no *wood* in his teaching, his *voice did not go out upon all the earth.*[17] But since the *bread* through the *wood* which was put into it received power, on account of this the word of his teaching has occupied the entire inhabited world. And then the *wood* was a symbol of the Passion of Jesus through which the bitter *water* becomes sweet. For I say that the Law, when uncomprehended, is bitter *water,* but when the *wood* of Jesus enters and the teaching of my Savior dwells, the Law of Moses is sweetened and becomes most pleasant when it is read and known.

3. Hence they said, *Come and let us put wood into his bread.* But they also say, *Let us erase him from the land of the living that his name will no longer be remembered.* So they killed him in order to obliterate his name. But Jesus knew how and why he dies. Hence, he said, *Unless a grain of wheat falls into the earth and dies, it remains alone; but if it dies, it bears much fruit.*[18] The result is that the death of Jesus like an ear of *wheat* propagates[19] and yields abundantly from what has been seeded, so that if hypothetically he had neither been crucified nor[20]

---

15. "In," not in Jerome.
16. Cf. Exod 15.25.
17. Ps 18.5 (19.4).
18. John 12.24.
19. Cf. Luke 8.8.
20. "Nor" (μηδέ), a correction from Jerome. S has μὴ δέ.

died, the *grain of wheat* would have remained alone and many would not have arisen from him. Pay attention then to his text, if this is not what he intends when he says: *The grain of wheat unless it falls into the earth and dies, it remains alone; but if it dies, it bears much fruit.* The death of Jesus has yielded all of this fruit, but if the death of Jesus has yielded such[21] fruit, how much more will the resurrection yield?

4. *Lord of hosts who judges righteous things, who examines loins and hearts, let me see your vengeance upon them.*[22] This is prayed for prophetically in order to see the *vengeance* of God *upon them.* For Jerusalem has been surrounded by troops and her desolation approaches,[23] and it is said to her, *Behold, your house is forsaken.*[24]

(2) Thus, *Let me see from your vengeance upon them, for to you I have committed my cause. On account of this the Lord says to the men of Anathoth, the men who seek my soul, the men who say, "Do not prophesy in the name of the Lord or you will die by our hands": "Behold I will visit them. Their young men will die by the sword and their sons and daughters will perish in*[25] *a famine, and there will be not a trace of them, because I will affix evil on the inhabitants of Anathoth in the year of my visitation of them."*[26] The name of Anathoth should be taken figuratively here, and the whole mystery of the Jews is stated allegorically in it. For *Anathoth* is translated as *obedience.*[27] Since, then, obedience[28] of God was in the people, as well as the kingdom of God, and it happened with respect to the kingdom that *the kingdom of God will be taken from you and given to a nation producing the fruits of it,*[29] according to this it happened also that the *men of Ana-*

21. "Such" (τοσούτους), a correction of Klostermann from Jerome. S has τούτους.
22. "Them" (αὐτῶν), a correction of Cordier from Jerome. S has αὐτοῦ. The Scripture verse is Jer 11.20.
23. Cf. Luke 21.20.     24. Matt 23.28.
25. "In," an addition of Klostermann from Jerome and LXX.
26. Jer 11.20–23.     27. Cf. *Onom. sacra* I.201.37.
28. "Since then obedience," an addition of Klostermann from Jerome.
29. Matt 21.43.

*thoth*, who were men in obedience, *sought the soul* not of Jeremiah but this is said concerning Christ. For history does not say that the men of Anathoth *sought the soul* of Jeremiah. We have the book of Kings, the Scripture mentions Jeremiah there.[30] Nothing such as this is stated in them, nor[31] in the Chronicles; for we have the book itself of the Prophet, the men of Anathoth have said nothing.

(3) *Those who seek my soul, who say, "Do not prophesy in the name of the Lord"*—the Jews hindered Jesus from teaching—*"or you will die by our hands": "Behold I will visit them. Their young men will die by the sword, and their sons and daughters will perish in a famine."*[32] They have not by then *perished* by the *sword*, but after the Advent, a *famine* now came upon them, *not a famine of bread or thirst of water, but a famine to hear the word of the Lord.*[33] For the *Lord Almighty* no longer *speaks*[34] with them. This *famine* is in order that prophecy would no longer exist. And why do I say prophecy? There is not any teaching.[35] Even if they bear the title "sage" a thousand times with them, the word of the Lord is still not among them, since the verse has been fulfilled: *The Lord took away from Judah and from Jerusalem the strong man and strong woman, the giant and the strong man,*[36] *and the soldier and judge and prophet and diviner and elder and captain of fifty and the admirable adviser and master builder and intelligent pupil.*[37] For he is no longer able to say, *Like a master builder I laid a foundation.*[38] The *builders* have passed over, have come to the Church, have laid the *foundation* Jesus Christ.[39] Those who came after them have also built on him.

---

30. Cf. 4 Kings 23.31, 24.18.
31. "Nor," from a suggestion of Klostermann from Jerome.
32. Jer 11.21.                      33. Cf. Amos 8.11.
34. Cf. Jer 6.9, 16; 7.3, 20–21, etc.
35. Jerome for this sentence has: "Neither teachers nor doctors have remained in the rest of Judea."
36. Jerome and LXX add here: "the strength of the bread and the strength of the water...."
37. Isa 3.1–3.                  38. 1 Cor 3.10.
39. Cf. 1 Cor 3.11.

## HOMILY 10

5. Thus, that *people* who are *forsaken* are *in a famine*. For, *I will bring evil on the inhabitants of Anathoth in the year of my visitation on them. You are righteous, O Lord, that I will complain to you. Moreover, I will speak my charges against you. Why*[40] *is it that the way of the impious prospers? All of those who break their promises flourish.*[41] Still we inquire if God who has given the Law and the Prophets is good when we see that the *way of the impious prospers* and he does not punish the *impious. All of those who break their promises flourish.* Those who speak against the demiurge,[42] who blaspheme him, *flourish, are planted and thrive, have given birth and have brought forth*[43] *fruit.*[44] How much *fruit* there is born of Marcion, how much of Basilides, how much of Valentinus![45] For it is this *fruit* which is prophesied and stated concerning the *impious* in the text: *They have given birth and they have brought forth fruit. You are near their mouth and far from their loins.*[46] They name the name of Jesus but they do not have Jesus. For they do not confess him as one must.

(2) *And you, Lord, you know me, you see me, you have examined my heart before you. Cleanse them for the day of their slaughter.*[47] What will I do in order to clarify this? By *cleanse* he means the punishments of those punished. For, *cleanse them for the day*, he said, *of their slaughter; cleanse them* by *slaughtering* them. *For the Lord disciplines him whom he loves, and chastises every son whom he receives.*[48]

6. *How long will the earth mourn and the grass of the field be dried up from the evil of the inhabitants in it?*[49] The Prophet here again talks as if the *earth* is alive, when he says that the *earth mourns* on account of the *evil* of those who walk on it. For

40. "Why," an addition of Cordier from Jerome.
41. Jer 11.25–12.1.
42. Those who believe that the creator is different from God.
43. "Have brought forth," an addition of Delarue from Jerome.
44. Jer 12.1–2.
45. All Gnostic thinkers whose doctrines Origen opposed.
46. Jer 12.2.   47. Jer 12.3.
48. Heb 12.6. Cf. Prov 3.11.   49. Jer 12.4.

each of us then the *earth* either *mourns* or rejoices. For either it *mourns* from the *evil of those who inhabit it* or it rejoices from the virtue *of those who inhabit it*. For each of us then the element itself either rejoices or *mourns*. But if the *earth* does so, perhaps also the rest of the elements. In a similar way I will also say so do water and the angel appointed over water,[50] in order that I might discuss the earth mourning or not mourning. For this body, the *earth*, does not *mourn* from the *inhabitants on it*, but please bear in mind that for the disposition of all things there is a certain angel appointed for the *earth*, another appointed for the waters, and another for the air and the fourth for fire.[51] So ascend with me in reason[52] up to the disposition which exists in animals, in plants, in the heavenly[53] stars. An angel has been appointed also for the sun and another for the moon, another[54] also for the stars. These angels with whom we are as long as we are on *earth* either rejoice[55] or *mourn* for us when we sin. The *earth mourns*, he says, from *the inhabitants on it*. He calls the angel for the *earth* itself by the same name, *earth*. For just as *greatly cursed is what is handmade and the one who made it*[56]—not that what is lifeless is itself *cursed*, but he means by "handmade" what tends carefully to the lifeless statue[57] and is called by that name—likewise I will say also that by the *earth* is meant the angel appointed over the earth. And by *water* is meant the angel appointed over water, according to what has been said, *The waters saw you, O God, the waters saw you and they were afraid, the deep stirred with many roars of waters, the clouds gave a sound, for also your arrows went through it.*[58]

50. Cf. Apoc 16.5.
51. Origen refers here to the very ancient view that the cosmos is composed of the four elements. See Schadel, 289, n. 110.
52. λόγος.
53. "Heavenly" (οὐρανίοις), a correction of Klostermann from Jerome. S has οὐνοῖς.
54. "Another," an addition of Klostermann and Nautin.
55. Here Klostermann adds, "if we act righteously...," from Jerome.
56. Wis 14.8.
57. Demons inhabit statues. Cf. *Cels* 7.64.
58. Ps 76.17–18 (77.17).

## HOMILY 10

7. *I have left behind my house, I have abandoned my heritage, I have given my beloved soul into the hands of its enemies.*[59] See with me that he who exists *in the form of God*[60] is in the heavens, see his supercelestial home. And if one wants to see even higher—for *I am in the Father*[61]—see that his home is God. He *leaves father and mother,*[62] the *Jerusalem above,*[63] and he comes into the earthly place and says: *I have left behind my house, I*[64] *have abandoned my heritage.* For that was his *heritage,* the country with the angels, the rank with the holy powers. *I have given my beloved soul into the hands of its enemies.* He has handed over his *soul into the hands of the enemies* of the soul, into the hands of the Jews who killed it, into the hands of the rulers who gathered together against him, into the hands of kings, when *the kings of the earth set themselves in array, and the rulers were gathered together against the Lord and against his Christ.*[65]

8. *My heritage has become for me as a lion in the forest.*[66] This *heritage* of his on *earth* which he has inherited behaved as a beast with him and the heritage became the Jews, furious against him *as a lion in the forest.* Do not be amazed if his *heritage* is then *as a lion in the forest.* Still now there are *in the forest lions* who want to curse Jesus and blaspheme him and lay traps for those who believe in him.

(2) Thus, *my heritage has become for me as a lion in the forest, he offered his voice against me, thus I hated him. Is my heritage not a cave of a hyena to me?*[67] He prophesies concerning this heritage: *My heritage* has it not become *a cave of a hyena*—a *cave of a hyena,* a most savage, death-devouring creature, which is around tombstones, which eats dead bodies?

---

59. Jer 12.7.  60. Phil 2.6.
61. John 14.11. Jerome adds, "and the Father is in me." Klostermann notes *Jo* 20.18 (16).
62. Matt 19.5.
63. Gal 4.26. Klostermann notes the parallel to *Comm in Mt* 14.17.
64. "I," a correction of Cordier. S has "you."
65. Ps 2.2 (Acts 4.26).  66. Jer 12.8.
67. "To me," an addition from LXX and Jerome. Jer 12.8–9.

(3) *Is my heritage not the cave of a hyena to me? Or*[68] *is there a cave against her round about? Go . . .*[69] Since they have become such, I command you, the angels, to go and gather together the beasts and deliver them to beasts. *Go and assemble all of the beasts of the field, and let them come to eat her.*[70] *The beasts of the field* came, they *ate* that people. Look at their hearts which are *eaten* by the opposing powers. If Jesus did not spare them but said, *Go, assemble the beasts,* how much less will he spare us? If we do not do the Law of God, the word of the Gospel, he will say again, *Go, assemble the beasts and deliver her.* But we do have the right to say in prayers: *Do not deliver to the beasts the soul which has confessed to you.*[71] Let us *confess* concerning our trangressions when we repent, and let us not be delivered to the *beasts,* but to the holy angels who will nurse us, who lift us up in their laps, who carry us from this age to the future age, in Christ Jesus, *to whom is the power and the glory for the ages. Amen.*[72]

68. "Or" (ἤ), a correction of Klostermann from LXX and Jerome. S has ὡς.
69. Jer 12.9.
70. Jer 12.9.
71. Ps 73(74).19.
72. 1 Pet 4.11.

## HOMILY 11

*Jeremiah 12.11–13.11*

On *"All of the earth was obliterated in destruction" and on the "waistcloth."*

**W**HO IS THE ONE WHO SAYS: *On account of me all of the earth was obliterated in destruction?*[1] Christ says this, since before his coming many sins had occurred in the people, but not of such a nature that they were altogether forsaken and delivered for a long time into captivity. But when they *filled up the measure of their fathers*[2] and continued denying the Prophets[3] and persecuting the righteous, killing the *Christ of God*,[4] then the verse *Your house is forsaken* has been realized. And *on account of* him they have suffered these things and *all of the earth was obliterated in destruction.*

2. But if one wishes to hear the passage *On account of me all of the earth was obliterated in destruction* in a higher way, note that, when Jesus came, the *earth* in you was *obliterated* in some sense. For it was *obliterated* when the[5] *members on the earth* were *put to death*[6] and the *earth* no longer produced its own works. There no longer arose in the righteous man the *works of flesh*, by which the *flesh* was flourishing, no longer *immorality*, no longer *impurity*, not *licentiousness*, not *idolatry*, not *sorcery*, and the rest.[7] But the Savior also says: *Why do you suppose that I came: to bring peace on the earth? I did not come to bring peace but a sword.*[8] For truly before he *came*, there was no *sword* on the

---

1. Jer 12.11.
2. Cf. Matt 23.32.
3. Cf. Matt 23.37.
4. Luke 9.20.
5. Jerome has "our" instead of "the."
6. Col 3.5.
7. Gal 5.19–20.
8. Cf. Matt 10.34.

*earth*, the *flesh* did not *desire against the spirit* nor the *spirit against the flesh*,[9] but when he *came* we were also taught what is of the *flesh*, and what is of the *spirit*, the teaching appearing on *earth* as a *sword*[10] divided the *flesh* and the *earth* from the *spirit*.[11]

(2) And the *earth was obliterated* when we *carry around the death of Jesus in the body*,[12] and no longer do we *live* according to the *flesh*, but the *spirit* lives, and we sow nothing *in the flesh*, but everything *in* that *spirit* in order that we may not *reap corruption* from the *flesh* but *eternal life* from the *spirit*.[13]

3. For it is said to the sinners: *Sow wheat and reap thorns*.[14] For even if they are acquainted with the words[15] of God, those who are not well acquainted with them, who neither live in a way required nor believe, *sow wheat and reap thorns*. But these things are especially understood[16] for the heretics who read the Scriptures and *reap thorns* not from the Scriptures but from their own inventions.[17]

(2) *Their offices will not profit them*.[18] Others have also discussed these matters before us, and since we do not[19] reject their discussion, we are bringing it up publicly with gratitude, not as having found it ourselves, but as having received a good lesson. If we attend to what is written, this word will help both you and us. Some of us suppose there to be by virtue of office some who preside over you such that some[20] want to reach for this office. But know that the *office* does not altogether save. For even many presbyters will be damned; even many laity will be proven blessed. Since there are some in the *office* who do not live in a way that they profit and hon-

---

9. Cf. Gal 5.17.  
10. Jer 12.12.  
11. Cf. Heb 4.12.  
12. Cf. Rom 8.13.  
13. Cf. Gal 6.8.  
14. Jer 12.13.  
15. "Word" (λογίοις), a correction of Klostermann. S has ἁγίοις. The Catena has λόγοις.  
16. "Understood" (ταῦτα νοῆσαι), a correction of Klostermann. S has κατανοῆσαι.  
17. ἐπίνοια.  
18. Jer 12.13.  
19. "Not" (οὐκ), a correction of Huet from Jerome. S has τοῦτ'.  
20. "Some" (τινὲς), a correction of Huet. S has τινὸς.

or the *office*, because of this, say the commentators, it is written: *Their offices will not profit them.* For to *profit* is not the same as to assume a position among the presbyters, but to live in a way worthy of the position, as the word demands. The word also demands that both you and we live in a good way, but if it can be said that *the powerful will be tested in a powerful manner*,[21] more is demanded of me than of the deacon, more from the deacon than from the laity, but from him who has undertaken the chief ecclesiastical office itself over all of us even[22] more is demanded. Therefore, hear the one who has been entrusted with great things, the Apostle, he says: *This is how one should regard us as servants of Christ and stewards of the mysteries of God. Moreover, it is required of stewards that they be found faithful.*[23] And so it is rare that a *steward* is found *faithful* and good. Jesus, *who knew all things before their inception*,[24] says: *Who then is the faithful and wise steward whom his master will set over his household to give them their portion of food at the proper time?*[25] Then he reproaches certain *stewards* and says, *But if that evil servant begins to say, "My master is delayed in coming," and begins to beat the menservants and the maidservants, and to eat and drink and get drunk, the master of that servant will come on a day when he does not expect him and at an hour he does not know, and will punish him and put his part with the unfaithful.*[26]

(3) These, then, are our views regarding *Their offices will not profit them.*

4. But let us consider next also the necessary blame, which is good to receive for the moral sphere, when the Prophet says, *Be ashamed of your boasting, of the reproach before the Lord.*[27] There are certain things in which we *boast* due to a lack of understanding, things which are not worthy of *boasting.* Just as someone *boasts* that he is rich and has acquired

21. Wis 6.6.
22. "Even" (ἔτι), is a correction of Klostermann. S has ἐπί.
23. 1 Cor 4.1–2.  24. Dan 13.42 (Sus 42).
25. Luke 12.42. Cf. Matt 24.45.
26. Luke 12.45–46; Matt 24.48–51.  27. Jer 12.13.

many possessions, it might be said to him, *Be ashamed of your boasting.* If someone boasts over a nobility which is external, it will be said to him: *Be ashamed from your boasting.* If someone boasts about the costliness of apparel, about the construction of a house which is built luxuriously, it is a *boasting* alien to the *boasting* of the saints. Hence, it will be stated to such a person, *Be ashamed of your boasting.* Hear the word of the Prophet Jeremiah who exhorts us not to *boast* not even with respect to wisdom: *Let not the wise man boast,* he says, *in his wisdom, neither the mighty man boast in his might nor the rich man boast in his wealth, but let the one who boasts boast in this, that he understands and knows that I am Lord.*[28] You yearn to *boast* by *boasting* not to hear: *Be ashamed of your boasting;* boast as the Apostle and say, *But far be it for me to boast except in the cross of our Lord Jesus Christ, by which the world has been crucified to me and I to the world.*[29] You want to *boast* so that it might not be said, *Be ashamed of your boasting?* Hear Paul when he *boasts* and learn when he says, *I will all the more gladly boast of my weaknesses, that the power of Christ may rest upon me.*[30] Hear of what boastful things he *boasts: countless beatings*—who among us can say this?—*far more imprisonments, often near death. Five times I have received at the hands of the Jews forty lashes less one, three times I have been beaten by rods, once I was stoned, three times I have been shipwrecked.*[31]

(2) We learn then also that there are differences of *boastings*, that some *boastings* are worthy of a *shame* for which the declaration of the Apostle could be said, *And the glory for them is in their shame.*[32] For what they ought to be *ashamed,* for these things they suppose that they are glorified.

5. After this let us consider what concerns the *waistcloth.* For, *thus says the Lord.* "*Go and buy for yourself a linen waistcloth and put it around your hips and do not*[33] *pass it through water.*" *And I bought the waistcloth, according to the Word of the Lord, and*

---

28. Jer 9.22–23.
29. Gal 6.14.
30. 2 Cor 12.9.
31. 2 Cor 11.23–25.
32. Phil 3.19.
33. "Not," an addition of Huet from Jerome.

*placed it around my hips, and the Word of the Lord came to me saying: "Take the waistcloth which is around your hips and arise and go to the Euphrates and hide it there in a cleft of the rock."*[34] After days he comes there, finds this rotted *waistcloth*, and the Lord offers what gives a clue to the explanation of the *waistcloth* when he says: *"Just as the waistcloth clings to the hips of man, so I cause to cling to me the house of Israel,"* says the Lord, *"that they may become for me a renowned people and a source for boasting and for glory; and they did not listen to me."*[35]

(2) Thus the Prophet takes the place of[36] God when the *linen waistcloth* is girded around his *hips*, as God is girded by the people. For *I have caused to cling* to myself, he said, this *people*. God speaks as if the *waistcloth* becomes the *people* of God. But why is the *waistcloth* of God *around his hips?* The one who is able reads Ezekiel and sees in the word that it is as if God is made corporeal,[37] and how those things *below* the hips are *fire*, and those things also *above* the hips are *electrum*.[38] Let me search out the reason why what is below the hips of God is *fire*. Those deeds arising from *hips* and *generation*, these are *fire*.[39] For, everything which is in generation has need of purification from fire; everything which is in generation has need of punishment. But what is above the hips and[40] has transcended generation, this is like the purest and most precious element in the world. For it is said that *electrum* is more valued than gold. Since then the Scripture

---

34. Jer 13.1–4.  35. Jer 13.11.
36. "Takes the places of" (παραλαμβάνεται), a correction of Klostermann from Jerome. S has περιλαμβάνεται.
37. Origen believes Scripture is depicting God in a corporeal way only to explain something about man, who is corporeal. Origen carries his allegory on the "waistcloth" to its logical end without entertaining the idea of a true "body" of God. The body of God is an image of conversion and maturity.
38. Cf. Ezek 1.27.
39. "Deeds" (πράγματα). No single term adequately translates the word γένεσις here. It involves simultaneously two ideas: the need for begetting and that we are creatures with a beginning.
40. "And," an addition of Klostermann from Jerome. Nautin includes it in his translation but ignores it in his Greek text.

uses examples so that it can teach that the body of God *above* is more precious and the body *below* is inferior, on account of this he introduced God as one composed of *fire* and *electrum*. In generation each of us is *fire* and is himself also a body of God.[41] We are not the *electrum*, but if we ascend and progress—for it is possible to pass from our present condition in what is *below* to one in which we become a body of God *above*[42]—when we step past the *fire* we will be *electrum*, what concerns the higher body of God.

6. Thus the *linen waistcloth clings* about his *hips*. Why? In order to make clear that the people are like a shelter of God. For against those who wish to accuse God, the people of God are placed, and they cover him like a shield and do not allow something wrong to be said in what concerns God. But whenever we sin, just as the Prophet puts aside this *waistcloth* and condemns it to the *Euphrates* river in order that it may perish there, so the sinner is thrown from the *hips* of God. And once banished, he is banished to the Euphrates river, the river of Mesopotamia, where there are Assyrians, enemies to Israel, where there are Babylonians, and there he is ruined. For since there are such rivers, the Prophet is sent from Judea to the Euphrates river to carry out the task and take off the *linen waistcloth*.

(2) But why is it also *linen?* Because it has its generation from earth.[43] For it is a plant which rises up from earth, then after it is cultivated, it is combed, washed and wiped clean and with great effort achieves a condition such that it may become a *waistcloth* or something else. And all of us then have our generation as the *waistcloth* of God, and since we have our generation from earth,[44] we have need of much

---

41. "In generation . . . God" is a reconstruction of Nautin from a text which, according to Klostermann, has a lacuna. The extant text in S reads: "And he himself is a body of God and in generation each of us is fire." Jerome's translation is missing the text: "And he himself is a body of God. . . ."
42. "For . . . above," is missing in Jerome's translation.
43. On linen, see Origen's comments in *Hom in Lev* 4.6.
44. "Earth" (γῆς), a correction from Jerome. S has τῆς.

## HOMILY 11

preparation so that we might appear yellow, so that we might be washed, in order that we might throw off the color of the earth. For the color of the *linen* just beginning is one thing, another thing is its color from the effort. And the color of the *linen* just beginning is darker, but it becomes most bright from the effort.

(3) Thus some such process also happens to us who are in generation. We are dark at the beginning in believing—hence in the beginning of the Canticle of Canticles it is said, *I am very dark and beautiful*,[45] and we look like the soul of an Ethiopian at the beginning—then we are cleansed so that we may be more bright according to the passage, *Who is she who comes up whitened?*[46] And we become *pure white linen*.[47] Then, when we are worthy to *cling* to God, we are also woven for the *waistcloth* of God. God does not take us off. He took off the first people, *the whole house of Judah* and *the house of Israel*.[48] It happened because they are no longer needed. For he no longer is girded by them. God girded himself with us in place of them. For God did not remain naked when he threw off that *waistcloth*, for he wove another *waistcloth* for himself. This *waistcloth* is the Church, the one from the pagan nations. Let her know that if God did not *spare* the first peoples, how much more will he not *spare* her if she sins,[49] if she is not worthy of the *hips* of God. *But he who clings to the Lord is one spirit*[50] with Christ Jesus, *to whom is the glory and the power for the ages. Amen.*[51]

---

45. Cant 1.5. See Origen's homily on this text in *Hom in Cant* 1.6.
46. Cant 8.5.
47. Cf. Apoc 15.6.
48. Jer 13.11.
49. Cf. Rom 11.21, 24.
50. 1 Cor 6.17.
51. 1 Pet 4.11.

# HOMILY 12

## Jeremiah 13.12–17

On "And you will say to this[1] people: 'Thus says the Lord God of Israel, "Every skin will be filled with wine,"'"[2] up to, "and your eyes will pour forth tears because the flock of the Lord was crushed."

THAT THE PROPHET is appointed to say for God ought to be worthy of God,[3] but it appears that it is not worthy of God when we rely on the letter,[4] for someone might say when hearing the letter: These texts are foolish. But the unspiritual man will say this, for *the unspiritual man does not receive what is of the spirit of God. For it is folly to him.*[5] Observe then the text which says: *And you will say*[6] *to this people, "Thus says the Lord God of Israel,"*—let what the Lord God of Israel says be worthy of the Lord God of Israel[7]—"*Every skin will be filled with wine.*' And it will happen, if they say to you: 'Are we so ignorant indeed that we do not know that every skin will be filled with wine?'"[8] And if[9] those who answer, holding to the literal word, say these things and state

---

1. "This," an addition of Klostermann from LXX and quotations in text.
2. "With wine," an addition of Cordier from Jerome. Nautin includes it in his translation but not in his Greek text.
3. In S, "not" follows "God," but it does not appear in Jerome.
4. γράμμα. The literal interpretation.
5. 1 Cor 2.14.
6. "You will say," a correction of Cordier from Jerome. S has "he will say."
7. "What the Lord God of Israel says," an addition of Klostermann from Jerome.
8. Jer 13.12.
9. "If," an addition of Klostermann from Jerome.

that they *know* that *every skin will be filled with wine*, they are lying. For not *every skin will be filled with wine*. In fact, there are skins filled with olive oil or other liquid, and some also remain empty.¹⁰ Thus, they lie. For not *every skin will be filled with wine*, and the people answer by saying: *Are we so ignorant that we do not know that every skin will be filled with wine?*—a question which will result, in accordance with our abilities, in this kind of explication. If we see the differences of the wines and the statements made concerning them, in them we will see consequently what is true concerning the *skins: Every skin will be filled with wine*. For either there is a certain, let us say, good *skin* among the skins, and it will be filled with wine to the degree of its own goodness, or there is a wicked *skin*, as compared with *skins* and by a judgment on what concerns them, and it will be filled with a wine of wickedness to the degree of its wickedness.

(2) Thus how is one to understand from the Scripture the different wines? Concerning the worse wines the following has been written: *For from the vine of Sodom their vine comes, and their shoots from Gomorrah. Their grapes from the grape of wrath, the cluster is of bitterness for them. Their wine is the desire of dragons and the incurable desire of asps.*¹¹ But concerning the better wines it says: *Your very strong cup intoxicates* me,¹² and *wisdom* summons to its wine bowl when it says, *Come, eat my bread and drink the wine which I have diluted for you.*¹³ Thus there is wine from Sodom and there is wine which *wisdom dilutes*. And again: *A vine arose for my beloved on a mountain-peak in a fertile area,*¹⁴ a *vine* called the Vine of Sorek, planted by God, a certain Chosen and Wondrous vine.¹⁵ But there is also the *vine* of the Egyptians which God beats according to what was written: *God has beaten down their vine with hail, and their sycamores with frost.*¹⁶

---

10. "And some also remain empty," an addition from Catena and Jerome.
11. Deut 32.32–33.    12. Ps 22.5.
13. Prov 9.1, 5.    14. Isa 5.1.
15. Cf. *Onom. sacra* I.199.76.    16. Ps 77(78).47.

2. And so, observe that in an allegorical sense all men are now able to contain *wine*. And[17] I call them, in light of this, *skins,* and I say that the bad is filled with the wine *of the vine of Sodom,* he is filled with Egyptian wine and wine of the enemies of Israel. But the holy one and he who has received help is filled with *wine* from the *Vine of Sorek* and the *wine* about which it is written, *Your very strong cup intoxicates,*[18] and again, the holy one is filled with *wine* which *wisdom dilutes.*[19]

(2) And so, understand these *skins* in terms of evil and virtue in order to envision how *every skin is filled with wine.* But if it is necessary to see the effects of evil and of virtue—punishments due to the evil, blessings and promises due to virtue—let us set down from the sacred Scriptures how the punishments and the promises are discussed as wine:[20] *Take the cup of this undiluted wine, and give to all of the nations to which I have sent you to drink*—he says this to Jeremiah,[21] and he adds to it—*and they will drink and vomit and go mad and fall.*[22] Hence he has called the punishments here *undiluted wine* which those deserving of *undiluted wine drink,* that is, an *undiluted* punishment. But there are others who *drink* a punishment which is not *undiluted,* but which has been *diluted.* For, *in the hand of the Lord is a cup filled with a mixture of undiluted wine, and*[23] *he poured it from this into this. Though its lees were not emptied out, all of the sinners of the earth drink.*[24] If you also wish to know the *cup of blessing*[25] which the righteous drink, the text from Wisdom then also suffices, in which it says: *Drink the wine which I diluted for you.*[26] But see with me the Savior on the Passover who goes up into *a large upper room furnished*[27] *and ornamented,* and who feasts with the disci-

---

17. "And" (καί). S has ἤ.
18. Ps 22.5.
19. Prov 9.1, 5.
20. "Wine" (οἶνος), a correction of Delarue from Jerome. S has οἰονεί.
21. "To Jeremiah" (Ἰερεμίᾳ), a correction of Nautin. S has Ἰερεμίας.
22. Jer 32.16.
23. "And," an addition from the Catena and Jerome.
24. Ps 74.9 (75.8).
25. Cf. 1 Cor 10.16.
26. Prov 9.5.
27. Mark 14.15.

ples and gives to them a cup, about which it is not written that he diluted. For Jesus, who cheers up the disciples with *undiluted* wine, cheers them up and says to them: *Take, drink, this is my blood,*[28] *which is poured out for you*[29] *for the forgiveness of sins.*[30] *Do this as often as you drink in memory of me;*[31] and, *Truly I say to you, I shall not drink again of this until that day when I drink it new with you in the kingdom* of God.[32] You see the promise which is the cup of the *New Covenant.*[33] You see the punishments as the cup of the *undiluted* wine, and another form of punishment as the cup which has been diluted so that in each person what he drinks is diluted according to the amount the worthwhile action mingles with the futile action. Notice that those who are strangers in every way to the worship of God and who do not commit themselves but live as it happens drink the *undiluted wine*—to which we apply the text from Jeremiah—while those who are not in every way apostates and sinners but are still unworthy[34] of the *cup of the New Covenant,* these people sometimes do better, sometimes the opposite acts,[35] and drink wine of *an undiluted mixture.*[36]

(3) For God *poured from this into this.*[37] What is *this?* I see two cups according to what was said: *He poured from this into this. Though its lees were not emptied out.*[38] Note the cup of his good works in the one hand of God, but, if you permit me to speak more boldly,[39] let the cup of your good works be in the right hand of God, then let the cup of your sins be in the left hand of God. For when you are about to be punished due to sins, even though there do arise in you more worthwhile acts, *the cup in the hand of the Lord* is *of a mixture of undiluted*

---

28. Cf. Matt 26.26–28.  
29. Luke 22.20.  
30. Matt 26.28.  
31. 1 Cor 11.25.  
32. Matt 26.29.  
33. Cf. 1 Cor 11.25.  
34. "Unworthy" (ἀναξίους), a correction of Huet from Jerome. S has ἀξίους.  
35. "Acts," an addition of Delarue from Jerome.  
36. Ps 74.9.  
37. Ps 74.9.  
38. Ps 74.9.  
39. The boldness is in talking about God as though he had "hands."

*wine. And he poured from this into this,* from the cup in the left to the cup in the right. For you are neither able to drink the cup of the good works, since you have not done only good works, nor are you able to drink only the cup of sins, for some worthwhile works have been practiced by you. Hence, *he poured from this into this.* The anger and the punishment are mixed for you in accordance with the pattern of your works, so that your punishment may either be more watery or more bitter and painful. For in accordance with the pattern, as aforementioned, the pain[40] from the cup of anger which is given proportionately for each of the sins is either weakened or not at all weakened when the sins are compounded with good works. But if you are wholly beautiful and good, you will say, *I will lift up the cup of salvation, I will call on the name of the Lord.*[41]

(4) So *every skin,* either beautiful or ugly, *will be filled with wine,*[42] and according to the fitness of the skin, wine will be put into the *skin* according to the purpose of those who are here named *skins.* Thus olive oil is not put into the *skins,* nor any other liquids, but every *skin* must be filled with *wine.*

3. Next with reference to those who have sinned, in light of the literal text, in *Jerusalem* then also in *Judea,*[43] he teaches with what wine God will fill those *skins,* the sinners. For it is written, *If they say to you: "Are we so ignorant we do not know that every skin will be filled with wine?" And you will say*[44] *to them: "Thus says the Lord: 'Behold I will fill all of the inhabitants of this land, and the kings, the sons of David who sit on his throne and the priests.'"*[45] He who is about to punish spares no one. Not even if someone were called a *prophet,*[46] he has sins, and will not be *filled* when the threats are spoken. Not even if someone were called a *priest* and believed that he had a stature of a more

---

40. Klostermann believes a lacuna is present in this sentence. "Pain" (πόνος), an addition of Koetschau. Others suggest "wine."
41. Ps 115.4 (116.13).  42. Jer 13.12.
43. Jer 13.13. The LXX text has Judah.
44. "You will say" (ἐρεῖς), a correction of Cordier from Jerome. S has ἐρεῖ.
45. Jer 13.12–13.  46. Jer 13.13.

honorable name among the people[47] does God spare him to the point that he does not punish him who has sinned. But what has been written down about them, the Apostle says, *was written down for us, for whom the end of the ages has come.*[48] Hence, if anyone among these *priests* sins—I am pointing to us presbyters[49]—or among those Levites who stood around the people—yet I mean these deacons—he will have this punishment. Yet again, we will shortly see, God willing when we read Numbers, but after an examination of the prophetic word, that there are some priestly blessings. For certain things about priests will be said there.

(2) Thus, God says that he *fills the priests and the prophets and Judah and all of the inhabitants of Jerusalem,* with *an intoxicant,* and *scatters man and his brother and their fathers and their sons.*[50] And let us also understand this passage in this way: God gathers together the righteous, but he *scatters* the sinners. Because of this also, whenever men were not *moving from the east,*[51] God did not *scatter* them. But when they *moved from the east* and *they said to one another: "Come and let us build for ourselves a city and a tower whose top will be*[52] *up to the heavens,"*[53] God said concerning this, *Come and when we go down let us confuse their language there.*[54] And so, each was *confused* and *scattered* to some place of the earth. And the people of Israel who did not sin also were in Judea, but after they sinned, they were *scattered* afterward from their inhabited place and *spread out*[55] everywhere.[56]

---

47. "People" (λαόν), a correction of Koetschau. S has ὅλον.

48. Cf. 1 Cor 10.11, 9.10.

49. Origen means that the presbyters of the New Covenant are comparable to the priests in the Old Covenant, even though they have a different name.

50. "And their sons," an addition of Cordier from Jerome. The text is Jer 13.13–14.

51. Gen 11.2.

52. "Will be" (ἔσται), a correction of Cordier from LXX. S has ἐστίν.

53. Gen 11.3–4.       54. Gen 11.7.

55. Cf. Gen 11.8.

56. Klostermann believes there is something missing in this sentence. Nautin corrects to the following: "They were scattered to some place of the earth and 'spread out' everywhere."

(3) Consider, please, that some such condition also concerns all of us. A certain *Church of the first-born* will be *enrolled in heaven*[57] where there is *Mount Sion* and the *city of the living God, the heavenly Jerusalem*.[58] Here the blessed will be brought together so that they may be together, but sinners are punished by not being there with the others. I know certain people in this life who like to deliver for punishment to some island and for torture the family members of someone of those who injured the kingdom. They *scattered* here the wife, here one son, to another place the other, so that the mother may not enjoy the company of the son, or the brother of the brother. Consider that some such condition occurs for the unrighteous. It is necessary that you a sinner, attended by God, taste something more bitter so that, once disciplined, you may be saved. And just as when you punish the servant or son who is punished by you but do not want simply to torment him, rather it is in order that you convert him by pains, so God, too, disciplines by the pains from sufferings[59] those who have not been converted to the Word, who have not been cured. For the purpose of training[60] he puts on what he puts on, according to the statement, *Through everything you will be taught by pain and whip, Jerusalem*.[61] Thus, in order that the pain which instructs increases, those who feel pain are *scattered* from one another so that this person and that person are not together at the same time. For the intensity of the pain would be lessened through a word of hope of each one with the other.

4. But if it is necessary to add also to that word another cause of the *scattering*, I also will offer this view: When evil ones associate with one another, they pay regard to and increase evil, just as when good ones associate with good, look

---

57. Cf. Heb 12.23.     58. Cf. Heb 12.22.
59. "Sufferings" (παθημάτων), a correction of Klostermann from Jerome. S has μαθημάτων.
60. "For the purpose of training" (ἐπὶ παιδείᾳ), a correction of Klostermann. S has ἐπεὶ παιδεία.
61. Jer 6.7–8.

after what is good. Thus the evil plan which would have been strengthened with similar kinds of persons is dissipated when the wicked are *scattered* from[62] one another. Because of this God arranges that the bad are not with one another, perhaps in Providence for them, that their evil ways not increase but, when dissipated, diminish.

(2) These are comments with respect to the text: *"I will scatter them, man and his brother, and their fathers and their sons in the same way," says the Lord.*

(3) *I will not regret and I will not spare and I will not pity their destruction.*[63]

5. The heretics attack such words when they say: "Do you see that the demiurge, the God of the Prophets, is the kind of being who says, *I will not spare and I will not pity their destruction?* How can this being be good?" But if I take as an example a judge who for the common good does not *show pity* and a tribune who for a good purpose is not merciful, I will be able, from this example, to persuade that God in order to *spare* many does not *spare* one. And I will also take as an example the healer, since he demonstrates that in order to *spare* the whole body, he does not *spare* one limb.

(2) Let us suppose that it is the appointed task for a judge to create peace and prepare matters beneficial for the people under him. Let there approach a youthful murderer who projects himself to seem personable and good. Let a mother approach who presents reasons for pity to the judge, that he might take mercy on her old age. Let the wife of this worthless man plead with him to be merciful; let his children who surround him cry out in need. In light of these things, what is fitting for the common good: to show mercy or not to show mercy upon this man? If he is shown mercy, he will repeat the same crimes. If he is not shown mercy, he will die, but the common good will be better off. So, if God *spares* the sinner and shows mercy to him and pities him such that he

---

62. "From," an addition of Blass, Koetschau, and Klostermann.
63. Jer 13.14.

not punish him, who would not be inflamed? Who[64] among the evil, when their own sins are stopped through fears of punishment, will not be inflamed, will not be worse?

(3) One can also see such things occurring in the churches. Someone sinned and after sinning prayed for return to communion. If he is shown mercy hurriedly, the common good will be inflamed, and the sin of others increases. But if a judge—in considering the case not as one who shows mercy repeatedly nor as one harsh, but as one who provides for the individual, but even more provides for the many beyond the individual—weighs the future loss to the common good of the person from the communion beside the allowance for his sin, it is clear that he will decide to reject the individual so he might save the many.

(4) Consider the healer also, how, if he *spares* surgery from what needs surgery, if he *spares* sterilization from what needs to be sterilized[65] because of the pains which accompany such aids, how the sickness festers and worsens. But if he in a more bold way proceeds to cut and cauterize, he will heal by not showing mercy, by appearing not to pity him who is cauterized and given surgery. So also God's plan is not for just one man but for the whole world. He oversees those things which are in heaven and what is everywhere on earth. He looks then to what is fitting for the whole world and for everything that exists. He looks also, as far as possible, to what is useful for the individual, yet not if it causes the profit for the individual at the expense of the world. Due to this an *eternal fire* was also *prepared*;[66] due to this a *gehenna*[67] was made ready; due to this an *outer darkness*[68] exists,[69] whose need exists not only for the punished, but especially for the common welfare.

6. But if you want to take Scripture as a witness that sinners are punished for the education of others, even if those

64. "Who," an addition of Klostermann from Jerome.
65. "What needs to be sterilized," an addition of Klostermann from Jerome.
66. Cf. Matt 25.41.   67. Cf. Matt 8.18.
68. Cf. Matt 8.12, 25.30.   69. Matt 8.12.

unabashed may be beyond treatment, hear Solomon in the Proverbs who says, *When a pest is being whipped, the fool will be more astute.*[70] He did not say that he who is being *whipped* will be more *astute* and more *sensible* through the whips, but he said that the *fool* will change from foolishness into common sense through whips employed on the *pest.* For this is signified here by the term *astuteness,* and the *fool* changes because he sees others who are *whipped.* Hence the punishment of others is useful for us if we become worthy of salvation through others who are punished. And just as the transgression of Israel was useful for the salvation of the pagan nations,[71] so the punishment of some[72] will be useful for the salvation of others. On account of this, God who is good said: *I will not spare and I will not pity their destruction.*[73]

7. Since the point of one part has been outlined, let us also see what the rest of the passage teaches us: *Hear and hearken, and be not proud, for the Lord has spoken. Give glory to the Lord our God before he causes darkness and before your feet stumble on the dark mountains. And you shall wait for light. And the shadow of death is there. And they shall be brought into darkness. But if you will not hear in secret, your soul will weep from the presence of pride, and your eyes shall pour down tears because the Lord's flock is crushed.*[74] He wants the same persons to *hear* and to *hearken,* for he is not satisfied that they only *hear* or that they only *hearken.* Therefore, he says: *Hear and hearken.* Then after this he orders them not to be *proud,* and he teaches what must be done. Let us learn then from the text what it is to *hear* and what it is to *hearken.*

(2) What you *hearken* to, you receive into the ears, and what you *hear*—if[75] it is in contrast to *hearken*—you receive perhaps in the mind. And since[76] among the texts in Scrip-

---

70. Prov 19.25.      71. Cf. Rom 11.11.
72. "Of some," an addition of Klostermann from Jerome. Nautin includes the addition in his translation but not in his text.
73. Jer 13.14.      74. Jer 13.15–17.
75. "If" (εἰ), a correction of Klostermann from Jerome. S has ἤ.
76. "Since" (ἐπεί), a correction of Wendland. S has ἐπί.

ture some are more secret and mysterious and some are immediately useful for those who are apprehending them, concerning those passages which are more secret I think it is said *hear,* but concerning those immediately useful passages which can help the hearer without interpretation, *hearken.*

(3) Thus, if we scrutinize the whole Scripture we will say as "bankers who become esteemed":[77] *Hear* this but *hearken* to this. Then,[78] when we *hear* and *hearken,* he enjoins us: *And be not proud.*[79] For, *everyone who exalts himself will be humbled.*[80] But the Savior when he says, *Learn from me, for I am gentle and lowly in heart, and you will find rest for your souls,*[81] teaches us not to be *proud.* For with other human evils, this sin is very much among us. For sometimes we are *proud* without any reason and about something which one has relatively no need to be *proud,* yet sometimes we are *proud* with plausible motives because there is some basis for pride. Still there is no sound reason to be *proud* over that thing.

8. But what I am saying will be evident in this way: There are some who are *proud* because they are sons of rulers and because they are descended from those who are great by earthly standards. Such ones, proud for purposeless and indifferent[82] matters, do not have a good explanation for what incites them to be *proud.* They are *proud* because they have the power to kill men and they are *proud* because they have acquired what among themselves is labeled such a dignified position that they can cut off the heads of men. *The glory* of such people is *in their shame.*[83] Others are *proud* about

---

77. Origen appears to cite something as Scripture which is not found in our canon, though it is cited by Clement of Alexandria and others. See Nautin, 2:30, n. 2, and Schadel, 294, n. 128.

78. "Then" (εἶτα), a correction of Klostermann from Jerome. S has δέχηται.

79. Jer 13.15.                      80. Luke 14.11, 18.14.

81. Matt 11.29.

82. "Indifferent." The term is also an ethical term used by the Stoics to explain what is neither good nor bad. See Schadel, 296, n. 129, and his reference to *Comm in Rom* 4.9, where Origen explains that what concerns the body and earthly things are in themselves neither good nor bad, but are indifferent.

83. Phil 3.19.

HOMILY 12   121

wealth—not about the true wealth but the wealth below—and others are *proud,* so to speak, about having a beautiful house or many fields. None of these things is worthy of discussion; there is no need to be proud over any of these things. But the plausible reason for being *proud* is when someone is *proud* because he is wise, and *proud* because he knows in his conscience from ten years old he did not touch sexual pleasures, and again another did not touch from the time of infancy, and again another is *proud* because he bore *chains*[84] for Christ. Here is a plausible reason which implies that one may be *proud* with good cause, but according to the true reason, no one can be *proud* for such things with good cause.

(2) Thus, it is not even for these reasons that one is *proud* with good cause. Paul had the material for him to be *proud* by his *visions,*[85] by the *things seen,*[86] by the *wonders and signs,*[87] by the troubles which he bore for Christ, by the churches which he built as one *making it his ambition* to found[88] a church *where Christ was not even known.*[89] All of these things were material[90] for him to be *proud*—if one must speak with justification of being *proud,* because it might seem proper if in some ways he was *proud*—but nevertheless, since to be *proud* in such things is not without danger, the good Father, as[91] he bestowed on him *visions* and *things seen,* so he gave to him in the guise of a gift *the angel of Satan so that he might harass* him, so that *he would not become too proud. And three times* he *sought the Lord about this, in order that* the angel of Satan, who was given to him according to the plan lest he be *proud, would leave* him,[92] and the Lord answered him—for Paul was

84. Cf. Eph 3.11.
85. 2 Cor 12.1.
86. Cf. Acts 16.10, 18.9.
87. Cf. Rom 15.19; 2 Cor 12.12.
88. "To found" (θεμελιοῦν), a correction of Blass and Klostermann from Jerome. S has θεμένου.
89. Cf. Rom 15.20.
90. "Were material" (ὕλη ἦν), a correction of Blass, Koetschau, and Klostermann from Jerome. S has ὕλην.
91. "As" (ὡς), a correction of Huet from Jerome. S has ἅς.
92. Cf. 2 Cor 12.7–8.

worthy of an answer from the Lord—and he said to him: *My grace is sufficient for you, for my power is made perfect in weakness.*[93]

(3) Thus there is nothing to be *proud* about.[94] For to sink to the state of being *proud* has its consequences according to the text: *Before ruin the heart of man is exalted and before glory it is humble.*[95] These words concern the text: *Hear and hearken, and do not be proud, because the Lord has spoken.*[96]

9. But let us see what he exhorts us to do after this: *Give glory,* he says, *to the Lord our*[97] *God before it darkens and before your feet stumble on the dark mountains. And you shall wait for light.*[98] He wants the one who *gives glory* to God to *give glory to God* when it is *light,* since the *glory* of God cannot be proclaimed when it *darkens* and darkness arises. When then does it *darken* and when does the coming darkness not arise? *Work while the light is in you.*[99] The *light is in you*[100] if you have in you the one who said, *I am the light of the world.*[101] As this comes forth in you, glorify God. But know that some sort of darkening can arise,[102] and it need not remain this darkening, but before it *darkens, give glory to God.*

10. Perhaps we will understand what has been written if we deal with a Gospel text spoken by the Savior which expresses it in this way: *Work while it is day. The night comes when no one can work.*[103] He has named here as this age the *day*—but of necessity I have added the word *here,* for I know that in other passages other meanings are revealed[104]—so he has

---

93. 2 Cor 12.9.
94. "About" (ἐπί), a correction of Klostermann. S has ἐπεί.
95. Prov 18.12.  96. Jer 13.15.
97. "Our," a correction of Klostermann. S has "your."
98. Jer 13.16.  99. Cf. John 9.4, 12.35.
100. "The light is in you," an addition of Klostermann from Jerome.
101. John 8.12.
102. "Arise" (γενέσθαι), a correction of Klostermann from Jerome. S has λέγεσθαι.
103. Cf. John 9.4.
104. Nautin, 2:36, n. 1, for example, offers a passage from Origen's homilies on Easter, where "day" for Origen indicates the future world and "night" the present world.

called this age the *day,* but the darkness and the night the consummation[105] because of punishments. For, *why do you desire the Day of the Lord? And it is darkness and not light,* says the Prophet Amos.[106] If you can envision after the consummation of the world what the gloom is, a gloom which pursues nearly all of the race of men who are punished for sins, you will see that the atmosphere will become dark at that time and no longer can anyone ever give glory to God, since the Word has given orders to the righteous saying, *Go, my people, enter into your rooms, shut your door, hide yourself for a little season, until the force of my anger has passed away.*[107]

(2) But if you can keep in mind that at the same time in these passages he has said, *for a little season,* and though that *little season* is a *little season* for God, it is not a *little season* for man. For one needs to see that what is *little* and what is great depends on each person. And I will show with an example that what is *little* or great depends on each person. For each living thing, whether an amount of food is *little* depends upon its structure and whether an amount of food is much depends again on its constitution.[108] And likewise what is *little* to man is great to another living thing. What is *little*, so to speak, to a man is much to an infant.[109] Likewise the whole period of human life and that of an old man are a *little* time compared to the whole period of all of the present era. Furthermore, the *little* of God is much to us, and a *little* is a whole era for God. Therefore, if he has said, *Go, my people, enter into your rooms, shut your door, hide yourself for a little season,*[110]

---

105. "Consummation" (συντέλεια) is a word used in Scripture and is translated (in the RSV) as "close" and "end" (in Matt 13.39, 40, 49; 24.3; Heb 9.26). It means more literally the final end. The Vulgate has *consummatio* which we have produced here. In Origen it can also involve, in light of Acts 3.21, the end. See his use of these terms in *Princ* 2.3.5.

106. Cf. Amos 5.18.     107. Isa 26.20.

108. In Jerome there is added here: "And what is little to some, is itself also much to another. What I speak is concerning animals."

109. "To an infant" (παιδίῳ), a correction of Klostermann, 349. S has παιδίου.

110. Isa 26.20.

one must understand that that *little season* is stated not in relation to the one who is ordered to *go* and *enter into his rooms*, but in relation to the one who commands these things, for whom the *little* is much to the other. For if it is necessary that some enter into their *rooms until the force of the anger* of God *has passed away*, whereas for others sins are *unforgiven* not only for *this* whole *age*, but also for the whole *future age*,[111] it is clear that the *little season* is extended to the lengths mentioned.

11. So, *give glory to the Lord our God.*[112] How do we *give glory to the Lord our God?* I will seek to *give glory to the Lord our God* not in sounds and phrases, but he who *gives glory to the Lord God* gives glory to him in actions. *Glorify God* in self-control, in righteousness, glorify God in beneficence. *Give glory to God* in courage and perseverance, *give glory to God* in beneficence[113] and holiness and the rest of the virtues. But if one holds these matters in this way and one does glorify God as such, do not think that I blaspheme when I state the matter from the opposite; for I will offer Scripture as a witness of these things. The prudent man *glorifies God,* the licentious man dishonors God. For he, like Nebuccadnezzar, overthrows the Temple of God[114] and *destroys the Temple of God*[115] and *dishonors God through transgression of the Law.*[116] This is even an apostolic text. Thus[117] the sinner adds no glory to God and asks questions about Providence, so that some doubt if there is Providence for nothing other than for evil. Take away evil and you are not offended by Providence. But those who are offended by Providence say this inside out: Why are there so many *adulterers* and so many *homosexuals,*[118] why so many atheists and so many impious? And sinners are

---

111. Cf. Matt 12.32.  112. Jer 13.16.
113. "Beneficence" is from S and repeats what was given in the prior sentence. Klostermann offers "piety" (εὐσεβείᾳ) from Jerome.
114. Jer 52.13.  115. Cf. 1 Cor 3.17.
116. Cf. Rom 2.23.
117. Here Jerome adds: "the righteous one glorifies God, the sinner. . . ."
118. Cf. 1 Cor 6.9.

those who engender contempt for Providence, offenses to God, blasphemy on him who created the world. Thus some give glory to God,[119] but those who do what is opposite to the glory of God through sins do not *give glory* to God.

12. *Give glory to the Lord your God before it darkens, before your feet stumble on the dark mountains.*[120] There are certain *dark mountains*, there are certain bright mountains.[121] Since[122] both of them are *mountains*, both are great. The bright *mountains* are the holy angels of God, the Prophets, Moses the servant,[123] the Apostles of Jesus Christ. All of these *mountains* are bright, and about these I think it was said in Psalms: *His foundations are in the holy mountains.*[124]

(2) But of what nature are the *dark mountains?* Those who *raise up prideful acts against the knowledge of God.*[125] The Devil is a *dark mountain*, the *rulers of this age who are abolished*[126] are *dark mountains*, and the little demon of lunacy was a *mountain*. And it was a *dark mountain* concerning which the Savior was saying, *You will say to this mountain. . . .*[127] For concerning lunacy, when the Word is sought and the disciples say, *Why could we not cast it out?* the Savior answered that *if you had faith as a grain of mustard seed, you will say to this mountain*—which you have raised up, about which you have inquired—*you will say to this mountain, "Move from here to there," and it will move:*[128] from *here*, away from the man, to *there*, to the place of its home. Thus those who stumble do not stumble on bright mountains but on *dark mountains*, whenever they go[129] with the Devil and his angels, the *dark mountains*.

(2) *And you shall wait for light.* One could actually connect

---

119. This phrase, without "have given," is an addition of Klostermann from Jerome.
120. Jer 13.16.
121. "There are certain bright mountains," an addition of Delarue from Jerome.
122. "Since" (ἐπεί), a correction of Delarue from Jerome. S has ἐπ'.
123. Cf. Num 12.7.
124. Ps 86.1.
125. Cf 2 Cor 10.5.
126. Cf. 1 Cor 2.6.
127. Matt 17.20.
128. Matt 17.20.
129. "Go" (γένωνται), a correction of Huet from Jerome. S has γένωμαι.

the text, *And you shall wait for light*,[130] with the passage, *Give glory to the Lord our*[131] *God*. If you *give glory to the Lord our God*[132] before *it darkens,* before your *feet stumble* on the *dark mountains,* it is clear that, even if it *darkens,* you will *wait for the light* and *the light* will overtake you. But another may say—I do not know whether he thinks soundly or not—that those who *stumble on the dark mountains*[133] *wait* along with the *dark mountains* as those who *wait for the light* of mercy. For this seems to be the meaning of, *And you shall wait for light.* But when anyone comes to the *dark mountains,* let us see what is *there:*[134] *a shadow of death.* Where the *dark mountains* are, *there* is *a shadow of death* arising from the *dark mountains* themselves.

13. *And they will be placed in darkness. But if you will not hear in a hidden way, your soul cries out from the face of insult.*[135] Among those who *hear,* some *hear in a hidden way,* others, even if they *hear,* do not *hear in a hidden way.* So what is it to *hear in a hidden way* other than what is said: *But we impart a secret and hidden wisdom of God, which God decreed before the ages for our glory?*[136] And again in another place it is said that *most of the works of God are in secret things.*[137] If I *hear* the Law, either I *hear in a hidden way* or I do not *hear in a hidden way.* The Jew does not *hear* the Law *in a hidden way.* Because of this he is circumcised outwardly, for he does not know[138] that *he is not a Jew who is one outwardly, nor is circumcision something outward in the flesh.*[139] But he who[140] *hears* of circumcision *in a hidden way* will be circumcised *in secret.*[141] He who *hears in a hidden*

---

130. "The text, 'And you shall wait for light,'" an addition of Klostermann from Jerome.
131. "Our," a correction of Klostermann. S has "your."
132. "If you give glory to the Lord our God," a correction of Klostermann from Jerome.

133. Jer 13.16.
134. Matt 17.20.
135. Jer 13.16–17.
136. 1 Cor 2.7.
137. Sir 16.21.

138. "Not know" (οὐκ εἰδώς), a correction from Jerome. S has οὐχὶ δ' ὡς.
139. Rom 2.28.
140. "But he who" (ὁ δέ), a correction of Huet from Jerome. S has οὐδέ.
141. Rom 2.29.

## HOMILY 12

*way* the matter ordained concerning Passover eats of Christ the Lamb. For *our paschal Lamb, Christ, has been sacrificed*,[142] and since he knows of what nature is the Flesh of the Word and since he knows that *it is truly food*,[143] he shares in this; for he has heard about the Passover *in a hidden way*. But due to this, this ordinary Jew killed the Lord Jesus and is liable today also for the murder of Jesus, since he did not *hear in a hidden way* either the Law or the Prophets. If you read about the unleavened bread, one can *hear* the commandment *in a hidden way*, one can understand the commandment *outwardly*. Since the Passover is near,[144] all among you observe the unleavened bread, the unleavened bread which is corporeal. You do not *hear* the commandment which says, *If you do not hear in a hidden way, your soul cries out*. And concerning the sabbath, women, by not *hearing* the Prophet, do not *hear in a hidden way*, but hear *outwardly*. They do not bathe the day of the sabbath, they go back *to the poor and weak elementals*,[145] as if Christ had not yet appeared, he who makes us mature and carries us across from the *elementals* of the Law to the maturity of the Gospel.

(2) Henceforth, let us give careful thought when we read the Law and the Prophets lest we succumb to the prophecy which says, *But if you do not hear in a hidden way, your soul from the face of insult will cry out*.[146] All of you who keep the Jewish fast so that you do not understand the *Day of the Atonement*[147] as that which is in accord with the coming of Jesus Christ, you do not *hear* the atonement *in a hidden way*, but only *outwardly*. For to *hear* the atonement *in a hidden way* is[148] to *hear* how God *put forward* Jesus as an atonement[149] for our sins, and that *he is an atonement for our sins and not for our sins alone, but also for the whole world*.[150] And if the Gospel parables are read and the hearer is among those[151] outside, he does not

---

142. 1 Cor 5.7.
143. John 6.55.
144. Cf. John 2.13.
145. Cf. Gal 4.9.
146. Jer 13.17.
147. Cf. Lev 25.9.
148. "Is," an addition of Cordier from Jerome.
149. Cf. Rom 3.25.
150. 1 John 2.2.
151. "Is among those" (ἢ τῶν), a correction of Klostermann from Jerome. S has αὐτῶν.

*hear* them *in a hidden way*. But if the hearer is[152] the Apostle or among those who enter *into the house*[153] of Jesus, he comes to Jesus. He learns also about the obscurity of the parable, and Jesus interprets it. And that hearer of the Gospel becomes one who *hears in a hidden way*, so that *his soul does not cry out*. For among those who do not *hear in a hidden way, the soul cries out*.

(3) Is it not amazing why he did not say, "You cry out if you do not hear in a hidden way," but, *your soul will cry out?* There is a certain kind of weeping when the soul alone *cries out*, and perhaps the Savior teaches about that weeping when he says, *There will be weeping*.[154] And if he says, *Woe to you who laugh now, for you shall mourn and weep*,[155] he speaks about that weeping which the Prophet threatens here also when he says, *If you do not hear in a hidden way, your soul will cry out from the face of insult*—and when you are *insulted*, then you *cry out—and your eyes will pour down tears because the Lord's flock has been crushed*.[156] If one views the state of the Jews now and distinguishes it from the ancient Jews, he will see how *the flock of the Lord has been crushed*. For this group was then the *flock of the Lord*, and since they *judged* themselves *unworthy*, the Word turned to the pagan nations.[157] Thus if that *flock of the Lord* was *crushed*, ought not we—we the *wild olive shoot* which was *grafted, contrary to nature*, onto a *cultivated olive tree* of the Fathers,[158]—fear more, lest he *crush* also this *flock of the Lord?* For it will be *crushed*, according to what is said by the Savior, when *because wickedness is multiplied, the love of many will grow cold*.[159] Whom does the word concern? Is it not said about Christians when it is said, *The love of many will grow cold?* Whom does that word concern, *When the Son of Man comes, will he find the Faith on the earth?*[160] Is it not about us? So let us take care to conduct ourselves in all things in order that, day

---

152. "Is" (ἡ), a correction of Klostermann. S has ἦν.
153. Matt 13.26.
154. Matt 8.12.
155. Luke 6.25.
156. Jer 13.17.
157. Cf. Acts 13.46.
158. Cf. Rom 11.17, 24.
159. Matt 24.12.
160. Luke 18.8.

## HOMILY 12

by day, this *flock of God* improves, is made sound, is healed, and he might send away from our souls everything which *crushes,* in order that we may be made mature in Christ Jesus, *to whom is the glory and the power for the ages. Amen.*[161]

161. 1 Pet 4.11.

## HOMILY 13

*Jeremiah 15.5–7*

*On "Who will spare you, Jerusalem?" as far as, "I was bereaved of children."*

E WANT TO understand the words said to Jerusalem with much foreboding, expressed thus: *"Who will spare you, Jerusalem? Or who will feel sad for you? Or who will return to plead for your peace? You have turned away from me,"* says the Lord, *"you will go back. And I will stretch out my hand on you and destroy you, and no longer will I forbear you.*[1] *And I will scatter them in a dispersion,"* then,[2] *I was bereaved of children.*[3]

(2) A difficulty has occupied me. I take as an example a certain proven enemy of a ruler of the earth. To such a person it is not possible to impart mercy lest someone offend the king who condemned him. And since[4] it is not possible to be merciful to such a person, some who *feel sad* for him do not rally around him lest by *feeling sad* they seem displeased with the king's judgment. If you have understood this, observe with me the one condemned by God for his many sins, even though angels who are assigned to help with the nature of humanity look on, consider this man as one who has received mercy from no one. For each of the angels, when they see that it is God who has condemned, that the Creator is the one who has turned away, that the nature of the sins are

---

1. LXX has "them" here.
2. "Then" (εἶτα), a correction of Klostermann, LXX and Hebrew. S and Jerome have εἶπα.
3. Jer 15.5–7.
4. "Since," an addition of Nautin.

such that they force—if I may speak[5] thus—the good God to cast the vote against the sinner, each of those who see do not *spare*, do not *feel sad*, do not *act with mercy*, do not go back to *plead for peace* for that sort of person.

(3) Suppose therefore this *Jerusalem*—for so it is stated by the letter[6]—has sinned against my Jesus, and has done such acts that Jesus could say about her: *Jerusalem, Jerusalem, you killed the Prophets and stoned those sent to you. How often would I have gathered your children together as a hen gathers her brood under her wings, and you would not. Behold, your house is forsaken.*[7] Let this *Jerusalem* be left behind as she has been left behind. The angels who have always helped *Jerusalem*, by whom also the Law of Moses, *ordained by angels through an intermediary,*[8] was ordained, let them leave behind *Jerusalem* and say: "Her sins have become great, they killed Jesus, they have laid hands on the Christ. Insofar as their sins were still little, we could still deem them worthy and plead for them; we could *spare* Jerusalem. Who will *spare* for this crime?" *If a man by sinning should sin against another man, then shall they pray for him. But if he sins against the Lord, who will pray for him?*[9] *Jerusalem* committed a sin, because of this she has been tossed into a *torrent*,[10] and it is said to her first, to this Jerusalem, *Who will spare you, Jerusalem? And who will be sad for you?* We do not *feel sad* for Jerusalem and for her misfortunes and for everything which happened to that people. *For in the trespass of those, our salvation has come so as to make them jealous,*[11] and since[12] their *trespass* was so great a sin that it was said through the voice of the Lord:[13] *Who will spare you, Jerusalem?* I[14] too say to her who

---

5. "I may speak" (εἴπω), a correction of Klostermann from Jerome. S has εἰ τοιαύτην.

6. Origen will now consider the literal interpretation.

7. Matt 23.37–38.   8. Gal 3.19.
9. 1 Kings 2.25.   10. Lam 1.8.
11. Rom 11.11.
12. "Since," an addition of Klostermann from Jerome.
13. "That . . . Lord," an addition of Klostermann from Jerome.
14. "I" (ἐγώ), a correction of Klostermann from Jerome. S has λέγω.

killed[15] my Jesus, *Who will spare you Jerusalem? And who will feel sad for you?*

2. I pass from the letter—since even it has taken a way which the Word has given[16]—to each soul already made worthy to see peace. For after divine studies, you have become *Jerusalem*, the prior place being Jebus. History says that the name of that place had been Jebus,[17] but afterwards the name changed and became *Jerusalem*.[18] The Children of the Hebrews[19] say that Jebus is interpreted as "what has been trampled." Jebus then is the soul which is *trampled* by hostile powers, has been changed, and has become *Jerusalem*, Vision of Peace.[20] If then you have sinned, when you have changed from Jebus to become Jerusalem, and you have *trampled upon the Son of God* and *held as profane the Blood of the New Covenant*[21] as she had, and you have ended up in grievous sins, it will also be said concerning you, *Who will spare you, Jerusalem? And who will feel sorry for you* if you become someone who betrays Jesus? When each of us sins, and especially if he sins grievously, he sins against Jesus. But if he is also an apostate, he does spiritually even more to Jesus the things that[22] *Jerusalem* did to him bodily. Therefore, *how much worse punishment do you think will be deserved by the man who has trampled upon the Son of God, and profaned the Blood of the Covenant by which he*

---

15. "Who killed" (ἀποκτείνασαν), a correction of Klostermann from Jerome. S has ἀπέκτενιας.

16. "Since . . . given": this translation, in accord with S and Nautin, is uncertain due to a probable textual problem.

17. "The . . . Jebus," an addition of Klostermann from Jerome.

18. Cf. Josh 18.28.

19. "Children of the Hebrews": it is not known to whom this title refers, if to anyone. Nautin, 2:57, n. 2, believes it refers to the author of the work on the translation of Hebrew names, and Schadel, 297, n. 134, believes it refers to the anonymous authors who handed down the Jewish traditional translations of names from the schools.

20. Cf. *Onom. sacra* I.203.2; I.169.66.

21. Cf. Heb 10.29.

22. "Spiritually . . . that" (πνευματικῶς ἅ), a correction of Klostermann from Jerome. S has π-ν-ι- ὅσα.

*was sanctified, and outraged the Spirit of grace?* If you have *trampled upon the Son of God and outraged the Spirit of grace, who will spare you? Who will feel sorry for you? Who will return to plead for what*[23] *is for your peace?*[24] The soul of the sinner has betrayed the Son of God himself who *pleaded for peace* for you. Who is able to beg again for *peace* after he has *returned?* Therefore, since we know that *it is impossible to restore again to repentance those who have once been enlightened, who have tasted the heavenly gift and have become partakers of the Holy Spirit, and have tasted the goodness of the word of God and the power of the age to come, if they commit apostasy, since they crucify the Son of God on their own account and hold him up to contempt,*[25] let us do everything lest it may be said also about us, *Who will spare you, Jerusalem? Who will feel sorry for you? Or who will go back to plead for your peace?*

3. But with each meaning of *Jerusalem*, the next also agrees: "*You have turned away from me,*" says the Lord, "*you will go back.*"[26] That you *turned away* from the Son of God, and by *turning away* from the Son of God you *turned away* from God, why is it even necessary to say? And seeing that Jerusalem in Judea—by which, through synecdoche,[27] it is possible to understand all of the Jews—*turned away* from Christ, because of this *you go back*. For there was a time when she was not *going back*, but going ahead. But now she *goes back*. *And in their hearts they turned toward Egypt*,[28] evidently so that they might *go back*. But concerning the difference between *she will go back* or *straining forward to what lies ahead,*[29] we will explain in this way. The righteous man *strains forward to what lies ahead* and forgets what lies behind.[30] It is clear that the one who prefers what is opposite[31] to the righteous remembers what

---

23. "What" (τά) is added to the scriptural text here perhaps, according to Husson, from Origen's recall of Luke 14.32. See Nautin, 2:58, n. 1.
24. Jer 15.5.      25. Heb 6.4–6.
26. Jer 15.6.
27. A technical term meaning that the whole can be inferred from the part.
28. Acts 7.39.      29. Cf. Phil 3.13.
30. Cf. Phil 3.13.
31. "What is opposite" (ἐναντίως), a correction of Delarue. S has ἐναντίος.

lies behind and does not *strain forward to what lies ahead*. But he who remembers what is behind hears wrongly when Jesus teaches and says, *Let him not turn back to take his mantle*,[32] hears wrongly when Jesus says, *Remember Lot's wife*,[33] hears wrongly when Jesus says, *No one who puts his hand to the plow and turns back is fit for the Kingdom of God*.[34] And it is written in the Law that the angels said to Lot when he came out from Sodom, *Do not look back to what is behind or remain in the surrounding countryside; save yourself in the mountain lest you are taken with the others*.[35] But this also holds a thought worthy of an angelic spirit:[36] *Do not look back to what is behind, strain forward* always to what is ahead. Since you have left Sodom, do not turn toward Sodom. Since you have left evil and sin, do not return to it *nor remain in the surrounding countryside*.

(2) Even if you keep[37] the former commandment which says, *Do not look to what is behind*, it is insufficient to be *saved* unless you have heard the second commandment which says, *Do not remain in the surrounding countryside*. For it is not necessary that the one just beginning to progress *remain in the surrounding countryside* of Sodom if he has gone through Sodom, but he who has gone through what it is to *remain in the surrounding countryside saves himself in the mountain*. According to the text, *Do not look back to what is behind nor remain in the surrounding countryside; save yourself in the mountain lest you are taken with the others*. If you do not want to be *taken* with the Sodomites, never turn to *what is behind nor*[38] *remain in the surrounding countryside* nor be in any other place than *in the mountain*. For there is the only place to be *saved*. And the *mountain* is Lord Jesus, *to whom is the glory and the power for the ages. Amen*.[39]

32. Mark 13.16.
33. Luke 17.32.
34. Luke 9.32.
35. Gen 19.17.
36. "Angelic spirit": Jerome has "spirit of God."
37. "Even if you keep" (κἂν τηρήσῃς), a correction of Klostermann from Jerome. S has καὶ τηρήσεις.
38. "Nor" (μηδέ), a correction of Blass, Diels, and Klostermann. S has μήτε.
39. 1 Pet 4.11.

# HOMILY 14

*Jeremiah 15.10–19*

On *"Woe is me, mother,"* up to, *"'Therefore,' thus says the Lord, 'if you will return, I will restore you.'"*

HEALERS OF BODIES, since they are around the sick and always give themselves freely to the cure of the sick in accordance with the purpose of the healing arts, view what is *terrible*[1] and touch what is *loathsome*, and[2] they reap *their own pains* by others' misfortunes[3] and their life is always in crisis. For they are never with those who are well but always with the wounded,[4] with those who have contagions, with those filled with pus, fevers, all kinds of illnesses. And if someone wants to prepare for medicine, he should not feel irritated nor should he neglect the purpose of the skill which he has adopted whenever he may be with the kind of situations we have just mentioned.

(2) I have stated this preface because the Prophets are like healers of souls, and they are always occupied wherever there are those who need treatment. For, *those who are well have no need of a healer, but those who suffer*,[5] but what healers suffer by[6]

---

1. "What is terrible" (δεινά), a correction from the Catena. S has τινά.

2. "And," an addition from Jerome and Hippocrates' text. See below.

3. Klostermann notes that this description is from Hippocrates, *De flatibus* I.569K.

4. "Wounded" (τραυματιῶν), a correction of Delarue from Jerome. S has τραυμάτων.

5. Luke 5.31.

6. "By" (ὑπό), a correction of Blass and Klostermann from Jerome. S has ὑπέρ.

unbridled[7] sick people this also Prophets and teachers suffer from those who do not want to be treated. For thence they are hated, as are those who prescribe against the choice of the wishes of sick people, as are those who restrain those who want to live licentiously and to pursue pleasures in their diseases, who do not want to take what is appropriate for the diseases. Thus the unbridled people among sick people flee from healers, often after they have blasphemed and abused them and done every sort of thing which an enemy would do to an enemy. For they forget, when they look on the agony of his way of life, on the agony of the impact from the knife of surgeons, not on the objective beyond the pain, that healers come as friends, and they hate healers as fathers only of pains, but not of the pains which bring to well-being those who are healed.

2. That people then was sick;[8] there were all kinds of diseases among those who had the name of the people of God. God sent to them the Prophets as healers. One of the healers was Jeremiah. He reproved the sinners since he wanted those who do evil to return, yet though needing to hear what was said they accused the Prophet and they accused before judges[9] similar to themselves. And always the Prophet was in judgments by[10] those who, with respect to his prophecy, had been cured but were not cured because of their own disobedience. It is due to them when he says: *And I said: "I will no longer speak nor name the name of the Lord." But it happened as a burning fire flaming in my bones, and I am weakened on all sides and I cannot bear it.*[11] And when he said, seeing himself as one who always is judged, abused, accused and falsely testified against, *Woe is me, mother, as what kind of man did you bear me?* he was not speaking as a *man* who judges but as *one who is*

---

7. "Unbridled" (ἀκολάστων), a correction of Klostermann from Jerome. S has ἀκολάστως.

8. "Was sick" (ἔκαμνε), an addition of Klostermann from Jerome. S has εἰ καί.

9. "Judges," a correction from the Catena and Jerome. S has "judge."

10. "By" (ὑπό), a correction from the Catena, S has ἐπί.

11. Jer 20.9.

*judged*, and not as one who disputes but one who *is disputed over all of the earth*.[12] And since those who are sick do not hear him when he advises for their good[13] and well-being, he says,[14] *I have not helped*.[15] And since he lent spiritual funds, they to whom he was speaking did not want to hear in order to owe for what they have heard. He says, *No one has ever owed me, I have not owed*.[16]

3. But in anticipation I have spoken these lines before I discuss the text, *I have not owed; no one has owed me*.[17] For the Scripture is in two texts. In most of the copies there is, *I have not helped; no one has helped me*, but in the most accurate copies and in accord with the Hebrew is, *I have not owed, no one has owed me*. So it is necessary both to discuss the text most common and carried in the churches, and not to leave undiscussed the view from the Hebrew Scriptures.

(2) He then preached the word, no one attended to what was said, just as the healer wastes drugs when the sick are unbridled and filled with their own desires, as if the healer too was saying: *I have not helped; no one has helped me*. Perhaps in benevolence there is a reciprocity between the person *helped* and the person who has *helped*, so that the one who speaks is also one who derives help, since *blessed is the one who speaks into the ears of those who hear*.[18] Thus as the teacher would derive help from this help from the hearers who progress and become better, he would receive help by *having fruits* in them,[19] and yet when he does not *have* this help from the Jews, Jeremiah says:[20] *No one has helped me*. For if it is necessary that the speaker *has fruit* in listeners, but the listener

---

12. Jer 15.10.
13. "For their good" (καλῶς), a correction from the Catena and Jerome. S has καλά.
14. "Well-being, he says" (ἰατρικῶς φησιν), a correction of Huet. S has ἰατρικῶι σφῆσιν.
15. Jer 15.10.
16. Jer 15.10. As Origen will explain in the next section, two different texts have been handed down for Jer 15.10.
17. Jer 15.10.   18. Sir 25.9.
19. Cf. Rom 1.13.
20. "And ... says," an addition of Klostermann from Jerome.

should misconstrue and be unconcerned with what was said, *No one has helped me* is stated, since he could not be helped from this help from which he would be helped, if the hearer who was helped became for the one who confers help a cause of progress and bliss.[21] And besides every teacher in the task of teaching, insofar as the learner is *intelligent,* is helped in what he teaches, in what he learns. And those who speak the lessons become stronger concerning those things which they have delivered when the *listeners,* if they are *intelligent,*[22] accept the words not generally, but investigate and inquire and examine the intention of what was said. Therefore, *I have not helped, no one has helped me.*

4. But since another discussion is also required on account of the more accurate variant readings that say, *I have not owed nor has anyone owed me,* let us thus also discuss what the literal text holds. He who *pays* to all their dues—taxes to whom taxes are due, revenue to whom revenue is due, respect to whom respect is due, honor to whom honor is due[23]—and *pays* duties to everyone so that with some he does not *owe* duties once he has honored, for example,[24] parents[25] as parents, brothers as brothers, sons as sons, bishops as bishops, presbyters as presbyters, deacons as deacons, the faithful as the faithful, catechumens as catechumens, if he *pays* all of the duties, he does not *owe.* But if he *owes* doing a duty, and has not done it, he cannot say, *I have not owed.* For since he *owes,* he has not *paid.*

(2) How then shall I also discuss, *No one owed me?* I was lending and was willing to give spiritual valuables, but they have turned themselves away from what was said and do not render themselves[26] debtors so that they can *owe.* On ac-

---

21. In this sentence, Origen has manipulated the same terms (ὠφελέω and ὠφέλεια), and I have tried to duplicate his efforts.

22. Cf. Isa 3.3.

23. Cf. Rom 13.7.

24. "For example," an addition of Klostermann from Jerome.

25. "Parents," an addition of Klostermann from Jerome.

26. "Themselves" (αὐτούς), a correction of Klostermann from Jerome. S has αὐτούς.

## HOMILY 14

count of this, *no one owes me.* For who received what was said so that from the receiving he became one who *owes* for what he has heard and claims, as one who *owes,* the interests on what was said?

(3) It is better then, in light of this, that the hearer take from the one who speaks the spiritual[27] funds and *owe* him than neither to receive, nor take, nor *owe.* For it is also set down in reproach: *Not one has owed me.*

5. But I do not think that the passage, *Woe is me, mother, as what kind of man did you bear me who is judged and disputed over all of the earth,*[28] can be said to be appropriate for the other Prophets in the way it can with Jeremiah. For many of the Prophets began to prophesy after they changed, after some time, after evil, after sins, but Jeremiah prophesied from youth. And one can give an example from the Scriptures. Isaiah did not hear, *Before you were formed in the womb, I knew you, and before you emerged from your mother, I glorified you, I established you as a prophet to the nations,*[29] nor did Isaiah say, *I do not know what to say because I am a youth,*[30] but when he saw the vision told about in his prophecy, he saw and said, *Woe is me, I am wretched for having unclean lips, I dwell in the midst of a people who have unclean lips and I have seen with my eyes the King, the Lord of hosts.*[31] And there was sent to me, he said, *one of the Seraphim; he touched my lips and he said, "Behold I have removed your transgression and this will purge your sins."*[32] Thus, after[33] sins which he did formerly, Isaiah later became worthy of the Holy Spirit and prophesied; and you may discover the resemblance to another, but Jeremiah is not the same.[34] For while still in swaddling clothes, clothed in the prophetic spirit, he prophesied from childhood.

(2) Therefore he was saying—for I first will discuss the

27. λογικός.
28. Jer 15.10.
29. Jer 1.5.
30. Jer 1.6.
31. Isa 6.5.
32. Isa 6.6–7.
33. "After," an addition of Klostermann from Jerome.
34. "But is not the same" (ἀλλ' οὐχ οὕτως), a correction of Klostermann from Jerome. S has ἄλλος οὗτος.

common view—*Woe is me, mother, what kind of man did you bear who is judged and disputed over all of the earth?*[35] But of those before me, someone[36] has pointed out this text by saying that he was saying these things not to his biological mother but to the mother who gives birth to prophets. But who produces prophets other than[37] the wisdom of God? Thus he said, *Woe is me, mother, what did you bear,*" O Wisdom! But the children of wisdom are told also in the Gospel: *And wisdom sends her children.*[38]

(3) Thus it may be said, *Woe is me, mother,* my wisdom, *what kind of man did you bear who is judged;* who am I to be *born* such a person, to be *judged,* to be *disputed* by arguments, by criticisms, by the teaching to *all* of those on *earth?* If Jeremiah says this, *what kind of man who is judged and disputed over all of the earth did you bear,* I do not have to discuss the words *over all of the earth.* For Jeremiah is not *judged over all of the earth.* Or will we say by forcing the phrase that *all over the earth* is instead of *all over* Judea? For his prophecy did not reach to *all of the earth* at the time when he prophesied. But perhaps just as in countless other passages we have shown that Jeremiah is spoken of instead of our Lord Jesus Christ, so also we can say here. In the beginning[39] I took note of the text, *Behold I have appointed you for nations and kingdoms, to root out and pull down and destroy and rebuild and plant.*[40] Jeremiah did not do this. But Jesus Christ has *uprooted* the *kingdoms*[41] of sin, and he has *pulled down* the buildings of evil and instead of those *kingdoms* he has made to rule[42] righteousness

---

35. Jer 15.10.
36. Klostermann suggests Philo, *De confusione linguarum,* 49.
37. "Other than," an addition of Klostermann from Jerome.
38. As written, no text such as this exists in the canonical Gospels. However, it appears to be a union of Matt 11.19 (variant reading), Luke 11.49, and Luke 7.35: "Yet wisdom is justified by all of her children." Nautin, 2:75, n. 3, suggests perhaps also the *Gospel according to the Hebrews.*
39. Cf. *Hom in Jer* 1.6.
40. Jer 1.10.
41. S adds here γῆς, "of the earth." It is missing from Jerome.
42. S adds here ἡμῶν, "our."

and truth in our souls. Thus just as it has been fitting to refer those passages more to Christ than to Jeremiah, I think in the same way also for both many other and these passages.[43]

6. One must speak first concerning *Woe is me*, due to what seems insulting. Can the Savior who calls others unhappy say, *Woe is me?* But let us produce from accepted texts which refer to none other than the Savior how he also wept for Jerusalem. And the sound of crying is the *woe*. And it is laid down in the Gospel that when he saw Jerusalem, *he wept for her*[44] and he said, *Jerusalem, Jerusalem, she who killed the Prophets and stoned those who were sent to her, how often would I have gathered your children*, and so on.[45] But evidently these things are also stated by the Savior in the passage, *Woe is me. For I have become as one who gathers straw in harvest and as one who gathers grape gleanings in the vintage, when there is no cluster for me to eat the first ripe fruit. Woe is me, soul! The devout man has perished from the earth and among men there are none who live rightly. All are being judged for shedding blood.*[46] For he came as one who *gathers straw for harvest* so that he might reap, and he found many sinners, and he said, *Woe is me that I have become as one who gathers straw for the harvest.* He came to gather in the fruit of life among men, but he found many sins among them, and due to this, he says, *And as one who gathers grape gleanings in the vintage when there is no cluster to eat the first fruits.* Also he states a view like these in another place when to the Father he says, *What profit is there in my blood if I go down to destruction?*[47] What extent have I profited men? What value have they made of the blood that I have shed for them? *What profit is there in my*[48] *blood if I go down?* From the heavens I have *gone down*, I came to the earth, I delivered myself for *destruction*, I have borne a human body. What value is it for them that he *lives rightly* for men? *What profit is there in my blood if I*

---

43. ". . . which are said now refer to the Lord," added by Jerome here.
44. Luke 19.41.   45. Matt 23.37.
46. Mic 7.1–2.   47. Ps 29.9.
48. "My," an addition of Klostermann from Jerome.

*go down to destruction? Will the dust give praise to you or declare your truth?*[49]

(2) Thus, such is what was said here first by the Savior: *Woe is me, mother, as what kind of man did you bear me.* The Savior says, *Woe is me, mother,* not to the extent he is[50] God, but to the extent he is[51] man, as in the Prophet: *Woe is me, soul, that the devout man has perished from the earth.*[52] But the soul was human, hence *it was troubled,*[53] hence it also was *sorrowful,*[54] but the *Word in the beginning with God*[55] was not *troubled,* that one would not say, *Woe is me.* For the Word was not liable to death, but the human nature is liable to this, as we have often demonstrated.

7. *As what kind of man, judged and disputed over all of the earth, did you bear me?*[56] If you see with me those martyrs who are *judged* in every place, those who submit to judges in each district, you will see in what way Jesus Christ is *judged* in each of the martyrs. For he is the one who is *judged* in those who *testify to the truth,*[57] and you will be persuaded, he says, to accept this when you see that you are not in prison when you are in prison, but himself, you are not punished when you are punished, but himself, you do not thirst, but himself. *I was in prison and you visited me, hungry and you gave me something to eat, thirsty and you gave me drink.*[58] Hence if a Christian is *judged* not for something else, not for his own sins, but because he is a Christian, Christ is the one *judged.* Thus, *over all the earth* Jesus Christ is *judged.* And as often as a Christian then is *judged,* Christ is the one *judged,* not only before proceedings such as these. But suppose a Christian is slandered

---

49. Ps 29.9.
50. "To the extent he is" (ἦ), a correction from Jerome. S has the article ὁ, which may be right.
51. "To the extent he is" (ἦ), a correction from Jerome. S has ἤ. See previous footnote.
52. Mic 7.1–2.                 53. John 12.27.
54. Matt 26.38.                55. John 1.2.
56. Jer 15.10.                 57. Cf. John 18.37.
58. Cf. Matt 25.36.

and[59] accused unjustly[60] for something, then too Christ is *judged* unjustly. *As what kind of man, judged and disputed over all of the earth, did you bear me?*

8. And you will understand in still another way how he is *judged* and *disputed all over the earth.*[61] Who then does not *judge* the word of the Christians? Who among the pagan peoples does not examine it, even if in a simple way? Who among the Jews does not speak things against the Christians? Who among the Greeks? Who among the philosophers? Who among the common folk? In every place Jesus is *judged* and brought to trial. And by some he is sentenced, but by others he is not sentenced. If he is not sentenced, he becomes accepted. You *open doors* for him, he will *enter* toward you, you believe in him, he *eats with you.*[62] But if you do not accept when hearing about Christianity, you have done nothing other than sentence Jesus as[63] one who is false, as one who has deceived men, as one who does not speak truly, because you have not believed in the doctrine[64] which he teaches.

(2) *As what kind of man, judged and disputed over all of the earth, did you bear me?* As many as disbelieve fully, they sentence him, but as many as do not disbelieve but are doubtful about him, they *dispute* concerning him. Jesus suffers twofold among men. He is sentenced by the unbelievers and he is *disputed* by the undecided. If you carry *the image of the heavenly* by putting away *the image of the earthly,*[65] you are not the *earth* which sentences him, nor are you the *earth* on which he is sentenced. No longer are you the *earth* which *disputes* him.

---

59. "And," I have added from Jerome.
60. "Unjustly" (ἀδικῶς), a correction of Nautin. S has ἃ δεῖ.
61. "And ... earth": placement of this sentence here by Huet comes from Jerome. S places the sentence after "common folk" below.
62. "He eats with you," an addition of Klostermann from Jerome, omitted by Nautin, but accepted by Schadel. Cf. Apoc 3.20.
63. "As" (ὡς), an addition of Klostermann from Jerome.
64. λόγος.
65. 1 Cor 15.49.

9. *My strength has failed among those who curse me.*⁶⁶ The Apostle says concerning the Savior that *he was crucified because of weakness,*⁶⁷ but also the Prophet says statements resembling these in the passage, *Lord, who has believed our report? And to whom has the arm of the Lord been revealed? We have brought it before him as a child, as a root in a thirsty land. We saw him, and he has no form or beauty, but his form was ignoble, failing more than the sons of men. A man who was in plague and in pain, who seemed to bear weakness because he turned his face from dishonor; he was dishonored and unconsidered. He bears our faults and for us he suffers. And we considered him to be in pain and in plague and in misfortune. But he was wounded because of our faults, and made weak for our sins. A chastisement for our peace was upon him. By his bruises, we were healed.*⁶⁸ Hence he took on the *weakness of our sins* and he carried us and came to those who *cursed* him, and his *strength failed among those who cursed* when he came down from the heavens. For at the same time he took on *the form of the servant* and *emptied himself,* as the Apostle said: *He emptied himself taking the form of a servant.*⁶⁹ Thus he said, *My strength has failed me among those who curse me.*⁷⁰

10. The Word himself granting, let us see if we can also say something more clear than what was said on the text, *My strength failed among those who curse me. He was the true light who enlightens every man who comes into the world.*⁷¹ *The true light* is the Son of God, *who enlightens every man who comes into the world.*⁷² And if he is endowed with reason⁷³ he has a share of the true light. But every man is endowed with reason. Among all the men who then have a share of the Word,⁷⁴ the *strength* of the Word increases in some, but in some it *fails.* If you see a passionate and sinful soul, you will see there the *strength* of the Word *failing.* But if you see a holy and just soul, you will see the *strength* of the Word bearing fruit day by day. And what is said about Jesus applies to the just. For it

66. Jer 15.10.
67. 2 Cor 13.4.
68. Isa 53.1–5.
69. Phil 2.7.
70. Jer 15.10.
71. John 1.9.
72. "The true light . . . world," an addition of Klostermann from Jerome.
73. λόγος.
74. λόγος.

was not only for himself that Jesus *progressed in wisdom and stature and grace with God and men*,⁷⁵ but also in each of those who accept progress *in wisdom and stature and grace* Jesus *progresses in wisdom and stature and grace with God and men.*

(2) Thus the Word, the Son of God, who is in the one who said, *Woe is me, mother,* and so on, says, *My strength fails among those who curse me.*⁷⁶ He who would *curse* the Word, this person outright receives the punishment for *cursing* the Word, for reproaching the teaching of Jesus. For the *strength* of Jesus *fails* in such a person, and the *strength* of the Word is not in him, so that again, from the opposite, if you praise Jesus and receive him, his⁷⁷ *strength* experiences the opposite to what it had experienced among those who *cursed* him. For just as there it *failed* among those who *cursed* him, so here it increases among those who praise him.

11. *Let it happen, Lord, if they go straight. Did I not stand before you in the time of their troubles?*⁷⁸ What does *Let it happen, Lord* mean? He who is able, let him by himself put together the text, *Let it happen,* such as this: "O Master, *Lord, if they go straight, let* the *strength happen* which *fails in those who curse me,* whenever after speaking ill of me, they, repentant,⁷⁹ turn to the straight path and travel it."

(2) *Let it happen, Master, if they go straight. Did I not stand before you?* Then he justifies himself concerning⁸⁰ those who have evil thoughts about him when he says, *Did I not stand before you in the time of their troubles?* He, the *expiation for our sins,*⁸¹ *stood before* the Father and pleaded for them *in the time of our troubles.* For he did not *stand* after the *time* of our *troubles,* but while *we were still*⁸² *sinners* Christ died for us.⁸³ *Did I*

---

75. Luke 2.52.
76. Jer 15.10.
77. "His," an addition from Jerome.
78. Jer 15.11.
79. "They, repentant," an addition from the Catena and in Jerome.
80. "Concerning" (περί), a correction of Blass, Koetschau, and Klostermann from Jerome. S has παρά.
81. 1 John 2.2.
82. "While we were still" (ἔτι ὄντων), a correction of Klostermann from Jerome. S has αἴτιον τῶν.
83. Cf. Rom 5.6.

146    ORIGEN

*not stand before you in the time of their troubles, in the time of their afflictions, for their good against the enemy.*[84] And in the *time of their afflictions,* he says, for this I *stood before* you *for* them *against the enemy.* But who is the *enemy* other than *our adversary the Devil*[85] who afflicted us? And evidently in the *time* of the hatred of that being against men, our Savior *stood before* the Father and begged concerning our own captivity,[86] so that we might be *redeemed* and *freed* from the *enemy.*[87]

(3) Let the Savior or the Prophet say these words, for the Prophet also can preach such things and pray for the people in the *time of their troubles.*

12. With respect to[88] these things God answered the people who were *accused* by the Prophet or by Christ, and he said these words to him: *An iron and brass covering is your strength,*[89] hard, unyielding, unbeaten. *An iron and a brass covering is your strength.*[90] *your strength* is like something able to cut and divide, a *strength* which is not for good.

(2) *And I will give your treasures for spoil, an exchange for*[91] *all of your sins.*[92] What *treasures* of the sinners does God *give for spoil,* and what *exchange for all of their sins* does God *give* them? Is it ever treasures stored up by them on earth? For each man stores up *treasures on earth* if he is bad, *in heaven* if he is good, as we were taught by the Gospel.[93] Or does he say to that people, "I intend to give *in exchange* your *treasures* because of your sins"? What kind of *treasures* of that people were *given in exchange*? Behold, one of the *treasures* is Jeremiah, another *treasure* is Isaiah, Moses was also a *treasure.* God took these *treasures* from that people, and through Christ,

---

84. Jer 15.11.   85. 1 Pet 5.8.
86. Cf. Isa 61.1–2; Luke 4.18.
87. Cf. 1 Pet 1.18; Titus 2.14; Col 1.13–14; 2 Tim 4.17–18; Luke 1.74, 24.21.
88. "With respect to" (ἐπί), a correction of Huet from Jerome. S has ἔτι.
89. Jer 15.12.
90. "Iron . . . strength," an addition of Klostermann from Jerome.
91. "For," an addition from Cordier and LXX.
92. Jer 15.13.   93. Matt 6.19–20.

who said, *The Kingdom of God will be taken away from you and given to a nation producing the fruits of it*,[94] he gave them to us.

(3) Thus, *I will give for our sins your treasures for spoil*,[95] and he *gave the treasures* of that people to us. For those first *believed the utterances of God*,[96] then after those people, we *believed*, since the *utterances of God* were *taken away* from them and were *given* to us. And we say that the passage, *The Kingdom of God will be taken from you and will be given to a nation producing the fruits of it*, was said by the Savior and fulfilled. Not that the Scripture was taken from them, but now they no longer have the Law and the Prophets, since they do not contemplate the meaning in them. For they possess the Bible, but how was the *Kingdom of God taken from* them? The meaning of the Scriptures was *taken away* from them. No longer is the interpretation of the Law and the Prophets preserved with them, rather they are ones who read and do not apprehend spiritually. For this was fulfilled through the coming of Christ: *I said to that people: while hearing you will hear but never understand, and though seeing, you see and never perceive. For the heart of this people has grown dull.*[97] What Isaiah said was also fulfilled, *The Lord will take away from Judea and from Jerusalem the strong man and the strong woman, the giant and the warrior, the judge and the prophet and the counselor and wise builder and the intelligent hearer.*[98] God took away all of these things from those people and he gave them, if we receive them, to us from the pagan nations.

(4) These thoughts concern *and I will give you treasures for spoil.* An exchange for all of your sins and in all of your territories, as if he were saying, *for your sins* which have extended to all of your *territories*. For there is no *territory* of that people which had not been filled with sin. And how was every *territory* of theirs not about to be filled[99] with sin when they kill, as

94. Matt 21.43.  
95. Jer 15.13.  
96. Rom 3.2.  
97. Isa 6.9–10; Matt 13.14–15.  
98. Isa 3.1–3.  
99. S adds here ἐπ' αὐτοῖς, but it is missing in Jerome, and ignored by Klostermann and Nautin.

far as they can, righteousness, if Christ is Righteousness; when they kill[100] wisdom, if Christ is Wisdom; when they kill truth, if Christ is Truth? For by sentencing to death the Son of God they rejected and killed all of those things. And my Lord Jesus, who rose from the dead, no longer appeared to those who killed him. For we do not possess in history that he appeared to those who killed him, but he appeared only to those who believe, after he rose from the dead.

13. *And I will enslave you among all of your enemies in a land which you have not known.* That people was *enslaved among their enemies* and it took place in a land which they had not known, *for a fire has been kindled out of my wrath, it will burn upon you.*[101]

(2) After this and the threatening words said to the people, he who[102] has prayed above finishes the prayer and adds these words to what has been said before: *You have known, Lord, remember and visit me and vindicate me from those who persecute me, without patience.*[103] And let the Prophet say these words when *persecuted* by those who accused him, and hated by those who do not grasp the truth. For he has *become an enemy* to those hearing by *speaking truth* to them.[104] And let our Savior also say these words, he who was also *persecuted* by the people. And he said, *without patience*. What is meant by *without patience?* You were *patient* always with the people in light of their sins, but with respect to those who have ventured against me, be *without patience*. And truly God was not *patient*. If you examine the times of the Passion and the fall of Jerusalem and the destruction of the city, and how God forsook that people since they killed Christ, you will see that he did indeed deal with the people *without patience*. But, if you wish, hear: From the fifteenth year of Tiberius Caesar to the destruction of the Temple forty-two years were completed.[105]

---

100. S adds here "the," but it is omitted by Klostermann and Nautin.
101. Jer 15.14.
102. "He who," an addition of Klostermann from Jerome.
103. Jer 15.15.  104. Cf. Gal 4.16.
105. Traditional dating of the destruction of Jerusalem. As Klostermann notes, Origen mentions it also in *Cels* 4.22, and Clement in *Str* 1.21.145, and Tertullian in *Adv Jud* 8.

For it was necessary to yield a little time for repentance, especially for those from the people who would believe from the signs and wonders which were to be done by the Apostles.

14. *Know that I was reproached on your behalf from those who disregard your words.*[106] Let us suppose that it is the Prophet who speaks and is despised for what he was saying, who is *disregarded* by the sinners. For he said, *I am continually mocked.*[107] Thus he is reproached by those who *disregard* the words which have been spoken through him by God, and he pleads to be assisted by God for this reproach when he says, *Know that I was reproached on your behalf by those who disregard your words. Bring them to an end.* Let the Prophet say this, but it is more fitting if the words, *Bring them to an end,* are said by the Savior. For the end came for Jerusalem and for the people due to events which happened from a plot of the people against our Savior.

(2) After these words, it is necessary—for the Prophets, by reproving and espousing the cause of the Word and speaking what is appointed by God, have suffered many things—to remind hearers concerning their own lives and their promises and our own choices so that, as far as we can, if we want to have a final rest with the Prophets, let us emulate the works of the Prophets. But what I am saying is this. Often in prayer we say, "Almighty God, give us the lot of the Prophets, give us the lot of the Apostles of Christ so that we may be found also with Christ himself." But when we say this, we do not realize what we pray. For in effect we are saying this: "Let us suffer what the Prophets have suffered, let us be hated as the Prophets were hated, give us the kind of words for which we will be hated, let befall us the kind of[108] misfortunes which befell the Apostles." For to say, "Give me a lot with the Prophets," yet not suffer the pains of the Prophets nor want to suffer, is unjust. To say: "Give me a lot with the Apostles," yet, truthfully speaking, not wanting to say, using Paul's expression, *far greater labors, with countless beatings, far more im-*

---

106. Jer 15.15.   107. Jer 20.7.
108. "The kind of" (ὅσαις), a correction of Blass. S has αἷς.

*prisonments, and often near death,*[109] and so on, is the most unjust thing of all. If then we want to be with the Prophets, observe the lives of the Prophets, that they were *judged,* they were *disputed,*[110] they were condemned for reproving, for blaming, for reproaching. *They were stoned, they were sawed in two, they were put to the test, they were killed with the sword, they went about in skins of sheep and goats, destitute, afflicted, ill-treated, wandering over deserts.*[111] Since there were many synagogues of Jews, they were also *wanderers over the desert and mountains and in dens and caves of the earth.*[112] What then is unexpected if someone who wants to emulate the prophetic life, who reproves, reproaches the sinner, is *ill-treated,* hated and schemed against?

(3) Just as it was necessary at the present that such a thing appear in the Church of God:[113] One condemned has been condemned; it was done by such a one who presides over such tasks.[114] It was necessary that an ecclesiastical vindication occur and it has occurred; the one who has taken the matter in hand has done what was necessary for him to have done. That condemned one goes around speaking malice about him who has vindicated the truth. But let us never[115] do this, let us never grant a hearing to those who, because they are cast out, speak malice about the one who has cast them out or about the person who agrees with the judgment. Those also among the unjust who are reproved and have become. . . .[116]

109. 2 Cor 11.23.
111. Heb 11.37–38.
110. Cf. Jer 15.10.
112. Heb 11.38.
113. "Just . . . God." Klostermann believes text is missing here. In what follows, Origen seems to be discussing the reactions to a rejection in his own church. The case is probably familiar to his audience.
114. "One condemned . . . tasks." Based on what Jerome has translated or paraphrased, Klostermann finds a lacuna here. Nautin makes no comment, but Schadel modifies the text, 305, n. 154.
115. "Never" (μή), a correction of Diels. S has μόνον.
116. The translation is uncertain due to a probable lacuna here, though Schadel connects this phrase with the next sentence. He writes: "When those among the unjust are reproved and a penalty has been imposed, the wonderful Apostles. . . ." But he has added the word "penalty," and it is not at all clear how this phrase fits with the next. Klostermann and Nautin accept the lacuna.

(4) The wonderful Apostles who were insulted many times for the truth say, *I am content with weaknesses, with insults and hardships, persecutions and calamities for the sake of Christ.*[117] I know that the basis of *hardships* is Christ when I am *insulted* if I know that I am *insulted* only for nothing other than for Christ, when I am in *hardships*, when I am abused if I know that the cause of abuse is none other than that I am a champion for truth and an *ambassador*[118] for the Scriptures so that everything happens according to the Word of God. For this I am blasphemed.

(5) And thus let all of us, as far as our ability allows, strive for the prophetic life, for the apostolic life, not avoiding what is troublesome. For[119] if the athlete avoids what is troublesome about the contest, the sweetness of the crown will never be his.

15. *And your word will be for gladness to me.*[120] It is not now but it *will be*. For since at present your word is for imprisonments, for judgments, for troubles, for slander, for pains, at the end of these it *will be*[121] gladness. *And your word will be for gladness to me and the joy of my heart because your name has been invoked upon me, O Lord Almighty.*[122] And even if Christ speaks, the name of the Father is *invoked upon* him.

(2) *I did not sit in the council of those who mock.*[123] If the Prophet ever saw that the *council* is not of those who are earnest but of those who *mock*, he avoided being part of that gathering more than[124] he sought eagerly for a gathering of those who *mock*. Thus you ought to understand the difference between the *council* of those who *mock* and those who are[125] earnest.[126] This *council* is earnest if it both does all with earnestness and worthy of earnestness and is in accord with

---

117. 2 Cor 12.10.      118. Eph 6.24.
119. "For," an addition of Cordier from Jerome.
120. Jer 15.16.
121. "Will be" (ἔσται), a correction of the Catena and Jerome. S has ἐστί.
122. Jer 15.16.      123. Jer 15.17.
124. "Than" (ἤπερ), a correction of Huet. S has εἴπερ.
125. "Not," is added here by S.
126. On this difference, see the philosophical discussion of Schadel, 305, n. 155.

what is said: a doctrine[127] in earnest, a life in earnest, and in everything is the *council* not of those mocking but those in earnest. But whenever the *council*, after abandoning earnestness concerning necessary things, is frivolous in the contests of this age and in the contests with evil, it becomes a *council* of *mockers*. Thus he said, *I did not sit in the council of those who mock, but I feared from the presence of your hand.*[128] Of the two choices set before me, to *sit in the council of those who mock* and to offend you, God, and not to please you, or to remove myself from the *council of mockers* and to do those things which were pleasing to you, I preferred to remove myself from the *council* and be your friend than[129] by doing the opposite become an enemy to your happiness.

(3) *I did not sit in the council of those who mock, but I had fear from the presence of your hand.*[130] And our Savior did not sit *in the council of those who mock*, but he rose up before them, and a sign that the Savior rose up from the *council of mockers* was when he said, *Your house is forsaken and desolate.*[131] For the Word of God has *forsaken* the *council* of the Jews, and has made for himself another *council* and a Church from the pagan nations.

16. *I sat alone.*[132] Even the literal words edify here. Whenever there may be a great number of sinners and they do not forbear the righteous living righteously,[133] there is nothing improper in avoiding the *council* of evil to imitate the one who said, *I have sat alone*, to imitate also Elijah who said, *Lord, they have killed your Prophets, they have pulled down your altars, and I was left alone, and they seek my life to take it.*[134]

(2) But perhaps if you examine more deeply the words, *I sat alone*, you will find a kind of sense worthy of the prophet-

---

127. λόγος.
128. "Hand," an addition from Jerome. Jer 15.17.
129. "Than" (ἤπερ), a correction of Huet from Jerome. S has εἴπερ.
130. Jer 15.17.   131. Matt 23.38.
132. Jer 15.17.
133. "Righteously" (δικαίως), a correction of Klostermann. S has καὶ ὡς.
134. 3 Kings 19.10, 14; Rom 11.3.

ic depth. Whenever we imitate the life of the masses so that it has not been set off and is not greater and more special than the masses, I cannot say, *I have sat alone,* but I *sat* with the masses. But when my life becomes hard to imitate so that I become so great that no one resembles my habits, my doctrine,[135] my practices, my wisdom, then I can say, because I am one of a kind[136] and no one imtitates me, *I sat alone.* Thus it happens also that you who are not a presbyter, you who are not a bishop, nor a person honored by some ecclesiastical title can say this, *I sat alone.* You can strive after and adopt a life so as to say, *I sat alone.*

(3) *For I was filled up with bitterness.*[137] If *the way which leads to life is narrow and hard,*[138] it is necessary that you be *filled up with bitterness* in this life; you can enjoy nothing sweet. Or did you not know that your feast comes with bitter herbs? For when you feast, he said that you eat *unleavened bread on bitter herbs.*[139] What the Word intends when he says that it is necessary that the one feasting with God eat *unleavened bread upon bitter herbs,* one must consider. Since the Apostle discussed *unleavened bread,* it is not my interpretation. But it is required that what follows the interpretation be similar to the apostolic discussion. The Apostle discussed matters concerning *unleavened bread* when he said, *Let us celebrate the festival not with the old leaven, the leaven of evil and malice, but with unleavened bread of sincerity and truth.*[140] It is necessary to explain the meaning of *bitter herbs* in accordance with the *unleavened bread* being *of sincerity and truth.* Have *sincerity and truth,* and *bitter herbs* will be with you, and you will eat with *bitter herbs* the *unleavened bread of sincerity and truth.* Just as Paul also ate the *bitter herbs,* since he ate the *unleavened bread of sincerity and truth.* How did he eat *bitter herbs?* As he says, *I have become your*

---

135. "Doctrine" (λόγῳ), a correction from the Catena and Jerome. S has βίωι.
136. "Of a kind" (τοιόσδε), a correction of Koetschau and Klostermann. S has τοῖς ὧδε.
137. Jer 15.17.
138. Matt 7.14.
139. Exod 12.8.
140. 1 Cor 5.8.

*enemy by telling you the truth.*[141] How did he eat *bitter herbs? In toil and hardship, often without sleep, in hunger and thirst, apart from other things.*[142] Or[143] was this not *truth* with *bitter herbs* un*leavened bread* with *bitter herbs?*

(4) Thus the Law said: *Eat unleavened bread with bitter herbs,* and did not say: "Eat unleavened bread with bitter herbs until you are *filled up,*" as it was said for other things: *Eat and be filled up.*[144] Yet,[145] the Prophet goes further, saying that he did not eat *bitterness,* but *I was filled up with bitterness.* To the extent that I can partake of bitter things, so I[146] most fully[147] partake of *bitter herbs.*

17. *Why do those who hate me prevail against me?*[148] He had many troubles, he suffered from those who did not[149] want to hear the truth and they were[150] more powerful[151] here in this age than he, since the Kingdom of God *is not from this age* but from greater places as the Savior said, *If my kingdom was of this world, my servants would fight, that I might not be handed over to the Jews.*[152] Those then who give pain to the Prophet *prevail against* him in *this world.* For with regard to their being strong, view the martyrs. The judge sits in the courtroom as one who judges and lives a soft life. The Christian in whom Christ is *judged,*[153] is *filled up with bitterness* and is oppressed by the unjust, and is condemned.

141. Gal 4.16.
142. 2 Cor 11.27–28.
143. "Or" (ἤ), an addition by Blass, Koetschau, and Klostermann. S has εἰ.
144. Joel 2.26.
145. "Yet," from Jerome.
146. "I" (με), a correction of Klostermann. S has μετά.
147. "Most fully" (πληρεστάτων), a correction of Nautin. S has πληρέστατον.
148. Jer 15.18.
149. "Not," an addition of Klostermann from Jerome. The Catena here has δυσαρεστουμένων.
150. "Were" (ἦσαν), a correction of Klostermann from Jerome. S has ἤκουσαν.
151. Following "powerful" S has "but." So this sentence might read in the S manuscript, "and they heard him, but they were more powerful here. . . ." But since Origen says in the previous phrase, if we accept the correction from Jerome, that they did not hear, it is an improbable reading.
152. John 18.36.
153. Cf. Jer 15.10. See *Hom in Jer* 14.7.

## HOMILY 14   155

18. *My wound is severe, whence shall I be healed?*[154] Those who *prevail against* me wound me, and *my wound is severe.* Either he prophesies the cross of the Lord—for the cross is a *severe wound,* depending on those who crucify him—or it is said concerning[155] all of the just in whom he receives a *severe wound.* Or hear this also for the Prophet, for he himself, too, has suffered what was written up in the prophecy. It admits this sense according to the text which says, *My wound is severe.*

(2) *Whence shall I be healed?* And if the Savior says, *Whence shall I be healed,* he prophesies the resurrection from the dead after the *severe wound;* but if it is taken for the just, the healing again comes after the *wounds.*

(3) *It has become to me like false water,*[156] *which does not have faith.*[157] For the *wound* does not remain, but passes away.

(4) *"Therefore,"* thus says the Lord, *"If you will return, I will also restore you."*[158] These words again are said to each person whom God exhorts to "return" to him. But for me there seems to be evident here a mystery[159] in *I will restore you.* No one is *restored* to a certain place unless he was once there, but the restoration is to one's own home. Just as if my limb has become dislocated, the healer tries to make a restoration of the dislocated limb. Whenever anyone is outside the fatherland, either justly or unjustly, and he is again able to exist according to the laws of the fatherland, he is *restored* to his own country. I understand the same also for the soldier who was thrown off from his own battalion and[160] was *restored.* Thus he says here to us who turn away[161] that if we *return,* he will *re-*

---

154. Jer 15.18.
155. "Or" and "concerning," additions of Cordier from Jerome.
156. "Like false water," an addition of Huet from Jerome.
157. Jer 15.18.   158. Jer 15.19.
159. As we have noted elsewhere, Origen sometimes uses this word to indicate a theological question which is not clearly enough spelled out for him in the Scripture or in the rule of faith. The question here concerns the final end or restoration (ἀποκατάστασις) of all souls.
160. "And," an addition of Lietzmann and Klostermann.
161. "Turn away" (ἀποστρέψαντες), a correction of Lietzmann and Klostermann from Jerome. S has ἐπιστρέψαντας.

*store* us. For such is also the end of the promise as it is written in the Acts of the Apostles in the text: *Until the time of restoration of all things which God spoke by the mouth of his holy Prophets from of old*[162] in Christ Jesus, *to whom is the glory and the power for the ages of ages. Amen.*[163]

162. Acts 3.21. The idea of "restoration" (ἀποκατάστασις), based around this text of Scripture, is a concept of mystery for Origen, an idea which involves the final return to God and presumes, as Origen mentions here, that man has fallen, and that, in an ordered universe, things would return to their origin. See *Hom in Lc* 39.2, *Jo* 1.16, and the sections in *De principiis* devoted to this subject. Also peruse the long speculative discussion of Schadel, 307, n. 159.

163. 1 Pet 4.11.

## HOMILY 15

### Jeremiah 15.10 and 17.5

*On "Woe is me," again in another view, and, "Cursed is he who trusts in man and who will rest upon the flesh of his arm."*

 HERE ARE THOSE who bless the Prophets and[1] who in blessing them pray to have a lot with the Prophets, gathering[2] from the prophetic words the remarkable qualities of their prophecy. By seeking, they could then persuade themselves—if they live under the same conditions, if also something hard will meet them in this life so that they might imitate the prophetic life—that they might bring about the final rest and the blessedness with the Prophets. So it is possible in many places to gather together the remarkable qualities of the Prophets, freedom, vigor, vigilance, vehemence. Yet when they were in those circumstances they were not thinking about freedom, only that they would reprove, that they as the Prophets in rebuke of sinners would convert from *speaking* the Word of God *with boldness*,[3] even if those who are reproved seem to be able to do what is very powerful. Still even if it is possible to do this[4] in many places, let us also see from[5] what was read today.

(2) The Prophet reproved many and the Prophet spoke to many. For, he appeared at a time when there were sin-

---

1. "And" (κἄν), a correction of Klostermann. S has καί.
2. "Gathering" (συναγαγόντων), a correction of Klostermann. S has συνόντες.
3. Cf. Acts 4.29–31.
4. Gather together the remarkable qualities of the Prophets.
5. "From," an addition of Ghisleri.

ners,⁶ as is evident from that fact that the Captivity happened during his times. Since he reproved many, since he was judged by many, he spoke out in a certain way.

2. For, let us see first from the prophetic word and then also according to the anagogical,⁷ whether we can understand the vigor and freedom and power and *boldness* of the Prophet in the former text: *Woe is me, mother, as what kind of man did you bear me who am judged and disputed over all of the earth?*⁸ O *mother, as* what have you given birth to me, *a man judged* before everyone on *earth,* and *disputed*⁹ before *all* of those on *earth?* For the prophetic office was set forth¹⁰ for the Prophet, both for this one and for Isaiah and for the rest: to teach,¹¹ to reprove and to convert. For that reason it is set forth also for this Prophet to *dispute,*¹² to reprove, to be able to *judge* and to be *judged* with sinners, to reprove the sins of the people. And whatever those from the people have done to them, why need even speak? After being reproved, they *stoned* one, *cut asunder* another,¹³ *killed* another *between the Temple and the altar;*¹⁴ they threw this one into the *pit of mire.*¹⁵ And above all our Savior also has done this better even¹⁶ than they, seeing that he is Lord of the Prophets. For since he was scourged and crucified and delivered¹⁷ by the

---

6. "There were sinners" (ἁμαρτολοὺς γενομένους), a correction of Ghisleri, Blass, and Koetschau. S has ἁματολος γενόμενος

7. For Origen the anagogical sense (literally, what is uplifting) of Scripture implies a deeper meaning, sometimes a mystery, often something hidden or referring to Christ.

8. Jer 15.10.

9. "Disputed" (διακρινόμενον), a correction of Blass. S has διακρίνεσθαι.

10. "Set forth" (προέκειτο), a correction of Ghisleri and Cordier. S has προσέκειτο.

11. Cf. Heb 11.37.

12. "To dispute" (διακρίνειν), a correction of Blass, Diels, and Klostermann. S has διακρίναι.

13. Cf. Heb 11.37.   14. Matt 23.34–35.

15. Cf. Jer 45.6.

16. "Better even" (κρειττόνως γε), a correction of Klostermann. S has κρεῖττον ὥστε.

17. Cf. Matt 20.18–19.

HOMILY 15                                      159

Jews or by the teachers of the Jews and the ruler of the people, he said, *Woe to you, scribes and pharisees, hypocrites.*[18] And he appends to each *woe: because of* such and such.

(2) And so, if[19] we are serious about the blessed ways of the Prophets, let us do these things so that we, due to speaking and being *judged* before many men, can say: *Woe is me, mother, as what kind of man did you bear me, a man judged and disputed over all of the earth?*

3. Yet this text can be prophetic in a more authoritative sense when it is applied to the Savior. For suppose that the Prophet does say this, but he will not truly speak this except perhaps as an hyperbole. He is not *judged over all of the earth*. But if I come to my Savior and Lord, and especially because of *for judgment he will come*[20] and *that you might be justified in your words and might conquer when you are judged*,[21] I shall see that my Savior and Lord intends to stand before the Father as one *judged* with all of us men. Again I say: he is "judged" with all men. He is judged, he himself is even examined, and it is he who avenges the truth, but not as one accused.

(2) *Woe is me, mother, as what kind of man did you bear me, a man judged and disputed over all of the earth?* The Prophet cannot say *over all of the earth*. But I know those who like, and not only like but also those who love, our Lord and Savior Jesus Christ,[22] who are angry[23] and say that the Savior does not[24] speak here,[25] because the language is incongruous for the

18. Matt 23.13.
19. "If," an addition of Klostermann.
20. John 9.39.                    21. Ps 50.6(4).
22. "Who like . . . who love": The contrast between "to like" (φιλεῖν) as an affection between friends and "to love" (ἀγαπᾶν) as an attachment beyond human affection Origen makes elsewhere. See *Jo* 19.4, *Or* 20.1 and *Fr in Lam* 11, where Origen says, "And we think that to love is more godly and, so to speak, spiritual, but to like is more corporeal and human." This latter text from Klostermann, the others from Nautin.
23. "Who are angry" (ἀγανακτοῦντας), a correction of Blass. S has ἀγανακτεῖν.
24. "Not," an addition of Klostermann.
25. "Here," I have added.

Son of God. But is it necessary to show that *woe is me, mother* is not unusual for the Son of God? *My soul is very sorrowful, even to death*[26] and *my soul is troubled,*[27] and similar passages in the Prophets to that here: *Woe's me, mother, what kind of man did you bear, a man judged and disputed over all of the earth?* Or when[28] the grape gleaning was lost[29] in finding the cluster, *woe is me, soul, for the godly man perished from the earth, and there is none among men who goes straight.*[30] Who says there, *Woe is me, soul, for I have become as one gathering straw in harvest?*[31] For did the Prophet *gather* and want to *gather?* Does the Prophet have a farm? But it is proper to no one to *gather* both all from the harvest and what has been planted except to the Lord and Savior Jesus Christ. Since there are many faults among the pagan nations, but also among those who are supposed to be from the Church, he laments and mourns for our sins when he says, *Woe is me for I have become as one who gathers straw.* Let each of us scrutinize himself. Is he an ear of corn? Will the Son of God discover something in him to pick or harvest? Do we find that some of us are those swept by the wind? Even if we have still a little in ourselves,[32] two or three kernels, our sins are many against us. Seeing that the churches, those so-called, are filled with sinners, he says, *Woe is me, for I have come as one who gathers straw in the harvest and as one gathering grape gleanings in the vintage.*[33] He came seeking fruit on the vine, for each of us is planted also as a vine *in a fertile place.*[34] And he *transplanted a vine out of Egypt,*[35] but *I have planted you as a fruitful vine completely true.*[36] He comes, he seeks in what way[37] to pick, he discovers some

---

26. Matt 26.38.  27. John 12.27.
28. "When" (ὅτε), is a correction of Klostermann. S has ὅταν.
29. Nautin adds here ἀντί ("instead of").
30. Mic 7.2.
31. Mic 7.1.
32. "Ourselves" (αὐτοῖς), a correction of Klostermann. S has αὐτοῖς.
33. Mic 7.1.  34. Isa 5.1.
35. Ps 79.9.  36. Jer 2.21.
37. "In what way" (πῶς), a correction of Ghisleri. S has "somehow" (πως).

*grape gleanings* and a few *clusters*, neither flourishing nor plentiful. Who among us has *clusters* of virtue? Who among us has offspring of God? *Lord, our God, how wonderful is your name over all of the earth.*[38]

4. These things I have spoken regarding[39] *Woe is me, mother,* as in a digression for me. That it is not unusual for the divinity of our Savior when he views the sins of men—for the Savior not as God but as man, not as Wisdom but as *soul*—to say now, *Woe is me,* I have provided that[40] text of the Prophet: *Woe is me, soul, for the godly have perished from the earth, and there exist none among men who go straight.*[41] The blessed *soul* came for[42] human life, he took up a body on behalf of men. If he sees sins, he says to the Father: *What use is there in my blood since I go down to destruction? Will the dust give praise to you?*[43] But let him not say about us, let the angels of heaven not say about us: *Woe is me!* If our Savior says, *Woe is me,* they also say, *Woe is me.* For they are not better than our Savior, and they see our faults. But blessed are those about whom the angels will not say, *Woe is me,* but call blessed. For there is *more joy in heaven over one sinner who repents than over ninety-nine* people who *need no repentance.*[44] May this be in consolation.

(2) *Woe is me, mother, as what kind of man did you bear me?*[45] What *mother* does he speak of? Is he not able to declare as women both *soul*[46] and Mary?[47] But if a person accepts these words: *My mother, the Holy Spirit, has recently taken me and carried me up to the great mount Tabor,* and what follows,[48] one is able to see his *mother.*

(3) *Woe is me, mother, what kind of man did you bear, a man judged and disputed over all of the earth?*[49] He is *judged over all of*

---

38. Ps 8.2.
39. "I have spoken regarding," an addition of Klostermann.
40. "That" (ἐκεῖνο), a correction of Ghisleri. S has ἐκεῖνος.
41. Mic 7.1–2.  42. "For" (ἐπί). Or perhaps "in"?
43. Ps 29.10. Cf. *Hom in Jer* 14.6.  44. Luke 15.7.
45. Jer 15.10.  46. Mic 7.1.
47. The soul is the incorporeal, Mary the corporeal "mother" of Christ.
48. *The Gospel of the Hebrews,* Frag. 4. See also *Jo* 2.12.
49. Jer 15.10.

*the earth,* and he is *disputed,* and he will say to each: I have done such and such, and my divine agency[50] has accomplished such and such, and I have waited for your salvation. When the Savior says this, what are we to do?

5. For he will certainly be *disputed over all of the earth.* I want to consider the next words. It can be applied according to one discussion both to the Prophet and[51] to the Savior. Let us see then the next words: *I have not owed nor has anyone owed me. The ruler of the world is coming, but he possesses nothing in me,*[52] and truly he did not *owe,* but each of us is a debtor for sins, and a debtor is one who has a *bond.*[53] After his *bond* has been *canceled,*[54] how many other *bonds* have they made?[55] *He has committed no sin, no guilt was found on his lips,*[56] he did not make a *bond.*

(2) But what about *No one has owed me?*[57] How can we discuss in terms of the Savior, *No one has owed me?* Even though we read it in this way, it is necessary also to know that many of the copies of the edition of the Septuagint do not have it in this way. And later, after we considered the remaining editions,[58] we knew it was a faulty copy. And yet the text will be discussed for both versions. How at any rate did it happen, with respect to *No one owed me,* that not one person owed him? He remitted all their debts. *A certain creditor had two debtors; one owed five hundred denarii, and the other fifty. When they could not pay, he forgave them both.*[59] Do you wish to know who are those *two debtors,* the one who owed five hundred and the other fifty? Among those who have believed in God

---

50. "Divine agency" (οἰκονομία), the divine work of salvation and redemption which he has accomplished as the Savior.

51. Addition of Cordier.      52. John 14.30.

53. Col 2.14.      54. Col 2.14.

55. Col 4.12–15 concerns the effects of Baptism and Christ's work. A "bond" was held against man by God, and then Christ released us on the Cross.

56. 1 Pet 2.22.      57. Jer 15.10.

58. "The remaining editions": Origen is here referring to the translations of Aquila, Symmachus and Theodotion. See *Hom in Jer* 14.3, Nautin, 2:124, n. 1, and his *Origène,* 310ff.

59. Luke 7.41–42.

there are two peoples: The people from the Jews, who did not believe in Christ, *owed fifty;* perhaps we from the pagan nations, more idolatrous than everyone, *owe five hundred,* to whom also the text[60] regarding the repenting prostitute is stated. Still someone may say, "How does the *five hundred* refer to that woman?" From the words, *and what sort of woman who touches him,*[61] to which[62] he replied to Simon, *A certain creditor had two debtors, one owed five hundred denarii, the other fifty,* and so forth. This has been said respecting *I owed no one and no one owed me,* which was necessary to clarify to you.[63]

(3) *I owed no one and no one*[64] *owed me. My strength failed among those who curse me.*[65] Even though he was killed *in weakness, he lives by the power of God.*[66]

6. Then since many words continue on, it would be necessary[67] to speak also concerning each of the statements; but, because time rushes on, it does not allow it. Let us then speak concerning the next words which were read: *Cursed is he who has hope in man.*[68] From this statement we will refute[69] those who suppose that the Savior was a man but not also[70] the Son of God. For they dared with many human evils to say even this, that the *only-begotten,*[71] the *first-born of all creation*[72] could not be God. For, *cursed is he who has hope in man.* It is

---

60. "The text" (τό), an addition of Ghisleri.
61. Luke 7.39.
62. "Which" (ὅ), a correction of Cordier. S has ὄν.
63. "To you" (ὑμῖν), a correction of Ghisleri. S has ἡμῖν.
64. "No one," an addition of Cordier.
65. Jer 15.10.     66. 2 Cor 13.4.
67. "Would be necessary" (ἦν), a correction of Ghisleri and Cordier. S has εἰ.
68. Jer 17.5.
69. "This statement we will refute" (τούτου ἐλέγξομεν), a conjecture of Klostermann. S has τοῦ. Text is missing here.
70. "But not also," I have added. As Nautin notes, there appears here to be a lacuna. Klostermann, however, does not comment and Schadel translates the text as: ". . . the Son of God, the Savior, was [merely] a man." He adds "merely." Nautin writes: ". . . the Savior was a man [and by no means] the Son of God." He adds "and by no means."
71. John 1.18.     72. Col 1.15.

evident that *cursed* are those who *have hope in man*. I may say that I do not have *hope in man*. When I *hope* in Christ Jesus, I do not know the *man*. Not only do I not know the *man*, but I do know Wisdom, Righteousness itself, a *man*[73] through whom *all things in heaven or on earth, either seen or unseen, whether principalities or authorities, were created*.[74] *Cursed is he who has hope in man*. Even if the Savior testifies that he whom he carried was *man*, even if he was also a *man*, he is now by no means a *man*. For *even though we knew Christ according to the flesh, we no longer know him thus*,[75] says the Apostle. Through him I no longer am a *man*, if I follow his words, for he says, *I said: "You are gods and all sons of the Most High."*[76] Hence just as he is the *first fruit of the dead*,[77] so he has become a *first-fruit* of all men who change into a *god*.[78]

(2) *Cursed* then *is he who has hope in man and rests on the flesh of his arm*,[79] whoever gives rule to the fleshly, he who if he acquires bodily strength, also serves as a soldier according to the flesh. But the holy person is not like this. For he does not *rest on the flesh of his arm*. For he has *always the death of Jesus in his body*,[80] and he puts to death *the members on the earth, immorality, impurity*.[81] Once he has put these to death, he does not *rest on the flesh of his arm*.

(3) *Cursed is he who has hope in man*. But at the same time it applies to those who have hope in people thought worthy. A certain friend of mine is a centurion; he is a governor; a certain friend of mine is also rich and is generous with me. This statement, *Cursed is he who has hope in man*, is also spoken

---

73. "A man" (ἄνθρωπος) in S. Klostermann, 349, conjectures that "man" should be corrected to λόγος here. Nautin adds it to his text. Blass eliminates it from his text. Schadel holds to the original, but translates "the man."

74. Col 1.16.      75. 2 Cor 5.16.
76. Ps 81.6.      77. Col 1.18.

78. Or: ". . . he has become a first-fruit of all men who turn round toward God." The previous sentence, however, Origen's inclusion of Ps 81.6, and the context of being "no longer a man" seems to favor the other translation of μεταβάλλειν.

79. Jer 17.5.      80. 2 Cor 4.10.
81. Col 3.5.

## HOMILY 15

against such a person. We hope in[82] no *man,* even though they seem to be friends of ours. For it is not in them but in our Lord we hope, that is, Christ Jesus, *to whom is the glory and the power for the ages of ages. Amen.*[83]

82. "In" (ἐπί), a correction of Blass. S has πρός.
83. 1 Pet 4.11.

## HOMILY 16

### Jeremiah 16.16–17.1

On *"'Behold, I am sending many fishers,' says the Lord,"* up to, *"A sin of Judah is written with an iron pen, with a point of a diamond; it is engraved on the tablet of their heart."*[1]

**I**T IS RECORDED IN THE GOSPEL according to Matthew that our Savior came beside the sea of Galilee and saw *Simon and Andrew, his brother, casting a net into the sea, for they were fishermen.* Then the word states that the Savior, when he saw them, said, *"Follow me, and I will make you fishers of men."* Immediately they left their nets and followed him,[2] and Jesus has *made* them to take up fishing for men.[3] And he found *two other brothers, James son of Zebedee and John his brother, in the boat with their father mending the nets, and he called them*[4] to the same knowledge,[5] and he *made* them also *fishers of men.* And if one considered those who hold from God a gift of word woven[6] as[7] a *net* and bound together[8] from the sacred Scriptures as a *casting net,* so that what is woven is thrown around the souls of the hearers, and he also consid-

---

1. "On . . . heart," an addition of Klostermann from Jerome.
2. Matt 4.18–20.
3. "Men," an addition of Koetschau and Klostermann from Jerome.
4. Cf. Matt 4.21.
5. "Knowledge" (ἐπιστήμη), a practical knowledge, meaning the total of skill and information required by people who perform a particular profession, as distinct from γνῶσις, which often involves a mystical or contemplative knowledge.
6. "Woven" (πεπλεγμένην), a correction of Klostermann from Jerome. S has πεπληρωμένην.
7. "As" (ὡς), a correction of Cordier from Jerome. S has ἤν.
8. "Bound together" (συγκειμένην), a correction of Huet. S has συγκειμένων.

ered[9] this as a skill which arises according to the knowledge which Jesus taught, he will see in what way not only then, but now, our Savior sends out *fishers of men*, having taught them so that we can come up from the *sea* and flee its harsh waves.

(2) But those fish, those without soul,[10] that come up in the dragnets and in the casting nets and in the small nets or in fishhooks, die a death without a life which succeeds death.[11] But he who was caught by the *fishers* of Jesus, and who comes up from the *sea*, he also dies, but he dies to the world, he dies to sin, and after having died to the world and to sin, he is made to live by the Word of God, and receives another life. Just as, if you could apprehend hypothetically when the soul of the fish changed, after coming out from the fishly body, it became something better than the fish—I have taken an example, let no one take as pretext what he did not hear[12]—you will then apprehend[13] something such as this. Having come up from the *sea*, falling into the *nets* of the disciples of Jesus, after you come out you change the soul, you are no longer a fish who struggles in[14] the salty waves of the sea, but your soul immediately changes and transforms itself and becomes better and more godly than what it was formerly. But that it does transform itself and change, hear Paul who says, *And we all with unveiled face, reflecting the glory of God, are being transformed to the same image from glory into glory, just as from the Lord, the Spirit.*[15] And this transformed fish which was caught by the *fishers* of Jesus, after it has abandoned the way of life in the sea, makes his way in the *mountains* so that he no longer needs the *fishers* who brought him

---

9. "Considered" (κατενόησε), a correction of Klostermann. S has κατανοῆσαι.

10. "Those without soul," is missing from Jerome.

11. "Without a life which succeeds death," missing from Jerome.

12. Origen does not want his hearers to think he teaches that people can in some way be or become fish.

13. "You will apprehend" (νοήσεις), a correction of Koetschau. S has νοήσῃ.

14. "In," an addition of Klostermann.

15. 2 Cor 3.18.

up from the *sea*, but he needs a certain second group called *hunters* who hunt from *every mountain* and from *every hill*.[16] Thus after you have come out of the *sea* and been caught in the *nets* of the disciples of Jesus, change from the *sea, forget*[17] it, go upon the *mountains* (the Prophets) and upon the *hills* (the righteous) and make your way of life there in order that, after these events, when the time of your final departure is close at hand, *many hunters* may be sent other than the *fishers*. But who could they be except those who are appointed[18] for taking over souls on the *hills*, those who are not set below? And see if this is not what the Prophet cried out mystically when he speaks and he suggested this meaning in the words, *"Behold, I send many fishers,"* says the Lord, *"and they will fish them, and after them, I will send many hunters, and they will hunt them upon every mountain and upon every hill."*[19]

2. Hence if you want to be caught by the *hunters*, see that you do not make your way of life in the valleys, nor live below somewhere, but seek the *mountains*.[20] *Ascend to the mount*, where Jesus was *transfigured, ascend to the mount* on which Jesus, *seeing the throng*, had gone up and the *disciples* followed him, where, *after he opened his mouth, he taught them saying, "Blessed are the poor in spirit, for theirs is the kingdom of heaven,"*[21] and the beatitudes which follow this.

(2) And it is impossible for these hunters to collect in any other place than from the *mountains* and the *hills* and from *the holes of the rocks*. For these three places are mentioned in the Prophet: *For I will send many hunters, they will hunt them upon every mountain and upon*[22] *every hill and out of the holes of the rocks*. From what place will I consider the *rocks* and the *holes in the rocks?* I come upon Exodus, I seek[23] to discover a trace of the discussion of the *holes of the rocks*, I discover there

---

16. Jer 16.16.  
17. Cf. Ps 44.11.  
18. "Appointed" (τεταγμένοι), a correction of Blass. S has ἐπιτεταγμένοι.  
19. Jer 16.16.  
20. Cf. Gen 14.10.  
21. Matt 17.1–2, 5.1–3.  
22. "Every mountain and upon," from LXX. S has ἀπό.  
23. "I seek" (ζητῶ), from Jerome. S has ζητῶν.

## HOMILY 16

Moses who wants to know God, and God promising him also saying, *Behold, I will put you into an opening of the rock and you will observe my back. But my face will not be visible to you.*[24] If you understand there the *rock* and you see there the *opening of the rock*, how he who stood[25] upon the rock and sees the *opening of the rock* sees God through the *opening of the rock*, he will also see many *rocks* and *holes*. Who then is that one *rock*? But Christ was the rock, for *they drank out of the spiritual rock which followed*,[26] and *he placed my feet upon a rock*, the thirty-ninth Psalm says.[27] Who is *the opening in the rock*? If you see the coming of Jesus, having understood him as the whole *rock*, you will see the *opening* in light of his coming, an *opening* through which what is behind God is contemplated. For such is understood in the text, *And you will see my back*.[28]

3. But I found[29] one *opening* of the one *rock*. I pass in explanation from the *opening* to the *hole* of the *rock*. Also I seek *many rocks*. If I come to the chorus of Prophets or Apostles or also the holy angels who have gone up above, I say that all imitators of Christ, as that one is a *rock*, become *rocks*.[30] And just as he has an *opening* through which is observed the *back* of God, in the same way when each has given a way to understand God through what is said by him, he makes an *opening* in himself, and a *hole*, if he also wants to name this *opening* otherwise. It is an *opening* or *hole* from which you will see the Law through Moses, and through Isaiah his prophecy, and through Jeremiah other words[31] of God. But if it will also be an angel who speaks as he spoke according to what is said in the text, *the angel*[32] *who speaks in me*,[33] I stand there also be-

---

24. Cf. Exod 33.22–23.
25. "Stood" (στάς), a correction of Blass and Klostermann. S has ἱστάς.
26. 1 Cor 10.4.      27. Ps 39.2.
28. Exod 33.23.
29. "I found" (εὗρον), in S. εὗρον a suggestion of Guéraud in Nautin.
30. "Rocks" (πέτραι), a correction of Blass, Lietzmann, and Klostermann from Jerome. S has πέτρα.
31. "Words" (λόγους), a correction of Cordier from Jerome. S has λόγος.
32. "In the text, the angel" (τῷ ὁ ἄγγελος), a correction of Klostermann and Cordier from Jerome. S has τῷ εὐαγγελίῳ.
33. Zech 4.1.

fore the angel and I see there a *rock* and an *opening* of the *rock* and I see[34] God in an angelic way.

4. But I need an example so that I can explain how it is that he who comes before an angel also sees God through an angel. For in Exodus, it is written, *An angel of the Lord appeared to Moses in a flame of fire from a bush. And Moses saw that the bush was aflame with fire and the bush was not consumed.*[35] And the Scripture did not say, as it said at the beginning, that *an angel appeared* (for it spoke in this way because there was an *angel of the Lord*), but, *I am God of Abraham and God of Isaac and God of Jacob.*[36] Thus God was there in the angel being contemplated, as God is known through the *rock* and the *opening* which is in it.

(2) Hence you do not know at what time the *hunters* are *sent*. Because of this fact you should never come down from the *mountains* nor abandon the *hills* nor be outside the *holes of the rocks*. For if you were discovered outside, it will be said to you who have existed outside and who speak of matters of one outside, *Fool, on this night they require your soul from you. And what you have prepared, for whom will it be?*[37] These words will be said to you. But these words will also be said to you if you should say, *I will pull down my barns and build larger ones, and I will say to my soul, "Soul, you have goods laid up for many years; rest, eat, drink, be merry."*[38] You see that the person below the *mountains*, below the *hills*, outside the *holes of the rocks*, how he is deceived even in his judgment about the *goods*, supposing these things to be *goods*. That is why he says, *And I will say to my soul, "Soul, you have goods laid up for many years."* He supposed that *goods* are grain and produce of the earth. For he did not see that the true *goods* are not in the accursed earth, but the true *goods* are in heaven. And since he thinks that the *goods* are what is on the earth, he has laid up *trea-*

---

34. "I see ... I see" (βλέπω ... βλέπω), corrections of Blass and Klostermann. S has βλέπων ... βλέπων.
35. Exod 3.2.
36. Exod 3.6.
37. Luke 12.20.
38. Luke 12.18–19.

sures on earth.³⁹ But if someone, persuaded by Jesus, passes from laying up *treasures on earth* to laying up *treasures in heaven*,⁴⁰ it will not be said to him, *Fool*,⁴¹ *on this night they require your soul from you*, but after the *hunters* come who seek not the animals below but those in the *mountains*, those in the *hills*, those sheltered in the *holes of the rocks*, they will *collect* them and carry them away from that hunt. Where? To the resting place of the holy and blessed ones in Christ Jesus.

(3) For, *my eyes*, he says, *are on all of the ways of them*,⁴² of such beings who make their life on the *mountains* and in the *hills* and in the *holes of the rocks;* and⁴³ God has *eyes on all of the ways*.

(4) Such beings *were hidden from my face*.⁴⁴ For the bad are *hidden* from the *face* of God. Adam *heard*, after his transgression, *the sound of God walking in Paradise in the afternoon*,⁴⁵ and he *hid*, but the holy man does not *hide*, but has a heart with openness with God due to the holy life. For *if our conscience does not condemn us, it has an openness with God, and whatever we ask we receive from him*.⁴⁶ Thus even though Adam sinned, he did not sin an excessively severe sin. Because of this *he hid from the face of God*.⁴⁷ But what did the more sinful and unholy Cain who murdered his brother do? *He went out from the face of God*,⁴⁸ so that in comparing evils the lesser evil is to *hide* from *the face of God*. For indeed he who is not past blushing but feels shame *hides* himself from God.

(5) Thus, these *did not hide from my face*. They who did

---

39. The order of phrases in this sentence is reversed from what is in S. See Nautin, 1:88. In S it reads: "He has stored up treasures on earth, and since he thinks that goods are on the earth." Klostermann keeps the original order but eliminates the "and," as does Jerome and Schadel, in order to make the sentence functional. Possibly there is a lacuna here.
40. Cf. Matt 6.19–20.
41. τί follows "fool" in S, but is missing in Jerome and Huet.
42. Jer 16.17.
43. "And," omitted in Jerome, the Catena, Nautin and Klostermann.
44. Cf. Gen 3.8.    45. Gen 3.8.
46. Cf. 1 John 3.21–22.    47. Cf. Gen 3.8.
48. Gen 4.16.

these things at some time⁴⁹ sensed they were in the midst of sins, and from sins of those in the *sea* they were *fished*.

5. Thus in order that those who were *fished* and have come to the *mountains* after this may not presume that these things arise in them from righteousness, the Word reminds not only them but us of our former sins. That is why, after the worthwhile deeds, it is said, *And their iniquities have not been hidden from my eyes*.⁵⁰

(2) The next sentence is likely to produce a challenge for us. For either we understand it as what follows the preceding,⁵¹ in which case⁵² we will rethink⁵³ carefully concerning the recompense for sins; or⁵⁴ it seems that it does not follow concerning what is *fished* and *hunted;* and so it puts us into a challenge which is not met. For he says, *And I will recompense first their wrongs and their sins doubly, for which they have profaned my land with the carcasses of their abominations and with their lawlessness, with which they filled my inheritance*.⁵⁵ Whether some scribes, by not understanding, removed the *first*, or whether the Seventy who supervised, removed it,⁵⁶ God would know. Nevertheless, by comparing the remaining translations, we discover a reliable text: *And first I will recompense their wrongs doubly*, in order that it might be clear that even though there may be those worthy of blessedness due to their second works, since they are men and are born in

49. "At some time" (ποτὲ), a correction of Klostermann from Jerome. S has τότε.

50. Jer. 16.17.

51. "It as what follows the preceding," an addition of Lietzmann and Klostermann from Jerome.

52. "In which case," my addition.

53. "We will rethink" (φροντίσομεν), a correction of Cordier from Jerome. S has φροντίσωμεν.

54. "Or" (εἴτε), a correction of Klostermann. S has εἰ δέ.

55. Jer 16.18.

56. "The Seventy who supervised [οἰκονομήσαντες] removed it": Nautin translates this phrase, in light of his interpretation of οἰκονομήσαντες, which means for him here a hidden or secret activity: "The Seventy removed it in view of an Economy." See 2:145, n. 2. Schadel without comment translates: "The Seventy have intentionally caused its removal."

sins, it is necessary *first* that they receive what is due for their sins. And observe if the word is not true. Who will not receive their due for sins if not he who, after believing and receiving forgiveness for sins—so that he hears Jesus saying, *Your sins are forgiven, sin no longer*[57]—sins no longer?[58] But if after forgiveness of sins and the divine agency of the *washing of the regeneration*,[59] we should sin—as we are the masses who are not as mature as the Apostles—and after sinning, we should also do something as we ought along with the sinning, what awaits us, one must ponder.

(3) What if we finish our life with sins but also with what is commendable, will we be saved through what is commendable and acquitted concerning those sins which were knowingly committed? Or will we be punished for the sins but receive no recompense for what is commendable? But neither the one way—where I say one does receive his due for what is base but does not receive his due for what is better—is in accord with God being just; nor is the other view—where I say that he receives his due for what is better but does not receive his due for what is base—in accord with God being just, who wants to purify and cut down evil. For suppose that you have built, after the *foundation* which Christ Jesus has taught, not only *gold, silver, and precious stones*—if indeed you possess gold and much silver or little—suppose that you have *silver, precious stone*, but I say not only these elements, but suppose that you have also *wood and hay and stubble*,[60] what does he wish you to become after your final departure? To enter afterwards then into the holy lands with your *wood* and with your *hay* and *stubble* so that you may defile the Kingdom of God? But again do you want to be left behind in the fire on account of the *hay*, the *wood*, the *stubble*, and to receive nothing due you for the *gold* and the *silver* and *precious stone*? This is not reasonable. What then?

6. It follows that you receive the *fire first* due to the *wood*,

---

57. Cf. Luke 5.20; John 5.14, 8.11.
58. "Sins no longer," an addition of Nautin.
59. Titus 3.5.   60. Cf. 1 Cor 3.11–13.

which consumes the *wood* and the *hay* and the *stubble*. For to those able to perceive, our God is said to be in reality *a consuming fire*. And the Prophet was silent about what *consuming* is when he said, *Our God is a consuming fire*,[61] but has left it for us to determine. Because he said, *God is a consuming fire*, there is something which is *consumed*. What then is the thing which is *consumed*? For he does not *consume* what is according to *the image and likeness*,[62] he does not consume his own creation but the accumulated *hay*, the accumulated *wood*, the accumulated *stubble*.

(2) The passage was a very difficult one. There were promises, and after the promises he says, *And first I will recompense their wrongs doubly*.[63] Of necessity he adds *first*. For *first* that which is wrong, then that which is righteous are rendered their due; for God does not render what is due the other way around. If *first* he renders what is due for the good things, it is necessary to interrupt the good things in order that we might receive the evil things. But now he renders what is due for the evil things,[64] in order that through the disappearance of evil things, he may bring an end to the punishment of those who suffer, so that after this, he may render what is due for the good things. Accordingly you find in the sacred Scriptures that God speaks *first* about those things which appear to be more severe, and after this what is better. *I kill and I produce life, I will smite and I will heal.*[65] He

61. Deut 4.24; Heb 12.29.
62. Gen 1.26. See also *Hom in Gen* 13.4 on the persistence of the image in man.
63. Jer 16.18.
64. "If . . . for the evil things," is Nautin's reconstruction of a text which he believes has several copyists' errors, 1:88–89. Nautin adds the words: "But now he renders what is due for the evil things. . . ." Schadel, 180, follows Nautin without comment. Klostermann, who corrects through Jerome, has: "If 'first' he renders what is due for the good things in order that we might 'receive the good things,' and now he renders what is due for the evil things, it is necessary to interrupt the good things in order that we might receive what is due for the evil things. [But first he will receive the evil things, and after this the good things,] in order that. . . ." He adds the words in brackets.
65. Deut 32.39.

## HOMILY 16

*makes pain, and again he restores. He has struck, and his hands will heal.*[66] It is for these reasons that he who understands and upholds with piety[67] these statements says: *Lord, who shall sojourn in your tabernacle? Or who shall dwell on your holy mountain? He who walks blameless and works righteousness, who speaks truth in his heart. He has not deceived with his tongue, and he has not done evil to his neighbor, and he has not taken up a reproach against those who are near him.*[68] But we *reproach* both those who repent and those who convert, though the Scripture says, *Do not reproach a man who turns away from sin.*[69] *He did not take a reproach against those near him. Before him, an evildoer is of no account, but he honors those who fear the Lord.*[70]

(3) All of us thus who have matter for that fire will receive *first* for our sins.

7. But someone among those who hear will ask to discuss also the word *doubly*.[71] For suppose that I receive *first* what is due for sins in order that, when I receive what is due for sins, after this what is said by the Apostle may be fulfilled: *If anyone's work will be burned up, he will suffer loss, though he will be saved, but only as through fire.*[72] Why do I at some time receive *doubly* what is due for sins? But one must say that a *servant who knew the will of the master and did not act according to his will be thrashed not a few times but many times.*[73] Therefore, it is worthwhile that those who sin from the pagan nations receive one time what is due for their sins, but we receive *doubly* what is due for our faults. *For if we sin deliberately after receiving the knowledge of the truth, there no longer remains a sacrifice for sins, but a fearful prospect of judgment, and a fury of fire which will consume the adversaries.*[74]

(2) These words were prophesied concerning those who are *fished* and will be *hunted*, and those who will *first* receive

---

66. Job 5.18.
67. "With piety," a correction of Klostermann from Jerome.
68. Ps 14.1–3.
69. Sir 8.6.
70. Ps 14.3–4.
71. Jer 16.18.
72. 1 Cor 3.15.
73. Cf. Luke 12.47.
74. Heb 10.26–27.

what is due *doubly* for their sins. After this the calling of the pagan nations is prophesied explicitly, not those who are being called but those who have been called, and not those who do not[75] know why they should confess and why they should express thanks,[76] but those who have already learned. For in the first statements we learn that they were called, *fished, hunted,* but in the second statements they will entrust themselves. Let us see what he prophesies concerning us who did learn already to pray, but who have learned even more.

8. *Lord, my strength and my help and refuge in the day of evils. To you the pagan nations will come from the last of the earth and will say: "How false were the idols our fathers possessed and*[77] *there is no help in them."*[78] *From the last of the earth* the pagan nations came to God, and the pagan nations said, *False were the idols our fathers possessed, and there is no help in them.* How are they *from the last of the earth?* There are some of the earth who are first and there are some who are *last.* Who are first,[79] first of the earth, not strictly first? The *wise of the world, the nobles,* the rich, the highly esteemed. Who are the *last?* "God chose the foolish of the world, the low, the despised, things that are not."[80]

(2) Thus, *the pagan nations will come from the last of the earth,* as if he was saying, from the worst of men on earth, from fools, from the low-born, from the despised, *and they will say: "How false were the idols our fathers possessed, and there is no help in them."* It is not that there is some kind of true *idol,* which is stated in contrast to the *false,* but they are *idols* which[81] are by nature *false, and there is no help in them.*

75. "Not," an addition of Klostermann.
76. "Why they should confess . . . thanks": These words will bring to the mind of Origen's listeners Baptism and the Eucharist.
77. "And," an addition of Lommatzsch from Jerome.
78. Jer 16.19.
79. S adds here, "the wise of the world." Nautin removes it.
80. Cf. 1 Cor 1.26–28.
81. "Which" (ἅτινα), a correction of Klostermann from Jerome. S has τινα.

## HOMILY 16

9. *If a man will make gods for himself....*[82] Not only do men *make gods for themselves* from statues, but you will also find men *making gods for themselves* from their imaginations. For such people can imagine another god and creator of the world other than the divine plan of the world recorded by the Spirit, other than the true world.[83] These all have *made gods for themselves,* and they have *worshipped the works of the hands.*[84] So, too, I believe is the case either among the Greeks who generate opinions, so to speak, of this philosophy or that, or among the heretics, the first who generate opinions. These have *made idols for themselves* and figments of the soul, and by turning to them *they worship the works of their hands,* since they accept as truth their own fabrications.

(2) The Word then, when it refutes all of those who *make gods for themselves* through the senses and the mind, says, *If a man will make for himself gods, and these are not gods. On account of this I will make manifest to them my hand in this time, and I will make known to them my power.*[85] In what other *time* except *this?* And pointing out the *time* of the coming of the Lord, he says,[86] *And they will know that my name is Lord.*[87]

10. Then there is another prophecy; I do not know how we do not find it in the Septuagint, but we do find it in the other translations. It is clear that it stood in the Hebrew, and it has been filled with the most essential things which are able to convert our souls, if we pay attention. And so it has the words: *A sin of Judah is written with an iron pen, with a point of diamond it is engraved on the tablet of their heart.*[88] It is [89] to surrender oneself to what is more obvious even to say: "These words were written about the Jews because *their* sin *is written.*"

---

82. Jer 16.20.
83. In S, after "world" add: "concerning divine dispensation of the world." Removed by Klostermann and Nautin.
84. Isa 2.8.   85. Jer 16.21.
86. "He says, 'And they will know,'" an addition of Cordier from Jerome.
87. Jer 16.21.
88. Jer 17.1 (Hebrew).
89. "It is," an addition of Klostermann.

But if you see, as we have often shown, Judah being said figuratively for Christ, perhaps *a sin of Judah* is the sin of us who believe in Christ who was from the tribe of Judah.[90]

(2) And if you can understand more mystically in another way, perhaps he prophesies concerning Judas the betrayer, that it is about him that the prophecy is stated: *A sin of Judah is written with an iron pen, with a point of diamond it is engraved on the tablet of the heart.* But again the *their* does not fit with that view.

(3) Perhaps then he was saying that if we become sinners, these events prophesied happen to us. We sinned, and our sin *is* not *written* outside us, but in our *heart,* and it is *written with an iron pen with a diamond point.* But that the sins which we sin have been engraved in us on account of sinning the circumstance itself will prove.[91] I do not perceive such a circumstance or such a sin; after I do it, I have its impression and it is as if the impression of my sin which is sinned is *written* on my soul. And if my sin was *written* in black ink, I would have wiped it off. But now it is *written with an iron pen,* it is written *with a diamond point,* it is *written on the tablet of our heart* so that I may come before the judgment seat and the prophecy may be fulfilled which says, *Nothing is covered that will not be revealed, or hidden that will not be known.*[92] My *tablet* was laid bare and the *heart* which has the letter engraved of my sin *with an iron pen with a diamond point,* and all read the impressions of my sins on my *tablet* and on my *heart. For nothing is covered that will not be revealed,*[93] but also *their conflicting thoughts accuse or perhaps excuse them,*[94] and *do not pronounce judgment before the time, before the Lord comes, who will bring to light the things now hidden in darkness, and will disclose the purposes of the heart.*[95] To whom does he *bring to light?* Not to him-

---

90. Cf. Apoc 5.5; Heb 7.14.
91. Origen wishes to show that the experience of sin can be unperceived because it does not affect, in line with Scripture, what is "outside," but the inner person, the heart.
92. Matt 10.26.
93. Matt 10.26.
94. Rom 2.15.
95. 1 Cor 4.5.

## HOMILY 16

self. For he knows *all things before their generation.*[96] But again to whom does *he bring to light?* To those who are about to see, on account of their purity, the sin of the one who has sinned, so that the sinners rise up *to reproach and everlasting shame;*[97] from which the God of the universe redeems us in order that we might rise up to glory in Christ, *to whom is the glory and the power for the ages. Amen.*[98]

96. Dan 13.42 (Sus 42).   97. Dan 12.2.
98. 1 Pet 4.11.

# HOMILY 17

## Jeremiah 17.11–16

*On "The partridge cried out," up to,*
*"And the day of man I have not desired, you know it."*

WE HAVE COME to the famous question to see what is the *partridge*, about which the Scripture now tells: *The partridge cried out; she has gathered what she did not lay, making her riches not with judgment. In the midst of her days, they will leave her behind; at her end she will be a fool.*[1] Out of what exists on the nature of animals it is necessary[2] to extract what may be recorded about the partridge, so that, by knowing something concerning the animal, we may know whether,[3] in order to classify now what is said about the partridge, it is in a better or worse category.[4] It is said that the animal is most malicious and wily and unscrupulous, and wants to deceive hunters. Often it rolls around at the feet of the hunter so that it might distract him as the animal who is near in order that he might not reach the nest. And if at that time it believes it has distracted the hunter and the little ones have fled the nest, then it also flies away. And the animal is exceedingly indecent so that the males fight with one another for intercourse, and males mount males. If then this animal is malicious, if also indecent, if also unscrupulous, if

---

1. Jer 17.11.
2. "It is necessary," an addition of Blass and Klostermann.
3. "We may know whether" (εἰδῶμεν πότερον), a correction of Klostermann from Jerome. S has μὲν πρότερον.
4. For what follows, cf. Aristotle, *Historia animalium* 9.8

## HOMILY 17

also deceitful, it is clear that to rank it as in the better category and to say that it can refer to the Savior appears to be impious. Thus one needs to see whether we may want to interpret it[5] for the adversary, if the[6] whole interpretation follows logically for us.

2. Well let us begin from the passage: *The partridge cried out, she gathered what she did not lay.* Likewise the Devil does not *gather* his own creatures, he does not *gather* what he has generated, but when he *cries out,* he *gathers* the creatures of another and he makes them his own.[7] *The partridge cried out* through Valentinus, *the partridge cried out* through Marcion, *the partridge cried out* through Basilides, through all of the heretics. For none of these could speak with the voice of Jesus. *My sheep hear my voice.*[8] But the *voice* of Jesus is in Paul and Peter; therefore, Paul said, *if you seek proof that Christ speaks in me.*[9] A *voice* of the *partridge* who has *gathered what she does not lay* is in those who lead astray and deceive the naive among believers because of their innocence and lack of preparation.

(2) Thus, *the partridge cried out, he gathered what he did not lay, making his riches without judgment.* The *partridge* was *rich.* See what kind of *riches* are his. Many become possessed by the *partridge,* by the power of the adversary. And he made his *riches* by neither caring about *judgment* nor by having *judgment,* but by acting without judgment. Therefore it is said that it is the *partridge who makes* his *riches without judgment.* But my Savior *makes* his[10] *riches* with *judgment* and his *riches* are judged and chosen.[11]

---

5. "It" (αὐτό), a correction of Koetschau. S has αὐτόν.
6. "The" (ἡ), a correction of Delarue. S has τῆι.
7. This concept of being owned by God or the Devil is a common one in Origen and other authors. Origen's way of expressing it is varied. Often he speaks of dimensions commonly shared such as the "image," the λόγος, being a son, a christ, etc. See the note of Huet in PG 13.455, n. 2. See also *Hom in Jer* 16.6.
8. John 10.27.   9. 2 Cor 13.3.
10. "His," an addition of Klostermann from Jerome.
11. Cf. 1 Pet 2.9.

3. Yet *in the middle of his days they will leave him behind.* We are all those who have come under the *partridge* who has *cried out.* For he *cries out* not only through those aforementioned but also all of those who generally deceive and who call forth for an ungodly religion, for teachings opposite to the truth. But *in the middle of his days* we have *left him behind.* For all of his *days* are the *days* of this age. But since Christ Jesus delivered *us from the present evil age,*[12] on account of this we have *left him behind in the middle of his days.*

(2) *And at his end he will be foolish.* For when was he prudent, that *at his end* he becomes *foolish?* But we will say that he was prudent. For, *the serpent was the most prudent of all of the animals which the Lord God made on the earth.*[13] He was *prudent* according to what is said in Isaiah, *For I will beat against the great mind, the ruler of the Assyrians.* For he said: *I will act in strength and in the wisdom*[14] *of understanding I will remove the boundaries of nations and spoil their strength, and I will shake the inhabited cities.*[15] If anyone is able, he can understand how *his end will be foolish.* After he was *prudent* in evil—for he was *the most prudent of all of the animals on earth*[16]—he became, in contrast to what was *prudent,* foolish in evil. You will understand truly what the words mean, *His end will be foolish,* if you know how it is also taught to you by the Apostle that you receive foolishness on behalf of your salvation. *If anyone among you,* he says, *seems to himself to be prudent in this age, let him become a fool.*[17] He has released you who before *cried out,* I am foolish and silly, so that you become *prudent.* If then there is a certain kind of blameworthy prudence wherein *the sons of this age are more prudent than the sons of light in their own generation,*[18] it is the good God who with reverse tactics overthrows

---

12. Gal 1.4.  13. Gen 3.1(2).
14. Due to a large lacuna in the Greek here, I offer a translation of Jerome's Latin. It should be noted that Jerome is usually accurate in his translation of the meaning of the text, but he often makes many little changes. His translations of some sentences are quite free.
15. Isa 10.12–13.  16. Gen 3.1.
17. 1 Cor 3.8.  18. Luke 16.8.

the hostile powers so that he may fulfill what was said, *His end will be foolish.* When will *his end be foolish?* Christ must *reign until God places all his enemies under his feet;* when he will have subjected all things to him, *the last enemy will be destroyed, death.*[19] When *death* will have been *destroyed,* then there will be the *end* of the *partridge, and his end is made foolish.*

4. This was said concerning the *partridge.* At the beginning of the second passage this was read: *The throne of glory, an exalted* position from the beginning, *our sanctification, the endurance of Israel. Lord, all who have left you are confounded when they depart, let them be written over the earth* because they have left the source of life, the Lord.[20] Blessed Isaiah the Prophet said when he saw the Lord and his Kingdom, *I saw the Lord of Sabaoth sitting on a high and exalted seat.*[21] And Jeremiah saw how God reigns on account of what he says when glorifying him: *A throne of glory, an exalted* place from the beginning, *our sanctification.* If you wish to understand that as referring to Christ, you will not offend, or if referring to the Father, you will not hold an impious opinion. For *the throne of glory,* an elevated place and from the beginning, is the Savior. The *throne of glory,* elevated[22] because his Kingdom is elevated, our *sanctification*[23] is Christ. *For he who sanctifies and those who are sanctified are all from one.*[24]

(2) *The endurance of Israel*[25] is our next subject. Just as the Savior is righteousness itself, truth itself, sanctification itself, so is he *endurance* itself. And there can be no way to be just without Christ, nor to be holy without him nor to endure without having Christ, for he is *the endurance of Israel.* And even if you apply these words to God,[26] you will not in this way be impious.

(3) *Lord, let all who have left you be dishonored when they have*

---

19. 1 Cor 15.25–26.  20. Jer 17.12–13.
21. Isa 6.1.
22. "Elevated," an addition of Nautin.
23. Here the lacuna ends and we return to Origen's Greek text.
24. Heb 2.11.  25. Jer 17.13.
26. "God." Jerome has "Father." See above.

184                          ORIGEN

*separated*.²⁷ Whenever each of us sins, through what he sins he *leaves* Christ. And if he *leaves* Christ, he *leaves* God.²⁸ For he who is unjust *leaves righteousness,* and he who is profane *leaves* sanctification. He who wars *leaves* peace behind and being under the Enemy he *leaves* the *redemption,* and being outside the Wisdom of God, he *leaves* behind *wisdom*.²⁹ Thus the Prophet prays for all who have *left* God, since he teaches us about what will happen to them when he says, *Let all who have left you be dishonored.* Insofar as they have *separated,* to that extent let them be *dishonored.*

(4) *Let them be written about on the earth*.³⁰ All men are *written about,* the holy in heaven, and sinners *on the earth.* It is said to the disciples by Jesus: *Be glad that your names are written in the heavens.*³¹ Accordingly one must rejoice if he becomes the sort of person whose name is inscribed *in the heavens.* But as the name of the holy are inscribed *in the heavens,* so also of those who conduct themselves in an earthly way, those who do not *pass through*³² the *land of Edom* but who possess the fields and the *vines* of the *land*³³ *of Edom,*³⁴ these names are *written on the earth* as belonging to those who have *left* God.³⁵

(5) *Let them be dishonored,* he says, *when they have separated,*

27. Jer 17.13.
28. Here is an example of the kind of modification which the text of the homilies has endured through a few centuries on an important text. In S it reads: "Whenever each of us sins, he leaves God, but when he leaves Christ, he leaves God." The Catena reads: "Each of us leaves Christ through what he sins, but if he leaves Christ, he leaves the Father." Jerome's Latin reads: "Whenever each of us sins, through what he sins he leaves Christ, and if he leaves the Son, he leaves the Father." My translation follows the modification of Klostermann (and Nautin) of these three texts.
29. Cf. 1 Cor 1.30.                              30. Jer 17.13.
31. Luke 10.20.
32. "Pass through" (παραπορευομένων), a correction of Klostermann from LXX and Jerome. S has πάνυ πορευομένων.
33. "Land" (γῆς), a correction of Klostermann from Jerome. S has τῆς.
34. Cf. Num 20.17–19.
35. Origen follows a traditional etymology here. The name "Edom" means "of the land" according to Philo, *Quod deus sit immutabilis* 144.

*let them be written on the earth.* For also *with the measure that you measure will you be measured.*[36] Each person is responsible for himself for what is *written.* If you seek what is [37] on *earth,* you do not seek what is in heaven. If your soul has bowed down over the things here, you are responsible for yourself, for Jesus says, *Do not lay up treasures for yourselves on earth, where moth and worm consume and where thieves break in and steal. But lay up for yourselves treasures in heaven.*[38] Do you *lay up treasures in heaven?* You are responsible for yourselves if your name is to be inscribed *in the heavens.*

(6) These words concern *Let them be written on earth,* and he says the cause: *because they have left behind the source of life, the Lord.*[39] And in the beginning the same Prophet was speaking under a mask[40] of God, *They have left me behind, the source of the water of life.*[41] And now, *they have left behind the Lord, the source of life.* Let us also then speak, if we do not want to *leave behind the Lord, the source of life,* with the voice of the genuine disciples of Jesus which they have spoken to the Master who said to them, *Do you not also wish to go away?* What then are we to say? *Lord,*[42] *to whom shall we go? You have the words of eternal life.*[43] There also the second passage ends.

5. Then again there is a prayer which goes on in this way: *Heal me and I will be healed, Lord. Save me and I will be saved, for you are my boast. Behold they say to me, "Where is the word of the Lord? Let it come." But I have not been weary of following you, and I have not desired the day of man, you know.*[44] It is to the healer who alone has come for those who are sick and who says, *Those who are well have no need of a healer, but those who are sick,*[45] that everyone who wants to be cured from the sickness of his

---

36. Matt 7.2.
37. "What is," addition of Blass, Koetschau, and Klostermann.
38. Matt 6.19–20.          39. Jer 17.13.
40. "Mask" (πρόσωπον). Translation from a suggestion of Schadel, 316, n. 190.
41. Jer 2.13.
42. "Lord," an addition of Klostermann from Jerome. S has καί.
43. John 6.67–68.          44. Jer 17.14–16.
45. Matt 9.12.

soul boldly speaks, *Heal me and I will be healed.* But if anyone else besides this one promises the healing of souls, you would not truthfully say to him, *Heal me, Lord, and I will be healed.* For also that woman who was hemorrhaging *had spent all that she had* for healers and *she could not be healed by any of them.*[46] For to none other of them was it reasonable to say, *Heal me, Lord, and I will be healed,* than to him alone, *the fringe of* whose[47] *garment*[48] she begins to touch. So I say to him: *Heal me, Lord, and I will be healed.* For if you heal, the end in the healing, the cure, will follow from you, so that I would be saved. And as many as may save,[49] I will not be saved.[50] The only true[51] salvation is if Christ saves me, for then *I will be saved. The horse is a false hope for deliverance,*[52] false also are all others besides God for salvation.[53] On account of this I might say to him: *Save me, Lord, and I will be saved,* and I say this if I can say also the next words after every *boast* which is renounced, *For you are my boast;*[54] or when I fulfill the commandment which says, *Let not the wise man boast in his wisdom, and let not the strong man boast in his strength, nor the rich man in his riches, let him who boasts boast in this, to understand and know that I am Lord.*[55] Blessed is he who has renounced every *boast* here below, such as in so-called noble birth and in beauty and in corporeal things, in riches, in vainglory, since he is content with one *boast,* that he may say, *For you are my boast.*

6. *Behold they say to me: "Where is the word of the Lord? Let it come." But I have not been weary of following you.*[56] Jesus says to

---

46. Cf. Mark 5.25–26; Luke 8.43.
47. "Whose," an addition from the Catena and Jerome.
48. Luke 8.44; Matt 9.20.
49. "And as many as [may] save" (ὅσοι δὲ ἂν σώσωσιν), a correction of Nautin. Blass and Klostermann have the text: "And as many [others] as do save ..." (ὅσοι δὲ ἄλλοι σώσουσιν), which Schadel follows. S has ὅσοι δὲ ἂν σώσουσιν.
50. This sentence is missing in Jerome.
51. Or from the Catena and S combined: "The only and true salvation...."
52. Ps 32.17.
53. "False also ... salvation," missing in Jerome.
54. Jer 17.14.   55. Jer 9.23–24.
56. Jer 17.15–16.

you: *Take up your cross and follow me,*[57] and, *Leave everything and follow me,*[58] and, *He who does not leave behind father and mother and follow me is not worthy to be my disciple.*[59] If then you become such a person so as to *follow* Jesus in every way, and you will *follow,* and to the extent you do *follow,* you will not be *weary.* For *there is no hardship in Jacob nor will distress be seen in Israel.* There is no toil in following Jesus; the *following* itself takes away the toil. In order that we may no longer be *weary,* since we are *weary* before beginning to follow him, that is why he himself says: *Come to me all who are weary and are heavy laden and I will give you rest.*[60]

(2) If then when we are *weary,* we come to him and follow him, we will say, *But I was not weary of following you.* But it follows that we say also to him: *I have not desired the day of man.*[61] There is a certain *day of man,* there is a certain day of God. Let each of us *desire* the day of resurrection of the holy rather than that day about which it was written, *Woe to those who desire the Day of the Lord. And it is darkness and not light.*[62] Who is the one who says, *And I have not desired the day of man?* The clarity of the Word will reprove us, for we have[63] *desired the day of man.* Often when we were ill and were absorbed in a vision[64] of the final departure, we exhort those friends who know us and we say: "Ask for a reprieve for me, ask for me to stay on in life." When we say these words we do not *desire* the holy day of God, but the *day of man.* Therefore when we have set aside the love of life and the desire for a *day of man,* we will seek to know that day in which we will gain the blessedness in Christ Jesus *to whom is the glory and the power for the ages. Amen.*[65]

---

57. Cf. Matt 16.24.
58. Cf. Matt 19.27, 9.9, 8.22.
59. Cf. Matt 10.37–38.
60. Matt 11.28.
61. Jer 17.16.
62. Amos 5.18.
63. S has "not" here. Klostermann and Nautin remove it.
64. S adds here "of death." Klostermann and Nautin remove it.
65. 1 Pet 4.11.

# HOMILY 18

## Jeremiah 18.1–16

*On "The word which came from the Lord to Jeremiah,
saying: 'Arise and go down to the house of the potter,'" up to,
"to assign their land to destruction and derision."*

NEXT IN WHAT WAS READ there are two visions of Jeremiah. Of these the former contains what concerns the clay vessel in the hand of the potter which is capable of reconstruction after crushing, for it is possible to remold it. But the other vision contains what concerns the earthen wine vessel which if broken has no remedy. For when it was clay, if it broke, even if it was already formed, it allows itself, since it was clay, to be kneaded a second time and be created a second time. But when, after being clay it becomes earthen and hardened by fire, then after the crushing of the earthen there could not be a remedy for it. What then these words portend we will consider first in an overview, then, if it is so ordained, we will examine it word by word.

(2) As long as we are in this life, because of our clay vessel, we are formed—I will name it in this way—like a pot,[1] and we are formed either according to evil or according to virtue. Indeed we are formed in this way so that our evil is admitted and crushed in order to become a new and better creature, and our progress is unbridled after the formation into a clay vessel. But when we have gone beyond the present

---

1. This word κεραμευτικῶς, translated, "like a pot," is apparently created by Origen.

## HOMILY 18

age, when we are at the end of life, whereupon we become whatsoever[2] we become by being put through fire, either under the fire of the *flaming darts of the evil one*[3] or under the fire of God, since also *our God* is a *consuming fire.*[4] If, I say, from one or the other fire, we become whatever we should become; if we are crushed—either we are crushed and perish from becoming the good vessel or from becoming the evil vessel—we are not remade[5] nor does our constitution admit of bettering. Because of this, insofar as here we are like those who are in the hands of the potter, even if the vessel falls from his hands, it admits of a remedy and can be remade.[6]

(3) I have spoken about these things in a little[7] more accessible sense before we make an examination of the rest[8] by reason, regarding the two forms of receptacles, the one of clay and not baked hard, and the second which has already become earthen.

2. But let us consider from the same text what is said about the clay receptacle in the hand of the potter and how he, the Word in the Prophet, the Lord who prophesies in him,[9] gives also not a few other bases for the interpretation of what concerns the mold in the hand of the potter.

(2) *The word which came to Jeremiah from the Lord said: "Rise up and go down to the house of the potter."*[10] Jeremiah is up, he has gone up above the clay vessels, the clay vessel is below, and the nature who manages the clay vessels, when he condescends for those who are managed, is below. On account

---

2. "We become whatsoever" (γενώμεθα ὁτιποτοῦν), a correction of Diels, Koetschau, and Klostermann. S has γενέσθαι ὅτι π' οὖν.
3. Cf. Eph 6.16.   4. Deut 4.24; Heb 12.29.
5. "Remade" (ἀνακτιζόμεθα), a correction from the Catena. S has ἀναγκαζόμεθα.
6. See 2 *Clem* 8.1–2.
7. "Little" (ὀλίγῳ) is a correction of Blass and Klostermann. S has ὁ λόγος.
8. "Rest" (λεῖπον) in S, but uncertain according to Klostermann. Nautin corrects to λεπτόν ("detail"), perhaps better.
9. Cf. *Ps-Barn* 16.9.
10. Jer 18.1–2.

of this the *word which came*[11] *to Jeremiah from the Lord said to him:* "*Rise up and go down to the house of the potter and there you will hear my words.*" It is said to Moses: *Go up to the mount and hear.*[12] It is said to Jeremiah: *Go down to the house of the potter and hear.* For each of those who *hear words*[13] either is taught about the things above or learns about the things below. If I am taught what is below,[14] I go down to the Word so that I may know the things below. But if I learn the things above, I go up to the Word for the things above so that I may meditate on what is there.

(3) But in order that you may follow everything which has been said to the extent of your abilities, I will use an example also from Scripture. And I will also offer with the example an exposition which will introduce you to the interpretation that has been granted. *In the name of Jesus every knee should bow, in heaven and on earth and under the earth, and every tongue will confess that Jesus Christ is Lord, to the glory of God the Father.*[15] And there is a certain wisdom pertaining to each of these realms: a wisdom concerning the heavens is how the heavenly matters have been ordered, a wisdom concerning what is under the earth, since the wisdom of God is also concerning the order of what is under the earth, as well as concerning what is on the earth. If I intend to grasp the wisdom which concerns heavenly things, I go up to the heavenly realms, as Moses had gone up to the top of the mountain in order that, in light of what was written, the voice out of heaven might become for him something audible. For he was about to be taught the heavenly ways for worship. For shadows and copies of divine mysteries are in the laws which were written above, as the Apostle taught when he said, *which serve*

---

11. "Came" (γενόμενος) is a correction of Nautin from LXX. S has λεγόμενος.
12. Cf. Exod 24.12.
13. "Words": other manuscripts have λόγον.
14. "If . . . below" (εἰ μὲν τὰ κατώτερα διδάσκομαι), an addition and correction of Klostermann. S has διδάσκων.
15. Phil 2.10–11.

*as a copy and shadow of the heavenly sanctuary.*[16] Thus, just as I who intend to be taught concerning heavenly matters go up, so, if it is necessary for me to learn concerning matters below the earth, even if I become a Prophet, I go down. And perhaps on account of this, Samuel, at the time when he was taught about what is below the earth, went down below and was in Hades, though he was in Hades not because he was sentenced but he came to be an observer and contemplator of the mysteries of matters below the earth.[17] Such a view can also be in what was said by the Apostle concerning wisdom, words which command us to know *what is the breadth and length and depth and height.*[18] You will know the[19] *height*, if you go up to the Word at his height. You will know the *depth* if you go down to the Word at his depth.[20] You will know the middle of the *height* and *depth* if you know the *breadth* and *length*. The intellect which is able to *follow* the Son of God comes to all directions when it is led by[21] the Word which teaches about all things, and it *follows* when it has renounced the world and has *taken up his cross.*[22] For the one who can say, *The world is crucified to me and I to the world,*[23] this[24] person can *follow* Jesus.

(4) It is necessary to explain the text: *Go down to the house of the potter, and there you will hear my words.*[25] For it is necessary to compare it to the text: *Go up and you will hear my words.*[26] For among those who hear, some *go up* so that they might be taught, but[27] they *go up* not altogether bodily. And some[28] *go down* and have the soul above for the purpose of seeing the Word who is above what concerns matters below. My Lord Je-

16. Heb 8.5.   17. Cf. 1 Kings 28.
18. Eph 3.18.
19. "The," an addition of Klostermann.
20. This sentence is an addition of Klostermann.
21. "By" (ὑπό), a correction of Blass. S has ἀπό.
22. Cf. Matt 16.24.   23. Gal 6.14.
24. "This" (οὗτος), a correction of Klostermann. S has οὕτως.
25. Jer 18.2.   26. Cf. Exod 24.12.
27. "But," an addition of Ghisleri.
28. "But some," an addition of Klostermann.

sus Christ himself has *gone up* and *gone down. For he who has ascended is also he who has descended. He is far above the heavens.*[29] If then you will comprehend the one who has *gone up* above, the Word who teaches concerning matters above, understand the one who *descends* to the things below, who teaches concerning matters below. Do not say: "Who will ascend into heaven"—that is, to bring Christ down—"or who will descend into the abyss"—that is, to bring Christ[30] up from the dead. But what does the Scripture say? *The word is near you, on your lips and in your heart,*[31] through which you ascend to heaven. And concerning the way up, *the word is near you,* and concerning what is below, *the word is near you.* For what can the holy man have in himself other than the Word which is everywhere? For, *the kingdom of heaven is within you.*[32]

3. Hence, the Prophet *goes down to the house of the potter* and described what he was viewing when he says, *And behold he was making a work in his hands, and the receptacle which he was making in clay in his hands fell. And he made another receptacle again, as it was pleasing in his view to make it.*[33] But I do not know what the Prophet saw when he was with *the potter.* For he saw the *potter* working. There was a clay vessel which appeared. The vessel *fell.* Why did he not say precisely, "The vessel slipped away from his hand." Did he not attribute the cause to the *potter?* But since the Word is for living vessels, which *fall* because of themselves, for this reason it is said, *The vessel fell from his hands.* You then, take heed for yourself,[34] lest after being in the *hands* of the *potter,* and still being molded[35] you *fall from his hands* because of yourself. For *no one snatches us away from his hands,* according to what was said

---

29. Cf. Eph 4.10.
30. S here adds, "to bring [Christ] up or who will go down into the abyss, that is Christ...." Evidently the text was copied by mistake.
31. Rom 10.6–8.   32. Luke 17.21.
33. Jer 18.3–4.
34. "For yourself" (σαυτῷ), a correction of Ghisleri. S has σαυτοῦ.
35. "Still being molded" (ἔτι πλασσόμενος), a correction of Klostermann and Cordier. S has ἐπιπλασσόμενος.

in the Gospel according to John.³⁶ Yet it is not written that just as no one *snatches us away*, no one also *falls* from his *hands*. For one who is self-determined is free. And I say: *no one* will *snatch us away from the hand* of God, no one can take us. But³⁷ we are able to *fall* from his hands if we are negligent.

4. And *the Word of the Lord came to me saying, "Can I not make you, house of Israel," says the Lord, "as the potter?"*³⁸ Each person according to his capacity understands the Scriptures. One takes the sense from them more superficially, as if from³⁹ the surface level of a spring. Another draws up more deeply as from a well, and both can be helped since the same thing to one is a spring, but to the other is a well. The Gospel validates this when it discusses what concerns the Samaritan woman. For there the same thing is called a *spring* and a *well*, and throughout the section it is called here a *spring*, and there a *well*.⁴⁰ But let him who is able consider in order that he sees that the same thing in substance is on the surface a *spring*, but is in a deeper sense a *well*.

(2) For me⁴¹ this is a preface to the future discussion about the clay receptacle which *fell from the hand of the potter* and was molded anew. Some have contemplated and understood these passages more simply. I will present for you the doctrine of those and the discussion. After this if we have something deeper, we will discuss this also. The events surrounding the resurrection can be revealed here, they say. For if the clay receptacle has *fallen from the hands of the potter* and from the same matter of the same clay he makes *it another receptacle as it was pleasing in his view*,⁴² God, the *potter* of our bodies, the Creator of our constitution, when this has *fallen* and been crushed for whatever reason, can take it up

---

36. John 10.29.
37. "But," an addition of Cordier.
38. Jer 18.5–6.
39. "As if from" (ὡς ἐξ), a correction of Klostermann. S has ὡσεί.
40. John 4.6, 11, 12.
41. "For me" (μοι), an addition of Klostermann. S has μου.
42. Jer 18.4.

and renew it and make it more beautiful and better, *another receptacle as it was pleasing in his view to make.*

5. Let this discussion also have favor. But let us hear the Lord himself when he describes it and says: *"Will I not be able to make you as this potter?" says the Lord. "Behold you are as the clay of the potter in my hands. I will pronounce a limit to a nation and a kingdom by cutting off and destroying them, and that nation will turn away from their evils which I spoke to it, and I will repent from the evils which I intended to do to them. And I will pronounce a limit to a nation and a kingdom in order to rebuild and replant, and they will do evil before me when they do not listen to my voice, and I will repent about the good which I intended to do for them," says the Lord.*[43] Let us see that this passage concerning the *house of the potter* refers not to certain matters concerning one person, but to two *nations.* For he says initially that[44] he intends to speak about *nations* so that he might suggest certain things to those able to hear secret mysteries. *I will pronounce a limit to a nation.* He examines the *limit* and the first *nation* about which he pronounces[45] the words of destruction because of their sins. And after he pronounces the words of destruction because of sins, nothing else is promised because, if they will repent, he will *repent* for the misfortunes which he intended to do to them. And again he speaks to the other, second nation that an entire nation *is rebuilt and planted.* And since this nation which is *rebuilt and planted* has the good promise, yet is able to sin, he says, after *pronouncing* these words, if they fall away from good works: *I will change my mind concerning the good which I intended to do for them.*

(2) Who then are the two nations, the former one named whom the Word threatens, and the second, to whom[46] he promised? Indeed he threatens so that if they repent, he

---

43. Jer 18.6–10.   44. "That," an addition of Huet.
45. "About . . . pronounces," an addition of Klostermann in light of what follows.
46. " . . . whom . . . to whom" (ᾧ . . . ᾧ), a correction of Ghisleri. S has ὡς . . . ὧν.

would not do the acts of the threat. He promises so that should the second nation fall afterwards and become not worthy of the promises, he will not form them. Concerning the two nations especially every plan of God for men in the world is set before us. That first nation is Israel, this second nation emerges after the appearance of Christ. God threatened the first nation what he threatened, and we see what concerns the threat of the first nation. It has been in captivity, their city was demolished, the holy sanctuary has been destroyed, the altar has been cast down, nothing is still retained of those old, holy customs among them. For God was saying to that nation: "Repent." And they did not repent. After saying this to these people, God speaks to this second nation about *rebuilding* it. But see, this nation are men who are able to err again. Because of this he also threatens this nation and says: "Even though I foretold what concerns the building and what concerns the planting and the tilling, and this nation also intends to sin, to her also who has sinned will happen those things which were stated for those others because of sins, and they will suffer if they should not repent."

(3) Scrutinize all of Scripture and you will discover that most passages concern these two nations. God selected the Fathers, he has given to them a promise, he brought from Egypt the people descended from the race of the Fathers, he was patient with[47] those who sin. He instructed them as a father, he prepared them, he gave to them a land of promise, he sent Prophets to them at the right time, he instructed them and turned them back from sins. He was always patient by sending those who cure; up till the Chief-healer came, the Prophet who surpassed prophets, the Healer who surpassed healers. They forsook and killed the one who had come when they said, *Take away, take away from the earth such a man, crucify, crucify him.*[48] Immediately wrath came on the

---

47. "With" (ἐπ'), a correction of Blass and Klostermann. S has ἐν.
48. Cf. John 19.15, 6.

nation, the *place*⁴⁹ where my Jesus *was crucified* was *made desolate*,⁵⁰ God selected another nation. See how *great the harvest is*, even though there are *few workers*. But also in another way God plans always that the *net* is thrown on the *lake* of this life, and *all kinds of* fish are *caught*. He sends out *many fishers*, he sends out many *hunters, they hunt from every hill.*⁵¹ See how great a plan it is concerning the salvation of the nations.

(4) *Note then the kindness and severity of God.* To the first nation who have also fallen, *severity*, but *to you*, the second nation, promises and *kindness, if you continue in his kindness. Otherwise you will all be cut off.*⁵² For the axe was laid to the root of the tree not only⁵³ once, the axe is ready to come again. And the *axe is laid to the root of the trees,* my Jesus said when he was prophesying about Israel against whom was the *axe*. He was the *axe* of the fruitless *tree* and he said, *Even now the axe is laid to the root of the trees.*⁵⁴ Whatever *tree* was not bearing fruit there he cut down, and threw it into the fire, and punished it. But now there has arisen another crop similar to the first, about which it was said, *When you bring them forth, plant them on the mountain of your inheritance, on your prepared place of dwelling.*⁵⁵ God *brought forth* his nation *on the mountain of* his *inheritance*. I do not seek *the mountain*, as Jews do, in materials⁵⁶ without souls. The *mountain* is Christ. In this one we were *planted*, on him we were firmly set.⁵⁷ See then if the master of the house was patient, lest when he comes he says: *Already three years I come to this figtree and it has not borne fruit. Cut it down. Why should it use up the earth?*⁵⁸ For he *uses up* the good *earth*, Christ, the mystery of the Church; he comes to the Synagogue also when he does not *bear fruit*.

49. Cf. Jer 40(33).10, 12.   50. Cf. Apoc 11.8.
51. Cf. Matt 9.37, 13.47; Jer 16.16. On the fishers and hunters, see also *Hom in Jer* 16.1.
52. Rom 11.22.
53. "Only" (μόνον), correction of Ghisleri and Cordier. S has μέν.
54. Matt 3.10.   55. Exod 15.17.
56. "Materials" (ὕλαις), a correction of Ghisleri. S has ὕλεσι.
57. "Firmly set" (ἐστηρίχθημεν), a correction of Blass, Koetschau, and Klostermann, 350. S has ἐτηρήθημεν.
58. Cf. Luke 13.7.

## HOMILY 18

6. *I will pronounce a limit to a nation or also to a kingdom.*[59] It may appear that the term *limit* is said[60] simply, but it does express something such as this: In the text, *I will pronounce to the nation or kingdom, limit* means the following: *I will demolish* is said as the *limit* for the first nation; *I will rebuild* you for the second nation. And again, *I will uproot* is said to the first, and *I will plant* to the second.[61]

(2) Since then the *limit* has been spoken, does the *limit* need to happen? God, who does not repent, is said to *repent*[62] according to the Scripture,[63] and let us pay close attention to the text, so that if we can defend how this is said, we may grasp the meaning. *I will pronounce,* he says, *a limit to a nation or a kingdom by cutting off and destroying them, and if that nation turns back from their evils which I have pronounced on it, I will also repent for the evils which I intended to do to them. And I will pronounce an end to a nation or to a kingdom in order to rebuild and plant, and they will do evil before me in order not to hear my voice, and I will repent about the good which I decreed to do to them.*[64] Concerning the repentance of God, we are demanded to defend ourselves. For to *repent* seems to be culpable and unworthy not only of God but also of the wise man. For I cannot conceive of a wise man repenting; rather when a man *repents,* supposing the customary use of the word, he repents for not having decided to be good. But God, a foreknower of what happens in the future, is unable not to have decided to be good and to repent for this.[65] How then has the Scripture brought forth this phrase which says, *I will repent?* I am not yet saying. And in Kings it is mentioned in the text, *I have re-*

---

59. Jer 18.7.
60. "Is said," an addition of Klostermann.
61. The word "limit" (πέρας) is hardly used in a simple sense, Origen is saying, but reflects God's "plan" with respect to the two nations. The "limit" has been reached for the one nation, issuing in destruction, whereas the other "limit" of the second nation has also been reached, and it issues in relationship with God.
62. Cf. Jer 18.10.         63. Cf. Jer 18.10.
64. Jer 18.7–10.
65. These ideas on repentance are similar to Stoic thought, as Schadel clarifies, 320, nn. 210–11.

*pented that I annointed Saul as king,*[66] and it is generally said concerning him, *And he repents for evils.*[67]

(3) But see what we are generally taught about God. Where *God is not as a man to be deceived nor as the son of man to be threatened,*[68] we learn through this text that *God is not as man*, but through another text that God is as a man, when it says, *For the Lord your God has taught you as a man teaches his son,*[69] and again, *As a man he takes on the manners of*[70] *his son.*[71] Hence whenever the Scriptures speak theologically about God in relation to himself[72] and do not involve his plan[73] for human matters, they say that he is *not as a man.*[74] For *there will be no limit to his greatness,*[75] and *he is more feared than all of the gods,*[76] and *praise him, all you angels of God; praise him, all his hosts; praise him, sun and moon; praise him, all stars and light.*[77] You can find numerous other passages, when you select from the sacred Scriptures, to which you can relate the words, *God is not as a man.*

(4) But whenever the divine plan involves human matters, it carries the human intellect and manners and way of speaking. And just as we, if we are talking with a two-year-old child, speak inarticulately because of the child—for it is impossible, if we observe what is fitting for the age of a full-grown man, and when talking to children, to understand the chil-

---

66. 1 Kings 15.11.      67. Joel 2.13.
68. Num 23.19.      69. Deut 8.5.

70. "Takes on the manners of": the word in the text is τροποφορεῖν, a word also found in the Nestle text of Acts 13.18. The LXX, however, as well as other manuscripts of Acts 13.18, have τροφοφορεῖν (to nourish or suckle). Perhaps the copyist or Origen has mistakenly recalled Acts 13.18 or perhaps the copyist erred in the transmission of both texts. For my translation see Origen's use of the term later in the section.

71. Deut 1.31. Cf. Philo, *Quod deus sit immutabilis* 53–54.

72. "In relation to himself" (καθ' ἑαυτόν), a correction from the Catena. S has κατ' αὐτόν.

73. οἰκονομία. Nautin writes about the word: "The word implies the idea of administration and plan, but connotes also that of adaptation, condescension and exception to strict rules," 2:199, n. 3

74. Num 23.19.      75. Ps 144.3.
76. Ps 95.4.      77. Ps 148.2–3.

dren without condescending to their mode of speech—something of this sort also seems to me the case with God whenever he manages the race of men and especially those still *infants*.[78] See also how we, mature men, change the name of things for babies, and we call "food" in a special way for them, and we call "drink" in another way of speaking, not using a vocabulary of adults which we use for adults of our age but a kind of childlike or babyish way of speaking. And if we name garments for children, we put upon them other names, as if we form a childlike name. Are we then for this reason immature? And if any of us should hear those who talk to children, will he say that this old man has become senseless, this man has forgotten his beard, the age of a man? Or is it granted that out of consideration when he converses[79] with the child he does not speak in an elderly or adult language, but in a childlike language?

(5) Now God also speaks to children. Even the Savior says, *Behold, I and the children which God has given me*.[80] It may be said to the old man who talks with the child in a childish way, or, to speak more dramatically, as a baby,[81] that he has *taken on the manners of*[82] his son and has taken on the manners of babes and has taken up its state. Likewise then, understand the Scripture when it says, *The Lord your God took on your manners as a man would take on the manners of his son*.[83] And those who have translated from the Hebrew, failing to find a suitable Greek term, seem to have concocted one,[84] as in many other places, and to have represented it as, *The Lord*

---

78. Cf. 1 Cor 3.1. Klostermann, 158, offers here a fragment from the homilies given in the Catena on the Pentateuch (PG 17.24): "He has embraced and condescended when he has claimed as his own our weakness. As a teacher speaks inarticulately with children, as a father tends his own children, so too when he puts on our ways and when he does them for what is more mature and higher."
79. "Converses" (ὁμιλοῦντα), a correction of Ghisleri. S has ὁμολογοῦντα.
80. Isa 8.17; Heb 2.13.
81. For an unweaned baby does not speak.
82. Deut 1.31. See prior note in this section.
83. Deut 1.31.  84. τροποφορέω.

*your God took on your manners,* (that is, he has taken on your manners) *as if some man would take on the manners of* (in light of this example which I have mentioned) *his son.* Since we really do repent, when he talks with us who repent God says, "I *repent,*" and when he threatens us, he does not pretend to be a foreknower, but he threatens as one speaking to babes. He does not pretend that he foreknows *all things before their generation,*[85] but as one who, so to speak, plays the part of a babe, he pretends not to know the future. And he threatens the nation on account of its sins and he says, *If the nation repents, I will repent.*[86] O God, when you were threatening, did you not foreknow whether the nation will or will not repent? When you were promising, did you not know whether the man or the nation to whom the word is directed does not remain worthy of the promises? Yes of course, but he pretends.

(6) But you can find many such anthropomorphic expressions in the Scripture, as also in the words: *Speak to the sons of Israel. Perhaps they will hear and repent.*[87] God has said, *Perhaps they will hear,* not as one who doubts.[88] For God does not doubt in order that he may say, *Perhaps they will listen and repent,* but in order that he might reveal to a great degree your self-determination and you not say: "If he foreknows that I am going to perish, it is a necessity that I perish. If he foreknows that I will be saved, I must surely be saved."

(7) He pretends then that he does not see your future so that he may preserve your self-determination by not foretelling or foreknowing whether you will repent or not, and he says to the Prophet, *Speak, perhaps they will repent.* For you will find numerous other passages where it talks about God *taking on the manners of* man. If you hear of the *anger* of God and his *wrath,*[89] do not suppose that *anger* and *wrath* are pas-

---

85. Dan 1(13).42.
86. Cf. Jer 18.8, 10.
87. Cf. Jer 33.2–3.
88. "As . . . doubts," an addition of Klostermann.
89. Cf. Deut 29.23, 24–27, etc.

sions of God. The purposes[90] of using this way of speaking are for converting and bettering the infant, since we also use a fearful expression with children, not from an actual state of mind but because of a purpose to cause fear. If we maintain what is kindly for the soul in our expression toward the babe, and we show the affection which we have for it, since we have not altered ourselves nor changed for the conversion of that one, we lose him and make him worse. So then it states that God is also said to be angry and wrathful in order that you can convert and become better. And he is truly neither angry nor wrathful, but you experience the effects of anger and wrath when you are in unbearable pains because of evil, whenever he disciplines by what is called the *anger* of God.

7. Next after the discourse concerning the two nations, the first, to whom the threat is given, and the second, to whom the promise is given, it says—he spoke evidently to the former—*And now say to the men of Judah and to the inhabitants of Jerusalem, "Thus says the Lord: 'Behold, I form evils against you.'"*[91] Because in my hand is what I *form against you*, it can fall. Make this to fall from my hand so that I will change and make good the evils which I *form against you*. You would not find: "Behold I form good against you." And next are statements analogous to them in order that after this it may appear that the good which he *forms* is lost from his hands in order that he can make these evil. No, he *forms evil* according to the example mentioned,[92] and after he *forms evil*, he arranges it—apart from the interpretation given for the text: *It fell from my hands*[93]—in order that, if it *falls*, I do not even know what sort of end of the evils which have been *formed* happens.

8. *Let each turn away from his evil way, and make more commendable your habits.*[94] It is true when the more simple people

---

90. "Purposes" (οἰκονομίαι), a correction of Cordier. S has οἰκονομία.
91. Jer 18.11.   92. In Jer 18.4.
93. Jer 18.4. See *Hom in Jer* 18.3.   94. Jer 18.11.

say: "Blessed are those ancient men, for they heard the Lord through the Prophet speaking, and the Lord spoke to them." And now through what has been written the Lord speaks to us:[95] *Let each turn away from his evil way.* The Lord himself addresses you when he says, *And make more commendable your habits.* But these, to whom the hortatory words have been spoken concerning repentance, respond. Let us consider what they answer, lest we also respond with these words. What then do they answer? *We will act like men, for we will go back to what we turned from, and each will do what pleases his heart of evil.*[96] And you may not speak in these words, but if your life is such that you sin, you too speak with power through evil acts according to the hortatory words, *Let us act like men, for we will go back to what we turned from, and each will do what what pleases his evil heart.*

(2) But what does *We go back to what we turned from* mean? Those who begin to *put the hand to the plow*,[97] and *strain forward to what lies ahead* in the field, and *forget what lies behind,* turn away from what is bad.[98] Hence whenever anyone, after he *puts the hand to the plow,* turns to *what lies behind,* he *goes back to what he turned from.* For he *goes back* to those acts from which he turned away, and he runs back again to those sins which he had abandoned. And therefore, among those who hear these words, either when as catechumens they abandon their pagan life or when as believers they already have progressed to *strain forward to what lies ahead,* if their life has become wicked, they also say nothing other than *We will go back to what we turned from, and each will do what pleases,* not merely, *his heart,* but his *evil* heart. For there is an *evil* heart and there is a good heart. Thus let no one go *back to what he turned from* nor do *what pleases his evil heart.*

(3) *"On account of this," the Lord says* to those who respond

---

95. "To us" (πρὸς ἡμᾶς), a correction of Klostermann from the Catena. S has ὡς.

96. Jer 18.12.   97. Cf. Luke 9.62.

98. Cf. Phil 3.13.

with these words, *"ask now among the nations, 'Who has ever heard of such abominable things which the virgin Israel has done again and again?'"*[99] And it seems that these words are also said in one sense, but if the Church from the pagan nations turns back to God, to the way which it must, it will be said: *Ask now among the nations, "Hear what abominable things the virgin Israel has done again and again."* For let us compare the life of those who sin with the life of those who turn back and believe, and we will see that those who have done *abominable* things kill *the Lord of glory*,[100] but these others, though they have done abominable things, have turned back to him who was killed and faced death by those first people for the sins of the world.

(4) *Ask*, then, *among the nations: "Who has ever heard of such abominable things which the virgin Israel has done again and again?"*

9. *Will breasts ever fail from a rock or snow from Libanus? Or is not water carried violently by the wind cut off? For my people have forgotten me, they have offered up incense in vain, and they become sick in their habits through eternal measures*[101] *in order to enter upon courses which have no path for walking, in order to place their land in destruction and eternal derision.*[102] He has spoken here of the differences of waters. First, in the text, *Will breasts ever fail from a rock?* And second, in the text,[103] *or snow from Libanus?* And third in the text, *Is water carried violently in the wind cut off?* These three forms of water are the sources of water which the soul of the just, similar to the hart, desires earnestly so that each might say, *In the way which the hart earnestly desires the sources of water, so my soul yearns for you, O God.*[104] Who then has become a *hart* hostile to the race of serpents, who suffers nothing from their arrow, as it is narrated

---

99. Jer 18.13.
100. 1 Cor 2.8.
101. See the fragment at the end of this homily.
102. Jer 18.13–16.
103. "In the text," an addition of Klostermann.
104. Ps 41.2.

concerning the *hart?* Who has thirsted in this way for God so that he might say, *My soul has thirsted for the living God?*[105] Who has thirsted in this way for the *breasts* of the *rock, and the rock was Christ?*[106] Who has thirsted in this way has thirsted for the Holy Spirit with the result that he might say: *In the way which the hart desires the source of water, so my heart yearns for you, O God?*[107] If we will not *thirst* for the three sources of water, we will not discover one *source* of water. The Jews appeared to have thirsted for one *source* of water, the God, but since they did not *thirst* for the Christ and the Holy Spirit, they have nothing to drink from God. The heretics seem to *thirst* for Christ Jesus, but since they have not *thirsted* for the Father, the God of the Law and the Prophets, because of this they never drink from Jesus Christ. And those who keep the one God, but who deny the prophecies, do not thirst for the Holy Spirit in the Prophets, hence they never drink from the paternal *source,* nor from the one who called out in the Temple and said, *If a man thirsts, let him come to me and drink.*[108]

(2) Thus *breasts* do not *fail from rocks,* but those *have forsaken a source of the water of life.*[109] A *source* of the water of life has not forsaken them. For God does not distance himself from anyone, but they who *distance themselves from him perish.*[110] God is nearer certain persons and meets with him who comes to him. When then the son after consuming the fortune has come back again, the father *meets with him;*[111] and he announces through the Prophets when he says: *I am as near to them as the undergarment of their skin.*[112] For he said, *"I am a God near at hand and not far off,"* says the Lord.[113]

(3) Thus *breasts, the waters of Jesus, will not fail from a rock,*

105. Ps 41.3.
106. 1 Cor 10.4.
107. Ps 41.2.  108. John 7.37.
109. Jer 2.13.  110. Cf. Ps 27.27.
111. Cf. Luke 15.12, 14, 20.
112. Apparently a quote from an apocryphal Ezechiel. Also quoted by Clement of Alexandria, *Paed* I.IX.84.3. See Nautin, 2:212, n. 1.
113. Cf. Jer 23.23.

*or snow from Libanus*,[114] the waters of the Father. For libanus is also the sacred incense, according to the Law of God, and *transparent libanus, equal to equal*,[115] is brought to the altar. And this mountain has the same name as libanus, and it is the *snow from Libanus* which comes down in the same way as the water of the Holy Spirit, concerning whom it is said, *Is the water carried violently in the wind cut off?* For he also is *carried in the wind*. He is not *cut off;* the water of the Holy Spirit does not flee, but each of us by sinning becomes a fugitive from drinking from the Holy Spirit.

10. *For my people has forgotten me, they have offered up incense in vain*.[116] Everyone who sins has *forgotten* God, but the righteous man says, *All of these things have come upon us and we have not forgotten you, nor have we been unjust in your covenant*.[117] But that people has really *forgotten* God and has *offered up incense in vain*. But what must be understood by *they have offered up incense in vain?* If we take up the statements made not long ago with respect to the Psalm, we will understand what the text *They sacrificed in vain* means. And such was what was said in the Psalm: *Let my prayer be as incense before you*.[118] Hence my prayer, a subtle thing composed from subtle thoughts[119] of a subtle heart, when our heart is not made gross, is sent up as *incense before God*. If then the prayer of the just man is *incense before God*, the prayer of the unjust man is incense but the kind of incense such that it would be said concerning it and the unjust one who prays: *He offered up incense in vain*. Just as concerning Judah it has been written, *Let his prayer be for sin*,[120] that one with respect to praying has *offered up incense in vain*.

(2) But who the one is who *offers up incense in vain*, let us

---

114. Jer 18.14.
115. Cf. Exod 30.34.
116. Jer 18.15.  117. Ps 43.18(17).
118. Ps 140.2.
119. "A subtle thing" and "from subtle thoughts," an addition from the Catena.
120. Ps 108.7.

probe still more. He said, *Three times a year shall every one of your males appear before the Lord your God*;[121] after which straightway there follows, *You shall not appear before me empty.*[122] Hence among those who come. . . .[123]

121. Exod 23.17.
122. Exod 23.15.
123. In extant manuscripts the homily is missing from hereon. Origen has promised to explore Jer 18.15–16. The following is a fragment of the Catena offered by Klostermann, 165: "The *schoinos* is a road measure with the Egyptians and the Persians. It is also spoken of in the Psalms, 'You have traced my path and my *schoinos*.' (Ps 138.3) But among *schoinos*, some are considered eternal, others temporary. For the worldly man travels a temporary *schoinos* around contemptible glory and riches and things here below. But he who travels the one who said, 'I am the way,' (John 14.6) travels the eternal *schoinos*, and it is the eternal because it does not consider the temporary but the eternal, and he travels until he comes to the end of these *schoinos*, the harbor at the home of God."

## HOMILY 19

### Jeremiah 20.1–7

On *"And the priest Paschor, the son of Emmer, heard,"* up to, *"You deceived me, Lord, and I was deceived."*[1]

IF THE SENSE OF THE SCRIPTURE, that which comes up in the eye when it comprehends the clarity of the sacred Scriptures.[2] These things are said to me in the prologue, which arouses and raises up both myself and those who listen to what was offered in the passages read, in order that we might ask that Jesus come and make clear to us and teach us now[3] what is written here.

11. Jeremiah prophesied, *and the priest Paschor son of Emmer heard* the words of the prophecy, and such other listeners heard Jeremiah, in light of what is reasonable in the context of what follows in the prophecy, though no other is immediately recorded except for Paschor. But he has taken care to say in the Scripture both whose son he was, Emmer's, and that he bore the title of a priest, and what position he had among the people, that he was *appointed governor of the House of the Lord in the time* Jeremiah was prophesying such words.[4] And it is recorded that, after he heard the words of the prophecy, Paschor *struck* Jeremiah, and he was not content just to have *struck* him, but also he threw him into a certain

---

1. The title and "On . . . was deceived" are additions of Klostermann.
2. The initial sections of this homily are not extant; what remains begins in section 10.
3. "Teach now" (διδάσκειν τὰ νῦν), a correction of Klostermann. S has διδάσκοντα.
4. Jer 20.1.

*pit*. He has taken care to say in Scripture also where this *pit* was: *in the gate of Benjamin*,[5] and that the *pit* was in a place where there was an *upper area*, and was the *upper area* of nothing other than the *House of the Lord*.[6] The Holy Spirit recorded that these events would happen in the prophecy to Jeremiah, but they would happen from Paschor. Then he said, *Paschor on the morrow*[7] *brought Jeremiah out of the pit*. And after being brought out Jeremiah said to Paschor: "It was not the Lord that called you this name, Paschor; another[8] name has been given to you. Just as Israel was given for Jacob, Abraham for Abram, Sarra for Sara, so also for you he has given the name *Exiled*.[9] And on account of this he called you Exiled, whereas *the Lord says: "Behold, with all I deliver you to exile"*? With whom? Not with your wives and your sons and your daughters, but *with your friends*. And when you are *delivered*[10] to exile, *your friends* will fall by a sword. Then as to the differences which exist between those who fall *by a sword*—if they fall from *swords* of enemies or from *swords* of others—he says that the friends of the one who threw Jeremiah into the *pit* will fall upon the sword *of their*[11] *enemies. And your eyes*, he says, *will see* these things prophesied. *But I also will deliver you, all of Judah, into the hands of the king of Babylon*, after these friends of yours suffer, *and they will exile them to Babylon and they will cut them down*.[12] For they *cut down* the king of Judah and those from Judah *by a sword*, yet it is no longer added, *of their enemies*, as in the former, who were said to be friends of Paschor. Then he says: *And I will deliver all of the power of this city and all of the treasures of the king of Judah and all of the fruits of this city into the hands of their enemies*, so that the enemies

---

5. "In the gate of Benjamin" is in the Hebrew, not in the LXX.
6. Jer 20.2.
7. "Paschor on the morrow," are taken from the Hebrew text.
8. "Another" (ἄλλο), a correction of Klostermann. S has ἀλλά.
9. Jer 20.3.
10. "You are delivered" (δοθῆς), a correction of Ghisleri. S has δοθῆ.
11. "Their" (αὐτῶν), a correction of editors. S has αὐτοῦ.
12. Jer 20.2–4.

will *plunder* the treasure and *take*[13] the aforementioned things and *bring* Judah and her king *to Babylon*.[14] But *you, O Paschor*,[15] *and everyone who lives in your house, go in captivity* to Babylon. And there *you will die, and there you and all of your friends to whom you have prophesied lies will be buried*.[16]

(2) It was necessary that the whole section be summarized and made clear, not its deep thought—if we comprehend it—but the literal text and the letter itself, which also one who is acquainted with the Scriptures carefully and not incidentally can understand, even in this way. What then do these words really mean? Here the challenge is to present the purpose of these Scriptures. And yet I confess that I by myself am not able to discuss these words, but I need, as I said before, the appearance of the power of Jesus, in the way he is Wisdom, in the way he is the Word, in the way he is the Truth, so that his appearance might make light on the countenance of my soul.

12.[17] The *enchanters* of the Egyptians have *wands* which want to discredit those of Moses and Aaron as not being from God, but the wands from God overturn those among the *sophists* and *enchanters*. *The wand of Aaron swallowed up them*.[18] For even without the *wand* of Moses it is sufficient for this.

(2) Then Paschor *struck Jeremiah the Prophet*[19] also with emphasis. *And he struck Jeremiah the Prophet*.[20] He even adds the phrase *the Prophet*. Here then he who *struck Jeremiah* struck *the Prophet*. And it is recorded in Acts that a man who was commanded by Ananias the high priest *struck* Paul; therefore, Paul said, *God shall beat you, you whitewashed wall!*[21] And up to

---

13. "Plunder" and "take," are in the Hebrew, not in the LXX.
14. Cf. Jer 20.5.
15. "O Paschor," is from the Hebrew text, not the LXX.
16. Jer 20.6.
17. A few lines are missing at the beginning of this section.
18. Cf. Exod 7.11–12.
19. "The Prophet," is in the Hebrew, not in the LXX.
20. Jer 20.2.   21. Acts 23.3.

the present the Ebionites, placed under the illegitimate high-priest of the Word,[22] beat the Apostle of Jesus Christ with slanderous words, and Paul said to such a high-priest of the Word that *God shall beat* you. And such a high-priest is *beautiful* on the surface and a *whitewashed wall,* but inwardly *full of dead men's bones and every uncleanness.*[23]

(3) But why am I speaking about Paul and Jeremiah? My Lord Jesus Christ himself said, *I have given my back for whips and my cheeks for blows, and my face I did not turn away from shame of spitting.*[24] The simple people know these things for the single time when Pilate whipped him, when the Jews schemed against him, but I see Jesus each day giving his *back for whips*. Enter into the synagogues of Jews, and see Jesus whipped by them with the tongue of blasphemy. See those who *gathered together*[25] from the pagan nations scheming against Christians, how they receive Jesus, he gives his own *back for whips*. Consider the Word of God being insulted, abused, hated by the unbelieving. See that this is how he gave his *cheeks for blows,* and the one who has taught *that if anyone strikes you on the right cheek give also the other,*[26] he himself practices it. Such people beat and whip him, and he is silent and does not speak. For it is recorded that he did not speak in the act of being whipped.[27] And Jesus up to this time *did not turn away his face from the shame of spitting.*[28] Who of those who despise the teaching does not up to now in a sense *spit* on Jesus who upholds it?

13. It follows that, when the Prophet was struck, it discussed those who were struck, such as the Apostle and anyone else who is struck; it presented also what concerned Je-

---

22. S has λόγον. Nautin corrects without comment to λόγου.
23. Cf. Matt 23.27.     24. Isa 50.6.
25. Ps 2.1–2.     26. Matt 5.39.
27. Cf. John 19.1, 9. Actually the New Testament makes no mention whether Jesus was silent while being whipped. Perhaps Origen is comparing Jesus to Anaxarchus and Epictetus whom Celsus believed showed no effect when they were being tortured. See *Cels* 7.53–54.
28. Isa 50.6.

sus himself. Thus, *Paschor struck Jeremiah the Prophet and threw him into the pit which was in the Benjamin gate of the upper area.*[29] The *pit* belonged to *Benjamin of the upper area.* Jerusalem is the inheritance of Benjamin in which the Temple of God was, as he who can understand[30] the sacred readings from the inheritance written up in the book of Nave will find.[31] Thus, since the Temple was in the inheritance of Benjamin—who is interpreted as the Son of Right, for there is nothing "left" concerning the Temple of God—on account of this he throws him *into the pit which was in the Benjamin gate of the upper area of the House of the Lord.*

(2) The *upper area* being in the *House of the Lord,* he threw the Prophet *into the pit.* Let us exhort ourselves, so that by taking Jeremiah now into the *upper area,* we will have ascended *in the House of the Lord.* And I will show from[32] Scripture that the *upper area* is the lofty and exalted sense when it testifies to the holy ones that they receive the Prophets in the *upper areas.* In the third book of Kings it is recorded that the widow who received Elijah the Prophet in Sarephta of Sidon entertained the Prophet *in* her *upper area,*[33] and in the fourth book the woman who receives Elisha made ready for him her house in the *upper area.*[34] And the sinner Ochozia fell from the *upper area.*[35] And Jesus commands you never to go down from the housetop. For he says, *whenever* such and such happens, then *let him who is on the housetop not go down to take what is in his house.*[36] Let him who flees in the persecutions never go up into the *housetop,* but *let him not go down from the housetop to take what is in the house.*

(3) It is good then to be in the *upper areas,* it is good to be on the *housetop* and to be anywhere above. But also the wonderful Apostles—as it is recorded of them in Acts when be-

29. Jer 20.2 (Hebrew).
30. "As . . . understand," an addition of Klostermann.
31. Josh 18.10–24.
32. "From," an addition of Ghisleri.   33. 3 Kings 17.19.
34. 4 Kings 4.10.   35. 4 Kings 1.2.
36. Matt 24.15–17.

ing together at the same place they were attentive to prayers and the Word of God—were in an *upper area*,[37] and since they were in an *upper area,* they were not below. On account of this *there appeared distributed to them tongues as of fire.*[38] But also Peter, at the time when he sent up the prayer to God, *went up to the housetop,*[39] and unless he had *gone up to the housetop* he would not see *something descending* from heaven *like a sheet let down on four corners* from heaven.[40] But also *Tabitha which means Dorcas,* who *did acts of charity,* was not below, but in the *upper room* where Peter, after going up, raised her from the dead.[41]

(4) But also Jesus, about to celebrate with the disciples the feast whose symbol we enact, the Passover, after they ask, *Where do you want us to prepare for you the Passover,* he says, *Go, when a man carrying a jar of water meets you, follow him. He will show to you a large furnished room spread,* cleaned, *made ready. There prepare the Passover.*[42] Thus no one who enacts the Passover as Jesus wishes is in a room below. But if someone celebrates with Jesus, he is in a great room above, in a furnished room made clean, in a furnished room adorned and prepared. But if you go up with him in order to celebrate the Passover, he gives to you the *Cup of the New Covenant,* he gives to you the *Bread of blessing,*[43] he makes a gift of his *Body* and his *Blood.* For this reason, let us exhort you: Move up into the higher area,[44] *raise your eyes on high.*[45] But to me too, if I teach the divine word, the Word says, "*Go up upon the high mountain, you who bring good news to Sion. Lift up your voice with strength, you who bring good news to Jerusalem. Lift it up! Fear not!*"[46]

(5) These words are regarding Paschor, for though there

---

37. Acts 1.13.
38. Acts 2.3.
39. Acts 10.9.
40. Acts 10.11.
41. Acts 9.36–37.
42. Cf. Matt 26.17; Mark 14.12–15; Luke 22.8–12. The word σαρόω (clean) is not in the Scripture.
43. Cf. 1 Cor 10.16.
44. Cf. Isa 37.24, 40.9.
45. Isa 37.23.
46. Isa 40.9.

was available *an upper area in the House of the Lord in the gate of Benjamin*, he did not bring up the Prophet into the *upper area*, but *he threw him into the pit* below.

14. *And it happened on the next day Paschor took Jeremiah out of the pit.*[47] O Lord Jesus, come again, make clear these things both for me[48] and for those who have come for the spiritual food. How did he *take Jeremiah out on the morrow from the pit?* For insofar as the *day of today*[49] has come—and *today* is all of this age[50]—the sinner has thrown the Prophet down into the *pit*. But if the *day* which has come ceases and the *morrow* comes, then, having repented, he brings him out from the *pit*.

(2) Then Jeremiah says to him what Paschor will suffer. What does he say to him? *He has not called your name Paschor but Exiled. For thus says the Lord.* Paschor will be exiled to Babylon, not only himself, but also *with his friends*, according to the extent of his sins.[51] For he is delivered to Nebuccadnezzar and he is carried off to Confusion[52] and is punished for his sins since *he threw the Prophet into the pit.*[53] Who then are the *friends* of *Paschor*, the name for the blackness of the mouth? All of those who receive his words, who were blackened by his mouth which has turned black, who accept the teachings of blackness.

(3) *And they will fall by the sword of their enemies.*[54] They who are assigned for giving punishments are those who have *swords* and who make them to *fall*. Concerning which the Word prophesied and said, *And your eyes will see. Your eyes*, he said, *will see* these things which are prophesied. *And I will deliver both you and all of Judah into the hands of the king of Baby-*

---

47. Jer 20.3.
48. "For me" (μοι), a correction of Ghisleri and Cordier. S has μου.
49. Gen 35.4.
50. After "age" S has ἐάν ("if"). Ghisleri removes it.
51. Jer 20.3–4.
52. Cf. Gen 11.9. "Confusion" is the meaning of the name Babylon, according to *Onom. sacra* I.174.91.
53. Jer 20.2.      54. Jer 20.4.

*Ion*.⁵⁵ If he has gone to live in Judah as a sinner in this way he is worthy to be possessed by the king of Babylon, the Confusion. He will be delivered to him, and the king of Babylon will accept the sinners. And the king of Babylon is Nebuccadnezzar according to history, but the Evil One according to the spiritual sense. And the sinner is handed over to this person, since he is alternatively, both the *enemy* and *avenger*.⁵⁶ But because the sinner is delivered to him, let Paul teach you, where he speaks about Phygelus and Hermogenes *whom I have delivered to Satan in order that they may learn not to blaspheme*,⁵⁷ and where he speaks about the one who has prostituted: *When you and my spirit are together with the power of the Lord Jesus, I have judged to deliver such a man to Satan for the destruction of the flesh so that the spirit may be saved on the day of the Lord Jesus Christ.*⁵⁸

(4) Thus Paschor, the one of the black mouth, is delivered *into the hands of the Babylonian king*, and they exile him to Babylon. *And they will cut them up with swords. And I will deliver all the strength of this city.*⁵⁹ It is easy to say that these things are prophesied about Jerusalem. For all of her *strength* and what is brought along are *delivered* to the king of the Babylonians. It is easy to say that these words are prophesied about *this city*, which was delivered to its enemies in the times of the Savior, and the sons of Jerusalem went away into captivity and the city was destroyed. But if you examine the circumstances and you see a city not as the stones, but as people, you will see that this very Jerusalem, the people, was delivered *into the hands of the king of Babylon* on account of impiety and sin with respect to Christ, and you are now Jerusalem. If then the Word now threatens Jerusalem, be fearful that you, if you sin, are⁶⁰ a sinner like Jerusalem and are being *deliv-*

---

55. Jer 20.4.   56. Cf. Ps 8.3.
57. 1 Tim 1.20. Origen cites 1 Tim, where the names are Hymenaeus and Alexander, but he uses the names of 2 Tim 1.15.
58. 1 Cor 5.4, 3, 5.
59. Jer 20.4–5.
60. "Are" (εἰ), a correction of Klostermann. S has ἡ.

*ered,* so that you may be Jerusalem no longer but become Babylon and Confounded, since Nebuccadnezzar the king of the Babylonians will have taken you over.

(5) *And all of the labors* of Jerusalem he delivers. How does he deliver *all of the labors?* If after suffering and struggling you succumb and sin, *all of your labors* have come into the *hands* of Nebuccadnezzar. How is it *all of your labors?* It will be said to you, if you fall after being worn out by many things on behalf of truth, *did you suffer so many things in vain?*[61] In particular those who in conscience have exhausted many *labors* on behalf of virtue ought to be afraid, lest because of some sin Nebuccadnezzar the king of Babylon takes over their *labors* to become Jerusalem. But in order that you may see more clearly how Nebuccadnezzar takes over the *labors* when Jerusalem sins, I will make use of words written in Ezekiel. They have it in this way: *If the righteous man turns away from his righteousness and commits a transgression, I will never remember the righteous things which he did.*[62] Why? Nebuccadnezzar takes over the *righteous* things which emerge after *labor* and Nebuccadnezzar the king of Babylon erases them.

(6) *And* he takes over *every honor*[63] of Jerusalem, when a man is in honor under God, and *while in honor has not understood*[64] and has sinned. If then you see[65] as one *in honor,* and as one called[66] into *honor* you again demean yourself through sins, the Babylonian king takes over the *honor* of Jerusalem.

(7) Now we consider, *And all of the treasures of the king of Judah.*[67] Jerusalem is rich, but if she sins, the Babylonian takes her *treasures.*

(8) *And they will plunder them and take them and carry them to Babylon. And you, Paschor, and all of those who dwell in your house, go to captivity in Babylon, and there you will die and there be*

---

61. Gal 3.4.  62. Cf. Ezek 18.24.
63. "Every honor," is from the Hebrew and is not in the LXX.
64. Ps 48.13(12).
65. "See" (ἴδῃς) in S. Nautin/Husson corrects to συνίδῃς ("are aware of").
66. "As one called" (κληθείς), a correction of Cordier. S has κληθῆς.
67. Jer 20.5.

*buried.*⁶⁸ The one who is overcome with confusion *dies* in Babylon. And the one who is affected in the opposite way, in being buried with Christ, he is *buried* in Babylon. For it is possible to be *buried* in a good way with Christ *through baptism.* According to the text, *we are buried with Christ and we are raised with him.*⁶⁹ Just as it is a mystery to be *buried with Christ,* so also it is a mystery, after becoming⁷⁰ a sinner due to a transgression, to be *buried* in Babylon.

(9) *And all,* he says, *your friends* go there, *those to whom you have prophesied lies.*⁷¹ He who discusses in an evil way about the sayings of God and throws the prophetic words into the *pit,* he prophesies, but he prophesies *lies.* For anyone who discusses the prophetic words, if he speaks truly, he both prophesies and prophesies truth, but if he lies, he is a lying prophet who speaks falsely of the prophetic words.

15. And the one section has indeed been completed, but let us now also begin the second. For it also contains matters immediately from the first phrase which did not occur before. And when attending to the text, let us again ask Jesus to come, and let us exhort him to come in a way more manifest and distinct, so that after he comes he may teach all of us whether the Prophet was speaking as one speaking truly, as it seems fitting to understand about a prophet, or as one speaking falsely in what follows, which it is not permitted to say concerning a holy prophet.

(2) And he says to God, *You have deceived me, Lord, and I was deceived; you were strong and prevailed. I have become nearly a laughingstock, every day I am continually being mocked. For I will laugh with my bitter word, I will call upon rebellion and misery. For the word of the Lord has become for me nearly a reproach and mockery every day. And I said, "I will never name the name of the Lord and I will never speak still with respect to his name." And there came about in my heart as a burning fire flaming in my bones, and*

---

68. Jer 20.5–6.  69. Cf. Rom 6.4.
70. After "becoming" S has ἐπί. Klostermann removes it.
71. Jer 20.6.

*I was weakened in every way, and I could not bear it, for I heard the reproach of many who gathered round* and who evidently say, *Conspire and let us conspire against him, we his friends. Watch his intention if he will be deceived and let us prevail against him, and we will take our vengeance upon him.*[72] But after they say these words, the Prophet says, *And the Lord is with me as a mighty warrior. On account of this they persecuted and could not understand. They were greatly disgraced for they did not understand their dishonor, these who through the age will not be forgotten.*[73]

(3) This is the second section of the reading. How then does the Prophet say, *You deceived me, Lord, and I was deceived?* Can God *deceive?* I am at a loss how I can accommodate the word. For if through God and his Word I do see something in it, what will be said requires suitable accommodation. After he ceased to be deceived the Prophet says, *You deceived me, Lord, and I was deceived,* since the basic matters and introductory things had emerged in deceit for him and, unless he was first deceived, he could not be instructed and introduced in religion in order to come later to the perception of the deceit.

(4) But it suffices to express a single useful example for what has been presented. When guiding children we speak to children, and we do not speak to them as we do to mature people but we speak to them as children who need[74] training, and we deceive children when we frighten children in order that it may halt the lack of education in youth. And we frighten children when we speak through words of deceit on account of what is basic to their infancy, in order that through the deceit we may cause them to be afraid and to resort to teachers both to declare and to do what is applicable for the progress of children.

(5) We are all children to God and we need the discipline of children. Because of this, God, since he cares about us, deceives us, even if we do not perceive the deceit before-

---

72. Jer 20.7–11.  73. Jer 20.11.
74. After "need" S adds διά. Huet removes it.

hand, lest as those who have gone beyond the infant we may no longer be trained through deceit but through acts. In one way the child is led into fear, in another way into progressing in age and crossing beyond the age of childhood. For if I am able when teaching children through deceit. . . .[75]

(6) . . . so that God who deceives may say, *I will train them in the hearing of their affliction.*[76]

(7) I will present the history of how God for salvation deceives and says certain things so that the sinner ceases doing what he might do if he had not heard certain of these words. Was the one who says, *Yet three days and Nineveh shall be destroyed,*[77] speaking as one who speaks truly or not, or as one who deceives by a deceit which converts? If that kind of conversion did not happen, was what was said no longer a deceit but already truth, and would there be a destruction which followed for Nineveh? It was up to those who hear. Either[78] they were deceived and believed in what was said as true statements to be beneficial and not be destroyed, or, if what was said does not come true and they were not deceived but concluded that what was said will not happen, to think of what was said as deceit and[79] not to undergo the *Yet three days and Nineveh will be destroyed,* but, I dare to say, something much more unpleasant than the *Yet three days and Nineveh will be destroyed.* For by hypothesis, if the Ninevites had not repented, after they have sinned, perhaps *Yet three days and Nineveh will be destroyed* would have happened. But suppose that it would not have happened this way, suppose a thing worse than this would have happened: they would have been delivered to eternal fire.

(8) Because of this another punishment according to the Law is stated for those who are brought up as children, but for those for whom *the fullness of time came,*[80] there are other

---

75. There is a lacuna here.   76. Hos 7.12.
77. Jon 3.4.
78. "Either" (ἤτοι), a correction of Klostermann. S has ἤ τοῖς.
79. "And," an addition of Delarue.   80. Gal 4.4.

forms of punishment. Compare the punishments of sinners according to the Law with the punishments of sinners according to the Gospel, and one will see that they as infants hear of punishments which accords with those infants, but we as mature in age hear of punishments more unpleasant. If then one has become an adulterer or adulteress, the threat is not hell, not eternal fire, but he will be stoned with rocks: *Let all of the synagogue stone him.*[81] When he has gone away, the adulterer found in these things will say, the adulteress found in these things will say: "Would that the Word will speak also for me; the people hurled stones at me and I would not give heed to the eternal fire." For not only the adulterer is *liable to the hell of fire,* but also the one who says to his brother, *you fool.*[82] But if the one who says to his brother, *you fool will be liable to the hell of fire,* to what will the adulterer be *liable?* I will seek for some punishment worse than the *hell of fire,* and perhaps I could say that the *hell* is for those who act involuntarily, the hell of those who are able to be purified, but just as for the good, the righteous—*what God has prepared for those who love him, does not arise in the heart of man*[83]—likewise what[84] he has prepared for sinners in fornication, in committing adultery, *does not arise in the heart of man.* For if it did *arise in the heart* for which[85] the one who said to his brother, *you fool,* becomes *liable,* it is evident that what is prepared[86] for those who have sinned more gravely is more than what arises in the *heart.* Yet I am unable to think of something more than hell, but I believe only that something more than hell is what is prepared for those who commit adultery.

(9) Thus I come also to the rest of the punishments ac-

---

81. Lev 24.16. This text, in fact, concerns a man who blasphemes, not an adulterer. Cf. Deut 22.24.
    82. Matt 5.22.                       83. 1 Cor 2.9; Isa 64.4, 65.17.
    84. "What," an addition of Delarue.
    85. "For which," an addition of Klostermann.
    86. "What is prepared" (ἠτοιμασμένον), a correction of Klostermann. S has ἡμαρτημένον.

cording to the Law, and I take the text of the Apostle which accords with these things, and which is silent about my punishment if I sin, for I do not want to accept to be deceived in a good way so that *you deceived me, Lord, and I was deceived.*[87] But what does the Apostle say? *Anyone who has violated the Law of Moses dies without pity before two or three witnesses. How much worse punishment will be deserved by the one who has spurned the Son of God?*[88] Name, O Paul, the *punishment.* I have said it, he says, but I do not speak about it. It is more than what is considered the punishment of those who sin in the Gospel, more than things heard, more than things thought. Because of this the Prophet was introduced as a child who heard and was afraid and was taught, and after this, when he became mature, he says, *You deceived me, Lord, and I was deceived.* And insofar as you are a child, fear the threats so that you may not suffer what comes beyond the threats, the eternal punishments, the unquenchable fire, or perhaps something more than this lays in waiting for those who have lived to the full outside of[89] right reason. Since all of these things exist, let us not by any means be tempted, but let us who are made mature in Christ Jesus become righteous, worthy of the heavenly feasts and our passover which is there for the spiritual elevation in Christ Jesus, *to whom is the glory and the power for the ages. Amen.*[90]

87. Jer 20.7.
88. Heb 10.28–29.
89. Or "contrary to" (παρά).
90. 1 Pet 4.11.

## HOMILY 20

*Jeremiah 20.7–12*

On *"You have deceived me, Lord, and I have been deceived"*
*(in another sense again) up to "understanding minds and hearts."*[1]

**EVERYTHING RECORDED** about God, even if it may be immediately unsuitable, must be understood worthy of a good God. For who will not say that what is brought up regarding God, that he has anger, that he uses wrath, that he regrets, and that he even now sleeps, does not seem unsuitable?[2] But each of these qualities, with the knowledge to hear *dark words*,[3] will be found worthy of God. For his anger is not fruitless, but just as his word instructs, so his anger instructs. He instructs with anger those who were not instructed by the word, and it is necessary that God use what is called anger as he uses what is named word. For his word is not such as the word of all others. For of no one else is the word a *living being*,[4] of no one else is the word *God*, for of no one else was the word *in the beginning with*[5] that one of whom it was the word, even if it was[6] only[7] . . . from a certain

---

1. Title and "On . . . hearts," additions of Klostermann.
2. Cf. Jer 38.26.
3. Cf. Prov 1.6.
4. From the *Acts of Paul*. Klostermann, 176, notes *Princ* 1.2.3 as another place Origen cites this text.
5. John 1.1.
6. "It was" (ἦν), a correction of Cordier. S has ἦ.
7. "Only" (μόνον), a correction of Nautin. S has μόνος. Klostermann believes there is a lacuna here and has retained μόνος.

*beginning*.[8] So indeed the anger of God is an anger[9] . . . of no one else,[10] an anger of none whatsoever, and just as the word of God has something of a nature alien beyond every word of anyone else—and what is *God* and what is a *living being* while being[11] a word, what subsists in itself[12] and what is subject to the Father, has an alien nature—so too, since once it was named as being of God, what is called anger has something alien and different from all the anger of him who is angry, so too his wrath also has something individual. For it is[13] the wrath of the purpose of the One who reproves by wrath, who wishes to convert the one reproved through the reproof. A word also reproves as a word instructs, but a word does not reprove in the way wrath reproves. For those who are helped by the reproof from the word will not need reproof from wrath.

(2) I was also saying[14] that a certain regret of God immediately seems unsuitable, since it was written, *I have regretted*[15] *that I annointed Saul as king*,[16] but inquire about the regret in a worthy way and do not suppose that his regret has some sort of relationship to the regret of those who have regretted. For as his word has something special, his anger has something[17] special, his wrath has something exceptional, and nothing in them is akin to words of the same sound. Likewise also his regret is a homonym to our regret. And a homonym is where the name alone is common, but its con-

---

8. This sentence remains unclear after all conjectures. Klostermann is probably correct in seeing a lacuna here. The difficulty lies in the mention of "beginning" twice in apparently different contexts or states. See the discussions of Nautin, 1:95, and Schadel, 328, n. 255.
9. Nautin notes here a small lacuna in S.
10. "No one"(οὔτινος). S has οὔντινος.
11. "While being," an addition of Klostermann.
12. "Itself" (ἑαυτόν), a correction of Nautin. S has ἑαυτῷ.
13. "It is" (ἐστί), a correction of Klostermann. S has εἶ.
14. "I was saying"(ἔλεγον), a correction of Ghisleri. S has ἔλεγχον.
15. "Regretted," not in LXX but in Hebrew.
16. 1 Kings 15.11.
17. "Something," an addition of Delarue.

cept,[18] according to the name of its substance, is other.[19] Thus only the name of a wrath of God and a *wrath* of anyone is common, and only an *anger* of anyone and the anger of God is common. So also with respect to regret it should be understood, and the one who is able will inquire: what does the regret of God accomplish? What has he accomplished? He deposed Saul who was ruling outside the Law, he set up a king for the people, one according to the heart of God. For he said through that good regret: *I have found a man according to my heart, David, son of Jesse.*[20]

(3) But all of these comments are for me a preface because the beginning of the reading from Jeremiah is expressed in this way: *You deceived me, and I was deceived.*[21]

2. For let us inquire whether, just as the wrath which is evil for all is perhaps the reproving work of God and the anger which is severe for all is perhaps what is called the educative work of God—and while the regret of all of us signifies weakness of reasoning of the person prior to the regret, for God his regret does not signify anything of God but the regret is taken for things outside him—we must understand that the deceit of God is of another kind from our deceit with which we deceive. What then is the deceit[22] of God of which the Prophet, after he understood, spoke, when he stopped being deceived, after he knew the benefit from the deception: *You deceived me, Lord, and I was deceived?*

(2) And first I will make use of the Hebrew tradition which has come to us by means of someone[23] who was fleeing on account of the faith of Christ and on account of having advanced beyond the Law,[24] and who had come where we live. Now he was saying something which appeared either a myth[25] or a discourse which could introduce those who hear

---

18. "Concept" (λόγος).  
19. Cf. Aristotle, *Categoriae* I.  
20. Ps 88.21; Acts 13.22.  
21. Jer 20.7.  
22. S here adds παρὰ τήν.  
23. The son of a rabbi to whom Origen refers in his *Letter to Africanus*, 7.  
24. "Law" (νόμος), a correction of Klostermann. S has λόγος.  
25. As Nautin, 2:256, n. 2, indicates, "myth" here is used in the Platonic sense, a story which reveals an idea of some inaccessible truth.

to *You deceived me, Lord, and I was deceived.* He was saying then something such as this: God does not tyrannize but rules, and when he rules, he does not coerce but encourages, and he wishes that those under him yield themselves willingly to his direction so that the good of someone may not be according to compulsion but according to his free will. This is what Paul with understanding was saying to Philemon in the Letter to Philemon concerning Onesimus: *So that your good be not according to compulsion, but according to free will.*[26] Thus the God of the universe could make what is supposed a good in us so that we would give alms from *compulsion* and we would be temperate from *compulsion,* but he has not wished this. Hence *not from reluctance or out of compulsion*[27] he enjoins us to do what we do, so that what occurs is from *free will.* In sum, God seeks a way, in a manner of speaking, whereby one[28] would want to do with *free will* what God wishes. The tradition then also was saying to me something like this: He wants to send Jeremiah who prophesies to all of the nations and before all of the nations to the people, but since[29] the prophecies have had something quite gloomy—for they imparted punishments with which each according to his deserts will be punished—and he knew the choice of the Prophet, who does not want to prophesy to the people Israel what is bad, for this reason he arranged to say: *Take this cup and make all the nations to whom I commissioned you drink.*[30] God then ordered Jeremiah to take the cup, but when he urged him in taking the *cup of unmixed wine,*[31] he says: "And I commission you to *all of the nations* with this *cup of unmixed wine."* But after Jeremiah heard that he was sent to *all of the nations*[32] as one who supplied them a cup of anger, a cup of punishments, since he did not guess that also Israel was about to drink from the cup of punishment, since he was de-

26. Philem 14.  27. 2 Cor 9.7.
28. "One" (τις), a correction of Ghisleri. S has τι.
29. "But since" (ἐπεὶ δέ), a correction of Ghisleri. S has ἐπειδή.
30. Jer 32.15 (25.15).  31. Jer 32.15.
32. After "nations" S adds ὅτι.

## HOMILY 20

ceived, he took the cup from which all of the nations drink. After he took the cup he heard: *And cause Jerusalem to drink first.*[33] Since then it seemed to be one way, and happened to him in another, for this reason he then said, *You deceived me, Lord, and I was deceived.*

(3) Note the resemblance also in this discussion to Isaiah. For that Prophet, who does not know what he will be ordered to say to the people, hears God say according to what is written, *Whom will I send and who will go to this people?* And he said in answer, *Behold, here I am, send me.* He hears, *Go and say to this people, "You will listen to the report, but you will not comprehend, and when seeing, you will not see and not perceive." For the heart of this people has grown dull,* and so on.[34] Since then he did not know what he would prophesy and that he would threaten such things to the people, he said, *Behold, here I*[35] *am, send me.* For this reason he said, in later passages, *the voice of one saying, "Cry,"*[36] and he did not respond as one willing to do what was ordered, but he said, *What will I cry?*[37] For he reacted cautiously lest again he hear something similar to the former prophecy, *Go and say to this people, You will listen to the report and you will comprehend.* Thus, *what will I cry? All flesh is grass and all its glory as a flower of grass,* and so forth.[38] In these words he heard nothing against Israel.

(4) That person[39] who delivered these things to us was speaking about *you deceived me and I was deceived.*

3. But I pray that what I receive from those who give I do not keep alone or bury *the talent in the earth*[40] of those who speak to me, nor return whatever useful *mina*[41] of those who teach *in a napkin,*[42] but make a gain from those lessons which

---

33. Jer 32.18.
34. Isa 6.8–10.
35. "I," an addition of Cordier.
36. Isa 40.6.
37. Isa 40.6.
38. Isa 40.6.
39. The person speaking from the Hebrew tradition. See above.
40. Matt 25.25.
41. A "mina" (μνᾶ) is a Greek monetary unit worth about one hundred drachmas.
42. Luke 19.20.

I receive from the one who grants them and who can deliver what is useful. I pray that I make the *mina* of a Gospel or of an Apostle or of a Prophet or of a Law many times greater. Then after I have heard these things, I examine for myself the statement, *You deceived me, Lord, and I was deceived,* and when I am examining I pray that I discover something true in regard to the passage.

(2) Perhaps then, as a father wishes to deceive a son in his own interest while he is still a boy, since he cannot be helped any other way unless the boy is deceived, as a healer makes it his business to deceive the patient who cannot be cured unless he receives words of deceit, so it is also for the God of the universe, since what is prescribed has to help the race of men. Let the healer say to the patient: "It is necessary that you have surgery, you must be cauterized, but you must suffer severely," and that patient would not continue. But sometimes he says another thing, and he hides that surgery, the cutting knife, under the sponge, and again he conceals, as I shall call it, under the honey the nature of the bitter and the annoying drug, wanting not to mislead but to heal the one who is cured.[43] With such remedies the whole divine Scripture is filled, and some of what is concealed is pleasant, but some of what is concealed is bitter. If you see a father who threatens as if he hates the son, and who says to the son frightful things and who does not show affection but who conceals love for the son, one knows that he wants to deceive the child. For it is not fitting for the son to be assured of the love of the father, the goodwill of his devotion. For he will be set free and will not be disciplined. That is why he hides the sweetness of the affection, and exhibits the bitterness of deceit.

(3) By analogy to the father and the healer, such is something of what God does. There are certain bitter things with which he cures the most righteous and wise. For it is necessary to punish every sinner for his sins. *Do not be misled, God is*

---

43. Cf. Plato, *Rep* 389b for this example of the surgeon.

## HOMILY 20

*not mocked,*[44] *neither the immoral nor the adulterer nor homosexual nor thief nor drunkard nor reviler nor robber will inherit the kingdom of God.*[45] If this was understood and viewed carefully by those who cannot see the surgical knife beneath the sponge, by those who are unable to understand[46] the bitter medicine beneath the honey, a person would become faint-hearted. For who among us has not been conscious of himself drinking without purpose and getting drunk? Who among us is pure from theft and from the desire to take what is necessary, not as one ought? But see what the Word says, *Do not be misled, for these persons will not inherit the kingdom of God.*[47] It is necessary that the mystery in this passage be concealed, so that most people may not become faint-hearted lest when learning the facts they may expect the final departure not as a rest but as a punishment. Or who will be found as Paul who can say, *It is better to depart and be with Christ.*[48] I cannot say this. For I know that if I leave, it is necessary that my *wood*[49] be burned in me, and I have reviler *wood*, and I have the *wood* of drunkenness, the *wood* of theft, and many other *woods* built up in my building.[50] You know that all of these things escape the notice of many of those who have believed, and it is good it escapes the notice. And each of us thinks, since[51] he has not been an idolater, since he has not been immoral—would that we were pure[52] in such areas—that after he has been set free from this life, he will be saved. We do not see that *all of us must appear before the judgment seat of Christ, so that each one may receive either good or evil according to what he has done in the body.*[53] We do not see what has been said: *You especially have I known out of all the tribes on the earth.*

---

44. Gal 6.7.
45. Cf. 1 Cor 6.9–10.
46. "To understand," an addition of Klostermann.
47. Gal 6.7; 1 Cor 6.10.
48. Cf. Phil 1.23.
49. Cf. 1 Cor 3.12.
50. Cf. *Hom in Jer* 2.3, 16.6.
51. "Since" (ἐπεί), a correction of Klostermann. S has ὅτι.
52. "Would that we were pure" (καθαρεύοιμεν), a correction of Cordier. S has καθαρεύωμεν.
53. 2 Cor 5.10.

*Therefore I will take vengeance upon you for all*—not just some and not others—*of your practices.*[54]

(4) So since the healer sometimes keeps hidden the surgical knife under the tender and soft sponge, and also the father conceals the affection through the appearance[55] of threat, and the deceits—some of which take away the tumors and varicose veins and whatever else weakens the condition of the body, the former removes the want of education and indolence—something then[56] such as this is what the Prophet has understood that God does in mystery, and he says, when he sees in what ways he was deceived for good reason by God, *You deceived me, Lord, and I was deceived.* It brought him to so great a grace that he prayed and said to God, "Deceive me, if this is beneficial."[57] For the deceit from God is one thing, the deceit from the Serpent another. See what the woman says to God, *The Serpent deceived me and I ate,*[58] and the deceit from the Serpent caused Adam and his woman to leave the Paradise of God. But the deceit which happened to the Prophet who said, *You have deceived me, and I was deceived,* brought him to a very great grace of prophecy, by increasing in him power, by bringing him maturity and by being able to serve the will of the Word of God without fearing man.

(5) Thus, when we also consider these things, both for the present and for the future,[59] let us also pray to be *deceived* by God, and let not the Serpent *deceive* us. And in another place there has been written something similar to this, for it

---

54. Amos 3.2.

55. "Appearance" (ἐμφάσεως), a correction of Klostermann. S has ἐμφράσεως.

56. "Then" (δή), a correction of Klostermann. S has δέ.

57. This translator, as well as Schadel, have translated as given in S. Nautin has expanded it as follows: "But the deceit which happens to the Prophet when he said, 'You deceived me, Lord, and I was deceived,' brought him to such a great grace of prophecy he prayed and said to God: 'Deceive me, if this is required.'"

58. Gen 3.13.

59. "For the future," an addition of Ghisleri.

is written in Isaiah, *For the Lord has mixed up for them a spirit of deviation.*[60] You know there also what the *spirit of deviation* does when *mixed* by God. But it is good that God has not given the *spirit of deviation* unmixed but, as the Prophet specified, *mixed* it.

4. I want to venture further and give an example of deceit helping. Due to this there are some who practice chastity and the most pure condition, and due to this others who practice monogamy, since they expect that he who has intercourse as if married is destroyed, he who remarries is destroyed. Let us distinguish among them what[61] is gained for the monogamist: that the one who remarries is *deceived* and supposes he is punished and is delivered to endless punishment so that monogamy and purity survive, or to know the truth and remarry? I suppose one is to say of every kind of person who sees the consequences that being pure is more blessed and that one should not remarry even when she is not *deceived*. And she should know that even the one who remarries shares in a certain sort of salvation, though surely not of such blessedness as great as the one who has been pure even though it is possible to remarry. But if one cannot do this, it is better to be *deceived* that those who remarry are destroyed and through the deceit to be pure than to recognize the truth and be in the lesser state, at the level of those who remarry. Some such idea you will find also for persons who practice chastity and complete purity, but many others can be found who are below us in the state of deceit and benefit us.

(2) For how many who are considered wise, when they discover the truth about punishment and therefore pass out of the state of deceit, have come to a worse life.[62] It would

---

60. Isa 19.14.
61. "What"(τί), a correction of Klostermann. S has ὅτι.
62. They come to a worse life because they learn the truth, that there is no physical punishment and the threats are a deceit. However, as Origen specifies in *Hom in Jer* 20.8–9, there are other non-physical kinds of punishments which are worse.

profit them to keep in mind, as they kept in mind formerly, *their worm will never die, their fire will not be quenched, they will be a spectacle for all flesh*,⁶³ and the *chaff will be burnt with an unquenchable fire*.⁶⁴ But if, when imagining something else beyond their first thought,⁶⁵ they tend to *presume upon the riches of the kindness and forebearance and patience of God*,⁶⁶ see if it is not truly because of this: since they supposed that they would not be deceived, they *stored up for themselves wrath in a day of wrath and of revelation and of God's righteous judgment*,⁶⁷ which they would not have *stored up* if they were deceived.

(3) These are thoughts regarding the deceit by God, since the Prophet said, *You deceived me, Lord, and I was deceived*.⁶⁸ But let us go on to the personal aspect regarding⁶⁹ *I was deceived*. Why did he not say only, *You have deceived me, Lord*, but has also added, *I was deceived*? One can at times think that someone strives for deceit, another guards himself from being deceived and is not deceived. But whenever a person strives to be deceived, and does not guard himself from being deceived but falls into deceit, he could say: *You deceived me, Lord, and I was deceived*. But since I also am concerned with the context, I should say something such as this: What if the Serpent speaks to me, even if he speaks a truth to me or even if he wants to deceive me, I should be suspicious of his words since I am sure that whether he deceives or tells the truth, he traps me. For his truth also entraps. There arises no benefit from the Serpent, since *an evil tree cannot bear good fruit*.⁷⁰ But if God speaks to me and I am confident that God is the one who speaks, I am prepared to commit myself. If he speaks the truth, I receive it. If he wishes to deceive me, I am deceived willingly, let God alone deceive me. And since I am

---

63. Isa 66.24.   64. Cf. Matt 3.12.
65. "Thought" (ἔννοιαν), a correction of Diels. S has "in which" (ἐν οἷς) here.
66. Cf. Rom 2.4.   67. Cf. Rom 2.5.
68. Jer 20.7.
69. "Regarding" (εἰς), an addition of Koetschau.
70. Cf. Matt 7.18.

committing myself, confident that God is the one who speaks and deceives, I also am not wasting my time, for I do not want[71] to be deceived by another but to be deceived by God. That is why I say not only that you have made the deception, but that I have also experienced the deception by you, and in accordance with this I say that *you have deceived me, Lord, and I was deceived.*

(4) But what follows after the matter concerning God deceiving and man as the one deceived? *You were strong and prevailed.*[72] He *is strong* over me then if he deceives me at my beginnings while still a youth in Christ, and since he *is strong* he can *prevail.* But if he has not been *strong,*[73] then I have need of pains. *You were strong and prevailed.*

5. Next he says after these words: *I have become a laughingstock, every day I am continually mocked.*[74] And concerning this passage I hear this: Jeremiah arose in a time of great sinners—the Captivity, in fact, happened near his time—and so there were sinners that mocked and laughed and scoffed whenever the Prophet was saying the prophetic prologue, *Thus says the Lord.* But since[75] those who hear were laughing and mocking the things said, he who was *deceived* and was helped from deceit is on guard to say, *Thus says the Lord.* As a result he who wants to deceive to bring benefit from the deceiving was also saying: I will say my own words to you, since you do not hear the words of the Lord. Thus those words were put forward to the hearers as words of Jeremiah and they were hearing words of God. But he who hands down the passage to me was saying these things to me when he examined the prologue and the beginnings of the prophecies. It is moreover also a beginning of the prophecy of Jeremiah before you, as the Septuagint hands it down, though it con-

---

71. "For I do not want" (θέλων), a correction of Klostermann. S has θέλω.
72. Jer 20.7.
73. "He is strong" (κρατήσῃ), a correction of Blass, Koetschau, and Klostermann. S has κρατήσῃς.
74. Jer 20.7.
75. "But since," an addition of Nautin.

siders something which I do not know: *The word of God which came to Jeremiah, the son of Chelkias from the priests.*[76] But in the Hebrew text and in the remaining manuscripts, it is rendered: *words of Jeremiah, son of Chelkias,* and all have agreed to the statement, *the words of Jeremiah, son of Chelkias.* Why then *words of Jeremiah?* Because the prologue for him was, in speaking to those who do not want to hear: "Hear my words."

(2) When such opportunities arise for us, when there appears an advantage for us, we also do it. Sometimes we preface our words to those[77] from the pagan nations when we want to introduce them to the Faith, and if we see that they have set themselves at variance with Christianity and abhor the name and hate to hear that this is the doctrine[78] of the Christians, we pretend to say that it is a useful doctrine not of the Christians. But when that doctrine is prepared by us according to our power, and we seem to captivate[79] the hearer who has not heard, as it happens, what was actually[80] said, then we admit that this praiseworthy doctrine was the doctrine of Christians and we accomplish something similar to the one who no longer said, *Thus says the Lord,* but, "Hear the words of me, Jeremiah."

(3) These statements concern the statement, *I have become a laughingstock.* And are we displeased if, while we are speaking, we are laughed at, where such a man as Jeremiah says, *I have become a laughingstock, every day I am continually mocked?* Why do I say Jeremiah? My Jesus also was mocked, for he said, *The Pharisees, who were lovers of money, heard all this, and they mocked him.*[81] But *the Lord mocked*[82] all of those who *mocked* the words of God.

(4) *I have become a laughingstock.* Behold in what way the

---

76. Jer 1.1.
77. "To those," an addition of Klostermann.
78. λόγος.
79. "Captivate" (αἱρεῖν), a correction of Ghisleri. S has ἐρεῖν.
80. "Actually," my addition.   81. Luke 16.14.
82. Ps 2.4.

Prophets lived their lives, how by being ridiculed, how by taking grave risks and by being cast down and stoned by the people, by being carried off, hated, banished, they also suffered and endured all things,[83] so that by *seeking* according to the will of God *the glory which comes from One only*,[84] by proclaiming the word, they would reach the end which is from God.[85]

(5) *One who is continually being mocked every day* is an accusation against those of that generation that the Prophet was not done being *mocked* for a few days, but every day he was continually *mocked*.

6. *For with my bitter word I will laugh.*[86] Laughter is a promise, a promise for which the patriarch Isaac was named. For his name translates as laughter.[87] But that a promise is laughter is evident from the text, *Blessed are those who now weep*, and the promise that *they will laugh*.[88] Just as it is a promise, *The sons of God will be called*,[89] and, *They shall see God*,[90] and *They shall inherit the earth*,[91] and *Theirs is the kingdom of heaven*,[92] so is laughter a promise to which the *weeping* which is *blessed* is the opposite. Yet inquire, in light of one or the other view, whether the *weeping* which is *blessed* accords with the good laughter, or whether the other weeping which is miserable, which is held in reserve for the contrary, is opposite to it. For, *woe on those who laugh now, for they shall mourn and cry*.[93] For the one is *weeping* which is *blessed*, the other is held in reserve for those who have lived in an evil way. And if that sort of weeping has some useful end, I do not know.

(2) Why do I speak? Hear Paul. When he taught, he made it his business in speaking that hearers were in pain, and he confesses that he especially rejoices whenever a person is in pain from him. For he said, *And who is there to make me glad*

---

83. "All things" (πάντα), a correction of Ghisleri. S has πάνυ.
84. John 5.44.
85. Cf. *Hom in Jer* 14.14, 15.1.
86. Jer 20.8.
87. Cf. Gen 21.1–7.
88. Luke 6.21.
89. Matt 5.9.
90. Matt 5.8.
91. Matt 5.5.
92. Matt 5.3.
93. Luke 6.25.

*but the one I have pained?*⁹⁴ And if a person is competent to move a soul of a hearer, especially one who has sinned, he prays to say such words, words which, when announced from their power and placement and divinity and sacred thoughts, will shake up the soul of the hearer and move⁹⁵ it to mourning and to weeping and to tears, so that the one who speaks rejoices whenever he sees the hall pleased and filled with what has been said. For where he *leads* to promises as through a *narrow and hard way* which is *in pain* to *life,*⁹⁶ he also leads through weeping to the laughter which is *blessed.* But when he does not accomplish this task, I am afraid he may say such words: *Woe on you who now laugh, for you will mourn and weep.*⁹⁷

(3) But why do I say this except in wanting to allude to what he says, *I will laugh with my bitter word,*⁹⁸ and to present a laughter of weeping and that weeping which those here who laugh weep, since God perhaps has made it his business to engender weeping in them?⁹⁹ For *there will be weeping and gnashing of teeth there,*¹⁰⁰ and God has made this his business since he sees that he who cries for his own sins, he who laments for his own transgressions, already has come to a perception of his own evils. Would that each of us for every sin would say, *Each night I will wash my couch, with my tears I will water my mattress.*¹⁰¹ Oh that each of us would speak for his own sins and cry, *My tears have become bread for me day and night!*¹⁰² If *my word* is more *bitter* here, and more *bitter* because I am afflicted through it, the hearers are disgusted. Whenever those who are reproved find oppressive the speaker I know that for my *bitter word* the end is to laugh, yet to laugh

---

94. 2 Cor 2.2.
95. "Will move" (κινήσουσιν), a correction of Klostermann. S has κινοῦσιν.
96. Cf. Matt 7.14.      97. Jer 20.8.
98. Jer 20.8.

99. Nautin, 2:279, n. 1, indicates that Origen alludes to an eventual salvation of the damned through purifying "weeping." In the context, this is a warranted assumption.

100. Matt 8.12.      101. Ps 6.7(6).
102. Ps 41.3(4).

as the laughter of the *blessed*. And perhaps the Prophet who has seen this said, *For I will laugh with my bitter word*. Already it is *with a bitter word* but not yet do I *laugh*, but *I will laugh with my bitter word*.

7. *I will call upon faithlessness and misery*.[103] The just *call upon* God, the unjust *call upon* Wisdom also. *For it will happen*, he said, *whenever you will call upon me I will not respond to you*[104]—the unjust at that point, but it is evident that the just call upon Wisdom sometimes—and *every one if he calls upon the name of the Lord will be saved*.[105] But here the Prophet said, *I will call upon faithlessness and misery*. Just as one calls upon God,[106] so will I call upon *faithlessness;* as one calls upon the Lord, so will I call upon *misery*. Is it something good Jeremiah *calls upon,* that he announces in saying, *I will call upon faithlessness and misery?* But it is necessary to consider the agreements which we make and their *faithlessness*, for agreements can be made sometimes in an evil way, and after making an agreement in an evil way, then indeed we *call upon faithlessness*. And so also if I consider the *wide and easy* way *which leads to destruction*[107] and that after going the way on it I will not be miserable, I change from the *wide and easy way* and come to the *narrow* and *hard*.[108] And when I am miserable, I say, *I will call upon misery*.

(2) I will show *faithlessness* in the agreements with the world and worldly matters so that I raise up heavenly agreements: *I will call upon faithlessness*. So also when I leave behind the life of the *wide and easy way*, and come to the *narrow* and *hard* so that I become as *miserable* as Paul,[109] I say:[110] *I will call upon misery*. For not every man will say, *Miserable man that I am. Who will deliver me from this body of death?*[111] But the person who has understood the *body of death*, who wants to

---

103. Jer 20.8.      104. Prov 1.28.
105. Joel 2.32.
106. "God" (θεόν), a correction of the Vatican manuscript. S has θεῶ.
107. Cf. Matt 7.13.      108. Cf. Matt 7.14.
109. Rom 7.24.
110. "I say" (λέγω), a correction of Delarue. S has λέγων.
111. Cf. Rom 7.24.

be *delivered* from the *body of death,* will say, *Miserable man that I am.* But the person, one of the masses, who indulges the body, who is faithless to the future age, does not say, *Miserable man that I am,* but he considers himself happy that he is a man and for being in the *body of death.* If I can therefore understand how Paul said, *Miserable man that I am,* though not as yet *calling upon misery,* I will *call upon* it from a lack of faith in the agreements with evil and I will say as Jeremiah, *I will call upon faithlessness and misery.* For he did not say: "I will call upon a faithlessness of God."

(3) I want to give an example from Scripture of a righteous lack of faith in an agreement in order to demonstrate that man can *call upon faithlessness* in act. Judith made an agreement with Holophernes that though she would leave for a certain number of days to pray to God, she also would present herself after these days at the marriage bed of Holophernes. Holophernes accepted the agreement. He freed Judith for her prayers outside the camp. What was it necessary that Judith do? To keep her agreement or show lack of faith in it? It is admitted that she showed lack of faith. For it was for God a blessed act to show *faithlessness* with Holophernes. Judith intended[112] to be faithless to the agreement with Holophernes, to say, *I call upon faithlessness.*[113] And so he *calls upon faithlessness.*

(4) It is fitting also that I be such a person in order that I say, *I call upon faithlessness;* and I *call upon faithlessness* with the Serpent, with the Devil. The Serpent once made an agreement with Eve. She was friendly to him and the Serpent to the woman, but God made it his business since he is good to destroy this agreement and to break up this evil friendship. And as the good God he says, *I will put emnity between you and between the woman, and between your seed and between her seed.*[114] Thus we should prudently listen how God makes an *enmity* with such a one, in order that he might make a friendship

---

112. "Intended," an addition of Klostermann.
113. Cf. Jth 12.6–7, 14.    114. Gen 3.15.

with Christ. For it is not possible to be friend at the same time with opposites, and just as *no one can serve two masters,* so no one can be a friend *to God* and *to mammon*,[115] a friend both to Christ and to the Serpent. But it must happen that to make a friendship with Christ is to make an *enmity* with the Serpent, and to generate a friendship with the Serpent is to generate an enmity with Christ.

(5) *I call upon faithlessness and misery.*[116] And in order that you will better understand *I call upon misery,* I will describe something[117] which happens with ascetics. For though to marry and not to have the concern of the flesh *revolting against the spirit*[118] oftentimes is an alternative, one prefers not to make use of the freedom to marry, but to be *miserable* and distressed, to *mortify* the body with fasts and *subdue* it[119] with *abstinence* from certain *foods*,[120] and in every way to *put to death the deeds of the body with the spirit.*[121] Does such a person not then *call upon misery,* since he is allowed to surrender himself to nourishment and pleasure and not to *call upon misery?* If a person then can imitate the Prophet, let him *call upon faithlessness* as we discussed, but also let him *call upon misery* through ascetical practices. And the history also concerning Jeremiah happens to be true, that he too lived in chastity. For the Lord said to him: *Do not take a wife, do not ever make children.*[122] And he lived in chastity. For he *called upon faithlessness and misery.*

8. *For the word of the Lord has become for me a reproach.*[123] Blessed Jeremiah, he who has no other *reproach* than *the word of the Lord.* But we who are wretched have *reproaches* not because of *the word of the Lord,* but because of our sins. We are reproached in what we fail and have failed, we are reviled for our evils. But the Savior does not want to reproach us with these sorts of reproaches when he says, *Blessed are you when*

---

115. Matt 6.24.  
116. Jer 20.8.  
117. "Something" (τι), a correction of Klostermann. S has ὅτι.  
118. Cf. Gal 5.17.  
119. Cf. 1 Cor 9.27.  
120. Cf. 1 Tim 4.3.  
121. Cf. Rom 8.13.  
122. Cf. Jer 16.1–2.  
123. Jer 20.8.

*they reproach you and persecute and speak every evil word against you for my sake.*[124] *Rejoice in that day and leap for joy.*[125]

(2) *The word of the Lord* then, he says, *has become a reproach and a mockery every day.*[126] One must then consider that the Prophets were men of good sense and not those who hide their personal sins as we do, and who do not speak just about those at that time but for those of all of the generations, if they have sinned. And I also hesitate to admit my sins before the few here, since those who hear will condemn me. But Jeremiah, after suffering something sinful, was not afraid, but recorded his sin. For it was a sin which was pronounced in the text: *Then I said, "I will never name the name of the Lord, and I nevermore will speak his name."* You were taught[127] to do *all things in the name of the Lord,*[128] to act in the *name of the Lord.* But you say, *I will never name the name of the Lord?* But what sort of *name* do you intend to *name? You will not mention in your hearts the names of other gods,*[129] and you say, *I will never name the name of the Lord, and I will never speak anymore for his name.* He speaks then as one who has suffered something inevitable for man, what we also take the risk to suffer often. And especially once someone has realized that because of the teaching and the word he has been in *misery* and suffered and hated, he often says: "I will withdraw, why remain in these circumstances? If I am also[130] in these circumstances from this, from teaching, from uttering the word, why should I not withdraw to the desert and peace?" The Prophet also has suffered something such as this when he says, *And I say, "I will never name the name of the Lord and I will never speak anymore for his name."*

(3) But it is a good Lord who after this prevents such sins of so great people. He did not allow the Prophet to speak truly when he spoke the foregoing, but in this he has also

---

124. Matt 5.11.  
125. Luke 6.23.  
126. Jer 20.8.  
127. "You were taught," a correction of Ghisleri. S has "he was taught."  
128. Cf. Col 3.17.  
129. Exod 23.13.  
130. "Also" (κἄν), a correction of Diels and Klostermann. S has καί.

## HOMILY 20

made Jeremiah to *call upon faithlessness,* and to be faithless to what was said. For he said, *I will never name the name of the Lord, and I will never speak anymore regarding his name.* But he said, *it arose in my heart as a burning fire, flaming in my bones, and I could feel it from all sides, and I could not bear it.*[131] The word of the Lord *arose burning* his *heart: And it arose in my heart as a flaming fire, burning in my bones.* He rejected[132] the sin which he had made when he said, *I will never name the name of the Lord, and I will never speak anymore about his name.* And Jeremiah rejected[133] the sin at the same time in the act of speaking. Would that I also, at the same time I sin and speak a sinful word, I would feel that a *fire arose* in my *heart burning* and *flaming* up so that I could not *bear* it.

(4) The Word intends to be daring here, but I do not know for what sort of audience it is fitting. He has said that there is a certain form of *fire,* an imperceptible fire, which punishes the one who is punished in the pain[134] which he cannot *bear.* For he said, *It arose in my heart as a flaming fire,* and *burning* not in *my heart* alone but also *in my bones, and it was present on all sides and I could not bear it.*[135] I fear that such is what awaits us, a *fire* which *arises* as it *arose* in the *heart* of Jeremiah, but we have not suffered it. If we had suffered this, and the two fires are set forth, this *fire* and the external fire which we see upon those who are burned by the governors of the nations, we would prefer that fire to this. For the former burns the surface, but the latter burns the *heart,* and what begins from the *heart* reaches to all the *bones,* and what reaches the *bones* comes to where the whole man is burned, and it comes in such a way that he cannot *bear* the *burning.* Who regarding this fire[136] can say, *I cannot bear it?* I know robbers who are able to endure this *fire,* the pain which is[137] from

---

131. Jer 20.9.
132. "Rejected" (ἀπέβαλε), a correction of Blass. S has ὑπέβαλε.
133. See previous note.
134. "In the pain" (τῷ πόνῳ), a correction of Klostermann. S has τοῦ πόνου.
135. Jer 20.9.  136. The sensuous fire.
137. "Which is," an addition of Blass and Klostermann.

this fire. The pain from the fire which Jeremiah has described is of a different sort; he says, *And it arose in my heart as a burning fire, flaming in my bones, and it spread everywhere and I could not bear it.* That is the *fire* the Savior kindles when he says, *I came to cast fire on the earth,*[138] and since the Savior kindles that *fire*, therefore he begins by a *fire* in those who begin to hear him and he first *casts fire upon* their *heart*. This is what Simon and Cleopas confess when they speak about his words: *Were not our hearts burning on the way while he opened up the Scriptures to us?*[139] Hence, the *hearts* of Simon and Cleopas *burn* with *fire*. Hear them speaking: *Were not our hearts burning?*

9. Who is already worthy to receive that *fire in the heart* in order that he might not receive it there? I want to describe the person who has this *fire in the heart*. I will describe two persons who have sinned the same sin generically—the abominable, the unclean fornication—and between these two who have fornicated, the one is not aggrieved nor feels pain nor is vexed, but experiences what was said in Proverbs concerning the adulterous woman *who having washed herself, if she does something, says she has done nothing wrong.*[140] See with me the other who after the mistake is unable to contain himself, but punishes the conscience, tortures the *heart*, is unable to eat and drink, who fasts not because of a judgment but because of grief of repentance. I will describe him as the kind of person who *appears sad all day long* and who wears himself down with suffering and who goes *wailing from the groaning of his heart,* who sees his sin reproved *before himself* on account of all which happened before.[141] And see that this sort of person punishes himself not only for one day nor one night but for a long time. Who do you say has hope before God? Is it that first person who has fornicated and does not care but *is callous* and also has hardened himself just as one who has *given himself up to licentiousness?*[142] Or is it this latter

138. Luke 12.49.
140. Prov 24.55 (30.20).
142. Cf. Eph 4.19.

139. Luke 24.32.
141. Cf. Ps 37.7, 9–10.

## HOMILY 20

person who after one sin goes into mourning, lamenting it? (2) This latter . . . [143] is with hopes. The more such a one *is burnt* by the *fire* of grief, the more he is shown mercy, and there is for him such sufficient time for punishment, as there is a time of punishment given to that person who fornicated and was grieved.[144] And since a time of punishment for this person is advantageous here, on account of this he has taken the trouble to punish the one who has fornicated, and when he has punished him with pain and seen sufficient pain, he says: *Lest such a person is overwhelmed with excessive pain, reaffirm love for him.*[145]

(3) Let each examine his own conscience and see in what way he has sinned, for he must be punished. Let each pray to God that this *fire* in Jeremiah comes to himself, then what came to Simon and Cleopas, so that he might not be kept for the other fire. For if he has never received the fire here but has also sinned and been unconcerned, he will be kept for that other fire.[146]

(4) *And there arose in my heart as it were a burning fire, flaming in my bones, and I faced it from all sides and I could not bear it, for I heard the reproach of many who gathered around me.*[147] O blameless, O blessed Jeremiah—excepting, I would say, this little sin and if he has done some other little one—reproached by *many*, but the *reproach* by[148] *many* was for him a hymn before God. For those who reproach were saying, *You conspire and we, all of his friends, conspire. Watch his intention and he will be deceived.*[149] They planned another deceit to deceive him mortally, one opposite to the deceit about which he said, *You deceived me, Lord, and I was deceived.*[150] But those who *conspire* against him say, *And we shall prevail against him, and we will take our vengeance on him.*[151] Those who were re-

---

143. Text seems to be missing here.
144. Cf. 2 Cor 2.5ff.
145. Cf. 2 Cor 2.7–8.
146. Cf. *Hom in Jer* 6.2.
147. Jer 20.9–10.
148. "By" (ὑπό), a correction of Ghisleri. S has ἐπί.
149. Jer 20.10.
150. Jer 20.7.
151. Jer 20.10.

proved for their own sins think that they were wronged, and because of this those who have thought they were wronged say, *We will take out our vengeance on him.* Those who *sawed* Isaiah *in two* also acted for some sort of reason as this.[152] For it is as ones who are wronged, after the prophecies were converting them and punishing them, were reproving, censuring, they *sawed* him *in two* and condemned him with a deadly decree.

(5) But Jeremiah said to those who *conspired: And the Lord is with me truly as a mighty man of war.*[153] If we become the sort of persons we need to be and we receive for our sins that *fire* which comes just as it came to Jeremiah and to similar persons, the Lord becomes after these events with us *truly a mighty man of war.* And *because of this they persecuted and could not comprehend,*[154] for the Lord was with the persecuted one, and the persecuted one could not be made subject to them. Perhaps then, as many things of Jeremiah refer to the Savior, can this not also be such? For, *You conspire and let us conspire against him,* is said also regarding the Savior, and the *Lord was with them truly as a mighty man of war.* That is why they, the Jews, the ones who persecuted him, *persecuted and could not comprehend; they were greatly confounded and did not comprehend their own dishonor.*[155] They who are dishonored in such a time do not speak of their sins, *which down through the ages will not be forgotten,* but they suppose[156] that their transgressions will be *forgotten* in this age. But let us realize that *down through the ages* their transgressions *will not be forgotten,* and when we realize this, let us recall the statement, *Do not become proud, but stand in awe. For if God did not spare the natural branches,* how much more *will he not spare* those who are contrary to the natural.[157]

---

152. Cf. Heb 11.37. Cf. *Ascens Is* 5.11–14.
153. Jer 20.11.
154. Jer 20.11. Here S adds text repeated below: "the Jews, the ones ... their sins." Removed by Klostermann and Nautin.
155. Jer 20.11.
156. "Suppose" (οἴονται), a correction of Ghisleri. S has οἶον.
157. Rom 11.20–21.

(6) *Lord*, then, *of the powers* is with us *testing what is just, understanding minds and hearts*.[158] The Lord *tests what is just* and he finds unworthy to *test* what is unjust, and is, shall I say, a banker of what is just and unjust.[159] But this Lord is one *who understands minds and hearts*. Here it is then written that he is one *understanding minds and hearts*. I seek what distinguishes the act to *understand minds and hearts*. And perhaps it is one thing to *understand minds and hearts* and another to *examine hearts and minds*.[160] He does not *examine the hearts and minds* of everyone, but of those who have sinned. For I understand—in what is signified by *to examine*—what is said in this life to those who are being put to the test. In the law-courts some[161] examine and some are examined, some also are in very grievous pains. Some punishers then examine sides, they examine bodies. But the Lord alone has a new way of examining. For he is one who examines *hearts*, and in the Lord alone there arises the *examining* of *hearts and minds*. Here the sides of thieves are examined according to a command of a governor, but there it is not from a command of God but by the Lord himself one is examined in *minds and hearts*—perhaps I say here that the one who is given command is the Son, but that the one who commands is the Father, and the Word is the one who examines *hearts and minds*. And I suppose that whenever he examines both *hearts and minds* the more grievous ones of all of the tests, of all of the pains, are those from the Word.

(7) Thus, let us do everything so that we might not be delivered over to that examination. Concerning which examination, I think that the worst to suffer are those who are delivered over to those mentioned in the Gospel as *torturers*.[162] For they are delivered over to many, perhaps to greater, tortures at the beginning, being not yet worthy to be delivered over to the Word who examines *hearts and minds*. The rich

---

158. Jer 20.12.  159. Cf. *Hom in Jer* 12.7.
160. Cf. Ps 7.10.
161. "Some," an addition of Klostermann and Cordier.
162. Matt 18.24.

man was that person not yet worthy to be delivered to him who *examines hearts and minds*. On account of this, he was tortured by more;[163] whether in the future that man does suffer this or not, let the one who is able examine. Nevertheless the things which await us for our sins are the *torturers* and he who examines *hearts and minds;* concerning which sins, if we do not get rid of them more quickly, we will be in these tortures. Hence after we rise up let us ask for the help from God, so we might be blessed in Christ Jesus, *to whom is the glory for the ages. Amen.*[164]

163. Cf. Luke 16.19, 28.
164. 1 Pet 4.11.

## HOMILY 27 (50)

*Jeremiah 27.23–29 (50.23–29)*

*(from Jerome's Latin translation)*

*On what was written, "How was the hammer of the whole earth broken and crushed? How was Babylon brought to destruction?" up to the place where it says: "Render to her according to her works; and do to her all that she has done, for she has stood up against the Lord God the Holy One of Israel."*

NOW, HE SAYS, *was the hammer of the whole earth broken and crushed? How was Babylon brought to destruction?*[1] One needs to inquire here who is the *hammer of all the earth* or in what way its brokenness is prophesied, since it was *broken* before it was *crushed,* so that after bringing together what has been written elsewhere about the *hammer,* when we find its name, we will also investigate the meaning of the name from these examples that we have brought forth.[2]

(2) At one time there was constructed a *house of God,* according to the third book of Kings,[3] and it was Solomon who built and erected it; and it was said here, as if in praise, about the *house of God,* that *hammer and axe were not heard in the house of God.*[4] Therefore as the *hammer is not heard in the house of God,* since the *house of God* is the Church, so the *hammer is not heard* in the Church. Who is this *hammer* who wants to obstruct, insofar as he can, the stones for building the Temple, so that, *broken,* they are not suited for its foundations. See with me if the Devil is not the *hammer of the whole earth.*

1. Jer 27.23.
2. On what follows, compare Fragment 30.
3. 3 Kings 6.1.   4. 3 Kings 6.7.

245

(3) I will also proclaim confidently that there is someone who cannot be affected very much by the *hammer of the whole earth*. And since the example was offered of a perceptible *hammer*, I will seek a material stronger than the *hammer* which does not feel the blows from it. In searching for it I find it too in what was written: *Behold a man standing above the adamant walls, and in his hand adamant.*[5] History records about *adamant* that it is stronger than every *hammer* striking it, remaining unbroken and unyielding. Even if the *hammer*, the Devil, stands above and the Serpent, who *as an indomitable anvil*,[6] may position himself below, still *adamant* endures nothing when resting *in the hand of the Lord* and in his regard. Thus the two opposites to this *adamant* are the *hammer* and the immovable *anvil*. Yet there is indeed among the nations a much-used proverb in the common language concerning those who are pressed by anxieties and extremely bad situations; they say: "They are 'between a hammer and an anvil.'" Still you can say that this refers to the Devil and the Serpent, who are always signified by names of this sort in the Scriptures for a variety of purposes. And you can say that the holy man, who is as an *adamant wall* or is *adamant in the hand of the Lord*, is not affected either by the *hammer* or by the *anvil*, but the more he is struck, the brighter will his virtue shine. They say that gem merchants, when they want to test adamant, since they are unaware whether it is adamant or not until it comes into contact with the hammer and the anvil, are indeed then persuaded that it is the most genuine adamant if the rock survives unscratched between the anvil and the hammer, if when the hammer strikes it from above and the anvil is placed below, the harder nature of the rock is unmarked. Such is a holy man before temptations. By those who do not know how to test rocks he is unknown; only God knows for certain the nature of the *adamant* rocks which is unknown by most. I myself do not know as yet whether with a *hammer* coming and hitting me I

5. Amos 7.7. 6. Job 41.15.

will be *broken* and *crushed,* smashed because I may not be *adamant.* Or will I certainly appear as true *adamant,* if with the attacks of persecutions, dangers, temptations I am not so much *broken* by the blows of the *hammer* as tested?

(4) And you yourself, go through the Scriptures and see if you are able to find an indication by God that he has promised that the *hammer* strikes one who ought [not][7] to be struck. I will offer an example, for to understand obscure passages, examples are employed. If there were not the *hammer,* there would not also be the *stretched out trumpet,*[8] which summons to the *feasts* of God in accord with the Law, which rouses up *to war* the souls of listeners by *its sound.*[9] A hammer is necessary to make the *stretched out trumpet.* That *hammer* has contributed very much to the stretched out *trumpet* Paul, that it may draw him through a variety of temptations and confirm him, that he can be hammered out and take on for listeners a form of a loud trumpet that does not give *an indistinct sound,* so that they are *made ready for battle.*[10]

(5) And since it is discovered that the opposing might is a *hammer* and the Serpent is an *indomitable*[11] anvil, whenever in the Scriptures I associate a name with *hammer* formed from [*bronze*][12] or any other material, I pursue the expression: Cain produced sons and from Cain arose[13] *the forger of bronze and iron.*[14] Therefore just as the Devil, who is the worker of all temptations, is called the *hammer,* he who serves him is a hammerer, the son of Cain. On every occasion you fall into temptation, I know that the *hammer* is the Devil and the hammerer he through whom the Devil pursued you. Hence in the betrayal of the Savior, the *hammer* is the Devil, the hammerer was Judas. And many were hammerers in that time in

---

7. "Not," I have added.      8. Num 10.1.
9. Num 10.9–10.      10. 1 Cor 14.8.
11. "Indomitable" (*improducibilis*), a correction of Nautin. Baehrens has *producibilis.*
12. Nautin inserts here "bronze" (*aereus*).
13. Nautin adds here "the hammerer."
14. Gen 4.22.

which the Lord suffered, when they cried out, *Take away, take away*[15] such a man from the earth; *crucify, crucify him*.[16] All are filled with *hammerers*. For whoever looks up to the Devil in his act and serves him to order to approve what is unjust and confound the just, all are *hammerers*. For that reason even if yersterday you were a *hammerer* and hold in your hand a *hammer*, now you learn that *hammerers* originate from Cain, the fratricide. Get rid of the *hammer* from your hand and pass over to a better *generation*,[17] which is spiritual, that of Seth, Enos, and the rest, who are proclaimed in the Scriptures with praises.[18]

(6) Nonetheless the end of the *hammer* is *brokenness* and *crushing*. One certainly needs to know that the Devil, declared by the Prophet to be the *hammer*, is not the *hammer* over a certain part of the earth but over the *whole earth*. And one needs to take the *whole earth* literally, since over every part of the earth his malice is spread and everywhere the *hammer* works evil. However, it must also be said that the Devil is *the hammer of the whole earth*, not the *hammer* of heaven; for the *hammer* is not fitting for fine substance, but for what is dense. If *you carry the image of the earthly*,[19] the *hammer* strikes you because you are *earthly*. If you sin and *you are earth and go to the earth*,[20] you experience the *hammer of the whole earth* working also in you.

(7) According to this interpretation, one needs to consider also that the *hammer of the whole earth* is the Devil because he uses his power against all earthly things. But one can understand that there is a lesser *hammer*, which is not the *hammer of the whole earth*, but of this or that part, if I may say, of the earth. And indeed when some opposing strength fights in me and struggles with me, yet not able to contend at the same time with the whole human race, like the Devil, then it is indeed the *hammer* in me but not the *hammer of the whole earth*, but yet the *hammer* in some sense of my *earth* alone.

15. John 19.15.
17. Gen 5.1.
19. 1 Cor 15.49.

16. Luke 23.21.
18. Cf. Gen 5.6ff.
20. Cf. Gen 3.19.

And since the *hammer of the whole earth* has been *broken and crushed*, what ought to be thought concerning the *hammer* of part of the *earth*? And likewise I think it worthy of amazement that the *hammer of the whole earth* has been smashed. For what is great if the *hammer* of part of the *earth* has been *broken* and *crushed*? But it is truly amazing that *the hammer of the whole earth* has been *broken and crushed*.

2. After this I seek who is the one who has *broken and crushed the hammer of the whole earth*, and I say that Moses could not have *broken and crushed the hammer of the whole earth*, nor before him Abraham nor after him Joshua nor any other of the Prophets. Who then could have *broken and crushed* so great a thing as the *hammer of the whole earth*? Who is this? Jesus Christ *broke and crushed the hammer of the whole earth*. And it is now in admiration that the Prophet says in the Holy Spirit: *How was the hammer of the whole earth broken and crushed?* First it was *broken*, then it was *crushed*. And since I have found that it is the Savior who has *broken and crushed the hammer of the whole earth*, I come to the Gospel and I observe his first temptation when the Devil said to him, *I will give all these things to you if you will fall down and worship me*, etc.[21] And I can say that in that time Jesus did not *crush the hammer of the whole earth*, but he *broke* it to an extent. When indeed *he departed from him until an opportune hour*,[22] and later came at the moment of the *opportune hour*, then *the hammer of the whole earth was crushed*, not only *broken*, as it was at first. And because *the hammer of the whole earth* was *crushed* which before had been *broken*, for that reason also it is *broken* through each of us when we are introduced in the Church and advance along to faith, yet it is *crushed* and crumbled when we will come to maturity. If you doubt who can *crush* the Devil to bring us to maturity, hear the Apostle blessing the just man with a blessing and saying: *May God quickly crush Satan under your feet.*[23] That *hammer* is one with soul; perhaps it is now furious

21. Matt 4.9.
22. Luke 4.13.
23. Rom 16.20.

against us. Because we make this known about it and it is *crushed* by us—for it was not just *broken* but also *crushed* through us—it seeks to *break and crush* us in retaliation. And it *crushes* many indeed, those who do not attend to themselves nor *guard their heart with all watchfulness*.[24] Since we truly trust in God, believe in Christ, the Son of God, let us not fear the Devil. Fear of God makes us fearless of the Devil, of anything suffered at his hands. But to speak not only generally but about our own selves: *How was the hammer of the whole earth broken and crushed?*

(2) After it was *broken* and crumbled, *Babylon came to destruction*. The city of Confusion is not scattered before *the hammer of the whole earth is broken and crushed*. Consider also the excellent order the Prophet has admirably used when he says, *How was the hammer of the whole earth broken and crushed? How was Babylon brought to destruction?* What was done first, he recorded first; what was second, he revealed subsequently. And it is necessary to observe this through each of the words of Scripture.

(3) When then does *Babylon* come to destruction? When every confusion of my soul is annihilated and the death of a son or a spouse no longer troubles me, when there is no one who can disturb me and provoke me to mourning, to anger, to concupiscence, to pleasure, when I remain unconfused by attending to the reason which steadies and controls me; then occurs in me what was said: *Babylon*, that is, complete confusion, *has been brought to destruction*.

(4) Now these things happen—that is, *the hammer of the whole earth* is *broken* and *crushed* and *Babylon* demolished—when the nations *are set over the hammer and Babylon*. For it was written: *In the nations are those who are set over you*,[25] that is, those who are from the nations are *set over you, O Babylon, are set over you, O Hammer,* so that *you are broken and crushed*. When were these things done? In the coming of my Lord Jesus Christ, when the Gospel was preached to *all the nations*.[26]

24. Prov 4.23.
25. Jer 27.23–24.
26. Matt 28.19.

Then the Father and the Son and the Holy Spirit are *set over Babylon and the hammer of the whole earth,* and what was said is fulfilled: *In the nations are those who are set over you.*

(5) *And you will be taken, Babylon, and you will not know it.*[27] Oh that *Babylon were taken* in each of us also. The captivity of *Babylon* can be understood from what precedes this, when, once *taken,* it is undermined, overthrown, made desolate so that nothing of confusion resides in us.

(6) *And you will be taken, Babylon, and you will not know it. You have been found and overwhelmed because you resisted the Lord.*[28] Has then only *Babylon resisted the Lord* and not instead all of the nations *resisted the Lord,* when after deserting the Creator they venerated idols? Or does he speak figuratively that every soul contrary to Jerusalem, the Vision of Peace, is *Babylon?* Consequently, the holy were also in Jerusalem, the sinners were in *Babylon.* And if the residents of Jerusalem sinned, they were sent to *Babylon,* and, if they turned to penitence while residing in *Babylon,* they were brought back again to Jerusalem.

(7) So, *Babylon is taken and did not know it;* in fact, Babylon has not *submitted to the Law of God, for she is not able.*[29] And *Babylon* has been *found,* and once *found* has been *overwhelmed,* and she was *overwhelmed* when she was *found* because she *resisted the Lord.*[30]

3. Then there is the beginning of another section. *The Lord has opened his treasure and brought forth the vessels of his wrath because there is need for the Lord of powers in the land of the Chaldeans, since their times have come. Open up their storehouses, explore it as a cave and spoil it so that there is nothing remaining; empty out all of its fruits, and let them go down to slaughter. Woe to them, since their day has come, the time of vengenance against them.*[31]

(2) Since I want to understand what is said by, *The Lord*

---

27. Jer 27.23.
28. Jer 27.24.
29. Cf. Rom 8.7.
30. Jer 27.24.
31. Jer 27.25–27.

*opened his treasure and brought forth the vessels of his wrath*, I search for other scriptural texts for the *vessels of anger*, and I find in an apostolic text of this Scripture nearly a complete comparison, and I find the Apostle offering for me there what the *vases of anger* are.[32] For he says, *What if, however, God, desiring to show his wrath and to make known his power, has endured with much patience the vessels of wrath made for destruction, in order to make known the riches of his glory for the vessels of mercy, which he has prepared beforehand for glory, even us whom he has called, not from the Jews only but also from the nations?*[33] Generally the Apostle has divided all people into two groups in saying there are some who are *vessels of mercy*, some who are *vessels of wrath*. For example, he has called the Pharaoh and the Egyptians *vessels of wrath*, while on the contrary he called himself who first *received mercy*[34] and those of the Jews and pagan nations who believed in that time, *vessels of mercy*.

(3) There are therefore in the *treasury* of God *vessels of wrath*. For it was written, *The Lord opened up his treasury and brought forth vessels of his wrath*.[35] What is that *treasury of the Lord* in which the *vessels of wrath* are found? Someone should perhaps ask whether there are only *vessels of wrath* in the *treasury of the Lord* and whether the *treasury* of God, which is the *treasury* of all things, does not have the *vessels of mercy*, or whether one needs to understand in another way the *treasury* of God where its *vessels of wrath are drawn*. I say with confidence that the *treasury* of the Lord is his Church, and in this *treasury*, that is, the Church, there are often concealed men who are *vessels of wrath*. The time will come then when *the Lord opens his treasury*, the Church. Now since it is shut, in the Church the *vessels of wrath* dwell with *vessels of mercy*, and the *chaff* are with the *wheat*,[36] and the *fish* who are to be destroyed and *thrown out* are kept with the *good fish* who have fallen into the *net*.[37] When he has *opened* it in the time of Judgment and then *brought forth the vessels of wrath*, perhaps

---

32. On this and following sentences, see Fragment 31.
33. Rom 9.22–24.  
34. 2 Cor 4.1.
35. Jer 27.25.  
36. Cf. Matt 3.12.
37. Cf. Matt 13.47–48.

he who is a *vessel of mercy* will say about the *vessels of wrath* who are leaving: *They went out from us, but they were not of us. For if they had been of us, they would have yet remained with us; but they went out from us, that it might be plain that they were not of us.*[38]

(4) The subject requires us to cast forth in some other direction; what we dare to say is something such as this. In the *treasury* of God there are *vessels of wrath*. Outside the *treasury* the sinful *vessels* are not *vessels of wrath*, rather they are less than *vessels of wrath*. For they are *servants who knew not the will of their Master and did not do his will*.[39] So he who has entered into the Church is either a *vessel of wrath* or a *vessel of mercy*; he who is outside the Church is neither a *vessel of mercy* nor of *wrath*. I seek for another name for him who remains outside the Church, and how I can determine with confidence that he is not a *vessel of mercy*. In this way, I can conversely state the view, moved from the truth of reason, that he is evidently not a *vessel of wrath*, but a *vessel* reserved for some other thing. Can I then prove by the Scriptures that he is neither a *vessel of mercy* nor *of wrath*, so that a second exposition can place before us something useful in the present context, and again surely hear in it what the text undertakes to expose? The Apostle says, *In a great house there are not only vessels of gold and silver but also of wood and earthenware, and some for noble use, some for ignoble. If any one purifies himself from what is ignoble, then he will be a vessel for noble use, consecrated, useful to the master, ready for any good work.*[40] Do you think that the *great house* is in the present, and in it are *vessels for noble use* and others *for ignoble use*? Or in that *house* which is to come are there *gold and silver vessels* which are *for noble use*? Will they be the *vessels of mercy*, while the rest, men in the middle, who are outside the situation of being either *vessels of wrath* or *of mercy*, can be, according to a certain profound dispensation of God, *vessels in the great house*, even though not *purified*, but earthen *vessels for ignoble use*, still necessary for the *house*?

(5) See, however, if I have the ability to establish this ex-

---

38. 1 John 2.19.    39. Luke 12.47–48.
40. 2 Tim 2.20–21.

ample from another testimony of Scripture: *Jechonias,* he says, *has been dishonored as if he was a vessel without use.* He does not say that he has a usefulness and his usefulness is *for an ignoble use,* but because he was from *the House of God* and he sinned, he had *no usefulness at all.* I have also another scriptural text in which it speaks of a certain sort of sinner: *And he will be like an earthen pot out of which you draw very little water and in which you bear coal.*[41] And so again it affirms that the *vessel* is not utterly necessary and not from every aspect unuseful.

(6) We therefore who are in this *House of God,* do we note that when *the Lord opens his treasury* we begin to be *purified,* if we have been at least *vessels of mercy,* the *vessels of wrath* rejected from us? Or is it not certainly now a fitting enough beginning for us, not only that we must not be *vessels of wrath,* but even that these, which are the *vessels of wrath,* be rejected from us? For it is some such thing as this that the Apostle Paul says to the Corinthians, *It is actually reported that there is immorality among you, and of a kind that is not found even among pagans; for a man is living with his father's wife. And you are arrogant! Ought you not rather to mourn? Let him who has done this be removed from among you.*[42] As if he had said: "Open up the *treasury* of God, let the *vessels of his wrath* depart!" For indeed *the Lord has opened his treasury and brought forth the vessels of his wrath.*

(7) I have read elsewhere as if the Savior was speaking—and I question whether it was someone who was a figure for the person of the Savior or if it was appended in his memory or if this may be truly what he said—the Savior there says, "Whoever is near me is near fire; whoever is far from me, is far from the kingdom."[43] For just as "whoever is near me is near" salvation, thus he "is near fire." And whoever hears me and once having heard me has done a transgression, is a *vessel of wrath prepared for destruction,*[44] when "he is near me, he is

---

41. Isa 30.15.   42. 1 Cor 5.1–2.
43. A text from the *Gospel according to Thomas.*
44. Cf. Rom 9.22.

near fire." Since "he who is near me, is near fire," if anyone, being on his guard becomes "far from me" and fears he is "near fire," let him know that such a person will be "far from the kingdom." An athlete, who having not enrolled in the competition, neither fears the whips nor waits on the crown. Yet once he has entered his name, if he does not win, he is flogged and rejected, but if he wins, he is crowned. Just so, he who has entered the Church—O catechumen, attend— he who accedes to the word of God, he has enrolled in nothing other than in the contest of religion, and once enrolled if he does not battle with integrity, he is struck with whips with which these others, who have not indeed enrolled in the beginning, are not flogged. If, however, he fights with courage to avoid the lashes and the reproaches, not only will he be freed from the wrongs, but he *will receive the incorruptible crown* of glory.[45]

4. *There is need for the Lord of powers in the land of the Chaldeans.*[46] An earthly locale, understood by means of its different aspects, can be called by many things, and the Savior too, under different aspects, has many names, since he may be one in substance[47] but varied in powers;[48] thus also, due to the wickedness of the human race, earthly matters, though they may be one in substance, are understood as many in their diversity. Yet what I say may be made more clear in this way, if by analyzing the example which is offered by the Savior, I then pass beyond it to those things which need explanation. There is one substance in my Lord Jesus the Savior. Though he is a single substance, he is a *healer* from one perspective, according to what was written, *Those who are well have no need of a healer, but those who are sick,*[49] from another perspective he is a *shepherd,*[50] by which he presides over what

---

45. 1 Cor 9.25.   46. Jer 27.25.
47. "In substance:" *in subjacenti.* Throughout this paragraph I have translated *subjaceo* as "substance." Literally it means "what is basic or lying under."
48. Cf. *Hom in Jer* 8.2, 15.6, 17.4 above.
49. Matt 9.12.
50. Matt 9.36; Mark 6.34; Ezek 34.12.

is irrational,[51] from another perspective a *king*,[52] by which he rules over the rational beings, from another perspective the *true vine*,[53] by which we men grafted to him *bear fruit*[54] abundantly and, cultivated by the *Father, the vinedresser*,[55] they are sustained by the abundance of the *true vine* by association with the unique root. From one perspective he is *Wisdom*,[56] from another *Truth*,[57] from another *Justice*.[58] Nonetheless he is one substance. In the way, therefore, that there are in the Savior, who is one substance, many perspectives for diverse names for him, so also earthly matters, though substantially one, are yet manifold in perspective.

(2) Frequently when speaking allegorically about Babylon we say that it is earthly matters which are those always riddled with faults. Similarly Egypt is what weakens us. As for the *land of the Chaldeans*, because they assign most of what happens on the earth to the stars, and whether they claim whatever sins or virtues done by us happen from their movements, we say that these are those who have committed themselves to such opinions. Every man then who believes in these opinions is *in the land of the Chaldeans*. If any of you follow the deliriums of the astrologers, he is *in the land of the Chaldeans*. If anyone computes the day of his birth and, believing in the differences in hours and calculation moments, supports this teaching according to which the stars for such and such reason make men immoderate, adulterers, chaste or whatever, this man is *in the land of the Chaldeans*. Now they hold that Christians are born from the course of the stars. Whoever among you has this understanding, whoever among you believes in these words, you are *in the land of the Chaldeans*. Hence when God threatens those who are *in the land of the Chaldeans*, he threatens these who consecrate themselves to genealogies and fate by asserting that all of these things that happen among mortals result either from

---

51. Cf. *Hom in Jer* 5.6.
52. John 18.37.
53. John 15.1.
54. John 15.2.
55. John 15.1.
56. 1 Cor 1.30.
57. John 14.6.
58. 1 Cor 1.30.

the movements of the stars or from necessity of fate. But God when advancing Abraham to better things said to him, *I am he who leads you from the land of the Chaldeans.*⁵⁹ For God is the power who also grants to us to leave the *land of the Chaldeans,* and we believe no other except him, by managing all things and ruling our life, metes out different kinds of circumstances, according to the qualities of the merits. For it is not the twinkling in some constellation either of Phaethon, as they say, or in the star of corrupt Ganymede that holds the causes of our affairs. And according to one line of reasoning certainly he who has believed in the calculations stated above is *in the land of the Chaldeans;* according to another he climbs up *on the roof and adores the army of heaven.*⁶⁰ However, we find in Jeremiah many menacing threats against these who *sacrifice to the army of heaven.*⁶¹

(3) Therefore, *there is need of the Lord of powers in the land of the Chaldeans, since their time has come.*

5. *Open up their storehouses,*⁶² evidently those of *the land of the Chaldeans.* Yet the *storehouses of the Chaldeans* are the teachings of horoscopes.

(2) *Explore it as a cave and destroy it.*⁶³ He who refutes the reckonings of birthdays, he who uses the word of truth against them, he who shows that nothing of what the astrologers say is true, he who teaches that the *unsearchable judgments of God*⁶⁴ are unable to be comprehended by men, he who affirms that the constellations are not the cause of what happens upon the earth, even less of what befalls to us Christians, he accomplishes the command of the Lord in saying: *Destroy it.*

(3) It is necessary to inquire what does what follows mean: *Let there be nothing left.*⁶⁵ *Do not annul some part,* he says, *of the Chaldeans,* then reserve another part. Therefore I command, "Do not leave even a speck in it. Dry up all of their fruit."⁶⁶ Who is

---

59. Cf. Gen 15.7.
61. Cf. Jer 19.13.
63. Jer 27.26.
65. Jer 27.26.
60. Wis 1.5.
62. Jer 27.26.
64. Rom 11.33.
66. Jer 27.27.

so blessed that he is able to *dry up all of the fruit of the land of the Chaldeans? And let them go down to slaughter. Woe to them, because their day comes and it is the time of vengeance against them.*⁶⁷

6.⁶⁸ After this again there is the next section of another pericope: *The voice of those who flee and save themselves again from the land of Babylon in order to announce in Zion the vengeance of our Lord God.*⁶⁹ He now prophesies about these who, having left the customs of their fathers and laws of the pagan peoples and their ancient lack of belief, come to the Word of God. For such in some sense is meant in what he says: *The voice of those who flee and save themselves again from the land of Babylon.* Oh that the *voice of those fleeing from Babylon, fleeing* vices, *fleeing* sins, would be yours, O catechumens! For it is a *voice of those fleeing and saving themselves again.* It is not enough *to flee from the land of Babylon,* but also *to save oneself again from the land of Babylon to announce in Zion the vengeance of the Lord our God,* so that by *fleeing from the land of Babylon* you come to *Zion,* the observatory,⁷⁰ the Church, *to announce in Zion,* that is, the Church, *the vengeance of the Lord our God,* a vengeance on his people.⁷¹

(2) *Proclaim in Babylon to many, to everyone who tends the bow.*⁷² It is significant that it posits *many.* For there are *many* who are *in Babylon,* yet few in Jerusalem. *For it was not because you are many that the Lord your God favored you; for you were the fewest of all peoples.*⁷³ It was well said to those on God's side: *You are fewest of all the nations.* Understand furthermore also this text: *There are few who are saved,*⁷⁴ but also this: *Strive to enter by the narrow door.*⁷⁵

(3) *By the wide and accessible announce to many in Babylon, to every one who tends the bow; let no one from her be saved.*⁷⁶ *Destroy, kill everything in Babylon.*⁷⁷ Recently we spoke concerning

---

67. Jer 27.27.
68. See Fragment 32.
69. Jer 27.28.
70. Cf. *Hom in Jer* 5.16.
71. Compare what follows to Fragment 33.
72. Jer 27.29.
73. Deut 7.7.
74. Cf. Luke 13.23.
75. Luke 13.24.
76. Jer 27.29.
77. Jer 27.16.

*infants* of Babylon,[78] of men of Babylon, of the *Babylonian seed.*[79]

(4) Therefore *let no one of Babylon be saved, render to him according to his works; according to all which he has done, do to him, since she has stood up against the Lord God the Holy one of Israel.*[80] Whenever you have in yourself thoughts which resist piety and the true Faith, you have in you Babylonians. But take *vengeance* and kill all sinners of the earth that is in you, all Babylonians, so that you, having been purified, can pass over to *Jerusalem, the city of God,*[81] in Christ Jesus, *to whom is the glory and the power for the ages of ages. Amen.*[82]

78. Cf. Ps 136.9.
79. Cf. Jer 27.16. Origen here refers to a prior homily, not now extant. See Fragment 26.
80. Jer 27.29.   81. Cf. Heb 12.22.
82. 1 Pet 4.11.

## HOMILY 28 (51)

*Jeremiah 28.6–9 (51.6–9)*

*(from Jerome's Latin translation)*

*On what was written: "Flee from the midst of Babylon" up to the place where it says: "Her judgment has reached up to heaven, elevated up to the skies."*

JUST AS OUR BODY bases itself in some place of the earth, in the same way also the soul according to its condition, is in a comparable place of the earth. What I am saying will become more clear in this way. Our body is in Egypt or in Babylon or in Palestine or in Syria or in some other place. Likewise the soul is in some place with the same name as the earth; one is in Babylon, another in Egypt, another in the region of the Ammanites; and so, according to the meaning of Scriptures, souls are spiritually differentiated with a diversity of places by the nature of their life.

(2) It is in *Babylon* when it is confounded, when it is disturbed, when devoid of peace it endures the war of the passions, when an uproar of malice rages around it; then, as we say, it is in *Babylon,* and the prophetic word refers us to that soul when it says, *Flee from the midst of Babylon and let every man save his soul.*[1] For as long as anyone is in *Babylon* he cannot be saved. Even if he has *remembered*[2] Jerusalem there, he mourns and says, *How will we sing the song of the Lord in a strange land?*[3] And because it is impossible, based in *Babylon,* to praise God with *instruments*—since the *instruments* there for the hymns

---

1. Jer 28.6 (51.6).   2. Cf. Ps 136.1.
3. Cf. Ps 136.4.

of God are indeed unused—accordingly it is said through the Prophet: *There upon the river of Babylon we sat, and we wept while we remembered Zion; among the willows in their midst we hung up our instruments.*[4] *Our instruments* have been *hung up*, as long as we are in *Babylon*, among the willows of the rivers of *Babylon*. If however we come to Jerusalem, to the place of the Vision of Peace, the *instruments*, which before were hanging unused, are then taken up into the hands, then we play the cither continually and there is no time when we do not praise God through the *instruments* which we have in our hands.

(3) Thus, as we began to say, the soul is always in some comparable place of the earth: just as the soul[5] of the sinner is in *Babylon*, so conversely the soul[6] of the just man is in Judea. Yet even in Judea itself it is assigned to varied places according to the quality of life and faith. For either it is in Dan, whose areas are at the borders of Judea, or in a little higher and better place than Dan, or in the central areas of Judea, or around Jerusalem, and there in the most beautiful spot of all, which rests in the midst of the city of Jerusalem. Yet he who is a sinner and is burdened with excessive crimes, he is in *Babylon*.

(4) One in a slightly less severe condition and not yet reaching up to the summit of sins sojourns in Egypt and in parts of Egypt. And just as those who are in Judea do not all have equal positions—one, in fact, is in Jerusalem, another in Dan, another in Nephtal, another in the border of Gad—so also for all those in Egypt. They do not dwell in equal places in Egypt: one lives in *Taphnis*, another is in *Memphis*, another in *Syene*, another in *Bubastis*,[7] places the Prophet Ezekiel, when he also explains the names of parts of Egypt, attests are sounds full of mysteries.

(5) If any reader is *a spiritual man who judges all things and he is judged by no one*,[8] not only will he allegorize the major re-

---

4. Ps 136.1.  
5. "The soul," I have added.  
6. "The soul," I have added.  
7. Ezek 30.13–18.  
8. Cf. 1 Cor 2.15.

gions as Judea and Egypt and Babylon, but also as smaller areas of the earth. And just as in Judea is Jerusalem and Bethlehem and its other cities, so in Egypt when he reads *Diospolis, Bubastis, Taphnis, Memphis, Syene,* he will understand figuratively the meaning of things. *Who is wise and understands these things? Or who is understanding and will know them?*[9]

(6) Who, in any case, even though established in the inner sense, can know the intention which the writings of the Holy Spirit have?

2. Now another matter is proposed: What is advised by the word of God for these who are in *Babylon: Flee from the midst of Babylon.* For you *flee* quickly at full speed, not gradually, not little by little. For this is to *flee. Flee from the midst of Babylon.* Whoever among you has a soul confounded by the passion of varied vices, to you is directed the word; and to me also it is ordered if indeed I am confused in mind and thus I am in *Babylon.* What then does God advise? He does not say: "Leave from the midst of Babylon," (this can be done gradually) but, *Flee from the midst of Babylon.*

(2) I also ask about the purpose of the expression, *from the midst.* Someone can indeed depart when he is in *Babylon,* but when he lingers on its far borders, he would seem in some measure to be on the outskirts of *Babylon.* It is another thing, however, to be situated in the middle of *Babylon,* so that from every direction there is an equal distance and thus one dwells in its center, as if in the midst of the heart of an animal. Just as the heart is the middle of the animal and the middle of the earth is termed the *heart of the earth* in the Gospel according to Luke,[10] so too it seems to me said in Ezekiel, *in the heart of the sea* as the position of Tyre,[11] and now that sinners ought to *flee from the midst of Babylon,* this is from its heart. Thus, *flee from the midst of Babylon.* By deserting the middle of *Babylon,* you can begin to be on its borders,

---

9. Hos 14.10.
10. The expression is found in Matt 12.40, not in extant texts of Luke.
11. Ezek 27.4.

## HOMILY 28

not *in the midst*. What seems obscure to you thus can be made more clear. He who is extremely immersed in vices, he is an inhabitant of the *midst of Babylon*. He who little by little leaves evil and turns his nature to what is better, will begin not so much to possess virtues but desire them. This person, even if he *flees from the midst of Babylon*, nevertheless, does not leave Babylon altogether.[12]

(3) According to interpretations of this sort it is fitting that one believes the sacred Scriptures have not even *one dot* which is empty of the wisdom of God. For he who orders a man like me saying, *You shall not appear before me empty*,[13] he acts this way to a greater extent. He speaks nothing which is empty. The Prophets who *received from his fullness*[14] sang of those things which were drawn from *fullness*, and due to that the sacred Books breathe the spirit of *fullness*. And there is nothing either in the Prophets, or in the Law, or in the Gospels, or in the Apostles, which does not come down from the *fullness* of the divine Majesty. For that reason the words of *fullness* breathe today in the holy Sciptures. They breathe to those who have the eyes to see what is heavenly and the ears to hear what is divine[15] and the noses to sense what contains *fullness*.

3. I have said these things because it was not simply stated, "Flee from Babylon," but with a necessary addition, *Flee from the midst of Babylon and let each save again his own soul*. It was appropriate first to *flee from the midst of Babylon*, then that each person *save again his soul* when he *flees*. It did not say in fact "save," but *save again*.

(2) The addition of *again* refers to a mystery: After once tasting salvation and then afterwards falling away from it on account of sins, we came to Babylon.[16] This is why it is appro-

---

12. A Greek fragment of the rest of this section is extant in *Philocalia* 1.1, translated below. See GCS 6.195–96.
13. Cf. Exod 23.15.      14. John 1.16.
15. Cf. Deut 29.3 (Rom 11.8).
16. Is this an allusion to the fall of pre-existent souls? If not, what then would be the "first" time one is saved?

priate that each save[17] his soul, so that he begins to recover what he lost, acording to the Apostle Peter who says thus: *As the outcome of our faith we shall obtain the salvation of our souls; concerning this salvation the Prophets who prophesied of the grace that was to be ours searched and inquired.*[18] Still it is in us to *flee from Babylon,* and it lies within our power, if we will, to set right what has collapsed.

4. Third it was commanded: *Do not be cast out for her iniquity.*[19] When anyone is *in the injustice of Babylon* and does not do penitence, then it follows that he is *cast out.* Note how the Scripture, even though a concept is translated from Hebrew to Greek, to the extent it can render the differences of words, it will express its meaning. It says actually in another place, *I have chosen to be rejected in the house of the Lord,*[20] and not *cast out.* In the present context it was not stated, "And do not be rejected for her injustice," but *Do not be cast out for her injustice.* For it is one thing to be *cast out,* it is another to be *rejected.* For what is in contempt and also neglected, this is not cast out, it is *rejected.* Yet what is inwardly outside of salvation and foreign to blessedness, this is *cast out.* This is what the divine Scripture expresses in another place when it says, *The leaders of my people are cast out from the home of their pleasures due to their ruinous inclinations.*[21] *For their offices will not profit them.*[22] And you yourself can gather together the texts if anywhere you discover the terms *cast out* and *reject,* so that by a comparison of the words you can with confidence develop the meaning, since the dispensation of Providence, even if it did not care greatly that the eloquence which is lauded in the Greek style follows in the Greek translation, nevertheless has cared to show what is significant and to explain their differences for those who peruse the Scriptures intently.

5. *Do not be cast out for the iniquity* of Babylon, *since it is the time of vengeance on her from the Lord.*[23] With wonderful insight

---

17. Nautin corrects without need: to "save again" (*resalvare*). Baehrens has *salvare.*
18. 1 Pet 1.9–10.
19. Jer 28.6.
20. Ps 83.11.
21. Mic 2.9.
22. Jer 12.13.
23. Jer 28.6.

it says that the penalties are inflicted for a revenge on those who suffer them. For whenever anyone is not vindicated, he is left unpunished. I recall frequently that I have spoken of what was written in the twelve Prophets: *And I will not visit on your daughters when they fornicate, and upon your daughters-in-law when they commit adultery.*[24] It is not then, as some think, that God punishes when he is wrathful, but, if it may be fitting to speak so, it is with great wrath from God when torments are not received. For he who is punished, even if he is chastened by what one may call the wrath of God, is punished for this purpose, so that he is improved. *Lord*, David says, *rebuke me not in your anger, nor chasten me in your rage,*[25] but even if you *rebuke, rebuke us in judgment and not in rage,* Jeremiah says.[26] Yet from a promise of God you also find a reproach given against certain people; when the penalty is promised to the sinful *sons* of Christ, that *mercy* is not denied. It was written: *If his sons abandon my Law, and do not walk in my judgments, if they profane my decisions and do not keep my Commandments, I will visit with a rod their transgressions and with scourges their iniquities; but I will not remove from them my mercy.*[27] When considering this, observe how he who up to the present commits the crime is not punished, since the punishment may not yet be deserving. The *visitation* of God is indeed exhibited in the torments on the one visited, yet when he who sins is[28] chastened, I do not know what is extended for a punishment.[29]

(2) Mention has been made of these things, regarding what was written: *For it is the time of his vengeance from the Lord.*

6. There follows: *He himself will render to him the retribution.*[30] It is not through servants that God will bring retribution to Babylon, but *he himself will bring the retribution* that is de-

---

24. Hos 4.14. See *Hom in Ex* 8.5.  
25. Ps 6.2.  
26. Jer 10.24.  
27. Ps 88(89).31–33.  
28. Nautin adds here: "not."  

29. Nautin adds "not" to the first clause of this sentence. He writes: "But to the sinner who is not chastened, I do not know what arrives in the guise of pain."

30. Jer 28.6.

served. I want to speak about the addition of the pronoun *himself* in the text. God himself has not rendered to all what they merit, but there are those to whom he renders through others, whether by punishing them or curing them through pain, as it is held in the Psalms: *He let loose on them the rage of his wrath, rage, wrath, and distress, sent down by the most evil angels.*[31] He *himself* does not render it upon them, but for their retribution he uses the services of *the most evil angels*. And perhaps like those punished for crimes he requites others not through bad angels but good ones. You will find many examples of this and like sort, if you search the Scriptures. Yet when he has rejected the offices of servants, God *himself* sets up the *retribution,* as he does now for Babylon.

(2) If I should remain silent, I fear leaving something obscure, which seems to me to be hidden, interposed in a clear passage. Nonetheless, at least one ought to hear a few words which touch on it. When there are wounds with easy and prompt cure, a healer sends his servant, he sends his disciple, so that the malady might be cared for through him; for the wounds are not great. It also happens at different times that one who is healthy might need an amputation and an iron for cautery, and yet the healer *himself* does not proceed to cure, but, choosing one from the disciples who is competent to cure, he uses his service. When, however, there are incurable diseases and gangrene has spread in the dead flesh and it is in such a bad condition that it is not for the hands of the servants or disciples, who approach him in the knowledge of the skill but lack the hands of the master *himself,* then the great master *himself,* who once having bound the limb, moves on to the cutting of the putrified wound. Similarly then, when there are lesser sins, God *himself* does not *render retribution* on the sinners, but makes use of other servants. When through his own doing an enormous illness overwhelms man, as it does now Babylon, which has been pierced with wounds by its own grave malice, then God *him-*

---

31. Ps 77(78).49.

*self* hastens to give *retribution*. You will also find something like this, if you seek further, concerning Jerusalem, concerning what happened to her after the Prophets because she turned against Christ.

7. So the contents of the first section finish. Let us see also what remains: *Babylon was a golden cup in the hand of the Lord, making drunk the entire earth. The nations drank of her wine; on account of this the nations became disoriented, and suddenly Babylon fell and she was broken.*[32] Nebuchadnezzar, wishing to deceive men through the deceitful *cup of Babylon*, did not mix the potion he was preparing in the *vessel of clay*, nor in what was a little better, in an iron, copper or pewter vessel, or what is superior to these, silver. Choosing rather a *gold* vessel in which he combined the potion so that whoever sees what is attractive about the gold, touched by the beauty of the radiant metal and drawn totally with the eyes by its splendor, does not consider what is inwardly hidden, and accepting the *cup*, drinks, ignoring that it is the cup of Nebuchadnezzar.

(2) You will understand what is called the *golden cup* in the present text if you note that the deadly words of the most evil teachings have a certain kind of arrangement of speaking, a kind of attractive eloquence, a kind of beauty of order, and if you know how each of the poets, who are thought along with their disciples as the most well-spoken men, have formed the *golden cup* and injected the venom of idolatry and the venom of obscenity, the venom of those teachings which slay the soul of man, the venom with the false name of knowledge. But my Jesus has done the opposite. For by knowing the *golden cup* of Satan and taking care that no one coming to his faith would ever worry that what he left behind was the *cup* of Christ and through a similarity of material would fear an error, he took care then that *we would have this treasure in clay vessels.*[33] I have often seen a *golden cup*, decorated with the beauty of words, and when I consider the

32. Jer 28.7–8. See Fragment 36.   33. Cf. 2 Cor 4.7.

venom of its teachings, I have perceived that it is the *cup of Babylon*.

8. *The golden cup of Babylon in the hand of the Lord*. It is not always the *golden cup* of Babylon, yet when it comes to vengeance and was placed *in the hand of the Lord*, then it becomes earth which was once *touched* in Job.[34] Yet it was not held immediately *in the hand of the Lord*, but only in the time of revenge, when the Lord will begin to render what is deserved, then it is *in* his *hand*.

(2) *Making drunk the whole earth*. This *golden cup of Babylon makes drunk the whole earth*. Yet how it *made drunk the whole earth* you may easily know if you have considered that all men are drunk.[35] We *become drunk* with anger, we *become drunk* with gloom, we *become drunk* and we obsess the mind with love, with desires and vainglory. Is it necessary to state how many potions it has mixed, how many *cups* of drunkenness it has offered?

9. *The golden cup of Babylon making drunk the whole earth*.[36] Observe that *the whole earth* is full of sin and you do not wonder how it is that *Babylon has made drunk the whole earth*. But if you see that the righteous man is not drunk from the cup of sinners, do not think that the Scripture is misleading which said, *making drunk the whole earth*, when this one is not *made drunk* by *Babylon* and yet still exists on the *earth*. Hear that the righteous may not be the *earth;* whereas that *golden cup makes drunk the whole earth*, the righteous, though he may be upon the earth, *has his abode in heaven*.[37] And on account of this it is no longer fitting to say to the righteous man: *You are earth and into earth you will go*.[38] But if it is necessary to speak more boldly, God says to the righteous man who remains upon the earth till now: "You are heaven and to heaven you will go," *for he bears the image of heaven*.[39] Let me therefore

---

34. Job 2.5. Fragment 36 is different here.
35. Cf. Gen 3.19. "You are earth. . . ."    36. Jer 28.7.
37. Cf. Phil 3.20.    38. Gen 3.19.
39. 1 Cor 15.49. Cf. *Hom in Jer* 8.2.

conclude that *the golden cup makes drunk the whole earth*, that is, we are *all made drunk* by it as long as we are *earth*.

10. *From its wine the nations drank; on account of this they are disoriented.*[40] Just as in these who *drink* the liquor *wine* which is in use, if they drink beyond thirst and beyond measure, we see a body movement of a drunk: feet wobbly, head and temples top heavy, mouth gaping, language which signifies the style of the drunk and lips having difficulty making words precise. It is like this to see those who *drink of the golden cup of Babylon*, how they *are agitated*, how they are unstable in step, how because of a crippled mind and thought which wanders they hold nothing with firmness, but always act with confusion[41] because they are uncertain. Why does divine Scripture speak about men in another place in this way? *Accordingly they were disturbed.*[42] We can interject something of mystery: why is it said about the sinner Cain that he *went away from the presence of the Lord and dwelt in the land of Nod east of Eden.*[43] In the Greek tongue *Nod* is translated as *disturbance*. For he who leaves God, he who deserts the inclination to think continually about him, that person today also *dwells in the land of Nod*, that is, he exists in the confusion of an evil heart and in the disturbance of the mind.

11. *The nations drank, accordingly they were disturbed, and suddenly Babylon fell and was broken.*[44] When did *Babylon fall suddenly?*[45] It seems to me that he has prophesied that the consummation of the world will happen *suddenly. For as in the days of the Flood they were eating and drinking, buying and selling, planting and building, until the Flood came and swept them all away,*[46] and *suddenly* the Deluge came—*likewise in the days of Lot*[47]—so also the consummation of the world will not happen in stages, but *suddenly*. With this ought to be compared,

40. Jer 28.7.
41. Cf. *Hom in Jer* 19.14 on the meaning of Babylon as confusion.
42. Cf. Ps 47.6.    43. Cf. Gen 4.16.
44. Jer 28.7–8.
45. Compare the following sentences to Fragment 35.
46. Matt 24.38–39.    47. Luke 17.28.

I think, what was written in Joshua, when by a single sound of a trumpet the crumbling city of Jericho suddenly perished;[48] and like this example *Babylon* also in the consummation of the age *will fall* and *suddenly* be *obliterated*.

(2) And these words were indeed spoken concerning the consummation. But if you come to the appearance of my Lord Jesus Christ and you see his great work—how he overturned the pagan teachings about idols so that he might remove from believers the yoke of their error—you will understand that at the time of his Passion *Babylon* crumbled *immediately* and *was broken down*. Each one of us should consider himself and observe if *Babylon* crumbled in his own heart. However, if the city of confusion has not fallen in someone's heart, in this person Christ has not yet appeared. For when he does come, *Babylon* is bound to fall. On account of this, taking refuge in the protection of prayers, request that Jesus come in your heart and *demolish Babylon* and cause to crumble all of her malice so that he might rebuild, in place of what was overturned and in place of *Babylon* which had been constructed before, in the governing power of your heart the holy *city of God Jerusalem*.[49]

12. *Wail for her, take balm for her corruption in case she may be healed*.[50] *Wail*, he says, *for Babylon*.[51] Then because every soul is able to receive salvation and no one is incurable with God, for that reason he gives to these who are capable of the migration to Jerusalem and able to carry the *balm* of the witness to make a plaster, the prescription so that they can offer a remedy. And to the extent they are strong with zeal they may restore Babylon to health. Let us, too, try to do this also when we pray to God to give us the rational *balm*. And we can learn from the rational *balm* to apply a poultice and oil and bands.[52] And when we apply them and imitate the Samaritan we *bind up the wounds*[53] of *Babylon* so that the

48. Cf. Josh 6.20.
49. Heb 12.22.
50. Jer 28.8.
51. Compare Fragment 37 with the following sentences.
52. Cf. Isa 1.6.
53. Luke 10.34.

wretched city may be healed, and once cured, she may cease to be what she had been. That is what it says: *Take balm for her corruption in case she may be healed.* Where are the heretics, where are they who, when they discuss certain natures, assert that matter is beyond hope and cannot by any means receive salvation? If there is a nature which should perish, what else of this sort will it be except Babylon? And yet God does not despise that city, for he commands the healers to place *balm* upon *Babylon in case she may be healed.*

(2) Certain of those then who had received the command, who *take the balm for the corruption of Babylon in case she may be healed,* do what the command said. They *took the balm for her corruption,* hearing what can happen, that Babylon might receive a cure. And since they did not accomplish what they thought—Babylon in fact by continuing in previous malice did not want to be cured—the good healers are satisfied and say: *We have cared for Babylon and she was not healed; let us leave her.*[54] See, O man, if God does not command at some time the angels that they may apply to the weakness of your souls the plasters of medicine in case they are able to heal you from illness, and the angels respond: *We have cared for* this *Babylon*—pointing out that your soul is *confused*[55] from passions—*and it was not healed.* They do not complain about their knowledge of the medical arts or the strength of the *balm,* but about you, who were unwilling to follow their orders, when they say, *We have cared for Babylon and she was not healed.*

(3) *Let us leave her.* The angel healers stood under the great healer God, wanting to cure our infirmities, wanting to free the soul from vices. We ourselves repulse them since we do not yield to their counsels. They see that their work is a waste; they confer with one another and say, *Let us leave her and go each to his own land.*[56] This means: medicine has been entrusted to us by God to care for the human soul, we

---

54. Jer 28.9.
56. Jer 28.9.

55. Babylon means "confused."

brought assistance, we applied medicine. There was much obstinance, it did not want to observe what we say, no effect resulted from our zeal, so *let us leave her and go each to his own land*, that is, to the place of his home and his own affairs. Take care, man, that the healer does not *leave* you, whether it is the angel of God or every man with whom is entrusted the care of the words in order to bring the medicine of salvation. For if he *leaves* you and says, *Let us go each to his own land, because its judgment is near in heaven,*[57] it is clear that his departure may be your condemnation as of one incurable and who does not want to be cured. Yet when he deserts you, what else will happen to you except what is wont to befall these who are deemed hopeless by healers, that by enjoying the inclinations of their own sickness they sink to a worse condition? Events similar to these occur also in the course of this life from the experiences of physicians. Any of them attacks infirmities as far as his skill permits, and he does not cease his work for a remedy. But if either the illness is so great that it fights against a cure or if the invalid himself through the impatience of the pain acts against what is proscribed, the physician in despair over such a man *leaves* him and retires, lest his dying in his hands may shift the blame for his demise on to himself. So, too then, if we die, not in the hands of holy angels who were appointed for our care by the Lord, they *leave* us out of despair for our soul and say, *There is no poultice nor oil nor band to apply.*[58]

(4) *Because his judgment was near in heaven, he was lifted to the skies.*[59] He who has a small sin is not brought up to heaven and the stars and does not bring about his *judgment*. For it is tiny and slight. Yet he who increases in wickedness, increases also in *judgment,* and likewise when he grows in vices and faults. And since he is lacking to the extent that *his judgment is lifted up to the heavens,* when he resists God through his own impiety he ascends to a higher place, God carries out his

---

57. Jer 28.9.  
58. Isa 1.6.  
59. Jer 28.9.

own *judgment* in a humiliation of the latter's *judgment* which *was exalted* by sin. And since he carries out *his judgment* he indeed humiliates the sin, but he gives to the righteous man a retribution worthy of his life in Christ Jesus, *to whom is the glory and the power for the ages of ages. Amen.*[60]

60. 1 Pet 4.11.

# FRAGMENTS ON JEREMIAH

# FRAGMENTS OF HOMILIES 21 AND 39 FROM THE PHILOCALIA

## I: Fragments from the Philocalia, Chapter 1

AND AS ALL OF THE GIFTS of God are far greater than the mortal being, so too the Word—who is precise about the wisdom of all these things since he is with the God[1] who arranges to write them, if the Father of the Word wishes—may arise in the soul which is utterly purified with all respect and with awareness of the human weakness about the basis of wisdom. But if a person dedicates himself rashly, without comprehending what is esoteric of the wisdom of God and of the Word who is *in the beginning with God*[2] and who is himself God, and that it is by means of the Word and God and by means of the wisdom with him that one must examine and discover these things, it must happen that he, by falling into myths and nonsense and fictions, submits himself to the danger which surrounds impiety. For that reason one needs to remember also the commandment from Solomon in Ecclesiastes concerning such things, which says, *Do not hasten to express a word before the face of God. For God is in the heaven above, and you are on the earth below. Therefore let your words be few.*[3]

(2) And it is fitting that one believe that the holy Scriptures do not have one dot empty of the wisdom of God. For if he will enjoin a man like me saying, *Do not appear before me empty*,[4] how much more will he himself say nothing empty. For the Prophets speak having received *from his fullness.*[5]

1. Cf. John 1.1.
3. Eccles 5.1.
5. Cf. John 1.16.
2. Cf. John 1.1.
4. Exod 34.20.

Hence all things breathe of his fullness. And there is nothing in Prophecy or Law or Gospel or Apostle which is not from fullness. On account of this, since it is from fullness, it breathes of the fullness in those who have eyes which see what is from the fullness and ears which hear what is from the fullness, and a sense organ for the sweet smell of what breathes from fullness.[6]

## II: Fragments from the Philocalia, Chapter 10

*On the thirty-ninth homily of those on Jeremiah, concerning "The Lord is unable to bear before the face of your evil."*[7]

1. And if in reading the Scripture you stumble on a good thought which is a *stumbling stone and a rock of offence*,[8] blame yourself. For do not despair that this *stumbling stone and rock of offence* have meanings so as to fulfill the saying, *And the one who believes will not be put to shame*.[9] Believe first and you will discover much holy aid beneath the supposed offence. For if we ourselves receive the commandment not to speak a *careless word as we will render an account of it on the day of judgment*,[10] and if we earnestly aspire, as far as possible, to make it so that every word coming out of our mouth works both on us who speak it and on those who hear it, what else is there need to understand about the Prophets than that every word spoken through their mouth was one which works? And do not be amazed if every word spoken by the Prophets works a work which is fitting for a word. For I think that every extraordinary letter written in the words of God works, and there is not *an iota or one dot*[11] written in the Scripture which does not work its own work in those who know to use the power of the Scriptures.

6. The first paragraph is from homily 39, the second from homily 21.
7. Jer 51.22.
8. Cf. Rom 9.32ff.; 1 Pet 2.7; Isa 8.14; Matt 18.7.
9. Rom 9.33; Isa 28.16.   10. Cf. Matt 12.36.
11. Matt 5.18.

2. And as with herbs, each has a power either for the betterment of the bodies or for something else, and it is not all who know for what each of the herbs is useful. But if some have obtained this knowledge, these folk take the time with herbs in order that they may know also when it is taken and where on bodies it is applied and how what is prepared benefits him who uses it. So too the saint is like a spiritual botanist who culls from the sacred Scriptures each *iota* and each simple event and finds the power of the Scripture and for what it is useful and that nothing of the Scriptures is extraneous. Yet if you wish to hear a second example for this: each member of our bodies has been made by God, the Craftsman, for some work, but it is not for all to know what is the power and use of the members, even the least significant. For those among healers who are involved in dissection are able to say for what use each part, even the smallest part, has been deemed by Providence. Notice for me that the Scriptures are in this way all of the herbs or one complete body of the Word. And if you are neither a botanist of the Scriptures nor a dissector of the words of the Prophets, do not suppose that what is from the Scriptures is extraneous, but blame more yourself than the sacred Scriptures when you do not discover the meaning of what has been written.

(2) This is mentioned as the prologue by me, though it can be generally useful for the whole Scripture in order that those who wish to pay close attention to the reading may persuade themselves not to dismiss a letter which is unexamined and unresearched.

# FRAGMENTS FROM THE CATENA

OR THE RIGHTEOUS is not in youth,[1] since *being perfected in a short time he fulfilled long years.*[2] For regarding one who is not in blamable ways the text says, *Do not say, "I am too young,"*[3] as was Roboam, who *forsook the counsel of the elders* and followed the ways of the younger men;[4] for that reason he also has not maintained the kingdom in the way he received it.[5]

2. The *caldron on the fire* is fired up from the *face of the north.*[6] For he is an enemy and also at the same time an avenger. Hence he who has sinned is *delivered to Satan* either in blasphemy *so that he might learn not to blaspheme,* or he is delivered *to Satan in fornication for the destruction of the flesh so*

---

1. As noted in our introduction, these fragments include all of those which do not duplicate texts already present in the extant homilies. It is a translation of the Greek text edited by Klostermann in GCS 6:199–232. His numbering is followed throughout. Three manuscripts are noted in his text: c (10th century A.D.), l (11th) and o (11th).

2. Wis 4.13.      3. Jer 1.10.

4. Cf. 3 Kings 12.13–14.

5. Nautin, 1:30, doubts the authenticity of this fragment because it has a different exegesis of Jer 1.10 than that given in *Hom in Jer* 1.6. Nautin may be right that this fragment is not from the homilies, but would the different exegesis be enough to prove that it is not Origen's thought? Origen often gave more than one interpretation to a text, depending on the context. This fragment may have been pulled from a work other than the homilies, perhaps from one which was discussing the text from Kings or the meaning of "youth" or some other passage from the Prophets. It is difficult to be certain, of course, since it is, after all, a fragment which is abridged and only one part of a discussion. We know that the fragments are usually abridgments and have on occasion been wrongly attributed, but, knowing only this much, and without much stronger evidence than Nautin offers here, we must take care in our judgment of them.

6. Jer 1.13.

*that the spirit may be saved in the day of the Lord.*[7] And whom does he *fire up?* The inhabitants but not the sojourners on *the earth.*[8] For he releases the *flaming darts*[9] on those who do not keep every watch over their hearts, as under such sins he brings flames.

3. About those who will *smite*[10] *them* he mentions a *lion* and a *wolf* and a *leopard.*[11] The meaning with respect to actions seems to be under what was spoken allegorically as *lions*, and the meaning with respect to knowledge is under those who want to mislead the discernment of the soul. For the *leopard* especially is said to pounce upon the eyes, and the *lion*, it is recorded, after it has grown old, prowls about *the cities*, wishing to hunt for men.[12] And it is also said that fire emerges from its bones when they are struck or ground up. Both the *lion* and the *leopard* may equally be also Nebuchadnezzar, who conquered the city and as a *leopard* removed its eyes—the king with his chiefs—but later on who also cut out the eyes of Zedekiah.[13] And Nebuzaradan, after he burnt the city to ashes, observed its bones.[14]

4. The statements which say, *a sacrifice to God is a broken spirit*[15] and *offer a sacrifice of righteousness,*[16] clearly give the means to investigate what the passage about *sacrifices* teaches.[17] And those who do not understand it in this way but have been excited over bodily sacrifices the Savior converts when he says, *But if you had known what this means: I desire mercy and not sacrifice, you would not have condemned the guiltless.*[18] And that there is such a principle concerning sacraments Paul taught in saying, *They serve as a copy and shadow of the heavenly.*[19]

---

7. 1 Tim 1.20; 1 Cor 5.5.
8. Jer 1.14; Gen 12.10. This distinction between inhabiting and sojourning is made also by Philo in *De confusione linguarum.* 1.416–17. See also Origen, *Sel in Gen* 12.10.
9. Eph 6.16.
10. "Smite" (παισόντων): c and o have πεσόντων.
11. Jer 5.6.
12. Jer 5.6. Cf. Aristotle, *HA*, 9.44.
13. Cf. 4 Kings 21.14, 25.7.
14. Cf. 4 Kings 25.8ff.
15. Ps 50.19.
16. Ps 4.6.
17. Cf. Jer 7.21.
18. Matt 12.7.
19. Heb 8.5.

5. *Turtledove, field swallow, and crane:*[20] the astute listeners and those competent to speak of the higher things *are watchful* that their own *comings* are made in *time*,[21] with the result that what is said reaches those who hear, as the *coming* of the *swallow* meets with the *coming* of the *turtledove*.

6. Aquila and Theodotion[22] rendered them: *For it is he who formed all things, and Israel is the rod of his inheritance.*[23] But if *Israel is the rod of his inheritance*, and he has said also that the nations are his *inheritance*, in light of the statement, *Ask from me and I will give you the nations as your inheritance*,[24] the nations will also be *Israel.*[25]

7. Though God justly does not hear those who do not hear him,[26] the demons will be unable to *save* the just in those who *burn incense* to them, whenever *the time of troubles* arrives.[27] Thus whenever God does not listen, it is dangerous to seek help from demons. But one must depend upon God who has turned away from us due to sins, yet who does not disregard the great and lasting refuge in himself.

8. He did not say, *I will not listen to* you, but to *them*, having also shown that, if at that time you ask on behalf of *them* who repent,[28] *I will listen.*[29]

---

20. Jer 8.7.  21. Jer 8.7.
22. These names refer to two other translations of the Old Testament besides the Septuagint.
23. Jer 10.16.  24. Ps 2.8.
25. This is another fragment which Nautin, 1:31–32, uses to bring doubt upon the usefulness of these fragments. He claims because Origen only mentions Aquila and Theodotion in the commentaries, and that the "nations" are not seen in this way in other works, that the fragment is not genuine. But there are two other possibilities: 1) that this fragment may be only one section of Origen's discussion on a text of Jeremiah (without necessarily being from the homilies) and 2) Origen may be creatively developing his interpretation of the "nations." We must be careful not to assume an exegete as creative as Origen cannot develop his ideas in a direction we may not have anticipated. The idea of the "nations" as the future Israel is not difficult to fit into Origen's thinking. See also my discussion above on Fragment 1.
26. Cf. Jer 11.11. The LXX has ἐπακούειν.
27. Cf. Jer 11.12.
28. "Who repent" (μετανοούντων). ο has μετανοοῦν.
29. Jer 11.11, 14.

9. The *forsaken* activity, he said.[30] For after God raises up his own Tabernacle, he is said to *destroy*.[31] Still in another sense the change from evil to virtue is a *destruction* worthy of the hand of God, according to the text, *I will set my hands upon you, and I will inflame you into purity*,[32] though prior to this the filth from sin in us is *destroyed*. Such also is the text: *I will scatter them*.[33] For since they in harmony acted impiously toward me, I will dissipate their evil, their gathering and harmony, just as he thus divided the tongues of the tower builders, having hindered what would increase the conspiring impiety.[34] And the statement, *They were made childless, they destroyed my people*,[35] holds an accusation against rulers and priests. For these people who were in the order of the Fathers became for the people barren of *children* when they substituted impiety for pious teachings. And perhaps it is not that he *destroys a people* who have formerly not *made childless* their own soul of offspring who have virtue. For no one who is good *destroys* another.

10. And the souls of the impious, who destroyed the *bridegroom*[36] Christ, could be the *widows*.[37] The *mothers*,[38] who bore them *in Christ* and who felt travail until Christ was *formed* in them,[39] and who raised them to young men on *solid food* after *milk*,[40] also *are distressed* for those who are destroyed.[41] Yet the number of *widows* is not as *the stars of heaven*,[42] but as *the sand of the sea*.[43] And according to the Scripture, the wives of those who fell[44] *most in number* in the war are *widows*, but the *mothers were distressed*.

11. He exhorts not to *bring burdens*[45] of sins nor say, *They have weighed me down as a heavy load*,[46] so that we might be-

30. Cf. Jer 14.5.
31. Jer 15.7.
32. Isa 1.25.
33. Jer 15.7.
34. Cf. Gen 11.7, 8.
35. Jer 15.7.
36. John 3.29.
37. Jer 15.8.
38. Jer 15.8.
39. Gal 4.19.
40. 1 Cor 3.2; Heb 5.13, 14.
41. Cf. Jer 15.8.
42. Heb 11.12.
43. Jer 15.8.
44. "Fell" (πιπτόντων): o has "die" (θνησκόντον).
45. Jer 17.24.
46. Ps 37.5.

come *kings* and *princes who have sat* steadfastly *on the throne of David*,⁴⁷ the Church of Christ, so that⁴⁸ it is said about us: *You placed on their head a crown from a precious stone.*⁴⁹ And such people also *ride upon chariots and horses*—when they restrain the body and keep under control the irrational movements—so that *the city* might be *inhabited for ever*,⁵⁰ and from every direction gift-bearers *will come* to it: *from the cities of Judah* (those who confess to God) *and from round about Jerusalem* (the peace of the Vision)⁵¹ *and from Benjamin* (the son of right,⁵² and right is all things which work according to virtue) *and from the plains country* (the one who has nothing *proud* raised up against *the knowledge of God*),⁵³ and *from the hill country* (the word of the Gospel), and *from the area to the south, the area which is opposite to what blows from the north;*⁵⁴ all come because of the virtue of those who rule and the most excellent behavior of the inhabitants. For, if they consume through the spirit all matter liable to the perpetual fire, these also will bring a *sacrifice* which is *holy, well-pleasing to God,*⁵⁵ the consecration of the soul, and rational *whole burnt-offerings,* for whom the *prayer* is *as incense, and the lifting up of the hands* is *an evening sacrifice.*⁵⁶ They also bring *frankincense,*⁵⁷ translated as Whitening, since they reject every dark condition, so that the words are fitting for them: *Who is she who comes up all white?*⁵⁸ For in this way they will be able to bring *praise to the house of the Lord, not having a spot or a wrinkle or any such thing*⁵⁹ which brings dirt on the Church of Christ. But if nothing such as this proceeds from us, we will endure the effects of the invited threat.

47. Jer 17.25.
48. ὡς. Other manuscripts have καί.
49. Ps 20.4.   50. Jer 17.25.
51. l has "the Vision of the peace."
52. For these meanings of Judah, Jerusalem, and Benjamin see *Onom. sacra* I.169.66; I.169.82; I.177.83.
53. 2 Cor 10.5.   54. Cf. Jer 17.26.
55. Cf. Rom 12.1; Jer 17.26.   56. Ps 140.2; Jer 17.26.
57. Jer 17.26.   58. Cant 3.6.
59. Cf. Eph 5.2.

12. The Apostle indicated the one who *builds a house with righteousness*[60] when he said: *You are a field of God, a building of God.*[61] But he also says that *no one can lay another foundation than that which is laid, which is Jesus Christ. But if anyone builds,* etc.[62] Therefore, through the one who taught him, the believer has Christ Jesus as a *foundation*. And if any person builds well, it is with *gold*, the teachings of truth, *silver*, the saving word, *precious stones*, a structure built from virtues.[63] And if anyone builds in an evil way by building what is bad for Jesus—I mean *wood, hay, stubble*[64]—how is he not impious? It is for him that the threat comes: *Woe*[65] *to him who builds his house without righteousness!*[66] The one who makes a structure up high, yet not according to reason and truth of God, he does not make *the upper chambers in judgment.*[67] And similarly one can also view those who teach either a true or a *falsely-called knowledge.*[68] Whereas Paul *builds the house*, the Church, *with righteousness*, he builds the *upper chambers*, Timothy and Luke and those such as them, *in judgment*.

13. And you could say that what was mentioned previously[69] might be applicable for false teachers. For on that account Solomon said, *He who produces treasures with a false tongue pursues idle things, and he will come to the snares of death.*[70] For such persons *build* for themselves *houses* in the name of the *Church* that are *filled with evil*[71]—with respect to them is spoken with irony: *You have built for yourself a well-proportioned house, spacious upper chambers.*[72] In them they were supposed[73] to build a place for refreshment. And through *the windows* you intend to enlighten your buildings with the light of knowledge, and you have formed the structure of the house

---

60. Jer 22.13.
61. 1 Cor 3.9.
62. 1 Cor 3.11–12.
63. Cf. 1 Cor 3.11–12.
64. 1 Cor 3.12.
65. "Woe" is not in LXX, but in the Hebrew.
66. Jer 22.13.
67. Jer 22.13.
68. Cf. 1 Tim 6.20.
69. Jer 22.13.
70. Prov 21.6.
71. Ps 25.5.
72. Jer 22.14.
73. "They were supposed" (ᾠήθησαν): o has ᾠήθης ("you were supposed").

with *wood* which will not decay, and you *painted* it with *vermillion* to intimate the blood of Christ.[74] But you *reign* if you also were *provoked in the cedar* of *your father*.[75] *Cedar*, a tree somewhat tall, conspicuous, adverse, is the Devil or the *prince*[76] of wicked doctrines, the *father* of the sinner. And those who have *built* such houses are lost in hunger, for they neither *eat* nor *drink*, and since they have not come to know Christ they have not *known righteousness*.[77] And *doing justice* is, he says, a special quality of those who have known God.[78] With such people neither the *eyes*, which do not see truth, nor the *heart*, which has been filled up with false teachings through which they *kill* their own souls by making others to fall, by *shedding innocent blood* with a false and deceitful tongue, are good.[79] And this is an event worse than the slaughter through swords.[80]

14. Jeremiah calls this son of Jehoiakim Jeconiah, and the Pharaoh Neco called the father of this man, though named Eliakim, Jehoiakim, whom Babylon, having carried off, *cast forth* before the gate, as the present Prophet and Josephus in the tenth book of his *Antiquities* say.[81] And the other editions have given the *signet ring* as a *seal*. And every person[82] who through repentance regains[83] what is *according to the image*[84] becomes a *seal*, a ring on the *right hand of God*.[85] For *good works*[86] are understood as on the *right of God*, who places the

74. Cf. Jer 22.14.   75. Jer 22.15.
76. A common title for the Devil in the New Testament, usually "prince of demons." Cf. Matt 9.34, 12.24; Mark 3.22, etc.
77. Cf. Jer 22.15–16.   78. Jer 22.15–16
79. Cf. Jer 22.17.   80. Cf. Jer 19.6–7.
81. Cf. Josephus 10.5.2 and 6.3; Jer 22.24; 4 Kings 23.34. Jehoiakim's son is called Jehoiachin in 4 Kings 23.34ff. In Jer 22.24 he is called Coniah and in Jer 24.1, Jeconiah. According to Kings, it is Jehoiachin who is carried off by the Babylonians, but according to Jeremiah 24, it is Jeconiah. It is possible that Origen in the original was explaining these differences, but their abridgment has obscured the purpose.
82. "Every person" (πᾶς): c has πως.
83. "Regains" (ἀναλαμβάνων): c has ἀναλαμπρύνων.
84. Gen 1.26.   85. Jer 22.34.
86. Cf. Eph 2.10; James 2.18, 20, etc.

*sheep at the right.*[87] The *father* gave this kind of *seal* to the profligate *son* who returned.[88] If Jeconiah had become this way, he would have been a model for those who are subjects of devotion. But it did not happen. Yet he seemed to be persuaded by what the Prophet said: *He who goes out to surrender to the Chaldeans who have besieged you shall live.*[89] For after he brought with him his *mother* and the *mighty men*, he left, deserting to the Babylonians.[90] But if he also displays the mature repentance, so that he becomes a *seal of righteousness in circumcision*, according to the divine Apostle,[91] so that, according to this, he seems to be *on the right hand of God*, he would be delivered, since he did pay a penalty for his recent sins, though one more moderate. For in Babylon, after he was chastized in prison and in chains, due to Evilmerodach, he was thereupon set free, becoming one who ate with the king, and thus in a foreign land he finished life.

15. He forbids them not merely to *listen to* a prophet[92] but *words of Prophets* when presented in imitation.[93] For he who hears a prophet like Moses hears not him but the Lord who speaks through him. But the false prophets *act in vain.*[94] For in not converting the hearer, when *they speak visions* of their own *heart*, they produce what is *vain.*[95] For an *intellect*[96] which involves itself in things without the will of God speaks a *vision of the heart not from the mouth* of the one who provides the means and enlightens to speak. But it is not in vain[97] whenever the *vision of the heart* and the word of the *mouth of the Lord*

---

87. Matt 25.33.
88. Luke 15.22.
89. Jer 21.9.
90. Cf. 4 Kings 24.12.
91. Rom 4.11.
92. "Listen to a prophet": o has "listen to prophets."
93. Cf. Jer 23.16.
94. Jer 23.16.
95. Cf. Jer 23.16.
96. 1 Cor 14.15. "Intellect": νοῦς. This is a more precise translation in Origen's thought than "mind," which is found in the familiar RSV translation of 1 Cor 14.15. For Origen, the νοῦς was not all of the brain's powers—as we tend to think when we read "mind"—but only the higher, spiritual force of the mind. The New English Bible has "intellect" in 1 Cor 14.14.
97. "Not in vain," I have added.

coincide. Hence he does not demean *the vision of the heart*, but only when it does not include the other. For he agrees with the one who says, *I pray with the mouth, but I also pray with the mind.*[98]

16. He prophesies concerning a *storm* and *anger* of the Lord which *comes down upon the impious.*[99] *The wrath did not turn away,* not by any means *until he executed it,* since it *turns away* when he *executed* it.[100] And what *the word of the Lord*[101] has not *executed,* the *wrath of the Lord executes.* And what the *wrath of the Lord executes* David says in the text: *Lord, do not reprove me with your wrath.*[102] Hence when he *reproves,* he does not stop until that point when he *executes* through what he *reproves,* since it is not *anger* until he completely disciplines. And he not only *executes,* but he *establishes* and secures.[103] But the enigma *from the intents of his heart* which is *in the latter days,* he says, will be *understood clearly* in what was said concerning *wrath* and *anger.*[104] Thanks then to him who revealed the matters which were concealed to us up till now.

17. For this reason, since they force my people back into wrong, they have not escaped my notice. For the one who has enabled the Prophet to know things everywhere, He himself knows much more. For *the Spirit of the Lord has filled all creation.*[105] And *in him we live and move and are,* as Paul said to the Athenians.[106] So also the text: *Do I not fill heaven and earth, says the Lord.*[107] For in power he *is near*[108] to all things. And prayers do not then arise for a god who is like one *far-off.*[109] But also concerning the Son it is said: *He was in the world and the world came into being through him.*[110] For he himself also is one who says, *I am a God who is near.*[111] For he also said, *When two or three are gathered in my name, I am in their*

98. 1 Cor 14.15.
100. Cf. Jer 23.20.
102. Ps 6.2.
104. Jer 23.20.
106. Acts 17.28.
108. Jer 23.23.
110. John 1.10.
99. Jer 23.19.
101. Jer 23.17.
103. Cf. 2 Cor 1.21; 1 Cor 1.8.
105. Wis 1.7.
107. Jer 23.24.
109. Jer 23.23.
111. Jer 23.23.

## FRAGMENTS FROM THE CATENA

*midst,*[112] and the one who says, *Behold I am with you all days until the close of the age.*[113]

18. For just as what belongs to our soul has nothing bereft of the body, but where sense perception[114] is, there too is soul—and it extends to the whole body—so also there is nothing empty of God. And likewise when he *fills*[115] all things, he does not *fill* the sinner, for he has been *filled* with unclean spirits. And such a one without the strength to be *filled* by God is one who is not released from others who *fill*. For *he fills* those on *heaven and earth*[116] who are worthy. For the *earth* and all things on it are not *of the Lord*, but only *the earth and its fullness,*[117] since certain things which are on it are not[118] a *fullness* of the *earth*. For a *fullness* of the *earth* is those who have been *filled* by the one who said, *"Do I not fill heaven and earth?" says the Lord.*[119]

19. Since the false prophets also avail themselves of the phrase, *Thus says the Lord,*[120] pretending to be the true Prophets, there is need of signs which distinguish each of them. Therefore there was, according to the Apostle, a gift of distinguishing *spirits,*[121] and he who possessed this gift distinguished spirits, both the divine and the bad ones, just as a moneychanger distinguishes genuine currency from counterfeit. But aside from this general knowledge, what was just said also suffices for distinguishing. For, *my word*, he says, is not empty and a nourishment for what is irrational, but it is like *wheat* and nourishment for what is rational.[122]

20. *What,* he said, *has straw in common with wheat,*[123] but not with barley? For the Lord has provided *bread of barley*[124] for

---

112. Matt 18.20.
113. Matt 28.20.
114. "Sense perception" (αἴσθησις) used once in the New Testament, Phil 1.9.
115. Jer 23.24.
116. Jer 23.24.
117. Ps 23.1.
118. "Not" (μή). c, l, and o have μέν.
119. Jer 23.24.
120. Cf. Jer 23.31, 2.2, etc.
121. Cf. 1 Cor 12.4–11.
122. Jer 23.28.
123. Jer 23.28.
124. Cf. John 6.9, 13.

those who are more irrational, but *bread of wheat* for the rational. On this account he did not also say now: *What has straw in common with* the barley, but *with the wheat*, since it specifically offers rational nourishment. It is also another sign that those with reason are *like an axe cutting rock*.[125] When[126] the reproved hearer burns so that he says, *Did not my heart burn within me*,[127] the *fire*[128] and the *wheat* are the Word. And if a listener is content with what concerns pleasure, he is *straw*. But the Word of God is also[129] an *axe*, forceful not only on trees, but also to split *rock*, not the *rock* which was understood with respect to Christ,[130] but the opposite one which it is necessary to split according to the text: *Rocks before the Lord will be crushed*.[131]

21. Just as he who buys a garment, perhaps from one who needs it, possesses it lawfully, but the one who has *stolen* it possesses it, but unjustly, so among those who offer words with a dishonest and defiled soul *steal*.[132] Concerning whom it might be said, *All who come before me are thieves and robbers, and the sheep did not hear them*.[133] Such is a person who uses the Gospel word, who is affected neither in faith toward it nor lives in accordance with it, but with an alien purpose uses the narrative of the word. For he is a thief and it will be said to him, *While you preach not to steal, you steal*.[134]

22. What the whole world is, this, according to a certain analogy, a single human being is. For you will discover that one is called a kind of heaven when he bears *the image of the heavenly*,[135] another *earth*, if he has *the image of earthly*. For it was said to the person who sinned, *You are earth*;[136] another has rivers in him *which lead to eternal life*[137] if he has the most fresh words, another which has a salt lake, full of waves,

---

125. Jer 23.29.
126. "When" (ὅταν): o has ἐάν.
127. Luke 24.32.
128. Cf. Jer 23.29.
129. "Also," an addition of Blass and Koetschau.
130. 1 Cor 10.4.
131. 3 Kings 19.11.
132. Jer 23.30.
133. John 10.8.
134. Rom 2.21.
135. 1 Cor 15.49.
136. Gen 3.20.
137. John 4.14.

which has a *dragon which God formed to deceive him.*[138] And by turn you will find that the sun and the moon and stars are mentioned, since *so it is with the resurrection of the dead.*[139]

Then after a little:

(2) But now the parable says he is a *very bad fig.*[140] For virtue sweetens him through ripening, as the whole soul, both spirit and body, is sweet from the quality which is instilled in it from virtues, but wickedness had made him evil and *inedible.*[141] But if anyone seeks[142] not *very good figs,* he seeks outside what concerns the mysteries of religion and the temple of God, just as the reverse is[143] for those not *very bad.* For if he comes to the discipleship itself *before the front of*[144] *the temple of the Lord, figs* are *very good*—the sort Christ knows how to produce—or *very bad.*[145] For the *fig* not outside what is bad throws out the words of God behind him. So around the temple of God and the holy teachings *two baskets*[146] lie. And the one who selects knows how he arranges each *basket,* since he does not sustain the qualities of the *bad fig* in order that the opposite would never mix with the very good. For *a little leaven leavens the whole lump.*[147] And perhaps the *basket of bad figs* is the hell of perpetual fire,[148] and the *basket* of *good figs* is the Kingdom of Heaven.

And after a little:

(3) But when has the Prophet seen[149] *the baskets?* After the Captivity, he said. For if you see the coming of the Savior and the Captivity of the people and us who are strangers by nature and now outside of Jerusalem due to the faith which is in God and sweetness of the truth, who become the good figs, you will see *the basket of good figs.* But if you should view

---

138. Ps 103.26.
139. 1 Cor 15.41–42.
140. Jer 24.1–2.
141. Jer 24.2. Cf. Prov 24.23.
142. "Anyone seeks" (ζητῇ τις): o has ζητῆς.
143. "The reverse is," I have added.
144. "The front of" (προσώπου): c has τοῦ.
145. Jer 24.1–2.
146. Jer 24.1.
147. 1 Cor 5.6.
148. Cf. Matt 5.22, 18.9.
149. "Has seen" (ἑώρακεν): o has τεθέαται.

those who are from a circumcision after this Captivity, you will see *the basket of bad and inedible figs*. And it is not enough that the *figs* are *very good*, but it also matters that they are *like* figs at *first season*.[150] For the one who is saved is not compared to a late *fig*.

23. Christ is a builder and architect, about whom it has been said in the Prophets, *He will build my city and he will turn back the captivity of my people*.[151] Thus the Lord said, *And I will build them up and I will not tear them down*.[152] For the God who is *good*[153] takes down certain buildings. For it is necessary that the building of unclean spirits be destroyed in us and a temple to God be built in this way from virtues and right teachings so that His glory can be seen in it. Yet he is also a tiller who *plants*[154] and one who *grafts*[155] on those who are worthy. For the Savior as a *root* who holds up all *branches*[156] said, *I am the true vine, you the branches, but my Father is the tiller. Every branch which abides in me and makes good fruit my Father prunes in order that it may bear more fruit. But every branch which abides in me but does not bear fruit my Father cuts off and throws it into the fire.*[157] That one who *abides in him and does not bear fruit* exists not among the pagan nations but among the faithful. It is the kind of person who says that he is faithful and yet errs without fear, who is probably *cut off*. But he *prunes* the one who *bears fruit* in order that, even though as a man he might overlook something, it would be set right.

24. The Septuagint, as we were saying, places this text under that which refers to the visions for the pagan nations.[158] But the other editions have the opposite. And the people Elam is Arabic for lying in the Red Sea.

25. For they thought against *archery* because they did not learn to shoot arrows.[159] *For I will place no hope in my bow and*

---

150. Jer 24.2.
151. Isa 45.13.
152. Jer 24.6.
153. Jer 24.6.
154. Jer 24.6.
155. Rom 11.17.
156. Rom 11.18.
157. John 15.1–2, 5–6. Cf. Matt 3.10, 7.19; Luke 3.9.
158. Cf. Jer 25.14ff.
159. Cf. Jer 25.15.

*my sword will not save me.*¹⁶⁰ And *nations* from every corner threaten to move against him; hence, he calls the *winds*¹⁶¹ from those places whence they originated. By analogy each of us is named by our condition Elamites or Idomites or Moabites or Egyptians or Israelites. And the strength to change from one of the *nations* to another is better or worse. For the spiritual *nations* knew to migrate to another. However each of us by analogy, in what he has treasured, drinks from the *cup* of anger of the Lord what is of *pure* or what is of *mixed wine.*¹⁶² For we all sin more or less. But as the name Israel arose for what it had done, when it stood strong for God in battle, so some are *Elamites,* meaning Those-Exposed-as-Blameworthy. For they are interpreted in this way.¹⁶³ And they are exposed as those whom, according to the Apostle, *God delivered to a base mind, to a passion of dishonor.*¹⁶⁴ And it is clear what are the *winds* about which the Word and Paul speak *so that we may no longer be those tossed to and fro and carried about with every wind of teaching by the cunning*¹⁶⁵ *of men, by the style of deceit.*¹⁶⁶ For He-Who-is-Exposed is carried about with every wind of teaching either of wrath or of desire. But the *four winds* are the principal things which arouse the soul of man—desire, fear, pleasure, pain—to which an *Elamite,* who has abandoned God, was delivered. But what is *the bow* of Elam in whom is *the head of the reign?* David himself answered this when he sang, *Behold the sinners have stretched their bow, they have prepared arrows for the quiver in order to shoot down in a dark moon the upright in heart.*¹⁶⁷

And after a little:

(2) But the Savior, after he appears, *brings upon the Elamites* who surround us *the four winds* so that he might *scatter* them.¹⁶⁸ For opposing powers are delivered to other op-

---

160. Ps 43.7.   161. Jer 25.16.
162. See *Hom in Jer* 12.2 on this analogy. Cf. Jer 32.1; Ps 74.9.
163. Cf. *Onom. sacra* I.186.1; I.56.1.   164. Rom 1.28, 26.
165. "Cunning" (κυβία): c has μεθοδεία.
166. Eph 4.14.   167. Ps 10.2.
168. Jer 25.16.

posing powers for punishment, as the Pharaoh is to Nebuchadnezzar. For if you shut up poisonous snakes, those weak from hunger are devoured by those more strong until the strongest one of all, filled up with the serpents whom he has eaten up, becomes the one called basilisk, which has a poison which dries up a fruit-bearing tree from a single look. So the wicked powers are punished by another until *death, the last enemy of Christ*,[169] has left behind the very last, the basilisk, concerning which he said, *You will tread upon the asp and the basilisk.*[170] For Christ, being mightier than the *basilisk*, has *trodden upon* him and given us *authority to tread upon serpents and scorpions.*[171]

26. There is a Babylonian man and a Babylonian infant, and it is necessary to struggle with them, that is, with either mighty forces or now with ruling passions. However, *Blessed is he who, after he has seized them, will dash the infants of Babylon to the rock*[172]—Christ[173]—before they grow up into men. And it is even more *blessed* to *destroy the Babylonian seed.*[174] In what manifests a Confounded[175] thought, is a seed opposite to that concerning which it has been said, *Blessed is he who has a seed in Sion*[176] and, *Blessed are those who sow by every water where the ox and the ass tread.*[177] It is more blessed to destroy not only a man and a boy, but even if[178] it is only a seed. For what is cultivated can bear fruit. But what sort of *water* is it in which it is necessary to *sow* the good *seed?* The baptismal water of rebirth. There *the ox and the ass tread,* the ox as what is pure and an Israelite, the ass as the impure one from the pagan nation. So these animals are symbols of the word announced to the Israelites and proclaimed to the pagan nations.

27. And the Babylonian *handles a sickle* not for saving but for cutting away at the holy land and *mowing down* church-

---

169. 1 Cor 15.26.
170. Ps 90.13.
171. Luke 10.19.
172. Cf. Ps 136.9.
173. Cf. 1 Cor 10.4.
174. Jer 27.16.
175. "Confounded": the interpretation of Babylon. See *Onom. sacra* I.174.91.
176. Isa 31.9.
177. Isa 32.20.
178. "Even if" (κἄν): c has καί.

es.[179] Before we suffer this let us *destroy*[180] him by obliterating the teachings of the heretics. Which was exactly what Paul says, *being ready to punish every disobedience*,[181] he who says *destroying every proud obstacle to the knowledge of God*.[182] Next he testifies to a power in the *Greek* doctrine, since every nation yields to what claims to be verified in every way.[183]

28. He said the sheep is like one who has *gone astray*.[184] And also in the Gospel he said, *The Son of Man came to search for and save the lost*.[185] And also in the parable only one is lost out of the hundred which the shepherd who dwelt with them came to find, who also, after laying it upon his shoulders, returned it to the ninety-nine.[186] *For we are all one body*[187] and one *sheep*. He who is the feet, and the head, and the rest, is the shepherd who, after he came, brought together bone with bone and joint with joint,[188] and after he united them, he took them up to his country. And the unity arises through love and truth and the choice of good.[189] Thus to his own Word he united all. But if some who are disobedient have appeared, they have acquired an incurable condition.[190] Thus every Israelite is one according to the true relationship, *for we are all one body and one loaf of bread and we partake of one spirit*.[191] But a *sheep* which *goes astray* is one who in word and practice does not join the hunt of what is proper, either by not *seeking* or by not *finding*.[192] And the one who knows and does what concerns the knowledge does not *go astray*. But the one who *goes astray* is *driven out* by *lions*. For *your adversary the Devil prowls around like a roaring lion, seeking someone to devour*.[193] And also already *young lions roaring to seize and seek from God food for themselves*[194] lay snares for the righteous,

---

179. Jer 27.16.
180. Jer 27.16.
181. 2 Cor 10.6.
182. 2 Cor 10.5.
183. Jer 27.16.
184. Jer 27.17.
185. Luke 19.10.
186. Cf. Matt 18.12ff.; Luke 15.3–5.
187. Cf. 1 Cor 10.17.
188. Ezek 37.1–14.
189. "Good" (ἀγαθῆς): o has ἀγάπης.
190. Cf. Deut 32.24; Prov 6.15.
191. 1 Cor 10.17; Eph 4.4.
192. Cf. Matt 7.7–8.
193. 1 Pet 5.8. Cf. *Hom in Jer* 5.16.
194. Ps 103.21.

wanting to *drive us out* from the mountains of peace.¹⁹⁵ But as David who took hold of the beard seized the *lion*,¹⁹⁶ so let us beg the spiritual David, Christ, when taking hold of the lion, to abolish also every Sanhedrin of beasts.

(2) But now he takes hold of two principal *lions*, the Assyrian and the Babylonian. According to the history in the fourth book of Kings, there are two. For Assyria *removed* the sons of Israel to Assyria *until today*,¹⁹⁷ but Babylon removed the sons of Judah *to Babylon*.¹⁹⁸ Except he did not say here first and second, but *first* and *last*.¹⁹⁹ For the first *lion* is the antagonistic Devil; he is a *murderer*.²⁰⁰ The very *last* lion at the completion of the age is *the man of sin, the son of perdition, who exalts himself above every so-called god or object of worship*.²⁰¹

29. Israel cannot be *restored to its pasture*²⁰² unless the two *kings* suffer what they need to suffer for the *revenge* of those who have suffered miserably.²⁰³ Yet you should not take the word in every way as referring to the Devil or to the Antichrist. For let me abolish in myself *Satan who is soon crushed under my feet*.²⁰⁴ And whenever you have taken out these two and those in between, he will *restore Israel to its pasture*. It is also when he will *feed on Carmel and on Bashan and in the hills of Ephraim and in Gilead*.²⁰⁵ Though such places are outside of Judea and outside of the land which was inherited, he has named these only.

30. He calls *Babylon* a *hammer worn away* by its own greed on *earth*.²⁰⁶ And when Solomon prepared the divine Temple, the third book of Kings said in praise that *a hammer and axe were not heard in the house of God*.²⁰⁷ But the Church of God is a house in which a *hammer* must not *be heard*. Yet the Devil is

---

195. Cf. Ps 71.3.
196. Cf. 1 Kings 17.34–35.
197. 4 Kings 17.23.
198. 4 Kings 25.7, 11.
199. Jer 27.17. Ziegler's text of LXX reads ὕστερος, but ancient witnesses have ἔσχατος.
200. John 8.44; 1 John 3.15.
201. 2 Thess 2.3–4.
202. Jer 27.19.
203. Jer 27.17–18.
204. Cf. Rom 16.20.
205. Jer 27.19.
206. Jer 27.23.
207. 3 Kings 6.12.

the *hammer of the whole earth,* and there is one who has no concern for it, as if some substance is beaten by it and does not suffer. For he said, *Behold, a man stood upon a wall of adamant and in his hand was adamant.*[208] Whoever is *adamant* is affected by no *hammer.* Even if the Devil as the *hammer* stands above and a dragon *as an unyielding anvil*[209] lies below, *adamant* in the hand of the Lord and under his protection will yield nothing. For the holy man is a *wall of adamant* and when he remains in the hands of the Lord, he is unsuffering, even if he was taken in the midst of *hammer* and dragon. And insofar as he is beaten, he displays his virtue brighter. For the Devil, ignorant of this kind of rocks, assays through many blows a kind of *adamant,* but God alone knows the nature of them well. If there was not a *hammer,* there would not be, according to the Law, a *beaten trumpet,*[210] rousing the hearers to the feasts of God or inciting the hearers to war. The *hammer* made Paul such through varied temptations, though Paul did not suffer from it, but in a great voice roused himself up to the war against evil. Thus the *hammer* bangs out temptation, but the *smith* from Cain, *manufacturer of brass and iron,*[211] is a servant to the *hammer.* Judas with respect to the Savior is such a person, and those who cry out, *Crucify, crucify him,*[212] are servants to the *hammer* because of such acts.[213]

31. The Apostle also knows *vessels of wrath*[214] *made for destruction so that he might make known the riches of his glory for vessels of mercy.*[215] And he has divided all men into these two *vessels,* those of *wrath,* those of *mercy,* those like the Pharaoh and the Egyptians, those like Paul and those who have believed. But what is the *treasury*[216] of the Lord in which are the *vessels of wrath?* Perhaps it is the Church in which such often go unnoticed. But there will be a time when he *opens*[217] the

---

208. Amos 7.7.  
209. Job 41.15.  
210. Num 10.2, 8, 9. Cf. *Hom in Jer* 5.16.  
211. Gen 4.22.  
212. John 19.15.  
213. Cf. *Hom in Jer* 27(50).1 (Latin) above.  
214. Jer 27.25.  
215. Rom 9.22–23.  
216. Jer 27.25.  
217. Jer 27.25.

Church. For now they have been shut up and the *vessels of wrath* share space with the *vessels of mercy,* and the *chaff* are with the *wheat,*[218] and in one net are the worthless and the chosen *fish.*[219] And *the Lord opens up his treasury* in the time of the judgment, when the *vessels of wrath* are thrown out, he who is a *vessel of mercy* may reasonably say: *They have gone out from us, for they were not from us.*[220] And outside the treasury the *vessels* who sin are not yet[221] the *vessels of wrath,* but inferior. For they are *servants who did not know the will of their Lord and did not do it.*[222] So they are *vessels* who are simply kept for other purposes.[223]

32. Some of the captives of the Jews come proclaiming the *vengeance* against *Babylon.*[224] And he may speak also concerning those who turn back from idolatry, which he calls *Babylon.* Whoever have come into *Sion,* the Watchtower,[225] the Church, they report the *vengeance for the Lord our God.*[226]

33. *Many* are in *Babylon,*[227] but very few are in Jerusalem. For it is said: *It was not on account of this that you are numerous, that the Lord God loved you. For you are fewer than all the nations.*[228] For there are really *few* who are *saved* and who *enter through the narrow door.*[229] And *all those who bend the bow* are *summoned against* the *wide and spacious*[230] *Babylon* to preserve nothing of her.[231]

34. Whenever a person has great thoughts which oppose piety, *many* are *Babylonians.* One must do away with such sins, since they are of the earth. The one who has been purified from these who avenges *the pride* of Babylon is in the city of God. For he supposed that he prevailed with his own power

---

218. Matt 3.12; Luke 3.17.  219. Cf. Matt 13.47–49.
220. 1 John 2.19.
221. "Not yet" (οὔπω), or "not at all."  222. Luke 12.47–48.
223. See above *Hom in Jer* 27(50).3 (Latin).
224. Jer 27.28.  225. See *Onom. sacra* I.174.90.
226. Jer 27.28. Cf. *Hom in Jer* 27(50).6 (Latin) above.
227. Jer 27.29.  228. Cf. Deut 7.7.
229. Cf. Luke 13.23–24.  230. Matt 7.13.
231. Cf. above *Hom in Jer* 27(50).6 (Latin).

and he demeaned God. For after the Temple was ablaze, the sacred vessels were given to the concubines for use.[232] Therefore in a *fire* he consumes the fruitless people, just as he would a *forest*. Accordingly he said to this one: *Behold, I am against you, the proud one, says the Lord of hosts.*[233]

35. He prophesies that the end will happen suddenly. *For just as in the days of the flood,*[234] and *in the days of Lot,*[235] all were attending to concerns of life *until the flood and the fire came and destroyed them all,* so will the swiftness of the end be. Of which Jericho which fell suddenly with a shout and a single blare of trumpets was a symbol.[236] But also *Babylon fell quickly*[237] around the time of the Passion of the Savior, since Christ abolished the teachings concerning pagan idols and redeemed from the pagan nations those who believed.[238]

36. The *cup* of Nebuchadnezzar is *golden* for the deceit of men in order that, after they receive it, because they view the gold *that is good to behold with the eyes and beautiful to consider* but do not count on the judgment which is in it, they drink.[239] For his villainous teachings are embellished with speciousness, baiting with a beauty of expression and a skilled method. And yet every workman who appears consummate has fabricated a *golden cup*, putting in the poison of idolatry, abuse and all sorts of carnal evils. But Jesus did not provide a *golden cup* lest it seem at all similar to that one—wherefore *we have this treasure in earthen vessels*[240]—but for the salvation in himself. And when the *golden cup, Babylon,* meets its vengeance, it is in the *hand of the Lord,*[241] in what once took hold of Job,[242] for *she causes all the earth to be drunk* from anger, from grief, desire, vanity—for whatever the sins are, all are also intoxicants, even as are *all of those shaken up from wine*[243]

232. Cf. Dan 5.2, 3.
233. Cf. Jer 27.29–32.
234. Matt 24.38–39.
235. Luke 17.28.
236. Cf. Josh 6.20.
237. Jer 28.8.
238. Cf. above *Hom in Jer* 28(51).11 (Latin).
239. Cf. Jer 28.7.
240. 2 Cor 4.7.
241. Jer 28.7.
242. Job 2.5.
243. Jer 28.7.

and having nothing stable. But the righteous man is not *earth*.[244] For though he is on *earth*, he has the *commonwealth in heaven*[245] and would not hear: *You are earth and to earth you will return*,[246] but more likely: "You are heaven and to heaven you will return; for you bear *the image of the heavenly*[247] and stand unshaken."[248]

37. But if Babylon was not declared hopeless—for then he would not have said, *if she will be healed by any means*[249]—what other kind of soul will we declare hopeless? And if she has not been saved, this occurred on account of herself,[250] since the best doctors spoke in their own defence and said, *We tried to heal Babylon and she was not healed. Let us forsake her.*[251] For it is not on account of them, nor on account of the healing skill nor on account of *resin*,[252] that this one is not healed. And these are angel-healers who are under the great Healer God and who want to heal those who are persuaded. And if not, they will say, *Let us forsake her, let each of us leave for his own land* and his own place and his own concerns, *for her judgment has reached to heaven*,[253] condemning her as incurable and as one who has yielded to what is hopeless. For the healers of the body abandon the incurable, lest perchance they should expire while in their hands. This then is what the angels do. And to the degree we sin, the *judgment* on us grows, and if it *mounts up to the stars*,[254] it is clearly for the holy ones. And then God *brings forth his judgment*[255] for the abasement of the *judgment* which raised itself so high from sin, by abasing the sin and rendering what is due.[256]

---

244. Jer 28.7.
245. Phil 3.20.
246. Gen 3.19.
247. 1 Cor 15.49.
248. Cf. above *Hom in Jer* 28(51).7–9 (Latin).
249. Jer 28.8.
250. "On account of herself" (παρ' αὐτήν), a correction of Blass. c and o have παρ' αὐτῇ.
251. Jer 28.9.
252. Jer 28.8.
253. Jer 28.9.
254. Jer 28.9.
255. Jer 28.10.
256. Cf. above *Hom in Jer* 28(51).12 (Latin).

38. And Isaiah prophesied: *Raise up a standard on the mountain of the plain; exalt the voice to them; beckon with the hand.*[257] And the Prophets have given these counsels to the Persians and Medes—as they were already stronger than Babylon—to raise up *on her walls*[258]—as she can be easily conquered—the signal of the war, through which they show the attack point for the soldiers. And he advises *to have the shields ready. The bows are for the Medes,* he said.[259]

39. And in agreement with the statement that *every man was made foolish from knowledge,*[260] Paul said, *Has God not made foolish the wisdom of this world?*[261] And *a time of visitation*[262] especially is the destruction of idolatry by the appearance of Christ. And the *vessels of war* which Babylon has *scattered*[263] are the experienced men of war of Israel and Judah, for the sake of which he threatens that no one is to be spared.

40. The demons are the *riders of horses*[264] who sit upon the fleshly pleasures. For the contests of Egypt also *threw horse and rider into the sea,*[265] but those which are harnassed in us are different passions which are opposed to the four virtues which build *chariots.*[266] And he who is wild and vigorous for evil is *man*. And she who is unrestrained in pleasure is *woman.*[267] And he who has *aged by wicked days*[268] is an *elder.*[269] And the *youths*[270] are those concerning whom Isaiah said, *The young will hunger and the youth will be weary, and the chosen ones will be powerless.*[271] But in contrast: *But those who wait on God with renewed strength, they shall put forth new feathers like eagles, they shall run and not tire.*[272] But now if he says that the *chosen ones*[273] are among evil, what sort of statement is: *His food also*

257. Isa 13.2. Cf. Jer 28.12.
258. Jer 28.12.
259. Cf. Jer 28.11.
260. Jer 28.17.
261. 1 Cor 1.20.
262. Jer 28.18.
263. Cf. Jer 28.17–20.
264. Jer 28.21.
265. Exod 15.1.
266. Jer 28.21.
267. Jer 28.22.
268. Cf. Dan 13.52 (Susanna)
269. Jer 28.22 (Hebrew).
270. Jer 28.22.
271. Isa 40.30.
272. Isa 40.31.
273. Not in Ziegler's text, but cited by him in notes, 295.

302                          ORIGEN

*was the chosen.*[274] Those *chosen* according to virtue were consumed by Nebuchadnezzar.[275] But he also had *maidens,*[276] the Hestiakans, the Pythians and the others. But also the soul who has not received the divine seed is a *maiden* to him. And he also refers to *shepherds*[277] who train by evil teaching those who follow them. But he refers also to *farmers*[278] who sow *weeds*[279] and those who till *thorns and thistles,*[280] the concerns of daily life among men. He refers also to *governors* and *rulers*[281] in evil, and *the battle for us is especially against them, against the rulers, against the powers.*[282] Thus for *all* of these God *requites*[283] in the presence of those just mentioned: *Come and let us declare in Sion the magnificent deeds of God.*[284]

41. On account of the height of the kingdom he calls Babylon a *mountain* which was *ruined* from idolatry and unjust works, through which it *destroyed* the others.[285] And it also was the city on high because of the river nearby from which some stairs went up to the city, the city being in two parts, and lying close to the river on each bank, with the walls also of the city being very high. And it mentioned a *hand,* the avenging power, the same power of his which destroyed something made from *rocks*[286] for security and for watch. And due to the fire having *obliterated* its *stones,*[287] they were useless, as there was not a stone to be put together for a firm building. And for the anagogical meaning, the Devil is named a *mountain,* as in the book of Zechariah: *Who are you, a great mountain before the face of Zorobabel?*[288] And concerning the one who has the *deaf and dumb* demon, the Savior said, *If you have faith as a grain of mustard seed, you will say to this mountain: "Move away," and it will move away.*[289] Thus the Devil is a *moun-*

274. Hab 1.16.
276. Jer 28.22.
278. Jer 28.23.
280. Cf. Matt 13.22.
282. Eph 6.12.
284. Jer 28.10.
286. Jer 28.25.
288. Zech 4.7.
275. Jer 28.34.
277. Jer 28.23; cf. 1 Tim 4.6.
279. Cf. Matt 13.25.
281. Jer 28.33.
283. Jer 28.24.
285. Jer 28.25.
287. Jer 28.26.
289. Matt 17.20.

*tain* which is *ruined* from his own evil and which *destroys* everyone to the extent they have their mind on what is earthly.[290]

42. The statement, *Consecrate the nations*,[291] is instead of: "Segregate them." For the service of God is holy, even if the one who is segregated with respect to it may be vengeful and profane. Such a person was Cyrus to whom He said through Isaiah: *But you have not known me*.[292] And he called some of those who fought against Babylon profane nations, among which he calls *Ararat*[293] of the Armenians.

43. And *the earth trembled*.[294] Though the men on it were in the past situated securely and had the most stable positions under the tyrannies and kingdoms, they now receive the *desolation* as an unfortunate and painful change. And every thought which had possessed the *Babylonian earth*,[295] after being shaken from the craving for such impiety and Confusion,[296] rejects such a condition to take up the spiritual and heavenly state.

44. For God was the one doing this, the one who spoke through Isaiah to Cyrus: *I will go before you and I will level mountains, I will break in pieces brazen doors and I will burst iron bars*.[297] For Babylon is recorded to have such gates around the outside, and to be seized from the descents into the river which was in the middle, each part joined by bridges joined to the paths which led up to the city, since the city was divided in line with each part. The history also says that, as those who conquered were around the outskirts of the city, while the others were taking part in a festival, they did not notice on account of the great size of the city when, as is likely, some *ran* toward the *report* but the rest were turning away from it to be there in the city filled with the noise.[298] And he

---

290. Cf. Jer 28.25.
291. Jer 28.27.
292. Isa 45.4.
293. Jer 28.27.
294. Jer 28.29.
295. Jer 28.29.
296. "Confusion," the meaning of Babylon. See *Onom. sacra* I.174.91.
297. Isa 45.2.
298. Cf. Jer 28.31. See Herodotus, I.180, 186, 191.

seems to say the *military corps*[299] are now houses. For in the sequence of events they were *joined* with others. Hence there follows next: *The houses of the king of Babylon*[300] and so forth; that is to say, the strongholds from those joined together in them.

45. Symmachus[301] says that they shall *lead him astray* and they shall *break in pieces his possessions*. And *they shall bring strain on him* and *empty out his possessions*.[302] For he continued in the souring of the wine, showing that it will be emptied of the good. The plenty indeed is not good for those who have boasted, as it is not for the *rich man* in *Hades*, on account of which he is punished.[303] But since the word *mixtures*[304] as for wine was mentioned, Aquila[305] rendered it κέρατα,[306] which was the original form of cup—for they drank from horns— whence also to say "to mix"[307] survived. The cities therefore are *vessels*,[308] and men and wealth are what is inside. As they are taken away, the *vessels* are filled up again. And the event *shames* the hopes with demons. But *the hope* with God *is not ashamed*.[309] And Jeroboam in Samaria placed heifers on Bethel.[310] And the one who does not say he is *strong*[311] is saved. For *a king is not saved through much power*.[312] And the *day of Moab* is the time of punishment, and *misfortunes* are the pains which will seize this person.[313] But worthy are all those in a *circle* to insult him. For this is what *shake the head* at him means, namely, with reference to his shame and pain.[314] For, *God opposes the proud*.[315]

299. Jer 28.32. "Military corps" (συστήματα): the translation of LXX is uncertain here. I have assumed a connection, albeit weak, to the Hebrew.
300. Jer 28.33.
301. One of the versions of the Bible in Origen's Hexapla.
302. Jer 31.12.
303. Cf. Luke 16.19ff.; Jer 9.23.
304. "Mixture" in Greek is κέρασμα.
305. The name of another column in Origen's Hexapla.
306. κέρατα are horns.
307. In Greek "to mix" is κέρασαι.
308. Jer 31.11.
309. Rom 5.5.
310. 3 Kings 12.29.
311. Jer 31.14.
312. Ps 32.16.
313. Jer 31.16.
314. Jer 31.17.
315. Prov 3.34; James 4.6.

46. He presents as an *arm*[316] either the sceptre or those under the ruler or hirelings. For the recompense are wages.[317]

47. He will *clap with his hands*.[318] He *has clapped with his hands* when he rejoices in Israel's troubles and boldly stands up against God. And those who have *trusted* in the *strongholds*[319] of the *cities*, when they *leave* them to *live* in the *rocks* which are set in mountain clefts, they are those who copy *doves* in their licentiousness and lawlessness.[320] For it matters when they hide in places from which those who want can easily rob the *nestlings*.[321] And the one who is consecrated to *Baal of Peor*[322] and who foolishly is attached to useless and vain idols is also licentious. Such a one was Moab. For *the fool said in his heart: there is no god*,[323] since he is either an atheist in every sense or he considers that one who is really God does not exist.

48. *Jerusalem*, according to what is often said,[324] is interpreted as the Church, which is a city of God built from *living rocks*,[325] from which anyone who sins, when delivered to Nebuchadnezzar, to Satan, is cast out. For Paul says concerning the fornicator, that he *delivers this man to Satan for the destruction of the flesh, that his spirit may be saved in the day of the Lord*.[326] And in the first letter to Timothy, concerning those who blaspheme, *whom I have delivered to Satan, that they may learn not to blaspheme*.[327] And let the one cast out of *Jerusalem* know that if he did not complete sufficient time doing what is necessary outside the Church, he would not be sent back to *Jerusalem*. And anyone who sins is cast out, even if he was not cast out by men. But it is necessary that he who is outside not neglect to *construct a house* and *to plant gardens*.[328] For when he does

---

316. Jer 31.25. "Arm" (ἐπιχείριον), the word is not in the LXX, which has ἐπίχειρον.
317. "Wages:" ἐπίχειρα. See previous note.
318. Jer 31.26.
319. Cf. Jer 31.7.
320. Cf. Jer 31.26–28.
321. Cf. Jer 31.26–28.
322. Cf. Num 25.5.
323. Ps 13.1.
324. Cf. *Hom in Jer* 1.3, 9.2, 18.14.
325. Cf. 1 Pet 2.5.
326. 1 Cor 5.5.
327. 1 Tim 1.20.
328. Jer 36.5.

not do these things nor complete the symbolic number of *seventy years*[329] which also belongs to the sabbath rest, he is not sent back to associate with the Church, but remains one condemned to be outside Jerusalem. But what it is to *take wives*,[330] the one who spoke concerning wisdom clarified: *I sought to make her my spouse, and I was a lover of her beauty.*[331] And it is necessary that he love this one, just as in the Proverbs of Solomon, it was advised, when he said: *Love her and she will exalt you.*[332] And he understands the other women beside wisdom as the rest of the virtues. So it will be possible that many will *take wives*, from whom it is necessary to *beget children.*[333] One begets from wisdom a word of wisdom as you also would build other things; from prudence, works of prudence that you may make in life and word prudent things; from righteousness, works of righteousness in community and in contracts. But also when you teach what is righteous and when you have begotten *sons* from the *sons and daughters, sons* as the divine thoughts and doctrines, and *daughters* as the practices, *you will make children* from righteousness.

49. Since Babylon was in control of a disrupted Jerusalem, it is likely that those who want to see the future took refuge in foreknowledge. But the *false prophets*[334] insist that they foretell from the Holy Spirit. And some of the others are *diviners*, others again interpret *dreams.*[335] For this reason it is necessary that we not follow in any sense every profane foreknowledge. For if the stars by chance do influence, we pray in vain. Hence he said, *If the astrologers of heaven have spoken, what does the Lord advise concerning you,*[336] and, *There will be no divination in Jacob, nor enchantment in Israel.*[337] So he who is worthy of divine foreknowledge belongs to a race. For he proposes it after *there will be no enchantment in Israel. In time it will be told to Jacob and to Israel what God will accomplish.*[338]

---

329. Cf. Jer 36.10.
331. Wis 8.2.
333. Jer 36.6.
335. Cf. Jer 36.8.
337. Num 23.23.

330. Jer 36.6.
332. Prov 4.6,8.
334. Jer 36.8.
336. A variant of Isa 47.13.
338. Num 23.23.

50. Every presbyter who does such things will be convinced of such things under a *king of Babylon*.[339] For if one who partakes of the eucharist unworthily will receive *judgment*,[340] how much more will he who sits in the presbytery, who is defiled in mind, and who corrupts the council of Christ? For what devout man who is seated with him will dare to say that *I have not sat with a council of vanity*[341] and the remainder?[342]

51. And you might say that he is also exhibiting his unique kind of goodness through which he brings severity upon those who are in need of it. Thus, after he has attended to the pain, *the city*, he says, *will be built at its height*.[343] What sort of *height*? *A city set on a hill cannot be hid*.[344] Whoever is one who thinks nothing lowly or human says pleasures and riches on earth are also a contemptible glory. For, *he rose with Christ and seeks the things above*.[345] When you do these things, your *city will be built at its height*.

52. As he speaks about a rare matter.

It is the custom in Scripture that, after what is bitter, to say kind things for encouragement, and after what is good to say more bitter words, in order that, when they have disdained the *wealth of the goodness* of God,[346] they may not store up for themselves *anger in a day of anger*.[347] Hence he said: *If anger comes, it will not withdraw unless God has accomplished what he wants*.[348] And if God wants, *anger* also occurs, in order that what God wants does occur. For if anyone does not want to be in the will of the Word of God, the *anger*[349] is unleashed on him. Thus let us not show a need for an *anger* or *wrath* which disciplines.

---

339. Cf. Jer 36.21.
340. Cf. 1 Cor 11.27, 29.
341. Ps 25.4.

342. The reader may here wish to turn to the *Letter to Africanus*, where Origen comments on Jer 36.22, 23. Klostermann gives the Greek fragment from the letter, 224, in a footnote. The complete letter is translated by F. Crombie in ANF, 10:371–87.

343. Jer 37.18.
344. Matt 5.14.
345. Col 3.1.
346. Rom 2.5.
347. Rom 2.5.
348. Cf. Jer 23.20.
349. Jer 37.23–24.

308     ORIGEN

53. For it is not through desert, as in former times, but through the law-abiding and the inhabited area. And also it is said allegorically in *consolation*[350] that *blessed are those who mourn, for they shall be comforted.*[351]

54. The far-off *islands*[352] tossed with the waves of life, these are *far* from truth before they come to the salvation. God *ransomed* Jacob.[353] For, *the yoke which was laid upon them has been taken away, and the rod which was on their neck,*[354] as Isaiah says. But it is clear also that he of the diabolic power holds us. For what can we do against the one who said both the other[355] statements, and *I will take in my hand the whole world as a nest?* Against whom we say through Christ: *Death, where is your victory? Death, where is your sting?*[356]

55. To those worthy of a blessing who weep, to those who speak in the Holy Spirit, let it be said, *Let your voice cease from weeping. There by the rivers of Babylon we sat, and we wept in our remembrance of Zion.*[357]

56. It was also written in Baruch: *Why is it that you are in the land of enemies? You are defiled with the dead.*[358] For whenever the righteous go about, it is a land of the holy. But whenever there are many sinners, it is the *land* of the *enemies*.[359] And so, he says, they shall *return*, since an *abiding* place[360] exists for your children to *return* to from a *land of enemies*, for those helped by you and for your fruits. And in Exodus also it is written that *God heard* the people, *their groans from their works*.[361] There is a similar view in what is set down here, but not concerning all, but concerning the *lamenting of Ephraim*.[362] And *Ephraim* is interpreted Fruit-Bearing.[363]

57. God *hears* the weeping voice of those who *repent*.[364]

350. Jer 38.9.
352. Cf. Jer 38.10.
354. Isa 9.4.
356. 1 Cor 15.55.
358. Bar 3.10.
360. Jer 38.16–17.
362. Jer 38.16–18.
364. Jer 38.18–19.

351. Matt 5.4.
353. Jer 38.11.
355. Cf. Isa 10.14.
357. Ps 136.1.
359. Jer 38.16.
361. Exod 2.23–24.
363. Cf. *Onom. sacra* I.164.67.

Why did he say, *Ephraim laments*[365] for sins? The third book of Kings indeed makes clear that while Rehoboam cruelly rules them, it was necessary that they who were waiting not revolt—*we had no part in David,*[366] they cried out. When Jeroboam led those who withdrew—it being the tribe Ephraim—he was the very one who, after he made the heifers, took away the ten tribes from the worship of God.[367] Regarding them, they are, of course, in distress as they repent and cry out, as they are disciplined for the conquest. *You have chastened me, Lord, and I was chastened.* For as any *calf* who has skipped away from the herd, I have gone away from your pasture, and I need your help. For if you refuse, I will be unable to return. And it is necessary that I repent prior to the conquest and be obedient to your Prophets. After the conquest I *repented.*[368] And when he *knew,* he *bemoaned.*[369] For how can anyone who is ignorant that he sins have *bemoaned,* who has done acts worthy of *shame* for sins and especially for licentious acts? Yet I *repented* for such a thing, as it was *shown* in other ways to you. The repentance of Ephraim is great, so that God takes up from his mouth the words of the confession, and he hears a voice which says *from youth you are my beloved son, Ephraim.*[370]

58. A certain Assyrian, Nebuchadnezzar, possessed all men, from whom Christ ransomed us. Hence Matthew said from Isaiah that he *proclaims release for the captives.*[371] For he did not according to historical fact proclaim it to the captives. But he also is the *righteous and holy mountain.*[372] For how could they be related to a lifeless thing? But if we are in him, in accordance with the statement, *And you are in me,*[373] we might build on the *righteous mountain.* And a person does this when he is in *Judea,*[374] which is translated, She-Who-Has-

---

365. Jer 38.18.
366. Cf. 3 Kings 12.16, 24.
367. 3 Kings 12.28.
368. Cf. Jer 38.19.
369. Jer 38.19.
370. Jer 38.20.
371. Luke 4.18; Isa 61.1. This text is not found in Matthew.
372. Jer 38.23.
373. John 14.20.
374. Jer 38.23, 24.

Confessed,[375] she who has confessed to God her sins and given thanks. For *speak first of your licentiousness, so that you might become righteous.*[376] For some *cities*[377] of God are both his *buildings* and his *fields*. For Paul says also, *You are a field of God, a building of God.*[378] For in it the mysteries and ineffable teachings about God are constructed, in this is a temple of God and the holy of holies, this is the metropolis of all of *Judea*.

59. It appears that the statement, *I will not reject Israel* is opposite to the one which says to them, *And the race Israel shall cease,*[379] unless the one has been said concerning the fleshly Israel, the other concerning the spiritual Israel. Yet the word "not" added to the phrase, *I will reject* is not from the rest of the translations,[380] but only from the Septuagint. But you will also consider it this way, that I will now reject, but if it was *exalted*, I *will not reject.*

60. We are all in *prison,*[381] and especially those who are tempted. Then someone *acquires a field,*[382] but not because he comes out of *prison*. And the *acquiring* is in the will of God for those who struggle well. And the brothers Chelkias, father of Jeremiah, and Hanamel, both were sons of Shallum. For the effect of [these] brothers is both peace and portion of God. For Chelkias is translated as Portion, Shallum, Peace.[383] And the fruit of the portion of God is the Raising-Up-of-God. For so Jeremiah is translated.[384] And the fruit of peace is the grace of God. This is clear for Hanamel.[385] Thus the grace of God which is a progeny of peace produces in the Prophet in *prison* his own *field*, according to the command of God.

61. He makes a *deed of purchase,*[386] which is equally the thoughts, the memories, the opinions, through which we

---

375. *Onom. sacra* I.193.13; I.203.99.
376. Isa 43.26.
377. Jer 38.23.
378. 1 Cor 3.9.
379. Jer 38.36, 37.
380. Or from the Hebrew.
381. Jer 39.7–8.
382. Jer 39.7.
383. Cf. *Onom. sacra* I.184.67; I.55.16.
384. Cf. *Onom. sacra* I.192.91.
385. Cf. *Onom. sacra* I.162.25.
386. Jer 39.10.

have created the *field*, that is, the labors of our way of life. For it is necessary that he who practices righteousness has known before about righteousness, which may be said also about the rest of the virtues. And God considers that the *deed* is placed with more permanence in a *vessel*.[387] For, *we have this treasure in earthen vessels*,[388] or in our own *vessels*, or in the meanness of the written text. Hence, the *ruler of this world* is deceived, when he has despised the doctrine of religion, since it was not in golden vessels beautifully adorned in text and in a most persuasive way of expression. Thus also it *lasted many days*.[389] For *my speech and my messages*, the one who possesses the *deed of purchase* says, *are not in plausible words of wisdom but in a demonstration of spirit and power*.[390] And Jeremiah, after he had done the injunction, gave thanks to God. And see the obedience of the Prophet before the advantage is apparent, which he does present when he foretells the regaining of the land. For the prophecy through works, by making evident the whole in the part, sets down what is heard as what is seen, and the future as the present.

62. It is not plausible that such a Prophet, who was consecrated *from the womb*[391] and was full of the Holy Spirit, offers thanks for the property purchased for *seventeen shekels*.[392] But note that it is the sabbath number, the symbol of rest, and ten means something perfect and akin to God—for there are tens referred to in the tenth day of the propitiations[393] and the first legal code is a decalogue—and he knew the *field*,[394] the place full of the fruits suitable for the holy. Such was the *field* of Jacob which Isaac smelled.[395] *Behold*, he said, *the smell of my son is like the smell of an abundant field which the Lord has blessed*. So it is with the one who *possesses the fruits of the spirit*,[396] so that he can *sow things of the spirit and harvest eternal life*. For Jacob does not smell the smell of vines or of figs,

387. Jer 39.14.
388. 2 Cor 4.7.
389. Jer 39.14.
390. 1 Cor 2.4.
391. Jer 1.5.
392. Cf. Jer 39.9.
393. Cf. Lev 23.27ff.
394. Cf. Jer 39.9.
395. Gen 27.27.
396. Gal 5.22.

but of *charity, joy, peace, patience, kindness, goodness, faith, self-control.*[397] In such light then Jeremiah gives thanks for the *field* when he says, *O Lord Who-Is.*[398] For he looks to the One who is really, by not looking *at the things seen but the things not seen.*[399]

63. Not only has Jeremiah recorded prophecies, but also his own experiences, where to some he teaches the mysteries of the Kingdom of Heaven, while to others he teaches examples of perseverance, though the false prophets experience due to flattery nothing such as this. So let us be prepared in a time of persecution to be posted with Jeremiah and the Apostle who was *in chains often.*[400] And because *the king had no power with them,*[401] he disclosed the purpose more benevolent than his. And it is not necessary that the *upright king* be led away by the evils around him. Yet often the party around those who prevail is useful, through whom God often does good.

64. I fear, he said, that I become ridiculous to the deserters.[402] For I make out of this a motive and worries. But as Jerusalem is delivered through sin, so also is the Church. And if anyone should rule her according to Ezekiah, he will be saved. But if one rules according to Zedekiah, King of Judah, he saves as one cast out, but by remaining he destroys her. Therefore, if any person, when he defiles the Church, should leave, he saves it and *his soul.*[403] But if someone is about to act according to Zedekiah in regard to the departure, *A little leaven leavens the whole lump.*[404]

65. Jeremiah said to him that *the women will say* as they are led to an exiled place: "Those who have spoken of peace with you *have deceived you,* since they will not surrender to the Babylonian."[405] But they are allied with you as those who are causes of the fall. For in every way he might be taken.

---

397. Gal 5.22–23.
398. Jer 39.17.
399. 2 Cor 4.18.
400. 2 Cor 11.23.
401. Jer 45.5.
402. Cf. Jer 45.19.
403. Cf. Jer 45.20.
404. Gal 5.9.
405. Cf. Jer 45.22.

And perhaps he might also blame the false prophets who in their doctrine promise peace. But the Prophet kindly concealed the truth from the princes, since the king was worried.[406] For he did not impede this now by being silent, having already read them the words in public.

66. The Prophet, receiving a choice in what place he wants to live, since Babylon was unconcerned, decides for Judah,[407] because he avoids the honor from the king, and because of those poor who cleave to farming, as he also could take care of the earth for the laborers and till the souls of them with prophecies.[408] For the Prophets were distributed, he in Judah, and Daniel and the three youths in Babylon.[409]

67. The good man suspects that there is nothing wicked in this plan,[410] since to murder those who have done wrong is not wicked. But why did God agree to raise up Gedaliah if there could be another way and the judgments of God unattainable?[411]

68. He connects *the incense* with *the Lord did not remember*.[412] It is clear then that it is concerning the burning of *incense* to idols that he speaks. For when they confessed this, the preceding is put forth. However, let us also examine whether anyone who burns *incense* to God, since it is not necessary, becomes a cause for the *land becoming desolate*.[413] Even if indeed you offer the sensuous *incense* approved by the Jews, but you possess virtue, you offer in a good way, since you possess what is harmonious with the inner fragrance. But if you offer with evil, in the sense that you taint in some way the fragrance which is outside, you transform it into something foul-smelling. This is when it cannot be said, *The Lord smelled a smell of fragrance*,[414] but the opposite. Yet a smell of fragrance before God is not of the creatures caught by Noah,

---

406. Cf. Jer 45.24ff.
408. Cf. Jer 47.4, 5.
410. Cf. Jer 48.2.
411. This fragment is believed to be from the writings of Chrysostom.
412. Jer 51.21.
414. Gen 8.21.
407. Jer 47.4, 5.
409. Cf. Dan 1.6.
413. Jer 51.22.

who are called *clean*,[415] but of his *righteousness* and *maturity*, which he was in his generation.[416] For God does not enjoy blood and sacrificial odors, as the demons do. Only let us who are *raised with Christ seek the things above*,[417] by taking into mind[418] the text: *Let my prayer come as incense before you.*[419] For according to John in the Apocalypse, he says, *The prayers of the holy are incense.*[420] But if we defile them with bad thoughts, then it corresponds with: *Let their prayer arise for sin*, or the reverse if we pray from righteousness. Since[421] he is among those who say on account of sin, *My bruises have come to stink and rot from the presence of my foolishness*,[422] the *incense* becomes foul-smelling. Therefore Isaiah said: *If you bring semidalis*,[423] *it is in vain; incense, it is an abomination to me.*[424] But how one has to pray, the Apostle taught when he said, *I desire that men pray in every place by raising holy hands without anger and quarreling.*[425] When the hands of Moses were raised, Israel prevailed, but when they were lowered Amalek prevailed.[426] He who *prays* in this way does not fail, since the word bears the truth: *While you are speaking, he will say: "Behold I am near."*[427] Therefore the *incense* of the *wicked*, he says, the *Lord can no longer bear*,[428] just as we, even if we can endure some foul odor, avoid an odor which is excessive. God also then, who has a limit of forbearance, does not pursue those who do not[429] repent. Which is what he has done regarding Noah, when he

---

415. Gen 7.2–3.
416. Cf. Gen 7.10. "Maturity" (τελειότης): that is, spiritual maturity.
417. Col 3.1.
418. "Mind" (νοῦς): I normally translate νοῦς "intellect" in Origen's anthropology, but here he is saying something equivalent to what is truly sincere, almost "take to heart." Actually the terms for "heart" (ἡγεμονικόν or καρδία) are intimately connected to the νοῦς in Origen's anthropology.
419. Ps 140.2.   420. Apoc 5.8.
421. "Since" (ἐπεί), a correction of Blass. c, l, and, o have ἐπί.
422. Ps 37.6.
423. σεμίδαλις: a very fine wheat flour.
424. Isa 1.13.   425. 1 Tim 2.8.
426. Exod 17.11.   427. Isa 58.9.
428. Jer 51.22.   429. "Not," added by editor.

*could no longer bear*[430] the foul odor of those who were then offensive.[431] Hence he said in the Prophets: *I have been silent, will I always be silent?*[432]

69. For just as the air hovering around rotting bodies, once it overwhelms and is corrupted, makes a plague for those who are present, and the countryside *becomes desolate*,[433] so the sins of souls produce a plague for souls.

70. Baruch, affected along with the people, laments bitterly, and prays God on their behalf.[434] Hence he receives the news of aid in bad terms when God thus says, *Those whom I will break down, I will again build up.* For first *he causes one to be in pain, and again he restores*,[435] and the passages with respect to these. For when the evils are not taken away before, the good is not received. For he destroys the wretched buildings of the faithless, as he is the master builder *of the true tabernacle which he set up and not man;*[436] about which Paul said, *You are a building of God.*[437] And as a farmer who has *plucked out*[438] the unproductive fruit—for *every plant which my heavenly Father has not planted will be uprooted*[439]—he *plants* a *fruit-bearing vine*, not according to one which *turned itself around* to what is *bitter* and *strange*, which he cut out so that he might produce it again as a *true* one[440] and a *crop of God.*[441] So he *broke down the wall* of the vine[442] *out of Egypt*,[443] according to David, for which he prays: *Look down from heaven and consider this vine.*[444] And these people are then disciplined by the help: *For he whom the Lord loves he disciplines.*[445] For *who is there to make me glad but the one whom I have pained?*[446] For *godly grief produces a repentance that leads to salvation.*[447] For because of

430. Jer 51.22.
431. Cf. Gen 7.8, 6.12ff.
432. Isa 42.14.
433. Jer 51.22.
434. Cf. Jer 51.32–35.
435. Job 5.18.
436. Heb 8.2.
437. 1 Cor 3.9.
438. Cf. Sir 40.16.
439. Matt 15.13.
440. Jer 2.21.
441. 1 Cor 3.9.
442. "Vine," I have added in light of the Scripture.
443. Ps 79.9, 13.
444. Ps 79.15.
445. Heb 12.6.
446. 2 Cor 2.2.
447. 2 Cor 7.10.

this *I am bringing evil upon all flesh,* upon those who *set their minds* on the earthly.[448]

71. For God finds the *souls* of the righteous.[449] For *the souls of the righteous are in the hands of God,*[450] but those who are among the sinners count as nothing.

448. Cf. Phil 3.19.  
450. Wis 3.1.

449. Cf. Jer 51.35.

# HOMILY ON 1 KINGS 28

# HOMILY ON 1 KINGS 28

## *1 Kings (1 Samuel) 28.3–25*

**W**HAT WAS READ IS LENGTHY, and since there is need to give a summary, here are[1] the sections. The order of events of what concerns Nabal the Carmelite was read first,[2] then the history which concerns David hiding with the Ziphites and being at variance with them, and then that Saul, wanting to seize David, came, and once he had come he bided his time. But David sneaked up on Saul and, while he and his guards were sleeping, he[3] took the *spear* and *pitcher of water*, and, after this, he lectured those who were entrusted to guard Saul and yet were found asleep.[4] Then next came the third section of the history: David fled to the King of Geth, and after a while David, after many exploits, found favor with him, to whom the King said, *I will make you head of my bodyguards.*[5] Following these events there is the famous history concerning the medium and Samuel, that the medium had apparently conjured up Samuel and that Samuel prophesied to Saul.

(2) There being four pericopes, each of which has not a few events and which can also, for those able to examine them, occupy hours not of just one service but of many, let our bishop point out one of the four in order that we may occupy ourselves concerning it.

(3) Let us examine, he says, what concerns the medium.

---

1. "Here are" (δ' εἰσίν), a correction of Blass. M has δίσιν.
2. 1 Kings 25
3. "He" (αὐτόν), a correction of Al. M has αὐτῶν.
4. 1 Kings 26.   5. 1 Kings 28.2.

2. Some histories do not affect us, others are necessary for our hope. And I state "histories" explicitly, since we are not at this point striving for the higher meaning useful for everyone who knows how to go higher or hear what is higher. Thus some things of history are useful[6] for everyone, some not for everyone, just as, for example, the history concerning Lot and his daughters.[7] If it has something useful according to the higher sense, God knows also to whom may be given the gift to examine those words, but if it is useful according to the historical sense, you may seek for yourselves.[8] For how do I profit from the history about Lot and his daughters? Likewise what profit is there to me that the history of Judah and Tamar and the events about it be spoken?[9] However, since the history about Saul and the medium affects all, there is a necessary[10] truth regarding its subject. For who, after departing this life, wants to be under the sway of a little demon, in order that a medium may bring up not just one who by chance has believed but Samuel the Prophet, about whom God said through Jeremiah, *Even if Moses and Samuel are before me, I would not listen to them.*[11] Concerning them the Prophet in hymns said, *Moses and Aaron are among his priests, and Samuel among those who call upon his name, they call upon the Lord and he listened to them; in a pillar of cloud he spoke to them,*[12] and elsewhere, *if Moses and Samuel stand and offer prayers,*[13] and so forth?

(2) Is it not the case then, if such a great man was[14] under

---

6. "Thus some things of history are useful," an addition of Klostermann.

7. Gen 19.30–38.

8. "Seek for yourselves" (ζητήσαις), a correction of Al. M has ζητήσεσαν.

9. Gen 38.1–30.

10. "Necessary" (ἀναγκαία): Klostermann suggests (ἀναγκαίως) "necessarily," which Nautin uses in his translation, but does not add to his Greek text. See, however, the first sentence of this section.

11. Cf. Jer 15.1–2, a variant reading?   12. Ps 98.6–7.

13. Another variant reading of Jer 15.1? Nautin, 176, n. 3, believes Origen remembers the text in two distinct forms, and cites *On Easter* 15.29–30 and 15.35–16.1.4 as another example.

14. "Was," an addition from Eustathius of Antioch, who wrote a work refuting the homily. See the text in *De engastrimutho*, ed. E. Klostermann (Bonn, 1912).

the earth and the medium did bring him up, that a little demon has sway over the soul of the Prophet? What can I say?[15] These things are recorded. Is it true or is it not true? To say that it is not true drives us to unbelief, it comes down on the heads of those who speak it. But to say it is true presents for us an enquiry and quandary.

3. And we well know that some among our brothers look askance at the Scripture and say: I do not believe in the medium. The medium says that she saw Samuel. She is lying! Samuel was not brought up. Samuel does not speak. Just as there are false prophets who say, *Thus says the Lord,* and *The Lord did not speak,*[16] so too this little demon lies when it proclaims that it brings up the one pointed out by Saul. For, *whom shall I bring up?* He says: *Bring up Samuel for me.*[17] These things are said by those who state that this history is not true.

(2) Samuel in Hades! Samuel, he who was special among the Prophets, who was dedicated to God from his birth,[18] who before his birth is said to be in the Temple, who at the same time he was weaned was clothed with the ephod and double cloak and became a priest of the Lord,[19] the child to whom the Lord when he speaks uttered his messages,[20] he was brought up by a medium? Samuel in Hades, Samuel in the underworld, he who succeeded Heli condemned by Providence for the sins and transgressions of his children?[21] Samuel in Hades, whom God listened to in the time of the harvest of wheat and allowed rain to fall from heaven?[22] Samuel in Hades, he who spoke openly about whether he took what he desired? He did not take the calf, he did not take the steer. He judged and condemned the people though he remained poor, he never desired to take anything from a people such as they.[23] Why is Samuel in Hades?

(3) Observe what follows from Samuel in Hades. Samuel

---

15. "I say" (εἴπως), a correction from T. M has εἴπομεν.
16. Cf. Jer 2.2, 23.17, etc.
17. 1 Kings 28.11.
18. 1 Kings 1.11.
19. 1 Kings 1.22, 2.18–19.
20. 1 Kings 3.4–14.
21. 1 Kings 2.31–3.21.
22. 1 Kings 12.17–18.
23. 1 Kings 12.1–6.

in Hades! Why not also Abraham and Isaac and Jacob in Hades? Samuel in Hades! Why not also Moses, who was coupled with Samuel according to the text, *Not even if Moses and Samuel stood, I will not listen to them?*[24] Samuel in Hades! Why not also Jeremiah in Hades, to whom it was said, *Before I formed you in the womb I knew you, and before you came out of your mother, I sanctified you?*[25] Isaiah is also in Hades, Jeremiah also in Hades, all of the Prophets in Hades!

4. The person who says these things does not like the struggles in admitting that Samuel is really the one who is brought up. And since it is necessary to be fair-minded in hearing the Scripture, though the word shouts against us[26] and can truly disturb and move us, let us see first whether the Scripture has been understood in some manner by him who does not admit this, or whether his attempt is from laudable intentions but speaks what is opposite to what is written.

(2) For what is it which has been written? *And the woman said: Whom shall I bring up for you?*[27] Whose expression is the one which says, *The woman said?* Is it the expression of the Holy Spirit, from whom the Scripture is believed to be recorded, or is it the expression of someone else? For the narrative expression, as those involved with all sorts of words also know, is above all the expression of the author.[28] And the author for all of these words has not been believed to be a man, but the author is the Holy Spirit who moves men.[29]

(3) Therefore the Holy Spirit says: *And the woman said: "Whom shall I bring up for you?" And he said: "Bring up Samuel for me."*[30] Who says, *And the woman saw Samuel and the woman in a loud voice cried out saying?*[31] We will say to that man who

---

24. Jer 15.1. See note above on this text.
25. Jer 1.5.
26. "Shouts against us" (καταβομβήσαντος ἡμῶν), a correction of Klostermann. M has καταπομπήσαντος ἡμᾶς.
27. 1 Kings 28.11.  28. Cf. *Sel in Gen* 41.1.
29. Cf. 2 Pet 1.21. Cf. *Hom in Num* 26.3.  30. 1 Kings 28.11.
31. 1 Kings 28.12.

shouts such words against us and has insisted that Samuel was not in Hades, *The woman saw Samuel,* the voice of the narrator said this.

(4) *And the woman in a loud voice cried out and said to Saul: "Why have you misled me? You are Saul!" And the king said to her: "What is it? Do not fear! What have you seen?" And the woman said to Saul: "I saw gods ascending from the earth." And he said to her: "What was their form?" And she said to him: "An elderly man ascended and he wore a double cloak, an ephod."*[32] She says that she saw also the priestly garment. I am aware that it says, though opposite to our text, *No wonder. For even Satan disguises himself as an angel of light. So it is not strange if his servants also disguise themselves as servants of righteousness.*[33] But what is it that *the woman saw? Samuel.* And why is it not said: "The woman saw a little demon that pretended to be Samuel"?

(5) But it was written that *Saul knew that it was Samuel.*[34] If it was not Samuel, it would be necessary to write: "And Saul supposed that it was Samuel." Yet now it is written: *Saul knew.* No one *knows* what does not exist.

(6) So, *Saul knew that it was Samuel.*[35] *And he fell on his face to the earth and did obeisance.*[36] Then again the narrator of the Scripture: *And Samuel said to Saul, Why have you troubled me that I should come up?*[37] *He said*—the Scripture, which one needs[38] to believe, is speaking—*Samuel said: "Why have you troubled me that I should come up?"* Then to this Saul answered: *I am distressed*[39] *greatly. The foreigners war against me, and God has departed from me and he does not respond to me anymore by the hand of the Prophets or in dreams and I have called you to show me what I should do.*[40] Again the Scripture has said none other

---

32. 1 Kings 28.12–14. "Ephod" is omitted in Nautin's translation, but not in his text. Klostermann retains it.
33. 2 Cor 11.14–15.     34. 1 Kings 28.14.
35. "That it was Samuel" is in Eustathius, but missing from M.
36. 1 Kings 28.14.     37. 1 Kings 28.15.
38. "Which one needs" (ἣ δεῖ), a correction of Klostermann. M has ἤδη.
39. "I am distressed," suggested by Klostermann in notes. See LXX.
40. 1 Kings 28.15.

than *Samuel* himself speaks: *And why have you asked me? The Lord has departed from you.*[41] Is it spoken truly or falsely when it states these things?

(7) *The Lord has departed from you and has acted against you and made another for himself, whose way he spoke in my hand, and he will rend the kingdom from your hand.*[42] And does a little demon prophesy about the Israelite kingdom? What does the contrary opinion say?

(8) See the kind of struggle which exists in the word of God, which has need of hearers who are able to hear both great and holy words, and secrets concerning the final departure, the former still unexplained and the latter not clear. But the word is still being examined.

5. For I say that the history and the examination concerning it are necessary in order that we can see what it holds for us after the final departure.

(2) *He has spoken by my hand and the Lord shall rend the kingdom from your hand and will give it to your neighbor David*[43]—and the little demon is not able to see the king David who has been appointed by the Lord[44]—*because you did not hear the voice of the Lord, you did not act upon the anger of his wrath against Amalek.*[45] Are these not the words of God? Are they not true? For actually Saul did not *act upon* the will of the Lord, but he treated well *King Amalek who lives,*[46] for which Samuel before his final rest and upon his final departure also reproached Saul.[47]

(3) *And because of this the Lord has done this sentence to you on this day. And the Lord will indeed give Israel into the hands of the foreigners.*[48] Is a little demon capable of prophesying concerning the entire people of God that the Lord is about to deliver Israel?

(4) *The Lord indeed will deliver the camp of Israel to the hand of foreigners. Make haste, Saul. Tomorrow both you and your sons will*

41. 1 Kings 28.16.
42. 1 Kings 28.17.
43. 1 Kings 28.15.
44. 1 Kings 16.1–13.
45. 1 Kings 28.18.
46. 1 Kings 15.9.
47. 1 Kings 15.16–23, 28.16–19.
48. 1 Kings 28.19.

*be with me.*[49] Can also a little demon know this, that after a king has been appointed with the anointing oil of a Prophet, that tomorrow Saul and his sons with him will forfeit their lives? *Tomorrow you and your sons with you.*

6. So these things show[50] that what is recorded is not false, and that Samuel is the one who ascended. What then is a medium doing here? What is a medium doing bringing up the soul of the righteous man? He who spoke the first line of thought avoids that.[51] For in order to appear to have no difficulties in the other words which are probed in the context, he also says: "It is not Samuel." Since the Scripture cannot lie, the little demon is lying. But they are the words of Scripture. They are not from the expression of the little demon itself, but from the scriptural expression: *And the woman saw Samuel.*[52] *Samuel*[53] *said*[54] what has been said to come from Samuel.

(2) How then may the words in this context, what concerns the medium, appear to be unraveled? I ask him who previously stated the former idea: Samuel in Hades and the rest of his statements. Let him reply to this point. Who is greater, Samuel or Jesus the Christ? Who is greater, the Prophets or Jesus the Christ? Who is greater, Abraham or Jesus the Christ? Now anyone who is among those who have once come to know the Lord Jesus Christ, the one proclaimed by the Prophets, will not deny that Christ is greater than the Prophet. Therefore, whenever you acknowledge that Jesus Christ is greater, has Christ been in Hades or has he not been there? Is it not true what is said in the Psalms, interpreted by the Apostles in their Acts concerning the Savior's descent to Hades?[55] It is written that what is in the fif-

---

49. 1 Kings 28.15–16.   50. "Show," addition of Huet.
51. "That" (ἐκεῖνο), an addition of Nautin. M has ἐκεῖνος.
52. 1 Kings 28.12.
53. "Samuel," a correction of Nautin. M has "Saul." Klostermann sees a lacuna here. He offers a text of Eustathius, but the meaning still is unclear. Origen's point: The Scripture itself says that it is Samuel, and the Scripture itself says that Samuel spoke.
54. 1 Kings 28.15.   55. Acts 2.27–31.

teenth Psalm concerns him: *Because you will not leave my soul in Hades, you will not allow your holy one to see corruption.*[56] So Jesus Christ was in Hades, but you fear to say that in fact he descends to prophesy and comes to the other souls.

(3) Then next, if he replies that Christ has descended to Hades, I will say: If Christ has descended into Hades, what was he doing: Conquering or being conquered by death? Of course, he went down into those regions not as a servant but as a master of those struggling there, as we were recently saying in commenting on the twenty-third Psalm: *Many calves have encircled me, grazing bulls are around me. They have opened their mouth against me, as a lion on a rampage and roaring. My bones have been dislocated.*[57] We remember, if we at least remember the holy Scriptures. For I remember what was said about them[58] regarding the twenty-first Psalm.

(4) So the Savior came down in order to save. Has he or has he not come down there as proclaimed by the Prophets? But was he proclaimed by the Prophets, and yet elsewhere he does not come down through the Prophets? Moses announces his sojourn with the human race,[59] so that our Lord and Savior speaks well of him: *If you believe in Moses, you believe in me. For about me he wrote. And if you do not believe in his writings, how can you believe in my words?*[60] And Christ dwelt in this life and Christ is proclaimed before he dwells in this life. But if Moses prophesies about him here, do you not want him to descend also there in order that he may prophesy that Christ has come? What then? Moses, but not the rest of the Prophets, not Samuel?[61] What is so amazing about healers going down to those who are ill, and what is so amazing that the chief healer should also go down to those ill? They were *many healers,*[62] but my Lord and Savior is the chief healer. For he also heals the inner desire, which cannot be cured

---

56. Ps 15.10.   57. Ps 21.13, 14.
58. "What was said about them" (αὐτῶν εἰρημένων) is in the received text. Nautin corrects to αὐτῶν [τῶν] εἰρημένων: "the words themselves said."
59. Deut 18.15–18.   60. John 5.46–47.
61. 1 Kings 3.20.   62. Mark 5.26.

by others, which when *none* of the healers *are able to cure*,[63] Christ Jesus cures her: *Fear not*,[64] be not alarmed.

(5) Jesus appeared in Hades, and the Prophets before him, and they proclaimed the coming of Christ.

7. Next I also want to point out something else from the Scripture itself. Samuel comes up and note that she does say that she saw the soul of Samuel. She does not say she saw a man.[65] She has been scared by this thing which she saw. What did she see? *I saw gods*, she says, *coming up from the earth*.[66] And perhaps Samuel has not only come up in order just to prophesy to Saul, but it is likely, just as here *with the holy he will be holy, and with an innocent man he will be innocent, and with one of the chosen he will be as one of the chosen*,[67] and here the ways of the holy are with the holy but not with the sinners. And if then at some point the way of life of the holy is with the sinners for the purpose of saving the sinners, so perhaps also you may speculate whether either the holy souls of the other Prophets in the coming up of Samuel come up together or[68] perhaps whether they were angels of their *spirits*[69]—the Prophet says, *the angel who speaks in me*[70]— or whether they were angels who came up together with the spirits. And every [place] is filled with those who need salvation, and *are they not all ministering spirits sent forth to serve for the sake of those who are to obtain salvation?*[71] Why do you fear to say that every place has need of Jesus Christ? Those who have need of Christ have need of the Prophets. But if he has no need of Christ, he has no need of those who prepare for the appearance and dwelling of Christ.

63. Luke 8.43.
64. Luke 8.50; Mark 5.36.
65. Nautin and Klostermann modify this and the preceding sentence with various additions. Here are their corrections, with additions in brackets. Klostermann: "Samuel comes up, and [what] does [the woman] say [to Saul] that she saw? She does not say that she saw a man." Nautin: "Samuel comes up and note [the woman] does [not] say she saw Samuel; [she does not say she saw] a soul. She does not say she saw a man."
66. 1 Kings 28.13.
67. Ps 17.26–27.
68. "Or," an addition of Nautin.
69. Cf. 1 Pet 3.19.
70. Zech 1.9.
71. Heb 1.14.

(2) And as for John, of whom there was none greater in those born among women, according to the witness of our Savior, who says, *There is no one greater among those born of women than John*[72] the Baptist, do not fear to say that he went down into Hades proclaiming my Lord, in order that he might say beforehand that he came down. For this reason, when he was in prison and he knew the final departure which was near to him, when he sent two of his disciples he did not ascertain the answer to *Are you the one who comes?* for he knew, but to *Are you the one who comes or do we wait for another?*[73] He saw his glory,[74] he spoke of many things concerning his wonderful nature, he bore witness to him[75] as the first, *the one coming after me has been before me.*[76] He saw his glory, *glory as the only-begotten from the Father, full of grace and truth.*[77] Though seeing such great things about Christ he hesitated to believe, he doubts, and yet he does not say: *Say to him, "Are you the Christ?"*[78]

(3) Now some who do not understand what was said say: "John, the one so great, did not know Christ, yet the Holy Spirit has departed from him. Yet he did know for whom he bore witness before his birth and in response to whom he *leapt* when Mary too came to him, as his mother testified when she said, *For behold, when the voice of your greeting came to my ears, the babe in my womb leaped for joy."*[79] So this is the John, who leapt before birth, who said, *He is the one concerning whom I said, "He who comes after me exists before me."*[80] *The one who sent me said to me, "He on whom you see the spirit descend and remain, this is the Son of God,"*[81] this John, he says, no longer knew Jesus Christ?

(4) For he did know him *in the womb*, but on account of an extraordinary glory. He has done something similar to Peter. In what way? He knew something great concerning

72. Luke 7.28.
73. Luke 7.20.
74. John 1.14–15.
75. Luke 9.32; John 1.15.
76. John 1.15, 30.
77. John 1.14.
78. Mark 14.61.
79. Luke 1.44.
80. John 1.15.
81. John 1.33.

Christ. Who am I, *who do men say that I am?*[82] He says: "They say such and such." "But what do you say?"[83] *You are the Christ, the Son of the living God,* for which he is also blessed, *for flesh and blood did not reveal* it to him, *but the Father in the heavens.*[84] Since then he heard great things concerning Christ and he assumed great things and he did not accept divine aid[85] which was given to him: *Behold we are going up to Jerusalem and it will be accomplished,*[86] and, *The Son of Man must suffer many things and be rejected by the chief priests and elders and be killed and on the third day be raised,*[87] he said: *God forbid, Lord.*[88] He knew great things about Christ, he did not want to accept the humiliation concerning him. Some such thing seems to me also for John. In prison, when he saw great things concerning Christ, he saw *heavens opened,*[89] he saw the *Holy Spirit descending from heaven* upon the Savior and remaining *on him*.[90] After he *saw* such a great *glory*[91] he doubted and perhaps he did not believe if one[92] so glorious would also come down to Hades and to the *abyss*.[93] Because of this he said, *Are you the one who comes or may we look for another?*[94]

8. I did not digress nor forget what was discussed, but we needed to establish this point because if the Prophets, the forerunners of Christ, all went down into Hades before the Christ, so too Samuel has gone down there. For he does not merely go down, but he goes down as a holy man. Wherever the holy man may be, he is holy. Is Christ no longer Christ, since he was once in Hades? Was he no longer Son of God, since he existed in an underworld place, *that every knee should bow in the name of Jesus Christ in heaven and on earth and*

---

82. Matt 16.13.
83. Matt 16.15.
84. Matt 15.16–17.
85. "Divine aid" (βοὴν τὴν θείαν), a correction of Klostermann. M has βοήθειαν.
86. Luke 18.31.
87. Luke 9.22.
88. Matt 16.22.
89. Matt 3.16.
90. Matt 3.16.
91. John 1.14.
92. "If one" (εἰ ὁ), a correction of Klostermann. T and M have διό.
93. Rom 10.7.
94. Luke 7.20.

*under the earth?*⁹⁵ So, Christ was Christ even when he was below; that is to say, while he was in the place below, he was above in purpose. So too, the Prophets and Samuel, even if they go down below where the souls are, they are able to be in a place below, but they are not below in purpose.

(2) I inquire: Have they prophesied the heavenly things? But I cannot give to a little demon such a great power that he can prophesy concerning Saul and the people of God and he can prophesy concerning David that he will become king. Those who say these things may seem to know what concerns the truth in the passage, but they do not find a way to present how a holy one too may come to the place of those ill on behalf of the Savior of those ill. Healers must appear in places of afflicted soldiers and where the foul smells of their wounds have been; healing beneficence sets this aside. So the word has set this aside with the Savior and the Prophets both in order to come here and to go down into Hades.

9. And one must also apply this to the text: if⁹⁶ Samuel was a Prophet and, after dying, the Holy Spirit left him, and the prophetic gift left him, then the Apostle does not speak truly when he says, *I prophesy in part and I know in part, but when the perfect comes, then what is in part will pass away.*⁹⁷ Thus the *perfect* is after life. And if Isaiah prophesied something, he prophesied *in part with all boldness.*⁹⁸ Yet about David it has been here testified about⁹⁹ what is *perfect* of prophecy.¹⁰⁰

(2) Samuel then did not discard the prophetic grace, and because¹⁰¹ he did not discard it, it thus belongs to him, that he might say, like those who speak in tongues, *My spirit prays*

---

95. Phil 2.10.
96. "If," an addition of Klostermann.
97. 1 Cor 13.9–10.   98. Cf. Acts 4.29.
99. "About" (ἐπί), from M. T has ἐπεί.
100. Because Samuel says that Saul will die and David will become king, and this actually happens, this is "perfect" τέλειος; it is accomplished exactly as he says.
101. "Because" (ὅτι), a correction of Blass. M has ὅτε.

*but my mind is unfruitful!*[102] And yet[103] he who speaks in a tongue does not edify the Church. For Paul too says that the one who prophesies edifies the Church, for he literally says it: *The one who prophesies edifies the Church.*[104] But if *the one who prophesies edifies the Church,* he has the prophetic grace—for he has not lost it since he did not sin. For only he who, after prophesying, has done something unworthy of the Holy Spirit so that he forsakes and flees from his heart, loses the prophetic gift, which David feared after his sin and said: *And remove not your Holy Spirit from me.*[105] If then the Holy Spirit prophesies and Samuel was a Prophet, *and the one who prophesies edifies the Church,* whom does he *edify?* Does he prophesy toward heaven? To whom? To the angels who have no need? *The strong have no need*[106] *of healers, but the ill.*[107] Some have need of[108] his prophecy. For a prophetic gift is not fruitless; none of the gifts of those in the holy man are fruitless. Therefore the souls of those who die, I may dare to say, have need of prophetic grace. But here Israel has need of the Prophet, and the one who died also, the one who has departed life, has need of the Prophets, in order that the Prophets may again preach to him about the coming of Christ.

(3) In fact, before the[109] sojourn of my Lord Jesus Christ, it was impossible for someone to come near to where the *Tree of Life* was. It was impossible to come near to those who were posted to protect the way of the tree of life: *He stationed the Cherubim and the fiery sword which turns about to protect the way of the Tree of Life.*[110] Who could make one's way? Who could make it so that the *fiery sword* pass through someone?

---

102. 1 Cor 14.14.
103. "And yet" (καίτοι), a correction of Klostermann. T and M have καὶ ὅτι.
104. 1 Cor 14.4.   105. Ps 50.13.
106. "Have no need," an addition of Blass.
107. Matt 9.12.
108. "Have need of" (δέονται), a correction of Jahn. M has δέχονται.
109. "Before the" (πρὸ τῆς), a correction of Pearson. M has προφήτης.
110. Gen 3.24.

Just as none[111] other can make one's way in the sea than God and the *pillar of fire*,[112] the pillar of light from God, just as no one can make one's way in Jordan except Joshua[113]—that Joshua was a figure for the true Jesus—so Samuel was not able to pass through the *fiery sword*, nor Abraham. For this reason too Abraham is seen by the one who is punished, and *the rich man in torments who raised up his eyes sees Abraham*[114]— though *he sees far off*, he sees—*and Lazarus in his bosom*. So Patriarchs and Prophets and everyone wait for the coming of my Lord Jesus Christ, in order that he might open up the *way: I am the way*,[115] *I am the door*.[116] He is the *way* for the *Tree of Life*, that it might happen: *If you pass through fire, you shall not be burned*.[117] What kind of fire? *He stationed the Cherubim and the fiery sword which turns about to protect the way of the Tree of Life*, with the result that the blessed await there handling God's business because of those unable to exist where the *Tree of Life* is, where the *Paradise* of God is, where God the gardener is,[118] where the blessed and the elect and the holy ones of God reside.

10. Hence there is nothing offensive in this passage, but everything is wondrously written and has been understood by those to whom God has revealed it.[119] And have we, those who have *come to the consummation of the ages*,[120] something beyond this, something more? If we depart hence, with excellent character and morals, without bearing burdens of sin, we are also they who pass through the *fiery sword*[121] and will not come down into the area where those who died before his appearance awaited Christ; but we, with nothing blasphemous, pass through the *fiery sword*, and *whatever sort of work*

---

111. "None," an addition of Klostermann.
112. Exod 13.22, 14.24.
113. Josh 3.11–17. "Joshua," a correction of Klostermann. M has "God." Joshua and Jesus are the same name in Greek.

| 114. Luke 16.23. | 115. John 14.6. |
| 116. John 10.9. | 117. Isa 43.2. |
| 118. Cf. Gen 2.18. | 119. Cf. 1 Cor 2.10; Matt 11.27. |
| 120. Heb 9.26. | 121. Gen 3.24. |

## HOMILY ON 1 KINGS 28

*each has done, the fire tests it. If the work of any man is burned up, he will suffer loss, though he himself will be saved, but only as through fire.*[122] So we pass through, and we have something further;[123] we are also unable, when we have lived well, to depart in a bad way. Neither the ancients nor the Patriarchs nor the Prophets said what[124] we can say if we live well. For *it is better to depart and be with Christ.*[125] That is why, having *something more*[126] and much *gain*[127] in coming to the *consummation of the ages,*[128] we who are *first* accept the *coin.* For hear the parable: Give the coin *beginning from the last.*[129] But the *first* believe that they will receive something *more.*[130] You then who have come *last* receive as one *first*[131] the *wages* from the *overseer*[132] in Christ Jesus our Lord, *to whom is the glory and the power for the ages of ages. Amen.*[133]

122. 1 Cor 3.13, 15.
123. Matt 20.10.
124. "What" (ὅ), a correction of Klostermann. M has οὐ.
125. Phil 1.23.  126. Matt 20.10.
127. Phil 1.21.  128. Heb 9.26.
129. Matt 20.8.  130. Cf. Matt 20.10.
131. Matt 20.16.  132. Matt 20.11.
133. 1 Pet 4.11.

INDICES

# GENERAL INDEX

*In these entries h precedes references to the Homilies followed by homily and section number. In the remaining entries p precedes references to the Fragments from the Philocalia; c, the Fragments from the Catena; and k, the Homily on 1 Kings 28. These entries are followed by section number.*

Aaron, h 19.12
Abraham, h 1.5, h 4.4–5, h 27.2, h 27.4, k 6, 9
actions, *see* works
*Acts of Paul*, h 20.1
Adam, h 8.1, h 16.4, h 20.3
adamant, h 27.1, c 30
adultery, h 19.15
afterlife, h 2.3, h 5.4, h 5.11, h 7.1–3, h 8.6, h 12.10, h 14.18, h 16.1, h 16.5–6, h 18.1, h 19.15, h 20.6, h 28.3, h 28.11, c 16, c 31, k 5, k 10
Age, h 17.3; completion of h 4.3, c 28
agreements, h 20.7
Ammanites, h 28.1
analogies and allegories, adamant, saint as, c 30; architect, God as, c 70; athlete, Christian as, h 27.3; axe, rational person as, c 20; axe, Word as, c 20; Babylonian man or infant, evil thoughts as, c 26; Babylonians, impious thoughts as, c 34; Babylonians, spiritual torturers as, h 1.4; basket of figs, Kingdom of Heaven as, c 22; botanist, saint interpreting Scripture as, p 2.2; branch, man as, c 23; bread, word as, h 10.2; Captivity, sinful state as, h 1.3–4; cedar, proud man or Devil as, c 13; child, man as, h 1.8; city, soul as, c 51, c 58; city, spiritual goal as, c 51; clouds, holy man as, h 8.3–5; debtor, sinner as, h 15.5; deed of purchase, thoughts, memories, or opinions as, c 61; Devil, Nebuchadnezzar as, h 1.3; earth or earthly, base desires as, h 11.2, h 11.6; farming, prophesying as, c 66; father, forefather as, h 9.4; field, human labors as, c 61; field, soul as, h 5.13, c 66; fig, man as, c 22; fish, repentent sinner as, h 16.1; food, Word as, c 19; foreskin, bad thoughts as, h 5.15; foreskin, pre-existent fault as, h 5.14; gardener, God as, k 9; God, soul as, c 18; grain of wheat, Christ as, h 10.3; hammer, Devil and evil as, h 27.1–2, c 30; healer, Christ as, k 6, k 8; healer, God as, h 12.5; healers, angels as, h 28.12; healers, Prophets as, h 14.1, k 6, k 8; hills, the righteous as, h 16.1; horses, passions as, c 40; house or building, soul as, h 1.15, c 12, c 23, c 58; house, Church as, c 13; Israel, Christians as, h 4.4; Jebus, soul as, h 13.2; Jerusalem, Church as, c 48, c 64; Judah, sinner as, h 4.2, h 4.5; king, God as, h 13.1; leopard, knowledge as, c 3; lightning, work of the holy as, h 8.5; lion, actions as, c 3; lion, Devil as, h 5.16–17, c 3, c 28; lion or leopard, Nebuchadnezzar as, c 3; location on earth, condition of soul as, h 28.1, c 11, c 25; maiden, soul as, c 40; migrant, spiritual man as, c 25; moneychanger, prophet as, c 19; mountain, Christ as, c 58; mountain, Devil or Babylon as, c 41; mountains, angels as, h 12.12;

337

## GENERAL INDEX

(analogies and allegories *continued*) mountains, pagan gods as, h 5.3; mountains, Prophets as, h 16.1; nations and kingdoms, bad movements in soul as, h 1.7, h 1.14; natural bodies and objects, angels as, h 10.6; Nod, land of, confused mind as, h 28.10; ox and ass, words proclaimed to Israel and pagan nations as, c 26; pagan gods, passions as, h 7.3; partridge, Devil as, h 17.1-2; plant or vine, soul or man as, h 2.1, c 70; plant, evil thought or act as, h 1.14; riders of horses, demons as, c 40; root, Savior as, c 23; seal, righteous one as, c 14; seeds, holy teachings as, h 5.13; servant, new convert as, h 4.5; smell of corpse, plague of sins as, c 69; smell, virtues as, c 62, c 68; snakes, evil forces as, c 25; soap, Word as, h 2.2; sons and daughters, good thoughts and practices as, c 48; soul, body as, h 28.1; stones, sinner as, h 4.5; straw, pleasure as, c 20; surgeon or healer, God as, h 20.3, h 28.6, p 2.2, c 37; sword, test of goodness as, k 9-10; temptations, prison as, c 60; thief, preacher of false ideas as, c 21; thorns and thistles, worries of daily life as, c 40; treasury, Church as, c 31; trumpet, Word as, h 5.16; universal, particular as, h 3.2; upper area, transcendent as, h 19.13; veil, barrier to good as, h 5.8-9; vessel of clay, man as, h 18.1; vessels, cities as, c 45; vessels, Scripture or man as, c 61; vessels, types of men as, h 27.3, c 31; waistcloth, people as, h 11.5; whole world, one man as, c 22; wife, wisdom as, c 48; winds, spirits as, h 8.5; wineskins, men as, h 12.2; wood, Cross as, h 10.2
Ananias, h 19.12
angels, h 1.1, h 5.2, h 10.6-8, h 12.12, h 13.1, h 13.3, h 15.4, h 16.3-4, h 19.14, h 28.6, c 37, k 7, k 9; as healers, h 28.12
anger of God, c 16, c 52
anthropomorphisms, h 18.6, h 19.15, h 20.1
Antichrist, c 29
apokatastasis, *see* restoration *or* afterlife
Apostle, the, *see* Paul
Apostles, h 12.12, h 14.13-14, h 16.3, h 19.13
Aquila, c 6, c 45
archery, c 25, c 33, c 38
Armenians, c 42
*Ascension of Isaiah*, h 20.9
ascetics, h 20.7
Asclepios, h 5.3
Assyria, Assyrians, h 11.6, c 28
astrology, h 27.4-5, c 49
atheist, c 47
atonement, h 12.13
aversions, h 18.8-9
awe, h 5.11

Babylon, Babylonians, h 1.4, h 11.6, h 19.11, h 19.14, h 27.1-2, h 27.6, h 28.1-2, h 28.10-11, c 14, c 26-27, c 30, c 32-35, c 37-38, c 43, c 49; curable, h 28.12, c 37; description of, c 41, c 44
Baal, c 47
Baptism, *see* Sacraments
Baruch, h 8.5, c 70
Basilides, h 10.5, h 17.2
basilisk, c 25
Beatitudes, h 16.2
beauty, h 17.5
beginning, h 20.1
behavior, c 21
belief or faith, h 6.1, h 8.5, h 14.12, p 1.1, p 2.1, c 21-22, c 41; true faith, h 4.3
Benjamin, h 19.13
blasphemy, profanity, h 5.11
blessed, h 6.2, h 15.1, h 17.6, h 20.6, k 9
blessing, c 55
blood, c 13
boasting, h 11.4, h 17.5
bodily sense of Scripture, h 1.7; *see also* Scripture

## GENERAL INDEX 339

body, h 7.3; extends to every soul, c 18; of death, h 20.7; under restraint, c 11

Cain, h 16.4, h 27.1, h 28.10, c 30
Captivity, h 1.3, h 19.11, h 19.14, h 20.5, h 27.2, c 22
catechumens, h 27.3, h 27.5
Chaldeans, h 27.4–5, c 14
chastity, h 20.4, h 20.7
Chelkias, c 60
children, h 18.6, h 19.15
Christ, Jesus, acts as signs of truth, h 5.3; Adam and, h 8.1; aspects, h 8.2, h 27.4; assumed opposites, h 8.9; begotten in each good thought and act, h 9.4; being in, c 58; builder, c 23; Church and, h 18.5; coming of, h 5.1–2, h 7.1, h 8.8, h 9.1, h 10.7, h 11.2, h 14.6, h 14.9, h 14.12, h 15.3, h 16.2, c 22, c 39, k 9, k 10; converter, c 4; council of, c 50; David and, c 28; death and, h 10.3, h 11.2, h 14.6, h 14.11, k 6; destroyer of idolatry, c 39; doubted by Peter and John the Baptist, k 7; expiation, h 14.11; final rest in, h 17.6; foundation, c 12; free will of, h 1.7; Hades and, k 6; healer, h 17.5, k 6, k 8; holy man and, h 9.1; in human soul, h 5.6, h 9.4, c 10; in martyrs, h 14.8, h 19.12; inspirer of exegete and preacher, h 19.10–11, h 19.15; Jeremiah and, h 1.6, h 14.5, h 19.13, *passim;* Jesus, h 1.7, h 8.9, h 10.8, h 11.3, h 13.1–3, h 14.6, h 14.8, h 27.2, h 28.7; John the Baptist and, k 7; Judah, h 4.2, h 5.16, h 9.1, h 9.4, h 16.10; judged (in the Christian), h 14.17; judgment on, h 15.3; killing of, h 14.13–14, h 15.5, h 18.5; knowledge of, h 1.8, h 10.1; Lamb, h 10.1, h 12.13; language of, h 15.3; Lord of Prophets, h 15.2; Man and God, h 14.6, h 15.6; Moses and, k 6; nature and aspects of, h 9.4, h 14.6, h 15.4, h 15.6, h 20.1, h 27.4; nothing impious, h 17.1; one Being before and after Incarnation, h 9.1; pagan teachings and, h 1.7, c 35; Passion of, h 10.2, h 14.13, h 28.11, c 35; Passover and, h 19.13; preexistence of, h 9.1; preparer, c 23; progress of, h 14.10; prophesies even when not in body, h 1.12; prophet, h 1.12, h 15.2, k 6; Prophets and, h 9.1, k 6; prudence of, h 8.2; Redeemer, h 14.11, h 15.4, c 35; Resurrection, h 14.12; return of, h 4.3; h 15.3; righteousness, h 14.12, h 17.4; rock, h 16.2, c 26; sanctification, h 17.4; Savior, h 1.6–8, h 1.11–12, h 5.2, h 7.3, h 8.1, h 8.9, h 9.4, h 14.6, h 14.9, h 15.2, h 17.5, k 6; shepherd uniting flock, c 28; shepherd who tends irrational, h 5.6; sin and, h 17.4; Son of God, h 8.1, h 9.4, h 13.2–3, h 27.2, c 17; soul depends on to grow, h 14.10, h 17.4; Soul of Jesus, h 10.7, h 14.6, h 15.4; Soul with Father, h 10.7; source, h 3.2, h 18.9; source of virtues, h 8.5–6; struck, h 19.12; teaching of, h 14.9–10; temptations of, h 27.2; throne of glory, h 17.4; truth avenger, h 15.3; Truth, h 14.12, h 17.4, h 19.11; victor over Devil, h 1.7, h 27.2, c 25; Way, k 9, k 10; weakness of, h 14.9; Wisdom, h 15.4; Word, h 9.1
Christianity, doctrine of, h 14.8, h 20.5
Church, h 4.3, h 5.16, h 7.3, h 9.1–2, h 9.4, h 10.4, h 11.3, h 11.6, h 12.5, h 14.15, h 18.5, h 18.8, c 27, c 31–32, c 48, c 64, k 9; built by righteousness, c 12; filled with sinners, h 15.3; hammer not heard in, h 27.1; overthrows devil, h 27.2; place of salvation, h 27.6; throne of David and Christ, c 11; treasury, h 27.3, h 27.6, c 31
circumcision, h 5.14–15, h 12.13, c 22
Cleopas, h 20.8
clergy, h 11.3, h 12.3, c 9, c 50

clouds, h 8.3–5
confession, h 5.10, h 10.5, h 10.8, h 20.8, c 57–58
confusion, h 28.10, c 43; as Babylon, h 27.2
conscience, h 6.2, h 16.4, h 20.9
consolation, h 15.4, h 17.6
consummation, h 7.1–2, h 12.10, k 10
contemplation, h 16.2
conversion, h 1.1, h 1.4, h 4.1, h 4.6, h 5.2–3, h 5.10–11, h 7.1, h 11.5–6, h 12.3, h 13.2–3, h 14.1, h 14.18, h 15.1–2, h 15.6, h 16.1–2, h 16.4, h 16.6, h 16.10, h 17.6, h 18.1, h 18.6, h 18.8, h 19.15, h 20.1, h 20.5, h 28.2, c 4, c 7, c 9, c 15, c 25, c 43, c 56, c 57
councils, h 14.15
covenant, h 9.2
creation, h 1.10, h 2.1, h 7.3, h 8.1, h 18.1, h 18.4
crucifixion, h 10.2–3, h 14.18
Cyrus, c 42, c 44

Dan, h 28.1
Daniel, c 66
David, h 20.1, c 28, k 1, k 9
Death, h 2.1, h 8.1, h 9.3, h 10.3, h 12.12, h 15.6, h 16.1, h 17.3, h 17.6, c 25, k 5, k 9–10
deceit, h 4.6, h 19.15, h 20.1–5, c 13, c 22, c 36
demiurge, h 10.5
demons, c 7, c 40–41, c 45, c 68, k 2, k 5
Devil, Satan, h 1.3–4, h 1.7, h 1.14–15, h 2.1, h 5.2, h 5.4, h 5.16–17, h 7.3, h 9.1, h 9.4, h 12.8, h 12.12, h 14.11, h 15.5, h 17.1–3, h 18.1, h 19.14, h 20.3–4, h 20.7, c 45; and death, c 54; deceiver, h 20.3, h 28.7; enflaming hearts, c 2; fall, h 5.17; holds us, c 54; hammer, h 27.1, c 30; lion, c 28; mountain, c 41; tempting Christ, h 27.2, c 13; wicked doctrines, c 29–30
disciples, h 16.1
divine agency, h 16.5

doctrine, h 5.13, h 5.15, h 20.5
drunkenness, h 20.3, h 28.8, c 36
earnestness, h 14.15
earth, earthly, h 8.1–2, h 9.3, h 10.6, h 11.2, h 11.6, h 14.8, h 14.12, h 16.4, h 17.4, h 18.2, h 27.4, c 2, c 18, c 34, c 41, c 70
Ebionites, h 19.12
economy of God, h 12.4–5, h 15.4, h 16.5–6, h 18.5–6, h 27.4
education, *see* teaching
Egypt, Egyptians, h 1.10, h 5.14, h 9.2, h 12.1–2, h 13.3, h 18.5, h 19.12, h 27.3–4, h 28.1, c 31, c 40
Elam, Elamites, c 24–25
elements, four, h 10.6
Elijah, h 14.16, h 19.13
Elisha, h 19.13
end, h 7.1, h 18.1, c 28, c 35; *see* after-life, age, restoration
Enos, h 27.1
ephod, k 3
Ephraim, c 56–57
esoteric life, teachings, h 1.10, h 4.1, h 4.3, h 5.2, h 5.4, h 7.1–2, h 8.8–9, h 10.4, h 12.13, h 14.16, h 17.2, h 18.2, h 18.4–5, h 19.14, h 20.3, h 20.6, h 20.8, h 28.3, h 28.10, c 16, c 58, c 63; in Scripture, h 12.7; restoration, h 14.18
Ethiopia, h 5.4
Eucharist, *see* Sacraments
Euphrates, h 11.6
Eve, h 20.3, h 20.7
evil, h 1.5, h 6.2, h 10.1, h 10.5–6, h 12.4, h 12.11, h 16.5–6, h 18.1, h 18.6–8, h 19.14, h 28.2; from evil to virtue, c 9; origin of, h 2.1
Evil-merocach, h 14
expiation, h 14.11
Ezekiah, c 64

faith, *see* belief
fall, of Devil, *see* Devil; of souls, *see* pre-existence
fasting, h 12.13
Father, the, h 5.13, h 8.1, h 9.4, h 10.1, h 10.7, h 12.8, h 14.11, h

## GENERAL INDEX 341

14.15, h 15.3, h 17.4, h 18.9, h
20.1, h 27.2, c 23
fear of God, h 27.2
feeling, h 6.2
fire, h 1.15, h 2.2–3, h 5.15, h 6.2, h
  11.5, h 12.5, h 16.5–7, h 18.1, h
  18.5, h 19.15, h 20.8–9, c 11, c 22,
  k 9; the Word, c 20
flattery, c 63
flesh, h 11.2, h 15.6; *see* polarities
food, c 10, c 19–20
foolishness, h 17.3; of earthly knowledge, h 8.7–9
foreskin, h 5.14
forgiveness, h 5.10, h 16.5, c 7
foreknowledge, h 6.2, c 49, c 61, c
  67; of Jesus, h 11.3; *see* Providence
fornication, h 20.9
four, elements, h 10.6; passions, c 25;
  virtues, 40
free will, h 5.8–9, h 17.4, h 18.3, h
  18.6, h 20.2, h 28.3, c 67; of
  Christ, h 1.7
friends, h 15.6
fullness of God, *see* God

Gad, c 28
Ganymede, h 27.4
Gehenna, h 12.5
generation, h 9.4, h 11.5–6
Gentiles, *see* pagans
Gedaliah, c 67
Geth, king of, k 1
gluttony, h 5.17, h 7.3
God, h 1.1, h 2.3, h 5.9, h 6.2, h 8.2;
  anger and reproof, differences between, h 20.1; anger of, c 16;
  avenger, h 28.5–6; benefits of, h
  3.2; body of, h 11.5; brings suffering before rewards, h 1.16, h 16.6;
  condescension of, h 18.6; consuming fire, h 18.1; craftsman, p 2.2;
  creator, h 13.1; creator of yet alien
  to earth, h 7.3; deception by, h
  19.15, h 20.2–3; finds souls of
  righteous, c 71; forsakes only with
  cause, h 1.4; fullness, p 1.1, c 18;
  gardener, k 9; good through bad,
  c 63, c 70; healer, teacher, father,
  h 20.3, h 28.6, h 28.12, c 37; holy ones,
  God alone knows, c 30; incurable
  and, h 28.12; judges in terms of
  the many, h 12.5; judgment of, h
  6.3, c 67; kind and severe, h 4.4;
  nearness of, h 18.9, c 17; not a
  tyrant, h 20.1; not cause of evil, h
  2.1; of Old and New Testament, h
  9.1; Offended by certain "smells,"
  c 68; One-who-is, c 62; plan of, h
  18.5–6; punishes according to
  need and merit, h 12.2; refuge, c
  7; regret of, h 20.2; repents, h
  18.6; Scripture and, h 18.6; source
  of true words, c 15; teacher, h
  10.1, h 19.15; will of, c 60; worthy
  men and, c 18
good, h 2.3; and shame, h 5.5; material versus spiritual, h 16.4, h 18.7;
  not destructive, c 9; punishes, c 51
Gospel, h 10.8, h 12.13
*Gospel of the Hebrews*, h 15.4
*Gospel of Thomas*, h 27.3
grace, h 1.7, h 1.12, h 3.2, h 5.4, h
  20.3, c 60, k 9
greed, c 30
Greeks, Greek thought, h 6.3, h 16.9,
  c 27
Greek translations, h 28.4

Hades, k 2
hammer, h 27.1–2, c 30
Hanamel, c 60
hearing, c 7–8; and hearkening, h
  12.7; in a hidden way, h 12.13;
  teachers and God, h 6.3, h 14.3;
  through Prophets, c 15
heart, h 1.16, h 5.9, h 5.13–15, h 6.3,
  h 16.5, h 16.10, h 18.8, h 18.10, h
  20.8–9; must work together with
  mouth, c 15
heaven, heavenly, h 8.2, h 16.4, h
  17.4, h 18.2, k 9
Hebrew text, h 14.3, h 16.10, h 18.6,
  h 20.5
Hell, h 19.15, c 22, k 2; *see* Hades
Heracles, h 5.3
heresies, heretics, h 1.16, h 4.4, h
  9.1, h 10.5, h 11.3, h 16.9, h
  17.2–3, h 18.9, h 28.12, c 27
heritage, h 10.8

Hermogenes, h 19.14
Hestiakans, c 40
history, h 1.2, h 5.15, c 28, c 58, k 2
Holophernes, h 20.7
holy ones, h 2.3, h 10.1, h 15.6, h 16.4, h 17.4, h 17.6, h 18.2, c 30, c 56, k 7–9; like a spiritual botanist, p 2.2
holy land, c 27
Holy Spirit, h 2.3, h 5.1, h 5.13, h 8.1, h 10.1, h 13.2, h 14.5, h 15.4, h 16.9, h 18.9, h 19.11, c 55, c 62, k 4, k 7, k 9; third Person of Trinity, h 27.2; writings of, h 28.1
hope, h 15.6, and Scripture, k 2

idol worship, h 1.16, h 4.5, h 5.3, h 7.3, h 9.2, h 10.6, h 16.8–9, h 20.3, c 29, c 32, c 35–36, c 39, c 41, c 47, c 68
image, earthly, heavenly, h 2.1, h 8.2, h 14.8, h 27.1, h 28.9, c 22, c 36; of God, h 1.10, h 2.1, h 16.6, c 14
imagination, creator of idols, h 16.9
imitation, h 4.5–6, h 14.14, h 15.1, h 20.5; of Christ, h 14.16, h 16.3; of Prophets and Apostles, h 20.7
impiety, c 9–10
incense, h 18.10, c 68
incurable, h 28.12, c 28, c 37
influences on Origen, h 20.2–3
inner man, h 1.13
intellect, mind, h 18.2, c 15
irrational, h 5.6, c 11
Isaac, h 1.5, h 4.4, h 20.6
Isaiah, h 1.14, h 8.3, h 9.1, h 14.5, h 14.12, h 15.2, h 16.3, h 20.2, h 20.9, k 3
Israel, Israelites, h 3.1, h 4.1–2, h 4.4, h 4.6, h 5.1, h 5.4, h 7.3, h 11.6, h 12.6, h 12.13, h 13.1, h 18.5, c 6, c 25, c 28, c 39; within us, c 29; see polarities

Jacob, h 4.4, h 17.6, c 54, c 62
Jebus, h 13.2
Jeconiah, c 14
Jehoiakim, c 14
Jeremiah, h 1.5–6, h 1.14, h 8.5, h 9.1, h 14.1, h 14.5, h 16.3, h 18.2, h 20.5, h 20.7–9, k 3; matured quickly, c 1; meaning of name, c 60; why he remained in Judah, c 61, c 63, c 66
Jericho, c 35
Jeroboam, h 4.1, c 45, c 57
Jerusalem, h 5.13, h 7.1, h 8.7, h 10.4, h 10.7, h 12.3, h 13.1–2, h 14.13–14, h 19.13–14, h 27.6, h 28.1, h 28.6, c 22, c 33, c 49, c 64; figure of the Church, c 48; peace, h 27.2, c 11
Jesus, see Christ
Jews, h 4.2, h 5.1, h 5.14, h 10.4, h 10.7–8, h 10.13, h 11.1, h 12.13, h 13.1, h 13.3, h 14.3, h 14.12–13, h 14.15, h 15.2, h 15.5, h 16.10, h 18.5, h 18.8–9, h 19.12, h 20.9, c 68
John the Baptist, k 7
Jordan, k 9
Josephus, c 14
Joshua, h 8.5, h 27.2, k 9
Judah, h 4.1–2, h 10.4, h 11.6, h 16.10, h 18.10, h 19.11, c 11, c 39, k 2
Judas, h 16.10, h 27.1, c 30
Judea, h 28.1, c 29
judgment, h 4.2, h 5.11, h 6.2, h 12.12, h 16.5, h 18.1, h 20.3, h 20.9, h 27.3, c 31, c 36–37; how God judges, h 12.5; life of judges, h 14.17; of God are unsearchable, h 27.5; on the arrogant, h 28.12
Judith, h 20.7
justice of God, h 3.1–2, h 4.4, h 13.1

knowledge, h 1.8, h 1.10, h 6.2, h 10.1, h 16.1–2, h 18.2, c 3, c 12–13, c 28, c 57; as foolishness, h 8.7–9; of God, c 11; prior to practice, c 61; worldly, c 39

last, h 8.4, h 16.8, k 10
last days, h 4.2
Last Supper and institution of Eucharist, h 12.2; see Sacraments
laughter, h 20.6
Law, h 10.8, h 14.16, h 16.3, h 27.2
Levites, h 12.3

## GENERAL INDEX 343

lightning, h 8.4
lions, h 5.16–17, h 10.8, c 3, c 28
literal sense, *see* Scripture
Logos, *see* Word
Lot, h 1.1, k 2
love, h 6.1, c 28; and human affections, h 15.3; unites man to God, h 5.2

Maccabees, h 7.1
man, h 16.5; as a god, h 15.6; as invalid, h 28.12; day of, h 17.6; different kinds of, h 27.3; drunk with passion, h 28.8; greater than Devil, h 5.17; microcosm, c 22; named according to his condition, c 25; powerless before Devil, c 54
Marcion, h 10.5
martyrs, martyrdom, h 4.3, h 14.7, h 14.17
marriage, *see* Sacraments
masses, h 14.16, h 16.5, h 20.7
maturity, h 1.7, h 4.1, h 5.10–11, h 6.2, h 8.7, h 12.13, h 18.5–6, h 19.15, h 20.3–4; diminishes power of Devil, h 27.2; masses not as mature as Apostles, h 16.5; of Noah, c 68; of repentance, c 14
Medes, c 38
medium, k 2, k 6
mercy, h 1.1, h 12.12, h 13.1, h 20.9
merit, h 12.2, h 27.4, h 27.6
Mesopotamians, h 11.6
Moab, c 47
money, *see* wealth
monogamy, h 20.4
Moses, h 1.10, h 1.12, h 5.3, h 5.8, h 8.3, h 9.1–2, h 12.12, h 13.1, h 14.12, h 16.2–3, h 18.2, h 19.12, c 15, c 68, k 3, k 6; cannot defeat Devil, h 27.2
mountains, h 12.12
mysteries, *see* esoteric life and teachings

Nabal the Carmelite, k 1
nations, *see* pagans
nearness of God, h 18.2, h 18.9, c 17, c 68
Nebuccadnezzar, h 1.3, h 5.6, h 7.1, h 12.11, h 19.14, c 3, c 25, c 40, c 48, c 58
Nebuzaradan, c 3
Neco, c 14
Ninevites, h 1.1, h 19.15
nobility, h 11.4, h 12.8, h 17.5
Nod, h 28.10

oaths, h 5.12
obedience, h 10.4, c 57, c 61
Ochozia, h 19.13
opposing powers, h 1.13
opposites, h 8.9

pagans, h 1.7, h 3.2, h 4.2, h 5.1, h 5.3, h 5.12–13, h 12.6, h 12.13, h 15.3, h 16.7–8, h 18.8, h 19.12, h 20.5, h 27.2, c 6, c 24, c 26, c 35; *see* polarities
partridge, h 17.1–3
Paschor, h 19.11, h 19.13–14
Passion of Christ, *see* Christ
passions, h 5.9, h 5.16, c 26; fleshly, c 40; four principal, c 25
Passover, h 12.13, h 19.13
patience of God, h 1.1, h 1.3, h 18.5
Patriarchs, k 9–10
Paul, h 1.16, h 8.4–5, h 8.7, h 10.1, h 11.4, h 12.8, h 14.16, h 17.2, h 19.12, h 20.3, h 20.6–7, c 30, k 9
peace, h 9.2, h 13.2, h 17.4, c 28; a deception, c 65; grace of God, c 60
penitence, *see* repentance
people of God, h 9.2–3
perfect, k 9; *see* maturity
perception, h 6.1
persecution, h 1.13, h 14.8, h 14.13–14, h 14.17–18, h 19.12–13, h 20.9, c 30, c 63; being like adamant, h 27.1; Christ is in one suffering, c 14.7
Persians, c 38
Peter, h 10.1, h 17.2, h 19.13, k 7
Phaethon, h 27.4
Pharaoh, h 1.10, h 5.6, h 6.3, h 27.3, c 25, c 31
Pharisees, h 4.4
philosophy, h 16.9
Phygelus, h 19.14
Pilate, h 19.12

344   GENERAL INDEX

polarities, alien and holy land, h 7.3; Babylon and Jerusalem, h 28.1, c 33; bitter and kind words or acts, c52; building of God and of Devil, h 1.15, h 10.4; buried with Christ and buried in Babylon, h 19.14; dark and bright mountains, h 12.12; day of man and day of God, h 17.6; day or light and night or darkness, h 13.3; death and life, h 1.16, h 9.3, h 16.1; deserted and inhabited, h 8.1, c 53; divine and evil spirits, c 19; earthen and gold vessel, h 28.7, c 36; eternal and temporary, h 18.10; evil and virtue, h 12.2, h 18.1; fire and electrum, h 11.5; first and last, k 10; flesh and spirit, h 5.15, h 8.1, h 11.2, h 20.7, c 59; friendship and enmity, h 20.7; going back and straining forward, h 13.3; good and bad odor, c 68–69; health and sickness, h 14.1, h 17.5, h 27.4, h 28.12; heavenly and earthly, h 2.1, h 8.2, h 10.7, h 14.8, h 14.12, h 16.4, h 16.8, h 17.4, h 18.2, h 28.9, c 22, c 36, c 43; here and there, h 1.9, h 20.9; inner and outer, h 1.10, h 1.13, h 4.3, h 12.13, h 16.10, h 20.8; Israel and Judah, h 4.1; Israel and pagans, h 3.2, h 4.2, h 5.1, h 5.4, h 5.12–13, h 12.13, h 14.12, h 14.15, h 15.5, h 18.5, h 18.8, h 27.2, c 6, c 26; land of the holy and land of the enemies, c 56; Law and Gospel, h 19.15; mature and immature, h 18.6, h 19.15; mountain and valley, h 16.1–2; rain and desert, h 3.1–2; rational and irrational, c 19–20; sensitive and insensitive to punishment, h 6.2; solid food and milk, c 10; spiritual and unspiritual, h 12.1; spiritually and bodily, h 13.2; strong and poor soul, h 6.3; superior and inferior, h 1.14–15, h 2.1; Temple of God and of idols, h 1.16; true and false, h 5.3, h 14.8, h 16.8, h 19.14–15; under and above, h 1.8, h 18.2, h 19.13;

universal and particular, h 3.1–2; vessels of wrath and of mercy, h 27.3, c 31; white and dark, c 11; *see* analogies, allegories
power, h 1.8, h 1.12, h 1.16, h 2.2, h 5.1–5, h 6.1, h 8.1–2, h 10.8, h 13.2, h 14.14, h 15.2, h 17.2, h 18.4, h 20.3, h 20.5–6, h 20.9
prayer, h 5.17, h 18.10, h 19.13, h 20.9, c 49, c 68
preaching, h 1.7, h 1.16, h 5.13, h 5.16, h 6.3, h 9.4, h 14.2–4, h 15.2, h 16.1, h 19.13–14, h 20.6, c 5; false, c 21; time required to discuss a text, k 1
pre-existence, h 1.11, h 2.1, h 5.14, h 8.1, h 15.4, h 28.3
pride, h 4.4, h 12.7–8, h 17.5, h 28.12, c 34, c 45; challenging God, c 11–12
priests, *see* clergy, Sacraments
progress in spiritual growth, h 11.5–6, h 12.13, h 13.3, h 14.3, h 14.10, h 15.6, h 16.1, h 18.1, h 18.6, h 18.8, h 19.15, c 9
promises, h 12.2, h 14.18, h 20.6
prophecy, h 19.14, c 61, k 9
Prophets, h 14.1–2, h 14.14, h 15.1–2, h 16.1, h 16.3, h 20.8, h 28.2, c 49, k 6–9; courage of, h 20.5; false, h 19.14, c 15, c 49, c 63, c 65; sign of true, c 19
Providence, h 6.2, h 7.3, h 16.10, h 28.4, p 2.2, c 67
prudence, h 8.2, c 48
*Pseudo-Barnabas, Epistle of,* h 18.2
*Pseudo-Ezechiel,* h 18.9
punishment, h 1.1, h 1.16, h 2.3, h 6.2, h 7.1–2, h 10.5, h 12.10, h 13.1, h 16.5–7, h 18.5, h 19.14–15, h 20.3, h 20.9, h 28.5, c 14, c 25, c 37, c 39, c 45, c 52, c 70; how and why God punishes, h 12.2–6; *see* afterlife
purification, purity, h 2.3, h 11.6, h 16.5, h 16.10, h 20.4, c 9, c 11, c 68
Pythians, c 40

ransomed by Christ, c 58

## GENERAL INDEX 345

rational, h 3.2, h 5.6, h 6.3, h 14.10, h 28.12, c 11–12, c 19–20; overcomes confusion and distractions, h 27.2
reason, *see* rational
redemption, h 5.17, h 7.3, h 10.1, h 12.13, h 14.5, h 14.9, h 14.11, h 16.10, h 17.4, c 35, c 58
rejected, cast out, h 7.3, h 12.5, h 14.14, h 27.3, c 31, c 48, c 59, c 64; difference between, h 28.4
remnant, h 5.4
repentance, h 1.1, h 1.4, h 2.1, h 4.4, h 5.3, h 5.5, h 5.10, h 5.17, h 7.1, h 10.8, h 13.2, h 13.3, h 14.11, h 14.13, h 14.18, h 15.4, h 16.5–6, h 18.5–6, h 18.8, h 20.6, h 20.9, h 27.2, h 28.4, c 8, c 14, c 48, c 57–58, c 68
rest, h 5.13, h 8.6
restoration, h 14.18, c 16, c 29; *see* afterlife
resurrection, h 1.16, h 2.3, h 8.6, h 10.3, h 14.18, h 17.6, h 18.4; *see* afterlife
retribution of God, c 40
riches, *see* wealth
right, c 11, c 23
righteous, righteousness, h 8.7, h 10.1, h 16.5, c 12, c 48, c 56, c 58, c 61, c 68
Roboam, h 4.1, c 1

sabbath, h 12.13
Sacraments, Baptism, h 1.16, h 2.3, h 16.5, h 19.14, c 26; Eucharist, h 12.2, h 12.12, h 19.13, c 50; Marriage, h 20.4; h 20.7; Orders, h 11.3, h 12.3, c 50; Penance, h 5.10, h 10.8, c 57–58; principle of, c 4
sacrifices, c 4, c 11, c 68
salvation, h 1.1, h 1.12, h 2.3, h 5.2, h 5.4, h 6.2, h 9.4, h 11.3, h 12.6, h 13.3, h 15.4, h 16.5, h 17.5, h 18.5, h 19.15, h 20.3–4, h 28.1, h 28.3–4, h 28.12, c 33, c 36–37, c 45, c 54, k 6–7; of Israel, h 4.6
Samaritan woman, h 18.4
Samuel, h 18.2, k 2

sanctification, h 17.4
Satan, *see* Devil
Saul, h 20.1, k 2
Savior, *see* Christ
*schoinos*, h 18.10, n 123
Scripture, h 1.6–7, h 5.15, h 6.3, h 10.1, h 12.13, h 14.12, h 14.16, h 16.10; allegorical, h 7.3; anagogical sense, h 15.2, k 2; anthropomorphisms in, h 18.6, h 20.1; author is Holy Spirit, k 4; bitter before kind, c 52; degrees of understanding and interpretations, h 18.4; different levels, h 1.7, h 19.11; difficulties, k 4, k 6; disturbing, k 4; does not always explain itself, h 16.6; encourages conversion, h 1.4, h 4.5; every dot important, h 28.2, p 1.1; hearing in a hidden way, h 12.3; higher sense, h 19.13, k 2; history and historical sense, h 1.2, k 2, k 4–5; interpretation must follow from text, h 17.1; lesson book, h 4.5; like a group of herbs or a body, p 2.2; literal (or bodily) sense, h 1.7, h 4.1, h 6.3, h 7.1, h 7.3, h 12.1, h 12.3, h 13.1–2, h 14.4, h 19.11, k 2; logic of, h 27.2; main theme is two nations, h 18.5; narrator of, k 4; need for help from Jesus, h 19.10; need of help to interpret, h 20.2; nothing extraneous, p 2.2; place names refer to condition of soul, h 28.1; proving through other texts, h 1.7; types in, h 1.6; unadorned to fool Devil, c 61; veil can confuse, h 5.8; view of God, h 18.6; we to blame if we do not comprehend, p 1.1
secret teachings, *see* esoteric life
seed, divine, c 40
senses, h 16.9; ruled by Christ, h 5.6
Septuagint, h 14.3, h 15.5, h 16.5, h 16.10, h 20.5, c 6, c 24, c 59
Serpent, *see* Devil
serpents, h 18.9
service of God, c 42
Seth, h 27.1
seven, c 48, c 62

Shallum, c 60
shame, h 5.5, h 5.7–8, h 11.4, h 16.4, c 45
sheep, c 28
shepherd, c 28
Simon, h 20.8
Simon Magus, h 5.3
sin, sinner, after forgiveness, h 16.5; all sin more or less, c 25; assumed by Christ, h 14.9; awareness of sin brings repentance, c 57; death and, h 9.3, k 9–10; delivered to Satan, c 2; destruction by words, h 1.7; determines kind of punishment, h 19.15; distances us from Holy Spirit, h 18.9; do not know Christ, c 13; effect of, h 1.3, h 10.1, h 15.3, h 17.4, h 20.8, k 10; filth destroyed first, c 9; forgets God, h 18.10; in faithful, c 23; kinds of, h 2.2–3, h 5.5, h 12.2, h 13.1–2, h 16.4, h 19.15, h 20.9, h 28.12; mixed with good, h 12.2; not filled with God, c 18; plague for souls, c 69; punishment of, h 12.2–6, h 16.5; treatment of, h 2.2; written on the heart, h 16.10
snakes, c 25
Sodom, h 1.1, h 8.7, h 12.1, h 13.3
soldier, h 15.6, h 17.4
Solomon, h 27.1
Son of God, h 8.1, h 15.3, h 15.6; see Christ
souls, h 6.3, h 8.1, h 10.8, h 16.1, h 16.10, c 40; connection with body, c 18; discernment of, c 3; endowment of, h 3.2; essentially good, h 2.1; mysteries and ineffable teachings constructed in, c 58; none incurable, h 28.12; spirit and body, c 22; spiritual diversity of, h 28.1
speaking in tongues, k 9
spirit, spiritual, h 2.2, h 8.1, h 8.5, h 11.2, h 12.1, h 19.14, h 20.7, h 27.1, c 11, c 19, c 62; see polarities
spirits, bad, h 5.2
stability (in thought and deed), c 16, c 36
struggle of Christian, h 14.14, h 19.14, h 20.8, h 27.3, h 28.1, c 25–26, c 30, c 57, c 59–60
stubbornness, h 28.12
suffering, h 6.2; upon entering Church, h 27.3
swearing, h 5.12
Silvanus, h 8.5
Symmachus, c 45

Tabitha, h 19.13
Tamar, k 2
teachers, teaching, h 5.13, h 5.15, h 6.2–3, h 10.1–2, h 14.1, h 14.3–4, h 17.3, h 18.2, h 18.5–6, h 19.15, c 5; bad, h 28.7; by punishment of others, h 12.6; evil, c 40; evil teachings are deceitful, c 36; false, c 12–13; false teachers kill their own souls, c 13; power of words determined by heart, c 21; temple built by right teachings, c 23; weak attracted to every, c 25
Temple, h 19.13
temptations, h 27.1, h 27.3, c 30, c 60
ten, c 62
three youths, c 66
theft, h 20.3
Theodotion, c 6
time, h 12.10
torturers, h 20.9
transformation, h 16.1
treasury of the Lord, h 27.3
truth, h 4.1, h 4.3, h 5.3, h 5.12, h 5.15–17, h 7.1, h 8.4, h 14.5, h 14.12–13, h 14.16–17, h 15.3, h 16.6, h 16.9, h 17.3, h 19.14, h 20.4, c 12–13, c 22, c 28, c 54, k 2–3
two nations, see polarities
Tyre, h 28.2

unbelief, k 2
underworld, k 3
unity, of love, truth, good, c 28

Valentinus, h 10.5, h 17.2
veil, over the heart, h 5.8, h 5.14–15
vessels, see analogies

GENERAL INDEX 347

virtue, h 6.1, h 8.1–2, h 10.6, h 12.2, h 12.11, h 15.3, h 18.1, h 19.14, h 27.1, h 28.2, c 9, c 11, c 23, c 30, c 40, c 48, c 61, c 68

way of the Lord, h 6.3
wealth, h 7.3, h 8.4, h 11.4, h 12.8, h 16.4, h 16.8, h 17.4–5, h 20.5, h 20.7, h 20.9, c 45, c 51
weeping, h 12.13; two kinds, h 20.6
whips of God, h 6.2
will of God, c 52, c 60
wine, h 12.1–2
wisdom, h 8.8, h 12.2, h 14.5, c 48; earthly wisdom, h 8.6–7, h 8.9, h 20.7; kinds of wisdom, h 18.2; meaning of, h 8.2
woman, c 40
woods, c 44
Word, h 2.2, h 5.15–16, h 6.3, h 9.1, h 10.1, h 13.3, h 14.6, h 16.9, c 52, k 8; all united to, c 28; as converter, h 15.1; as examiner at judgment, h 20.9; as inner teacher, h 18.2; beginning, h 20.1; being persecuted, h 19.12; in preacher, h 19.13; in soul of man, p 1.1; knowledge of, h 1.8; share of the, h 14.10
words, power of, h 1.16
works, behavior, h 3.3, h 5.2, h 5.7–8, h 6.3, h 8.2, h 8.4, h 9.3–4, h 12.2, h 12.11, h 18.5, h 18.9, h 20.7, h 27.6, c 3, c 14, c 61
world, h 14.17, h 16.1, h 18.2, h 20.7
worth, worthiness, c 45; to be filled by God, c 18; *see* merit
wrath, anger, c 25; difference between, c 16; on those who resist will of God, c 52

youth in Christ, h 20.4

Zedekiah, c 64
Zion, h 27.6, c 32
Zephites, k 1

# INDEX OF HOLY SCRIPTURE

*In these entries h precedes references to the Homilies followed by homily and section number. In the remaining entries p precedes references to the Fragments from the Philocalia; c, the Fragments from the Catena; and k, the Homily on 1 Kings 28. These entries are followed by section number.*

## Old Testament

Genesis
1.26: h 1.10; H 2.1; H 16.6; c 14
1.27: h 1.10
2.15: h 1.10
2.18: k 9
3.1: h 17.3
3.8: h 16.4
3.13: h 20.3
3.15: h 20.7
3.19: h 8.1f; h 27.1; h 28.8f; c 36
3.20: c 22
3.24: k 9
4.16: h 16.4; h 28.10
4.22: h 27.1; c 30
5.1: h 27.1
5.6: h 27.1
6.12: c 68
7.2–3: c 68
7.8: c 68
7.10: c 68
8.21: c 68
11.2: h 12.3
11.3–4: h 12.2
11.7–8: c 9
11.7: h 12.3
11.8: h 12.3
11.9: h 19.14
12.1: h 1.5
12.10: c 2
14.10: h 16.2
15.7: h 27.4
17.1: h 9.3
18: h 1.4

19.12: h 1.1
19.17: h 13.3
19.30–38: k 2
20.7: h 1.5
21.1–7: h 20.6
27.27: c 62
35.4: h 19.14
35.11: h 9.3
38.1–30: k 2

Exodus
2.23–24: c 56
3.2: h 16.4
3.6: h 16.4
4.21: h 6.3
7.8: h 5.3
7.11–12: h 19.12
10.27: h 4.5
12.8: h 14.16
13.22: k 9
14.24: k 9
15.1: c 40
15.17: h 18.5
15.25: h 10.2
23.13: h 20.8
23.15: h 18.10; h 28.2
23.17: h 18.10
24.12: h 18.2
29.45: h 9.3
30.34: h 18.9
33.22–23: h 16.2
33.23: h 16.2
34.20: p 1.1
34.34: h 5.8

34.35: h 5.8

Leviticus
14.33: h 1.15
14.40: h 1.15
23.27: c 62
24.16: h 19.15
25.9: h 12.13
26.21: h 7.1–2
26.23–24: h 7.1

Numbers
10.1: h 27.1
10.2: h 5.16
10.2, 8–9: c 30
10.9–10: h 5.16; h 27.1
12.7: h 12.12
16.5: h 1.8
18.17: h 5.7
20.17–19: h 17.4
23.19: h 18.6
23.23: c 49
25.5: c 47

Deuteronomy
1.31: h 18.6
4.24: h 16.6; h 18.1
7.5: h 1.16
7.7: h 27.6; c 33
8.5: h 18.6
16.21: h 4.4
18.15, 18: k 6
18.15, 19: h 1.12
19.15: h 1.7

348

# INDEX OF HOLY SCRIPTURE 349

22.24: h 19.15
29.3: h 28.2
29.23, 24–27: h 18.6
32.1–2: h 8.3
32.24: c 28
32.21: h 9.2
32.32–33: h 12.1
32.39: h 1.16; h 16.6

Joshua
3.11–17: k 9
6.20: h 28.11; c 35
18.10–24: h 19.13
18.28: h 13.2

1 Kings (1 Samuel)
1.11: k 3
1.22: k 3
2.18–19: k 3
2.25: h 13.1
2.31–3.21: k 3
3.4–14: k 3
3.20: k 6
12.1–6: k 3
12.17–18: k 3
15.9: k 5
15.11: h 18.6
15.16–23: k 5
16.1–13: k 5
17.34–35: c 28
25: k 1
26: k 1
28: h 18.2
28.2: k 1
28.3–25: k 1
28.11: k 3–4
28.12: k 4; k 6
28.12–14: k 4
28:14: k 4
28.15: k 4–6
28.15–16: k 5
28.16: k 4
28.16–19: k 5
28.17: k 4
28.18: k 5
28.19: k 5

3 Kings (1 Kings)
6.1: h 27.1
6.7: h 27.1
6.12: c 30

12: h 4.1
12.13–14: c 1
12.16, 24: c 57
12.28: c 57
12.29: c 45
17.19: h 19.13
18.44: h 8.3
19.10, 14: h 14.16
19.11: c 20
19.18: h 5.4
20.29: h 6.2

4 Kings (2 Kings)
1.2: h 19.13
4.10: h 19.13
16.10: h 7.3
17.23: h 4.1; c 28
21.14: c 3
23.24: c 14
23.31: h 10.4
24.12: c 14
24.18: h 10.4
25.7, 11: c 28
25.8: c 3

Judith
12.6–7, 14: h 20.7

Job
2.5: h 28.8; c 36
5.18: h 1.16; h 16.6; c 70
14.4–5: h 5.14
26.7: h 8.1
41.15: c 30
41.16: h 27.1

Psalms
2.1–2: h 19.12
2.2: h 10.7
2.4: h 20.5
2.8: c 6
4.6: h 5.9; c 4
4.7: h 6.1
6.2: h 28.5; c 16
6.7: h 20.6
7.10: h 20.9
8.2: h 15.3
8.3: h 19.14
9.30: h 5.16
10.2: c 25

13.1: c 47
14.1–3: h 16.6
14.3–4: h 16.6
15.10: k 6
17.26–27: k 7
17.30: h 5.16
17.42: h 1.15
18.5: h 10.2
20.4: c 11
21.13,14: k 6
21.31: h 9.3
22.5: h 12.1–2
23.1: c 18
25.5: c 13
27.27: h 18.9
29.9: h 14.6
29.10: h 15.4
32.16: c 45
32.17: h 17.5
33.16: h 6.1
33.17: h 5.11
35.6: h 8.3–4
37.5: c 11
37.6: c 68
37.7, 9–10: h 20.9
39.2: h 16.2
41.2: h 18.9
41.3: h 18.9; h 20.6
43.16: h 5.8
43.18: h 18.10
44.3: h 1.12
44.11: h 9.4
47.6: h 28.10
48.13: h 19.14
50.6: h 15.3
50.12: h 8.1
50.13: h 8.1; k 9
50.19: c 4
67.12: h 1.16
67.32–33: h 5.4
71.3: c 28
73.9: h 4.2
73.19: h 10.8
74.9: h 12.2; c 25
76.17–18: h 10.6
77.47: h 12.1
77.49: h 28.6
78.8: h 5.10
79.9: h 15.3
79.9, 13: c 70
79.15: c 70

# INDEX OF HOLY SCRIPTURE

(Psalms *continued*)
81.6: h 15.6
83.11: h 28.4
86.1: h 12.12
88.21: h 20.1
88.31–33: h 28.5
90.13: c 25
93.10: h 10.1
95.4: h 18.6
98.6–7: k 2
103.2: h 8.2
103.20–21: h 5.16
103.21: c 28
103.26: c 22
108.7: h 18.10
115.4: h 12.2
128.5: h 5.5
134.7: h 8.3
136.1: h 28.1; c 55
136.4: h 7.3; h 28.1
136.9: h 27.6; c 26
138.3: h 18.10
140.2: h 18.10; c 11; c 68
144.3: h 18.6
148.2–3: h 18.6

Proverbs
1.6: h 20.1
1.24: h 8.2
1.28: h 20.7
3.11: h 10.5
3.19: h 8.2
3.34: c 45
4.6, 8: c 48
4.23: h 27.2
5.22: h 9.4
6.15: c 28
8.25: h 9.4
9.1, 5: h 12.1–2
18.12: h 12.8
19.25: h 12.6
21.6: c 13
24.33: c 22
24.55: h 20.9

Ecclesiastes
5.1: p 1.1
7.20: h 8.1
7.23–24: h 8.7

Canticle of Canticles
1.5: h 11.6
3.6: c 11
8.5: h 11.6

Wisdom
1.7: c 17
1.13–14: h 2.1
2.24: h 2.1
3.1: c 71
3.11: h 8.1
4.13: c 1
6.6: h 11.3
7.26: h 9.4
8.2: c 48
12.10: h 1.1; h 7.1
14.8: h 10.6

Sirach
8.6: h 16.6
16.21: h 12.13
21.15: h 6.1
22.27: h 6.2
23.2: h 6.2
25.9: h 6.3; h 14.3
40.16: c 70

Isaiah
1.2: h 8.3
1.6: h 28.12
1.6–7: h 2.2
1.13: c 68
1.25: c 9
2.8: h 16.9
3.1–3: h 10.4; h 14.12
3.3: h 14.3
4.4: h 2.2
5.1: h 12.1; h 15.3
5.4–6: h 1.4
5.6: h 8.3
6.1: h 17.4
6.5: h 1.14; h 14.5
6.6: h 1.14
6.7: h 1.14
6.6–7: h 14.5
6.8–10: h 20.2
6.9–10: h 14.12
7.14: h 1.7
7.16: h 1.7

8.14: p 2.1
8.17: h 18.6
9.4: h 6.2; c 54
10.12–13: h 17.3
10.14: c 54
11.1: h 2.3
11.2–3: h 8.5
26.20: h 12.10
28.16: p 2.1
30.15: h 27.3
31.9: c 26
32.20: c 26
37.23: h 19.13
37.24: h 19.13
40.6: h 20.2
40.9: h 19.13
42.14: c 68
43.2: k 9
43.26: c 58
45.2: c 44
45.4: c 42
45.13: c 23
47.13: c 49
50.6: h 19.12
53.1–5: h 14.9
53.7: h 10.1
54.1: h 3.2; h 9.3
58.6: h 9.4
58.6–7: h 9.4
58.9: c 68
61.1: c 58
64.4: h 19.15
65.17: h 19.15
66.8: h 9.3
66.24: h 20.4

Jeremiah
1.1: h 20.5
1.2: h 1.2
1.4: h 1.5
1.5: h 1.5; h 1.10–12; h 1.14; h 14.5; c 62; k 3
1.6: h 1.6–9; h 14.5
1.6–7: h 1.13
1.7: h 1.6; h 1.9
1.7–8: h 1.6; h 1.13
1.8: h 1.13
1.9: h 1.14; h 1.16

## INDEX OF HOLY SCRIPTURE

1.9–10: h 1.6; h
   1.8–9; h 1.14
1.10: h 1.6–7; h
   1.14–16; h 14.5;
   c 1
1.13: c 2
1.14: c 2
2.2: c 19; k 3
2.13: h 17.4; h 18.9
2.20: h 4.4
2.21: h 2.1; h 15.3;
   c 70
2.22: h 2.2
2.31: h 3.1–2
3.5: h 4.4
3.6: h 4.1; h 4.4;
   h 4.6
3.6–8: h 4.1
3.7: h 4.1; h 4.5
3.7–8: h 4.5
3.8: h 4.1; h 4.4
3.8–9: h 4.6
3.8–10: h 4.1
3.10: h 4.6
3.10–11: h 4.1
3.12: h 4.2
3.18: h 4.1
3.19–20: h 5.1
3.21: h 5.1
3.22: h 5.1–3
3.23: h 5.3–4
3.24: h 5.5–7
3.25: h 5.8; h 5.10
4.1: h 5.11–12
4.1–2: h 5.2;
   h 5.11–12
4.2: h 5.11–12
4.2–3: h 5.13
4.3: h 5.13
4.4: h 5.14–15
4.5: h 5.15–16
4.6: h 5.16
4.7: h 5.16–17
4.8: h 5.17
5.3: h 6.1–3
5.3–5: h 6.3
5.6: c 3
5.18: h 7.1–2
5.19: h 7.3
6.7–8: h 12.3

6.9: h 9.4; h 10.4
6.16: h 10.4
7.3: h 10.4
7.20–21: h 10.4
7.21: c 4
8.7: c 5
9.22–23: h 11.4
9.23: c 45
9.23–24: h 17.5
10.12: h 8.1–2
10.13: h 8.3–6
10.14: h 8.7
10.16: c 6
10.24: h 28.5
11.1: h 9.1
11.2: h 9.1–2
11.2–4: h 9.2
11.3: h 9.4
11.4: h 9.2–3
11.4–5: h 9.3
11.5: h 9.4
11.6: h 9.4
11.6–9: h 9.4
11.9–10: h 9.4
11.10: h 9.4
11.11: c 7
11.12: c 7
11.11, 14: c 8
11.18: h 10.1
11.19: h 10.1–2
11.20: h 10.4
11.20–23: h 10.4
11.21: h 10.4
11.25–12.1: h 10.5
12.1–2: h 10.5
12.2: h 10.5
12.3: h 10.5
12.4: h 10.6
12.7: h 10.7
12.8: h 10.8
12.8–9: h 10.8
12.9: h 10.8
12.11: h 11.1
12.12: h 11.2
12.13: h 11.3–4;
   h 28.4
13.1–4: h 11.5
13.11: h 11.5–6
13.12: h 12.1–2
13.12–13: h 12.3

13.13: h 12.3
13.13–14: h 12.3
13.14: h 12.4; h 12.6
13.15: h 12.7–8
13.15–17: h 12.7
13.16: h 12.9; h
   12.11
13.16–17: h 12.13
13.17: h 12.13
14.5: c 9
14.7: h 14.8–10;
   h 14.14; h 14.17
15.1: k 3
15.1–2: k 2
15.2: h 15.4–5
15.5–7: h 13.1
15.5: h 13.2
15.6: h 13.3
15.7: c 9
15.8: c 10
15.10: h 1.6;
   h 14.2–3; h 14.5
15.11: h 14.11
15.12: h 14.12
15.13: h 14.12
15.14: h 14.13
15.15: h 14.14
15.16: h 14.15
15.17: h 14.15–16
15.18: h 14.17–18
15.19: h 14.18
16.1–2: h 20.7
16.16: h 16.1; h 18.5
16.17: h 16.5
16.18: h 16.5–7
16.19: h 16.8
16.20: h 16.9
16.21: h 16.9
17.1: h 16.10
17.5: h 15.6
17.11: h 17.1
17.12–13: h 17.4
17.13: h 17.4
17.14: h 17.5
17.14–16: h 17.5
17.15–16: h 17.6
17.16: h 17.6
17.24: c 11
17.25: c 11
17.26: c 11

352　INDEX OF HOLY SCRIPTURE

(Jeremiah *continued*)
18.1–2: h 18.2
18.2: h 18.2
18.3–4: h 18.3
18.4: h 18.4; h 18.7
18.5–6: h 18.4
18.6–10: h 18.5
18.8: h 1.4
18.8, 10: h 18.6
18.7: h 18.6
18.7–10: h 18.6
18.10: h 18.6
18.11: h 18.7–8
18.12: h 18.8
18.13: h 18.8
18.13–16: h 18.9
18.14: h 18.9
18.15: h 18.10
19.13: h 27.4
20.1: h 19.1
20.2: h 19.11–14
20.2–4: h 19.11
20.3: h 19.11; h 19.14
20.3–4: h 19.14
20.4: h 19.14
20.4–5: h 19.14
20.5: h 19.11; h 19.14
20.5–6: h 19.14
20.6: h 19.11; h 19.14
20.7: h 14.14; h 19.15; h 20.1; h 20.4–5; h 20.9
20.7–11: h 19.15
20.8: h 20.6–8
20.9: h 14.2; h 20.8
20.9–10: h 20.9
20.10: h 20.9
20.11: h 19.15; h 20.9
20.12: h 20.9
21.9: c 14
22.13: c 12–13
22.14: c 13
22.15: c 13
22.15–16: c 13
22.17: c 13
22.24: c 13

23.16: c 15
23.17: c 16; k 3
23.19: c 16
23.20: c 16; c 52
23.23: h 18.9; c 17
23.24: c 17–18
23.28: c 19–20
23.29: c 20
23.30: c 21
23.31: c 19
24.1–2: c 22
24.6: c 23
25.11: h 4.1
25.14: h 1.12
25.14: c 24
25.15: c 25
25.16: c 25
27.16: h 27.6; c 26–27
27.17: c 28
27.17–18: c 29
27.19: c 29
27.23: h 27.1–2; c 30
27.23–24: h 27.2
27.24: h 27.2
27.25: h 27.3–4; c 31
27.25–27: h 27.3
27.26: h 27.5
27.27: h 27.5
27.28: h 27.6; c 32
27.29: h 27.6; c 33–34
27.29–32: c 34
28.6: h 28.1; h 28.4–6
28.7: h 28.9–10; c 36
28.7–8: h 28.11
28.8: h 28.12; c 35; c 37
28.9: h 28.12; c 37
28.10: c 40
28.11: c 38
28.12: c 38
28.17: c 39
28.17–20: c 39
28.18: c 39
28.21: c 40

28.22: c 40
28.23: c 40
28.24: c 40
28.25: c 41
28.26: c 41
28.27: c 41
28.29: c 43
28.31: c 44
28.32: c 44
28.33: c 44
28.34: c 40
30.29: h 1.12
31.1: h 1.12
31.7: c 47
31.11: c 45
31.12: c 45
31.14: c 45
31.16: c 45
31.25: c 46
31.26: c 47
31.26–28: c 47
32.1: c 25
32.15: h 20.2
32.16: h 12.2
32.18: h 20.2
33.2–3: h 18.6
36.5: c 48
36.6: c 48
36.8: c 49
36.10: c 48
36.21: c 50
37.18: c 51
37.23–24: c 52
38.6: h 1.13
38.9: c 53
38.10: c 54
38.11: c 54
38.16: c 56
38.16–18: c 56
38.18: c 56
38.18–19: c 57
38.20: c 57
38.23: c 58
38.24: c 58
38.36–37: c 59
39.7–8: c 60
39.9: c 62
39.10: c 61
39.14: c 61
39.17: c 62

## INDEX OF HOLY SCRIPTURE 353

40.10, 12: h 18.5
44.20: h 1.13
45.5: c 63
45.6: h 15.2
45.19: c 64
45.20: c 64
45.22: c 65
45.24: c 65
47.4–5: c 66
48.2: c 67
51.21: c 68
51.22: P 2.1; c 68–69
51.32–35: c 70
51.35: c 71
52.13: h 12.11

Lamentations
1,8: h 13.1

Baruch
3.9–13: h 7.3
3.10: c 56
3.15: h 7.3

Ezekiel
1.27: h 11.5
11.19: h 4.5
16.51–53: h 8.7

18.24: h 19.14
27.4: h 28.2
30.13–18: h 28.1
36.26: h 4.5
34.12: h 27.4

Daniel
1.6: c 66
5.2–3: c 34
9.2: h 4.1
9.5: h 5.10; h 8.1
12.2: h 16.10
13.42: h 11.3;
   h 16.10
13.52: c 40

Hosea
1.9: h 9.2
2.25; h 9.2
3.4: c 42
4.14: h 28.5
7.12: h 19.15
14.10: h 28.1

Joel
2.13: h 18.6
2.26: h 14.16
2.32: h 20.7

Amos
3.2: h 20.3
3.12: h 5.17
5.18: h 12.10; h 17.6
7.7: h 27.1; c 30
8.11: h 10.4

Jonah
3.4: h 1.1; h 19.15

Micah
2.9: h 28.4
7.1–2: h 14.6; h 15.4
7.1: h 15.3
7.2: h 15.3

Habakkuk
1.16: c 40

Zephaniah
3.9–10: h 5.4

Zechariah
1.9: k 7
4.1: h 16.3
4.7: c 41

New Testament

Matthew
3.10: h 18.5; c 23
3.12: h 1.15; h 20.4;
   h 27.3; c 31
3.16: k 7
4.8: h 1.14
4.9: h 27.2
4.18–20: h 16.1
4.21: h 16.1
5.1–3: h 16.2
5.3: h 8.2; h 20.6
5.4: c 53
5.5: h 9.3; h 20.6
5.8: h 20.6
5.9: h 20.6
5.11: h 20.8

5.11–12: h 1.13
5.14: c 51
5.18: p 2.1
5.22: h 19.15; c 22
5.34: h 5.12
5.37: h 5.12
5.39: h 19.12
5.45: h 3.2
6.19–20: h 8.2
6.20: h 5.13
6.24: h 20.7
7.2: h 17.4
7.7–8: c 28
7.13: h 20.7; c 33
7.14: h 4.3; h 14.16;
   h 20.6–7

7.18: h 20.4
7.19: c 23
7.22–23: h 1.8
7.23: h 1.8; h 1.10
7.24: h 20.7
7.25: h 1.15
7.26: h 1.15
8.12: h 12.8;
   h 12.13; h 20.6
8.18: h 12.5
8.22: h 17.6
9.9: h 17.6
9.12: h 17.5; h 27.4;
   k 9
9.20: h 17.5
9.36: h 27.4

354    INDEX OF HOLY SCRIPTURE

(Matthew *continued*)
9.37: h 18.5
9.38: h 5.13
10.26: h 16.10
10.34: h 11.2
10.37–38: h 17.6
11.15: h 1.10
11.19: h 14.5
11.27: k 10
11.28: h 17.6
11.29: h 12.7
12.7: c 4
12.32: h 12.10
12.36: p 2.1
13.8: h 5.13
13.14–15: h 14.12
13.22: c 40
13.25: h 1.14–15; c 40
13.26: h 12.13
13.28: h 1.14
13.30: h 1.15
13.46: h 8.6
13.47: h 18.5
13.47–48: h 27.3
13.47–49: c 31
13.49: h 4.3
13.57: h 1.13
15.13: h 1.14; h 1.16
15.16–17: k 7
15.19: h 5.15
16.13: k 7
16.15: k 7
16.22: k 7
16.24: h 17.6; h 18.2
17.1–2: h 16.2
17.20: h 12.12; c 41
18.7: p 2.1
18.9: c 22
18.12: c 28
18.20: c 17
18.24: h 20.9
19.5: h 10.7
19.27: h 17.6
20.8: k 10
20.10: k 10
20.11: k 10
20.16: h 4.3; k 10

20.18–19: h 15.2
21.43: h 10.4; h 14.12
22.10: h 2.3
22.32: h 9.3; h 11.1
23.8–9: h 10.1
23.13: h 15.2
23.27: h 19.12
23.28: h 10.4
23.34–35: h 15.2
23.37: h 11.1; h 14.6
23.37–38: h 7.1; h 13.1
23.38: h 7.1; h 14.15
24.12: h 12.13
24.12–13: h 4.3
24.15–17: h 19.13
24.24: h 4.3
24.38–39: h 28.11; c 35
24.45: h 11.3
24.49–51: h 11.3
25.23: c 14
25.25: h 20.3
25.30: h 12.5
25.36: h 14.7
25.41: h 5.2; h 12.5
26.17: h 19.13
26.26–28: h 12.2
26.28: h 12.2
26.29: h 12.2
26.38: h 14.6; h 15.3
28.19: h 27.2
28.20: h 9.1

Mark
4.19: h 5.13
4.28: h 5.13
5.26: k 6
5.26–27: h 17.5
5.36: k 6
6.34: h 27.4
9.35: h 8.4
13.16: h 13.3
14.12–15: h 19.13
14.15: h 12.2
14.61: k 7

Luke
1.35: h 1.8
1.44: k 7
2.52: h 1.7; h 14.10
3.8: h 4.5
3.9: c 23
3.16: h 2.3
3.17: c 31
4.13: h 27.2
4.18: h 14.11; c 58
5.20: h 16.5
5.31: h 14.1
6.20: h 8.4
6.21: h 20.6
6.23: h 20.8
6.25: h 12.13; h 20.6
7.20: k 7
7.28: k 7
7.35: h 14.5
7.39: h 15.5
7.41–42: h 15.5
8.8: h 5.13; h 10.3
8.14: h 5.13
8.43: h 17.5; k 6
8.44: h 17.5
8.50: k 6
9.20: h 11.1
9.22: k 7
9.32: h 13.3; k 7
9.62: h 5.13; h 18.8
10.19: c 25
10.20: h 17.4
10.34: h 28.12
11.49: h 14.5
12.18–19: h 16.4
12.20: h 16.4
12.34: h 5.13
12.42: h 11.3
12.45–46: h 11.3
12.47: h 16.7
12.47–48: h 27.3; c 31
12.49: h 20.8
13.7: h 18.5
13.23: h 27.6
13.23–24: c 33
13.24: h 27.6
13.26: h 1.8
13.27: h 1.9
14.11: h 12.7

# INDEX OF HOLY SCRIPTURE 355

14.18–20: h 5.2
14.20: h 5.2
15.3–5: c 28
15.7: h 15.4
15.12, 14, 20: h 18.9
15.22: c 14
16.8: h 17.3
16.12: h 7.3
16.14: h 20.5
16.19: c 45
16.23: k 9
17.21: h 18.2
17.28: h 28.11; c 35
17.32: h 13.3
18.8: h 4.3; h 12.13
18.11–12: h 4.4
18.14: h 12.7
18.31: k 7
19.10: c 28
19.20: h 20.3
19.41: h 14.6
21.20: h 7.1; h 10.4
22.8–12: h 19.19
22.20: h 12.2
24.32: h 20.8; c 20

John
1.1: h 9.1; h 20.1;
   p 1.1
1.1–2: h 1.8
1.2: h 1.8; h 14.6
1.9–11: h 9.1; h
   14.10
1.10: c 17
1.14: h 1.8; h 9.1;
   k 7
1.14–15: k 7
1.15: k 7
1.16: h 28.2; p 1.1
1.18: h 15.6
1.30: k 7
1.33: k 7
2.13: h 12.13
3.29: c 10
4.6, 11, 12: h 18.4
4.14: c 22
4.35: h 5.13
5.14: h 16.5
5.20: h 16.5
5.23: h 5.8

5.44: h 20.5
5.46–47: h 9.2; k 6
6.9, 13: c 20
6.55: h 12.13
6.67–68: h 17.4
7.37: h 18.9
8.12: h 12.9
8.39: h 4.5
8.44: h 9.4; c 28
9.4: h 12.9–10
9.39: h 15.3
10.8: c 21
10.9: k 9
10.11: h 5.6
10.14: h 5.6
10.16: h 4.6
10.27: h 5.6; h 17.2
10.29: h 18.3
11.25: h 9.3
12.24: h 10.3
12.27: h 14.6
12.31: h 7.3
12.35: h 12.9
14.6: h 18.10; h
   27.4; k 9
14.10: h 1.9
14.10–11: h 1.8
14.11: h 10.7
14.20: c 58
14.23: h 8.1
14.30: h 15.5
15.1: h 27.4
15.1–2, 5–6: c 23
15.2: h 27.4
18.36: h 14.17
18.37: h 14.7;
   h 27.4
19.1, 9: h 19.12
19.6: h 18.5
19.15: h 18.5; c 30
49.8: h 9.1

Acts
1.13: h 19.13
2.3: h 19.13
2.27–31: k 6
2.41: h 9.3
3.21: h 12.10
3.22–23: h 1.12
4.4: h 9.3

4.26: h 10.7
4.29: k 9
4.29–31: h 15.1
7.39: h 13.3
7.52: h 1.13
8.9–10: h 5.3
9.36–37: h 19.13
10.9: h 19.13
10.10: h 19.13
13.14: h 5.1
13.22: h 20.1
13.26: h 4.2; h 5.1
13.33–35: h 5.1
13.46: h 4.2; h 5.1;
   h 12.13
14.15: h 4.3
16.10: h 12.8
17.28: c 17
18.9: h 12.8
23.3: h 19.12

Romans
1.13: h 14.3
1.26: c 25
1.28: c 25
2.4: h 4.4; h 20.4
2.5: h 20.4; c 52
2.15: h 16.10
2.21: c 21
2.23: h 5.8; h 12.11
2.28: h 12.13
2.29: h 12.13
3.2: h 14.12
3.25: h 12.13
4.11: c 14
5.5: c 45
5.6: h 14.11
6.4: h 1.16; h 19.14
6.12: h 1.7
7.24: h 20.7
8.3: h 7.3
8.6: h 8.1
8.7: h 27.2
8.13: h 8.1; h 11.2;
   h 20.7
8.14: h 9.4
8.15: h 4.5
8.25: h 9.4
9.22: h 27.3
9.22–23: c 31

# INDEX OF HOLY SCRIPTURE

(Romans continued)
9.22–24: h 27.3
9.32: p 2.1
9.33: p 2.1
10.6–8: h 18.2
10.7: k 7
11.2: h 5.4
11.3: h 14.16
11.4: h 5.4
11.5: h 5.4
11.8: h 28.2
11.11: h 4.2; h 4.5;
   h 5.4; h 7.1;
   h 12.6; h 13.1
11.17: h 12.13; c 23
11.18: h 4.4; c 23
11.20–21: h 20.9
11.21: h 4.4; h 11.6
11.21–24: h 4.4–5
11.22: h 4.4; h 18.5
11.24: h 4.4; h 11.6
11.25–26: h 4.6;
   h 5.2; h 5.4
11.33: h 27.5
12.1: c 11
13.7: h 14.4
15.19: h 12.8
15.20: h 12.8
16.20: h 27.2; c 29

1 Corinthians
1.8: c 16
1.20: h 8.9; c 39
1.24: h 1.6; h 8.2;
   h 9.4
1.25: h 8.8–9
1.26–28: h 16.8
1.30: h 8.2; h 17.4;
   h 27.4
2.4: c 61
2.6: h 12.12
2.7: h 12.13
2.8: h 8.8; h 18.8
2.9: h 19.15
2.10: k 10
2.14: h 12.1
2.15: h 28.1
3.1: h 18.6
3.2: c 10
3.6: h 5.13

3.8: h 17.3
3.9: h 1.15; c 12;
   c 58; c 70
3.10: h 10.4
3.11: h 10.4
3.11–12: c 12
3.11–13: h 16.5
3.12: c 12
3.12–13: h 2.3;
   h 20.3
3.13, 15: k 10
3.15: h 16.7
3.16: h 1.16
3.17: h 12.11
3.19: h 8.9
4.1–2: h 11.3
4.5: h 16.10
4.9: h 8.4
5.1–2: h 27.5
5.3–5: h 19.14
5.5: h 1.3; c 2;
   c 48
5.6: c 22
5.7: h 12.13
5.8: h 14.16
6.9: h 12.11
6.9–10: h 20.3
6.10: h 20.3
6.17: h 11.6
8.7: h 6.2
9.10: h 12.3
9.25: h 27.3
9.27: h 20.7
10.4: h 16.2; h 18.9;
   c 20; c 26
10.11: h 12.3
10.13: h 19.13
10.16: h 12.2
10.17: c 28
11.25: h 12.2
11.27: c 50
11.29: c 50
12.4–11: c 19
12.8–9: h 8.5
12.10: h 14.14
13.1: h 1.8
13.9–10: k 9
13.9–12: h 8.7
13.12: h 6.3; h 8.7
13.13: h 6.1

14.4: k 9
14.8: h 27.1
14.14: k 9
14.15: c 15
14.38: h 1.8
15.22: h 8.1
15.23: h 8.6
15.24: h 7.3; h 9.1
15.25–26: h 17.3
15.26: c 25
15.41–42: c 22
15.49: h 2.1; h 8.2;
   h 15.8; h 27.1;
   h 28.9; c 22; c 36
15.55: c 54

2 Corinthians
1.1: h 1.16
1.21: c 16
2.2: h 20.6; c 70
2.5: h 20.9
2.7–8: h 20.9
3.15: h 5.8
3.16: h 5.8
3.18: h 5.8; h 16.1
4.1: h 27.3
4.3: h 5.8
4.7: h 28.7; c 36;
   c 61
4.18: c 62
5.10: h 20.3
5.16: h 15.6
5.21: h 10.1
6.14: h 1.16
7.10: c 70
9.7: h 20.2
10.5: h 12.12; c 11;
   c 27
10.6: c 27
11.14–15: k 4
11.23: h 14.14;
   c 63
11.23–25: h 11.4
11.27–28: h 14.16
12.1: h 12.8
12.7–8: h 12.8
12.9: h 11.4; h 12.8
12.12: h 12.8
13.3: h 17.2
13.4: h 14.9

## INDEX OF HOLY SCRIPTURE

Galatians
1.4: h 17.3
3.4: h 19.14
3.19: h 13.1
4.4: h 19.15
4.9: h 12.13
4.16: h 14.13;
  h 14.16
4.19: c 10
4.23: h 5.15
4.26: h 5.13;
  h 10.7
4.27: h 3.2; h 9.3
5.9: c 64
5.17: h 11.2;
  h 20.7
5.19–20: h 11.2
5.22–23: c 62
6.7: h 20.3
6.8: h 11.2
6.14: h 11.4;
  h 18.2

Ephesians
1.19: h 1.9
2.3: h 5.14
2.6: h 1.16
2.10: c 14
2.12: h 4.2
3.11: h 12.8
3.18: h 18.2
4.4: c 28
4.6: h 5.2
4.10: h 18.2
4.13: h 1.13
4.14: c 25
4.19: h 5.5; h 20.9
4.27: h 1.14
5.2: c 11
6.12: c 40
6.16: h 18.1; c 2
6.24: h 14.14

Philippians
1.21: k 10
1.23: h 20.3; k 10
1.28: h 4.3
2.6: h 10.7
2.7: h 1.7; h 8.8;
  h 14.9

2.10: k 8
2.10–11: h 18.2
3.13: h 13.3; h 18.8
3.19: h 5.2; h 11.4;
  h 12.8; c 70
3.20: h 8.2; h 28.9;
  c 36
3.21: h 5.14
9.19: h 7.3

Colossians
1.15: h 1.8; h 15.6
1.16: h 15.6
1.18: h 15.6
2.3: h 8.5–6
2.9: h 1.6
2.14: h 15.5
2.15: h 9.1
3.1: c 51
3.5: h 11.2; h 15.6
3.9–10: h 5.13
3.17: h 20.8
4.12–15: h 15.5

1 Thessalonians
1.1: h 8.5
2.9–10: h 5.3
5.8: h 4.2

2 Thessalonians
1.1: h 8.5
1.4: h 5.16
2.3–4: c 28

1 Timothy
1.20: h 1.3; h 19.14;
  c 2; c 48
2.8: h 5.9
2.15: h 4.5
3.15: h 5.16
4.3: h 20.7
4.6: c 40
6.20: c 12

2 Timothy
1.7: h 6.1; h 8.5
1.15: h 19.14
2.19: h 1.8; h 1.10
2.20–21: h 28.3
3.12: h 1.13

Titus
3.3–6: h 5.1
3.4: h 1.1
3.5: h 16.5
3.6: h 5.1

Philemon
14: h 20.2

Hebrews
1.3: h 9.4
1.14: k 7
1.4–5: h 1.8
2.11: h 17.4
2.17: h 1.12
2.13: h 18.6
4.12: h 2.2; h 11.2
5.13–14: c 10
5.14: h 3.2
6.1: h 9.3
6.4–6: h 13.2
7.14: h 4.2; h 5.15;
  h 9.1, h 16.10
8.2: c 70
8.5: h 7.1; h 18.2;
  c 4
9.26: h 1.8; k 10
10.26–27: h 16.7
10.28–29: h 19.15
10.29: h 13.2
11.12: c 10
11.37: h 15.2; h 20.9
11.37–38: h 14.14
11.38: h 14.14
12.6: h 1.16; h 10.5;
  c 70
12.22: h 12.3;
  h 28.11
12.23: h 12.3
12.29: h 16.6; h 18.1
15.22: h 27.6

James
2.18, 20: c 14
4.6: c 45

1 Peter
1.9–10: h 28.3
2.5: c 48
2.7: p 2.1

(1 Peter *continued*)
  2.9: h 17.2
  2.22: h 15.5
  3.19: k 7
  4.11: h 1.16; h 2.3; h
    4.6; h 5.17; h 6.3;
    h 7.3; h 8.9; h
    9.4; h 10.8; h
    11.6; h 12.13; h
    13.3; h 14.18; h
    15.6; h 16.10; h
    17.6; h 19.15; h
    20.9; h 27.6; h
    28.12; k 10

5.8: h 14.11; c 28
5.8–9: h 5.16

2 Peter
  1.21: k 4

1 John
  1.5: h 9.4
  1.15: h 2.3
  2.2: h 12.13;
    h 14.11
  2.19: h 27.3; c 31
  3.8: h 9.4
  3.15: c 28

3.21–22: h 16.4
5.16–17: h 2.2

Apocalypse
  2.10: h 4.3
  3.12: h 9.2
  5.5: h 16.10
  5.8: c 68
  11.8: h 9.2; h 18.5
  16.5: h 10.6
  17.14: h 8.6
  20.6: h 2.3

www.ingramcontent.com/pod-product-compliance
Lightning Source LLC
Chambersburg PA
CBHW032024290426
44110CB00012B/666